SHARIAH GOVERNANCE SYSTEMS OF ISLAMIC BANKS

Theory and Practice

Advances in Research on Islamic Economics and Finance

Series Editor: Toseef Azid
(Qassim University, Saudi Arabia & Wayne State University, USA)

Published

Vol. 3: *Shariah Governance Systems of Islamic Banks: Theory and Practice*
by Md. Kausar Alam, Abu Umar Faruq Ahmad, Toseef Azid &
Eiman Ahmed Mohammad Khaleel Al Hashmi

Vol. 2: *Islamic Economic Institutions in Indonesia: Are they Successful in Achieving the Maqasad-al-Shari'ah*
edited by Toseef Azid, Muhammad Syafii Antonio, Zafar Kayani &
Murniati Mukhlisin

Vol. 1: *Economic Empowerment of Women in the Islamic World: Theory and Practice*
edited by Toseef Azid & Jennifer L Ward-Batts

Advances in Research on Islamic Economics and Finance – Vol. 3

SHARIAH GOVERNANCE SYSTEMS OF ISLAMIC BANKS
Theory and Practice

Md. Kausar Alam
BRAC University, Bangladesh

Abu Umar Faruq Ahmad
Islamic Cooperative Finance Australia Limited, Australia

Toseef Azid
Qassim University, Saudi Arabia

Eiman Ahmed Mohammad Khaleel Al Hashmi
Zayed University, UAE

NEW JERSEY · LONDON · SINGAPORE · GENEVA · BEIJING · SHANGHAI · TAIPEI · CHENNAI

Published by

World Scientific Publishing Co. Pte. Ltd.

5 Toh Tuck Link, Singapore 596224

USA office: 27 Warren Street, Suite 401-402, Hackensack, NJ 07601

UK office: 57 Shelton Street, Covent Garden, London WC2H 9HE

Library of Congress Cataloging-in-Publication Data

Names: Alam, Md. Kausar, author. | Faruq Ahmad, Abu Umar, author. | Azid, Toseef, author. |
 Khaleel Al Hashmi, Eiman Ahmed Mohammad, author.
Title: Shari'ah governance systems of Islamic banks : theory and practice / Md. Kausar Alam,
 BRAC University, Bangladesh; Abu Umar Faruq Ahmad, Islamic Cooperative
 Finance Australia Limited, Australia; Toseef Azid, Qassim University, Saudi Arabia;
 Eiman Ahmed Mohammad Khaleel Al Hashmi, Zayed University, UAE.
Description: New Jersey : World Scientific, 2025. | Series: Advances in research on
 Islamic economics and finance ; vol 3 | Includes bibliographical references and index.
Identifiers: LCCN 2024025399 | ISBN 9789811292903 (hardcover) |
 ISBN 9789811292910 (ebook) | ISBN 9789811292927 (ebook other)
Subjects: LCSH: Banking law (Islamic law) | Financial institutions--Religious aspects--Islam. |
 Corporate governance--Religious aspects--Islam.
Classification: LCC KBP940.2 .A43 2025 | DDC 346/.167082--dc23/eng/20241022
LC record available at https://lccn.loc.gov/2024025399

British Library Cataloguing-in-Publication Data
A catalogue record for this book is available from the British Library.

Copyright © 2025 by World Scientific Publishing Co. Pte. Ltd.

All rights reserved. This book, or parts thereof, may not be reproduced in any form or by any means, electronic or mechanical, including photocopying, recording or any information storage and retrieval system now known or to be invented, without written permission from the publisher.

For photocopying of material in this volume, please pay a copying fee through the Copyright Clearance Center, Inc., 222 Rosewood Drive, Danvers, MA 01923, USA. In this case permission to photocopy is not required from the publisher.

For any available supplementary material, please visit
https://www.worldscientific.com/worldscibooks/10.1142/13830#t=suppl

Desk Editors: Kannan Krishnan/Catherine Domingo Ong

Typeset by Stallion Press
Email: enquiries@stallionpress.com

Foreword

I believe and acknowledge that this book is a crucial undertaking on the topic of Shariah Governance Systems of Islamic Banks. The authors presented a comprehensive alternative Islamic narrative that is highly sought after, particularly in the field that is rapidly growing in importance. Malaysia, along with other Muslim countries, is at the forefront of this global Islamic effort. This detailed and well-written book will serve as a valuable resource for staff, students, policymakers, Islamic banking professionals, practitioners, and the wider society in understanding and implementing the *Shariah* governance system in Islamic banking, which has a significant impact on Muslims worldwide.

The field of Islamic banking has been steadily evolving in recent years amid significant global changes such as international economic crises, globalization, the fourth industrial revolution, increasing digitalization, and applications of artificial intelligence. Additionally, factors like global financial and environmental crises, the COVID-19 pandemic, and conflicts in regions have had lasting impacts on the perception, implementation, governance, and development of Islamic banking, like all other emerging Islamic alternatives based on Shariah, operates within established global narratives, systems, management structures, governance processes, and ecosystems that are rooted in current capitalist, liberal, and man-made narratives.

To promote the Islamic alternative effectively in this setting, one must comprehend the broader aspects of narratives, worldviews, cultures, governance structures, and their underlying value systems. Islamic banking practitioners, professionals, and experts should be aware that the goal is to establish a comprehensive system, environment, culture, and practice for Islamic banking and economic life, rather than just offering partial alternatives in various aspects.

We may still learn from existing models and practices, but there is a clear need for a holistic alternative that includes all necessary components such as techniques, ecosystems, policies, governance, management, services, goods, products, education, and training. Only when we realize that the partial alternatives we provide must be connected to the larger objectives and the entire ecosystems we are aiming to establish, can we go in the correct direction. Any alternative we propose in any subject matter or field must be connected to the broader Islamic system of life we aim to establish, rooted in the Islamic worldview as a comprehensive way of life rather than a creed that is private and personal.

This book introduces innovative concepts of corporate governance for the banking sector, especially in Islamic banking, focusing on values-based and integrated approaches. Muslim academics, specialists, professionals, and practitioners need to oversee and promote Islamic economics and finance systems as universal and replicable systems that benefit the entire world, not only Muslims. If Islam is considered a mercy to all mankind and its teachings and values are universal, then our narrative, systems, ideas, and solutions should likewise be global and universal. We should not exclusively target the Muslim demographic. The *Shar'iah* and Islamic worldview should be presented as a universal worldview for safeguarding religion, intellect, life, progeny, and wealth. It should offer the knowledge, guidance, and frameworks necessary to safeguard human beings, society, civilization, the environment, and the lives of all. The book specifically discussed the issues the corporate sector encountered, highlighting its shortcomings and the need for change to adapt to changing market and societal dynamics. The corporate sector needs to redesign its model to incorporate elements that enhance its flexibility, adaptability, and resilience in response to local, regional, and global environmental, economic, and socio-political changes and crises.

For instance, it was often noted that companies with low capital, but large debt levels were compelled to exit the market during crises. This had a detrimental effect on the expansion of this sector and hindered the process of research and innovation. Stakeholders are consistently worried about the effectiveness of the capital market, resource allocation for long-term investments, and corporate governance to ensure sustainable company practices. Stakeholders are increasingly requesting enhanced corporate governance and standards to ensure their protection, as well as greater

Foreword vii

compliance, disclosure, and transparency, especially during emergencies such as the recent pandemic.

Economists and business experts acknowledge the stock market's significance in delivering equity capital to enterprises, which enhances financial stability and helps fulfill commitments to employees, creditors, and suppliers. It allows households to manage their savings, investments, and plan for retirement. During recent crises, many smaller enterprises failed to survive and were delisted, exacerbating economic problems in several economies. Policymakers are formulating measures to support the growth of smaller enterprises and encourage their participation in the innovation process.

In the business world, stakeholders advocate for robust ethical corporate governance that is resilient and essential for the efficient functioning of capital markets. This includes safeguarding shareholders' rights and reducing capital costs through research and innovation.

The Islamic system is characterized by distinct ethical principles and practical rationality beyond its religious rationale, particularly in its approach to handling debt. Debt should only be used for necessities, not for luxuries, limiting opportunities for extravagant spending. It is a well-known occurrence that money is not regarded as a commodity and interest is not allowed, which means that prohibiting interest increases the circulation of funds for production.

A significant demand has been made by investors, board of directors, and other stakeholders to enhance the ethical and moral standards in corporate governance models. The ethical framework provided by Islam offers a governance structure based on pure ethical and moral standards that encompass both current life and the afterlife. The current book explores the theoretical foundation of *shari'ah* governance in relation to the Islamic financial system. The text provides a comparative analysis of conceptual *shari'ah* governance and the global *shari'ah* governance structure. It also outlines the legal actions taken by authorities in various countries, especially those in Muslim nations. The book presents a valuable opportunity for both academia and industry practitioners to study Shariah governance systems and theories in one comprehensive source. The book discusses theories about governance systems, global corporate governance models, and their practical ramifications.

To advance Islamic Banking, we must promote *ijtihad* and innovation to introduce new products and solutions that go beyond the traditional teachings of our esteemed scholars. Islamic banking scholars, educators, and specialists must address current problems and conditions to produce relevant answers while preserving the originality of Islam and its value system. Therefore, it is crucial to enhance Islamic banking and finance education to offer guidance and knowledge to individuals engaged in teaching, research, practice, training, consultancy, and problem-solving in these areas. The governance of Islamic banking systems is a crucial component of restructuring the Islamic economic and financial systems. These systems are components of the broader Ummah system, which encompasses political, social, cultural, educational, technological, and civilizational aspects. Hence, we always need to keep in mind the bigger picture and the higher narrative so that we will not lose sight while sinking into the details of Islamic banking and finance.

Additionally, it is essential to emphasize that humans, as vicegerents on earth, are the fundamental basis for establishing any systems of administration, management, leadership, and others. Therefore, while addressing issues related to the economy, politics, finance, or banking, it is essential to constantly go back to the human factors. Ultimately, issues concerning policy, systems, technology, governance, and management all trace back to human elements. Hence, we must enhance the Istikhlaf (vicegerent) Governance System of Islamic banking. We should always support and develop *khalifa* (vicegerent) who can effectively oversee the governance of Islamic banking. This will help reduce problems and transform the Islamic banking systems and values into practical solutions, dynamic culture, and real living systems.

Datuk Prof. Dr. Abdelaziz Berghout
Dean of International Institute of Islamic Thought-
International Islamic University Malaysia (ISTAC-IIUM)
And Former Deputy Rector, IIUM

Preface

This book describes the theories related to corporate and *shari'ah* governance frameworks of the global Islamic finance industry. It provides the conceptual models of *shari'ah* governance and global *shari'ah* governance systems. It also provides their historical background of development. The book illustrates the steps taken by the regulatory authorities in different countries. As there is a shortage of books on *shari'ah* governance in comparison to corporate governance, this book will be a great opportunity for academia as well as industry practitioners to learn the *shari'ah* governance systems and theories from one book. Locally, Malaysia has published a few books but there are no sufficient books in this field internationally. Earlier published books only illustrate the fundamental issues without highlighting the overall issues related to *shari'ah* governance. This book is diversified from the previous books as it provides the overall governance systems, theories, and global corporate governance models. This book targets the global market as Islamic finance is growing and regulators as well as academicians are increasingly interested from all over the world. The subject of *shari'ah* governance is relevant irrespective of jurisdiction.

The first chapter of the volume gives precise definitions of concepts describing corporate governance systems of financial institutions, definition, development, role, systems, and principles of corporate governance and discusses the key participants of corporate governance in the financial sector. This chapter also discusses the concept from an institutional theory perspective, issues surrounding the regulation in banks, the role of international regulatory bodies, and their significance in the development of corporate governance. In Chapter 2, the concept of corporate governance from an Islamic perspective is discussed. This chapter also discussed the different dimensions of *shari'ah* governance in Islamic financial institutions (IFI).

In Chapter 3, theoretical explanation of *shari'ah* governance is analyzed. The different theories from the perspective of *shari'ah* governance framework are also deliberated, for example, theories such as agency, stewardship, stakeholder, accountability, institutional, and their applications. Besides the aforementioned, this chapter throws light on the role of IT and legitimacy in the *shari'ah* governance. Chapter 4 is focused on the development process of corporate governance in the IFIs and the role of international standard-setting agencies. This chapter explained the legal instruments and their importance in corporate governance particularly in the Islamic finance industry. It also presented the corporate governance framework of Bank Negara Malaysia as an example. At the end, the resolution framework is discussed. *Shariah* governance framework, its mechanism, basic pillars of *shari'ah* governance model, and different suggestions and recommendations related to the Islamic financial industry are presented in Chapter 5. The next, Chapter 6, turned the attention of the readers toward the *shari'ah* governance model from a regulatory perspective. It discussed the different approaches, for example, reactive, passive, minimalist, proactive and interventionist, and general approach to *shari'ah* governance system. This chapter examines the different steps of the *shari'ah* governance process. The purpose of Chapter 7 is to investigate the structure of the models of *shari'ah* supervisory board and analyze the functions of the supervisory board. This chapter also explored the issues and challenges faced by the *shari'ah* supervisory board. Chapter 8 analyzed the *shari'ah* risk management and compliance system, for example, the risk profile of the Islamic intermediation, possible implications of *shari'ah* risk, different types of risks, and many other issues related to *shari'ah* risk. Chapter 9, discussed how the *shari'ah* audit system works, and what are the requirements for professional accounting qualifications particularly with reference to the critical economic perspective. Also, this research provided a detailed discussion of the *shari'ah* audit evidence and its methodology. In the end, Chapter 10 surveyed the different aspects and dimensions of *shari'ah* reporting and disclosure system, i.e., Islamic social reporting, the role of Accounting and Auditing Organization for Islamic Financial Institutions (AAOIFI), harmonization of Islamic accounting standards with International Financial Reporting Standards (IFRS), and the alternative components for the reporting of Islamic financial institutions.

About the Authors

Dr. Md. Kausar Alam works as an Assistant Professor at BRAC Business School, BRAC University, Dhaka, Bangladesh. He completed his PhD from the Department of Finance and Accounting, School of Business and Economics, Universiti Putra Malaysia (UPM). He completed his MBA & BBA from the Department of Accounting and Information Systems, Jagannath University Dhaka. He published numerous articles and book chapters in several international journals in accounting, finance, and Islamic finance. His research works have been published in Journal of Applied Accounting Research, Asian Review of Accounting, Pacific Accounting Review, Journal of Public Affairs, Journal of Islamic Accounting and Business Research, ISRA International Journal of Islamic Finance, Qualitative Research in Organizations and Management, International Journal of Ethics and Systems, International Review of Financial Analysis, Journal of Economics Finance and Administrative Science, Heliyon, Applied Economics, Asian Journal of Accounting Research, PSU Research Review, Journal of Asian Finance, Economics and Business, International Journal of Sociology and Social Policy and Asian Economic and Financial Review. His research interest areas are Accounting, Islamic Accounting, Shariah governance, integrating reporting, institutional theory, Islamic banking, corporate governance, legitimacy theory, legitimacy, working capital, and Islamic social finance governance. He already published more than 50 research articles and three book chapters. Some of his research works are in progress with reputed international journals. He received research grants from BRAC Business School.

Abu Umar Faruq Ahmad was Associate Professor at Islamic Economic Institute in King Abdulaziz University, Jeddah. And currently working as Adjunct Professor, Guidance College, Texas, USA. He has a significant number of published peer-reviewed refereed journal articles, books, chapters in edited books, conference proceedings, and other intellectual contributions to his credit on *Shariah* compliance of Islamic banks' products and structures, Islamic economics, the opportunities and challenges of Islamic finance, case studies of Islamic banks and financial institutions, Islamic insurance and reinsurance, Islamic microfinance, Sukuk, and dispute resolution in Islamic banking and finance, among others. He presented papers at international conferences held in the USA, Ireland, Australia, UAE, Saudi Arabia, Turkey, Brunei, Qatar, Sudan, Nigeria, Malaysia, Indonesia, Bangladesh and Pakistan. His current editorial roles include serving as founding editor, senior editor, editorial advisory board member of a plethora of internationally reputed refereed journals including some of those published by Emerald Group Publishing, UK.

Toseef Azid is a professor of Economics at the College of Business and Economics, Qassim University, Saudi Arabia. He holds a PhD in Economics from University College of Wales, Aberystwyth, UK (1993), and Masters in Economics from Quaid-i-Azam University (1979). He received COT Scholarship from government of Pakistan to study at UCW, Overseas Research Scholarship from the British government, and a Fulbright Award Scholar in Residence (2006) where he worked on a research project on "Economics of Middle Eastern Countries". He taught at Markfield Institute of Higher Education UK (2005–2006, 2007, and 2012). He also taught in Pakistan, Brunei, UK, USA, and Saudi Arabia. His research focuses on technological change, development Economics, labor economics, Islamic economics, and Islamic finance. He published more than 70 papers in local and international journals. He participated in several conferences held in Iran, Saudi Arabia, Turkey, Canada, Australia, Indonesia, Malaysia, Bahrain, Qatar, and Pakistan. His eight books as co-editor include *Labor in an Islamic Setting: Theory and Practice, Social Justice and Islamic Economics: Theory, Issues and Practice, Foundations of a Sustainable Economy: Moral, Ethical and Religious Perspectives and Labor Economics in An Islamic Framework* published by Routledge, UK, *Corporate and Shariah Governance in the Muslim World: Theory and Practice*, and

Monetary Policy, Islamic Finance, and Islamic Corporate Governance: An International Overview published by Emerald, UK; *Economic Empowerment of Women in the Islamic World: Theory and Practice* and *Islamic Economic Institutions in Indonesia: Are They Successful in Achieving Maqasad i Shariah?* published by World Scientific Publications, Singapore.

Eiman Khaleel Alhashmi is currently an assistant professor in the College of Humanities and Social Sciences, Zayed University, UAE. She received her PhD with first class honors with distinction in "Investment of zakat and its role in development of the Islamic world" from Cairo University, Dar Aloluom college, (Egypt) with excellent with highest honor (2012). Eiman published a book titled *The Provisions of Zakat and Its Latest Developments: A Contemporary Scientific Study* and a number of papers in referred journals, including *How to Eliminate Poverty by Zakat, Difference of Contemporary Fiqh Council's Resolutions on Zakat Fund Investment Is a Diversity Difference or Antagonism Difference; Fiqh Councils between the Agreement and Disagreement, Images of Contemporary Usury Transactions*, and participated in a range of forums on Islamic economics and finance. She also presented various academic as well as research-based papers at several national and international conferences. Her research activities are currently, *Waqf* (endowment), *Maqasid al-Shariah* (legitimate purposes), *zakat*, Islamic *shari'ah*.

Contents

Foreword	v
Preface	ix
About the Authors	xi
List of Figures	xxv
List of Tables	xxvii

1. Corporate Governance Systems of Financial Institutions
                                                  1

1.1	Introduction	1
1.2	Conceptual Definition of Corporate Governance	2
1.3	Corporate Governance	4
1.4	Corporate Governance in Financial Institutions	5
1.5	Good Corporate Governance	6
1.6	Development History of Corporate Governance	7
	1.6.1 United States of America (USA)	8
	1.6.2 United Kingdom (UK)	9
	1.6.3 Germany	9
	1.6.4 Japan	10
	1.6.5 China	10
1.7	Principles of Corporate Governance	11
	1.7.1 The 10 Fundamental Principles of Corporate Governance Stated in ASX	13
	1.7.2 The OECD Principles and Its Explanation	14
1.8	Role of Corporate Governance	14

1.9	Key Participants of Corporate Governance in Financial Sectors	15
	1.9.1 The Evolving Roles of the Key Players	18
1.10	Corporate Governance Theories	19
	1.10.1 Agency Theory	20
	1.10.2 Stewardship Theory	21
	1.10.3 Stakeholder Theory	21
	1.10.4 Transaction Cost Theory	22
	1.10.5 Legitimacy Theory	24
	1.10.6 Accountability Theory	25
	1.10.7 Signaling Theory	26
	1.10.8 Economic Theory	27
	1.10.9 Entity Theory	28
	1.10.10 Proprietary Theory	29
	1.10.11 Resource Dependency Theory	29
	1.10.12 Managerial-Class Hegemony Theory	30
1.11	Corporate Governance from an Institutional Theory Perspective	30
1.12	Corporate Governance Systems	32
	1.12.1 The European Model	33
	1.12.2 The Anglo-Saxon Model	34
	1.12.3 Germanic Corporate Governance System	36
	1.12.4 Latin Corporate Governance System	37
	1.12.5 Japanese Corporate Governance System	37
	1.12.6 Chinese Corporate Governance Model	39
	1.12.7 Islamic Corporate Governance Model	40
	1.12.8 Discussion on Overall Models	41
1.13	Issues Surrounding the Regulation in Banks	42
	1.13.1 The Positive Impact of Regulation on the Corporate Governance of Banks	43
	1.13.2 The Adverse Impact of Regulation on the Corporate Governance of Banks	45
1.14	International Regulatory Bodies	47
	1.14.1 The Organization for Economic Co-operation and Development	48
	1.14.2 The Basel Committee on Banking Supervision	49
	1.14.3 International Accounting Standards Board	51
	1.14.4 Regulatory Issues Pertaining to Basel II	51
1.15	Conclusion	52

2. Corporate Governance Concept from an Islamic Perspective 55

2.1	Introduction	55
2.2	Governance	55
2.3	Why Governance Matters?	57
2.4	Shariah Governance	59
2.5	Shariah Governance in IFIs	60
	2.5.1 Definition and Objectives of Shariah	62
	2.5.2 The Sources of Shariah	64
	2.5.3 Muamalat (Human Relations)	64
	2.5.4 Accountability from the Islamic Perspective	65
	2.5.5 The Principles of Islamic Finance	66
	2.5.6 Shariah Compliance of IFIs	71
2.6	Role of Shariah Governance in IFIs	73
2.7	Objectives of the Shariah Governance	74
2.8	The Importance of Shariah Governance	75
2.9	Internal Governance Mechanism in Islamic Financial Institutions	80
2.10	Foundational Dimension of Shariah Governance	83
	2.10.1 Tawhid and Shura-Based Model	84
	2.10.2 Stakeholder-Oriented Approach	87
	2.10.3 Conventional Corporate Governance vs Shariah Governance	91

3. Theoretical Explanation of Shariah Governance 93

3.1	Introduction	93
3.2	Theory Used in Shariah Governance	97
3.3	Agency Theory and SGF	99
3.4	Stewardship Theory and SGF	101
3.5	Stakeholder Theory and SGF	102
3.6	Institutional Theory Framework	104
3.7	Application of Institutional Theory to SGF	111
3.8	Application of Institutional Theory in Islamic Banks and SGF	115
3.9	Conceptual Framework for Shariah Governance Using IT	117
3.10	Background of the Legitimacy	122
3.11	The Construction of Legitimacy	124
3.12	SG-System, Internal Legitimacy and Social Acceptance.	127

xviii *Shariah Governance Systems of Islamic Banks*

3.13 Legitimacy of Islamic Financial Institutions SGF and Social Acceptance 129

3.14 SG and Accountability Theory 133

4. Historical Development of *Shariah* Governance and International Standard-Setting Agencies   **135**

4.1 Introduction 135

4.2 The Development of Corporate Governance in IFIs 135

    4.2.1 Tabung Hajji: Achieving One's Goals 138

4.3 Frameworks for Islamic Banking General 140

4.4 Need for Good Corporate Governance in the Muslim World 141

4.5 The Development of Standards and Regulatory Guidance in the World 142

4.6 Current Legal and Regulatory Framework Practice 144

4.7 International Standard-Setting Agencies 146

    4.7.1 Accounting and Auditing Organization for Islamic Financial Institutions 149

    4.7.2 International Financial Service Board (IFSB) 151

    4.7.3 Islamic Development Bank (IDB) 152

    4.7.4 International Islamic Financial Market (IIFM) . . . 153

    4.7.5 International Islamic Rating Agency (IIRA) 154

    4.7.6 International Islamic Centre for Reconciliation and Commercial Arbitration 155

    4.7.7 General Council of Islamic Banks and Financial Institutions (GCIBFI) 155

4.8 Legal Instruments 156

    4.8.1 Basel I 156

    4.8.2 Basel II 156

    4.8.3 Basel III 157

4.9 The AAOIFI Governance Standards 159

    4.9.1 Shariah Supervisory Board: Appointment, Composition, and Report 160

    4.9.2 Governance Standard for IFIs No. 2: Shariah Review 161

    4.9.3 Governance Standard for IFIs No. 3: Internal Shariah Review 163

Contents

4.9.4	Governance Standard for IFIs No. 4: Audit and Governance Committee	164
4.9.5	Governance Standard for IFIs No. 5: Independence of Shariah Supervisory Board	167
4.10	The IFSB Guiding Principles	167
4.11	Bank Negara Malaysia (BNM) Shariah Governance Framework	169
4.12	Importance of International Standard	171
4.13	Resolution Framework	173

5. *Shariah* Governance Framework in Islamic Banks — 177

5.1	Introduction	177
5.2	Shariah Governance Framework in Islamic Banks	177
5.3	Shariah Governance Mechanism in Islamic Banks	179
5.4	Conceptual Framework of Shariah Governance Systems	184
5.5	Central Banks' Role in Islamic Banking Governance	187
5.6	Four Basic Pillars of a Shariah Governance Model	188
5.6.1	Management and Supervision	188
5.6.2	Shariah Advisory Board	189
5.6.3	Shariah Compliance and Review	190
5.6.4	Transparency and Disclosure	190
5.7	Shariah Governance Framework Model	191
5.7.1	Decentralized Shariah Governance Model	192
5.7.2	Centralized Shariah Governance Model	194
5.8	The Problem of SGF in the World	197
5.9	Need for a Special Shariah Governance Code	201
5.10	Recommendation: Envisioned Model Shariah Governance Code	202

6. *Shariah* Governance System — 207

6.1	Introduction	207
6.2	The Shariah Governance Model from a Regulatory Perspective	207
6.2.1	Reactive Approach	208
6.2.2	Passive Approach	208
6.2.3	Minimalist Approach	209
6.2.4	Proactive Approach	209
6.2.5	Interventionist Approach	209

6.3	Shariah Governance Process		210
	6.3.1	Appointment	211
	6.3.2	Composition	211
	6.3.3	Qualification	211
	6.3.4	Shariah Compliance Process	211
	6.3.5	Shariah Compliance Review	214
	6.3.6	Shariah Audit	215
	6.3.7	Shariah Coordination	217
	6.3.8	Shariah Report	218
6.4	General Approach to Shariah Governance System		219
	6.4.1	Competence	219
	6.4.2	Independence	220
	6.4.3	Confidentiality	220
	6.4.4	Consistency	220
6.5	Conclusion		220

7. Model of *Shariah* Supervisory Board and Its Functions **221**

7.1	Introduction	221
7.2	Institutionalization of Shariah Supervisory Board	221
7.3	Importance of Shariah Supervisory Board	223
7.4	Models of the Shariah Supervisory Board	224
	7.4.1 Internal Shariah Supervisory Board	225
	7.4.2 External Shariah Supervisory Boards	225
7.5	The Role and Function Internal of SSB	227
7.6	The Role and Function of CSSB	233
7.7	The Supervision of Islamic Banking in Practice	234
7.8	Issues and Challenges of the Shariah Supervisory Board	236
	7.8.1 Independence of Shariah Supervisory Board	238
	7.8.2 Competence, Conflict of Interest, and Confidentiality	239
	7.8.3 Disclosure and Transparency	240
	7.8.4 Shariah-Compliant vs Shariah-Based	241
	7.8.5 Consistency	242
	7.8.6 The Remit of Various Institutions of Shariah Supervisory Boards	242
	7.8.7 The Commitment of Dedicated, Qualified Directors Who Understand and Can Assess Shariah	243

Contents

	7.8.8	Demarcation of Responsibility and Accountability between Board, Management, and SSB	243
	7.8.9	Investment Policy to Comply with Shariah Criteria	244
	7.8.10	Investors' Protection	244
	7.8.11	Financing	244
	7.8.12	Harmonization of Shariah Rulings	245
	7.8.13	Vigilance and Oversight of the Supervisor	245
	7.8.14	The Absence of Proper Shariah Governance	245
	7.8.15	Accountability	246
7.9	Conclusion		246

8. *Shariah* Risk Management and Compliance System — 247

8.1	Introduction		247
8.2	The Risk Profile in Islamic Financial Intermediation		249
8.3	Shariah Risk and Possible Implications		255
	8.3.1	Shariah Risk Definition	255
	8.3.2	Possible Shariah Risk Implications	255
	8.3.3	Shariah Risk Causes and Events	258
	8.3.4	People	258
	8.3.5	Processes	260
	8.3.6	Systems	262
	8.3.7	External Causes	263
	8.3.8	The Responsibility of the BOD and Senior Management	265
	8.3.9	Role of Banking Supervisors	266
8.4	Risk Management in Islamic Financial Institutions		268
	8.4.1	Credit Risk	268
	8.4.2	Equity Investment Risk	269
	8.4.3	Market Risk	269
	8.4.4	Liquidity Risk	269
	8.4.5	Rate of Return	269
	8.4.6	Operational Risk	270

9. *Shariah* Audit System — 271

9.1	Introduction	271
9.2	What is Shariah Audit?	271
9.3	Why Do We Need Shariah Audit?	274

9.4	Characteristics of Shariah Audit	276
9.5	Objectives and Scopes of Shariah Audit	276
9.6	Issues in Shariah Audit	278
9.7	Professional Accounting Qualifications: Critical Economic Perspectives	279

	9.7.1	Background Analysis	279
	9.7.2	Critical Economic Perspectives	281
	9.7.3	Shariah Accounting/Auditing Qualifications: A Market Gap	283
	9.7.4	Shariah Accounting and Auditing Qualifications in the Market	283
	9.7.5	Limitations and Market Gap	285
	9.7.6	External Shariah Audit	287
	9.7.7	Ethical and Divine Qualities of an Auditor	288

9.8	Shariah Audit Evidence	289

	9.8.1	Definition of Audit Evidence and Its Main Features	289
	9.8.2	Sources and Techniques of Audit Evidence	290
	9.8.3	Documentation of Audit Evidence	291

9.9	Shariah Audit Methodology Examination, Reporting and Documentation Phase	291

	9.9.1	Shariah Audit Methodology	291
	9.9.2	Examination Phase	293
	9.9.3	Reporting Phase (Nature of the Audit Report)	293
	9.9.4	Audit Documentation Phase	296

9.10	Challenges in Implementing Shariah Audit	297
9.11	Conclusion	298

10. *Shariah* Reporting and Disclosure System   299

10.1	Introduction	299
10.2	Islamic Social Reporting	300
10.3	The Roles of AAOIFI	301
10.4	Harmonization of Islamic Accounting Standards with IFRS	303

	10.4.1	The International Accounting Standards Board	304
	10.4.2	The Roles of IASB	305
	10.4.3	The Challenges for Islamic Accounting Standards	305

10.5	The Alternative Components for Islamic Banking Reports	307
10.6	Conclusion	310

Appendix   311

References   317

Index   359

List of Figures

1.1	Corporate Governance Structure in Conventional Financial Institutions	5
1.2	European Model of Corporate Governance	34
1.3	The Anglo-Saxon Corporate Governance Model	35
1.4	Germanic Model of Corporate Governance	36
1.5	Japanese Model of Corporate Governance	38
1.6	Chinese Model of Corporate Governance	39
1.7	Corporate Governance Structure for IFIs	41
2.1	Tawhid and Shura Based Corporate Governance Model	86
3.1	A Conceptual Paradigm for Examining SGF Using IT	120
5.1	Scope of the SGF	186
5.2	Four Pillars of SG System	189
5.3	SG in GCC	193
5.4	Shariah Governance Standards for Centralized Framework	195
5.5	Proposed Centralized SGF	198
6.1	Proposed Organizational Framework for Shariah Secretariat	213
6.2	Reporting and Auditing Process of Islamic Banks in Bangladesh	217
8.1	Risk Profile in the Operational Activities of IFI	250
8.2	Possible Implications of Shariah Risk	257
8.3	Shariah Risk Events Grouped under the Four BCBS Operational Risk Causes	264
9.1	External Shariah Audit Structure	288
10.1	Form of ICRs as Amended of IFASB	308

List of Tables

3.1	An Overview of the New Institutional Theory Framework.	111
4.1	Key Elements of Shariah Governance in the IFSB-10.	168
4.2	Institutional Arrangement in the Shariah Governance System.	172
5.1	The Key Participants in CG in IBs.	180
5.2	Institutional Arrangement in the SG System.	185
10.1	Summary of Ethical Principles and Contents of ICR.	309

CHAPTER 1

Corporate Governance Systems of Financial Institutions

1.1 Introduction

Corporate governance (CG) has become a global phenomenon. The financial crashes and scandals that have affected almost every nation have made sure that interest in this subject keeps rising. Globally, nations are either developing new codes of behavior or guidelines or updating those that already exist. Global governance standards, like the introduction of the Organization for Economic Co-operation and Development (OECD) principles, which were first published in 1999, have been updated and revised in 2004 to reflect changes in CG. Many issues, including whether boards should be accountable to broader groups of stakeholders and, if so, who these groups are; the compensation of the board of directors (BOD); the role of institutional investors; the connection between the company and its auditors; and numerous others, continue to be the subject of debate. However, certain fundamental themes have begun to emerge, including the significant role that independent non-executive directors can play and the suitability of key board subcommittees, such as the audit and compensation committees. There is also a growing realization that companies cannot operate in isolation from the broader society in which they are situated and must consider the desires of groups other than shareholders in order to ensure their long-term viability. The purpose of this volume is to emphasize, through a variety of case studies, the evolution of CG in a number of countries across the globe and to illustrate its application in specific case-study companies.

1.2 Conceptual Definition of Corporate Governance

The word corporation comes from the Latin phrase *corpus*, which means body, mass, or aggregate. The term *corpus* may also be used to refer to a body or collection of policies. According to the *American Heritage Dictionary*, a corporation is a legal entity whose members have separate advantages, rights, and liabilities. CG is the relationship among a company's management, directors, shareholders, and other stakeholders, as defined by the OECD (2004). The Cadbury Code (1992) defines CG as the management and oversight of a business. In addition, CG is the relationship between a corporation's multiple stakeholders (chief executive officer, management, shareholders, and employees) that defines the direction and performance of the organization (Monks and Minow, 1995). Moreover, Bandsuch *et al.* (2008) defined CG as a formalized set of values and procedures followed by the business owners, administrators, and management in its diverse operations and interactions with its stakeholders. Holder-Webb *et al.* (2008) define CG as the inclusion of an effective board, strong shareholder rights, and thorough disclosures in business management. CG is an international concern. Jensen and Meckling (1976) while focusing on candor and disclosures relating to CG as mechanisms of checks and balances outlined the importance of mitigating agency risks resulting from the segregation of control and ownership in contemporary companies.

Consequently, CG is a tool that enables investors, the capital providers of the organizations, to make sure that their investments are well-managed and profitable (Shliefer and Vishny, 1997). CG is the connection between corporate administrators, executives, equity providers, and organizations that save and invest capital in order to generate earnings. It is also concerned with the correct form, structure, and relationships of corporate committees, shareholders, managers, and other stakeholders. Further, CG is a framework of laws, contracts, and cultural standards that regulate the structure of corporate decision-making, and is concerned with achieving a balance between economic and social goals and individual and communal goals (Choudhury and Hoque, 2006). In addition, CG distinguishes organizations in which decision-makers, typically directors, are distinct from actual ownership.

Basel Committee on Banking Supervision of the BIS (the BIS-Committee) has issued the most widely accepted concept of CG within the conventional financial world. In fact, the BIS Committee issued two guidelines for CG. The first, "Enhancing CG for financial organizations," was published in February 2006, and the second, "Principles for improving CG," was published in March 2006. The Committee's guideline from 2006 was based on the OECD's 2004 promulgation of CG principles. The long-standing principles of the OECD are designed to guide participants and authorities of financial markets and assist governments in evaluating and improving their regulatory structures for CG (Mizushima, 2014). According to Fotiuh (2010), the concept of CG was introduced as a result of an increasing awareness of the need to safeguard the rights of all stakeholders, including minority shareholders. According to a 2010 report by Fotiuh, good CG encourages the flow of investments, diminishes the cost of capital, and fosters robust capital markets.

Since the introduction of limited liability corporations in the early 19th century, CG has existed in some capacity (Vinten, 2001). But until the development of agency theory (Fama and Jensen, 1983a), which is predicated on the separation of corporate ownership and control, the phenomena was not noticed (Berle and Means, 1932). Also, it wasn't until the middle of the 1970s that the phrase "CG" was developed (Cheffins, 2011). As a result of the separation, corporate management (control) has a fiduciary responsibility to uphold the trust, safeguard the proprietors' interests, and maximize shareholder value. The agency problem, which arises from the separation of ownership and control, is one of the most contentious and fundamental issues in modern CG. According to Fama and Jensen (1983b), the primary cause of the problem is a conflict of interest between principals (shareholders) and agents (management). The contemporary concept of CG is broader and multidisciplinary in nature, incorporating multiple organizational functions such as management, finance, accounting, business law, ethics in business, and economics concurrently. In addition, it addresses other corporate aspects, such as transparency, accountability, disclosure, social responsibility, fairness, and the relationship between the BOD, shareholders, and other stakeholders (Abdalla *et al.*, 2012). In addition, it specifies the regulations, policies, methods, and organizational structure necessary to effectively direct and control the organization (OECD, 2004). Due to its multifaceted nature, there is currently no definition upon which all parties concur. Nonetheless, the OECD (2004) defines it as "a system for directing and controlling organizations." The World Bank (2013) provides a more precise and widely accepted definition of CG as follows: CG is the system of rules and incentives that direct and control the administration of a company. It refers to the manner in which the board, company management, shareholders, and other stakeholders share rights and responsibilities.

The instruments of CG systems, according to Morin and Jarrell (2001) and Dittmar *et al.* (2003), include shareholders, managers, the board, executive management, suppliers, consumers, regulatory bodies, and the court. Effective CG is anticipated to protect stakeholder interests, prevent agency conflicts, and keep agency costs to a minimum (Haniffa and Hudaib, 2006). Four essential forms of CG procedures are described by Jensen (1993) as follows: (1) internal and external controls, (2) internal and external controls, (3) external controls, and (4) competitiveness in the product market. Shleifer and Vishny (1997) illustrate the benefits and drawbacks of each governance mechanism as they concentrate on incentive contracts, legal protection for investors against managerial self-dealing, and ownership by major investors. The CG mechanisms are divided into the two following categories by Denis and McConnell (2003): (1) internal governance mechanisms, such as BOD and ownership structure and (2) external governance mechanisms, such as the acquisition market and the legal regulatory framework. Farinha (2003) looks at two types of disciplinary (or governing) processes. The first is external punishment mechanisms, which include the danger of takeovers, product market rivalry, managerial labor market, manager-to-manager mutual monitoring, as well as security analysts, the judicial system, and the value of reputation. Large and institutional shareholders, the BOD, insider ownership, remuneration packages, debt policy, and dividend policy are the internal disciplinary mechanisms. Although policies and documentation are important, they are not enough to guarantee efficient governance. When it comes to promoting corporate transparency and accountability, deeds speak louder than words (Ahmad and Omar, 2016).

1.3 Corporate Governance

The term "CG" refers to the network of interactions between a company's top leadership, its shareholders, and other interested parties. CG additionally provides the framework for establishing a company's objectives, as well as the means for achieving those objectives and monitoring performance (OECD, 2004). Monks and Minow (1995) define CG as the relationship between various stakeholders, including chief executive officers, shareholders, the BOD, and employees, that influences the direction and performance of an organization. According to Shleifer and Vishny (1997), CG is an established framework of management accountability to stockholders. It is the relationship between diverse stakeholders, such as shareholders, managers, the board, executive management, vendors, consumers, regulatory bodies, and the judiciary, both within and outside of the company (World Bank, 2013; Morin and Jarrell, 2001; Ahmad and Omar, 2016; Dittmar et al., 2003).

1.4 Corporate Governance in Financial Institutions

Governance entails preserving, directing, leading, supervising, and managing corporations. The BOD or supervisory board, the managers, the shareholders, and the depositors are internal participants (Salacuse, 2003); outside stakeholders include government regulatory bodies, staff, vendors, customers, partners, the stock market community as a whole, and the court that imposes the remedies available for violating the rules of governance (Choudhury and Alam, 2013, 2019; Salacuse, 2003). Figure 1.1 illustrates the CG structure of financial institutions.

This is an amalgam of the Anglo-Saxon and European models, with only the governing council and corporate objectives differing. In this case, the BOD is accountable to shareholders, and lawmakers, and banks are regulated by banking regulations and commercial law.

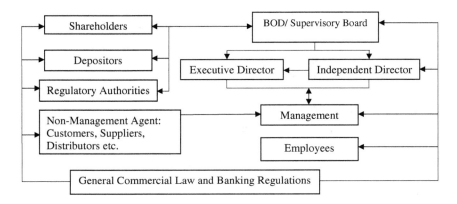

Figure 1.1: Corporate Governance Structure in Conventional Financial Institutions.
Source: Choudhury and Hoque (2004); Nienhaus (2007); Modified from Hasan (2011a).

1.5   Good Corporate Governance

The attribute of excellence could be beneficial to an organization's effectiveness (Wahab and Rahman, 2013). Competent CG has always been regarded as a crucial function for business environment stakeholders. Despite the fact that the purpose of CG varies from company to company and country to country, the primary concern is to promote a sound code of mechanism to elevate and regulate the organization. However, as a result of the contemporary business environment, CG structures change rapidly (Abu-Tapanjeh, 2009). Due to the absence of sound governance in organizations, there are numerous cases involving corporate controversies, such as Enron, Parmalat, and WorldCom via Global Crossing, among others. In an effort to reestablish public confidence in the CG of organizations, policymakers have enacted preventative measures by enhancing the existing guidelines. According to the World Bank (2013), a country with good CG ensures the sustainability of economic development and enhances investor confidence, safeguards minority shareholders, and promotes better decision-making and improved relations with key business stakeholders. Good CG involves the development of mechanisms and practices that assure the accountability of corporate management and enhance firm performance. Companies with strong CG may have a positive impact on firm performance at the micro level (Brammer *et al.*, 2007; Brown and Caylor, 2006; Bhagat and Bolton, 2008). According to Meyer (2004), systematic governance entails altering the signals within an organization so that employees act appropriately despite the need for oversight. Sound CG practices are now essential to global efforts to stabilize and strengthen healthy capital markets and safeguard investors. There are numerous studies linking excellent CG to improved performance. There is empirical evidence indicating countries that have instituted strong CG mechanisms have more robust corporate sector growth and a greater ability to attract capital. According to Fianna and Grant (2005), effective CG serves to reconcile the divide between the interests of a company's stakeholders by boosting investor confidence and reducing the cost of capital. In addition, they note that it facilitates the company's compliance with its legal obligations and the formation of relationships that create value for its stakeholders. Additionally, Coles *et al.* (2001) and Durnev and Han (2002) discovered that companies with superior CG are valued higher. Nevertheless, there is a developing consensus that CG continues to necessitate renovation and revision. The issue of effective CG is therefore still up for debate (Abu-Tapanjeh, 2009).

In order to restore public confidence in the CG practice in organizations, it is suggested that policymakers will need to enact new regulations that will at least prevent similar incidents from occurring. In pursuing their aims and objectives, corporations should implement "best practices" that result in the satisfaction of shareholders' and other stakeholders' rights. Consequently, a robust CG structure is deemed indispensable to a company's success, and its importance cannot be overstated. As for financial institutions, such as banks, their opaque and regulated characteristics distinguish the way they govern themselves from that of their non-financial counterparts (Hagendorff *et al.*, 2007; Mülbert, 2009). This could be explained by the nature of the banking industry, which collects funds from customers and then uses individual funds; consequently, it is crucial to implement a governance structure that adheres to the credibility of the financial market and safeguards the socioeconomic health of the global economy as a whole. On the other hand, one could predict that improper and weak governance in banks would result in catastrophic outcomes, such as economic devastation and a decline in investor trust (Hassan, 2012).

1.6 Development History of Corporate Governance

Given the scope of the issue, there may never be a comprehensive historical account of CG as it has existed since the incorporation of the corporation creating the potential for disagreements among investors and managers (Wells, 2010). The founding of the East India Company, Hudson's Bay Company, Levant Company, and other notable chartered corporations in the 16th and 17th centuries can be linked to the history of CG. It would be difficult to discuss every relevant facet of this history in a methodical manner. *A History of CG Around the World* serves as an example of the point. Despite having 687 pages, the publication only covers 11 nations and goes into great detail about a particular CG issue and ownership patterns.

This chapter concentrates on the process by which disputes about managerial accountability, board structure, and shareholder rights became channeled through the term "CG" rather than providing a generic history of CG. In doing so, it depicts how a phrase that was only popular in the United States in the 1970s became the subject of debate among academicians, regulators, executives, and investors worldwide within 25 years. The chapter

8   *Shariah Governance Systems of Islamic Banks*

recounts developments between the mid-1970s and the end of the 1990s, by which time "CG" was well-established as a jargon term in academic and regulatory circles.

The United States went through a continuous economic development after World War II, and its illustrious firms expanded quickly. Internal CG was not a major issue in the midst of widespread economic prosperity, and the term CG was not frequently employed (Cheffins, 2009; Greenough and Clapman, 1980). Managers led and directors and shareholders followed in the "managed corporations" that dominated the US economy at the time. Given that top executives heavily affected the choice of directors, it was reasonable to assume that boards would be supportive of management in the absence of a full-blown company crisis (Seligman, 1987). The retail investors that predominated share registers were "renowned for their apathy to everything but dividends and the approximate price of the stock," according to stockholders (Manning, 1958).

CG was included in the Federal Securities and Exchange Commission's (SEC) formal reform agenda in the middle of the 1970s. In 1976, when the term "CG" appeared for the first time in the *Federal Register* (Ocasio and Joseph, 2005), the official journal of the federal government, the S.E.C. began to consider managerial accountability issues as part of its regulatory mandate. In 1974, the SEC initiated proceedings against three outside directors of Penn Central, a railroad that had diversified into pipelines, hotels, industrial parks, and commercial real estate, alleging that they had exaggerated the company's financial condition in violation of federal securities law by failing to uncover a variety of misconduct committed by Penn Central executives (Schwartz, 1976). Many criticized the board's inaction after Penn Central declared bankruptcy in 1970 (Seligman, 1987).

1.6.1 *United States of America (USA)*

Between the conclusion of World War I and the end of World War II, the 1930s witnessed a remarkable democratization of shareholding. The advantages of democracy and diversification are contingent on the size of the stock market. Popular publications on share ownership and media coverage of Wall Street personalities drew wealth from the middle class into the stock market, immensely deepening it and making the risk of diversification for authority more appealing than elsewhere. The American response to the Great Depression destroyed much of the remaining family capitalism. After the crisis of 1929, the Insull and Van Sweringen business organizations, which resembled two enormous pyramids, collapsed. In the public's perception, the correlation between these high-profile failures and the Great Depression's overwhelmingly strong corporate control justifies a barrage of progressive reforms. According to 1937 data on block holding in the top 200 listed US companies, a series of regulatory reforms governing financial institutions, insurance firms, mutual funds, and pension funds prevented any of these organizations from accumulating significant CG influence. The hostile acquisitions of the 1980s disrupted this arrangement in some form and caused some institutional investors in the United States to clear their airways, the majority of American firms have remained independent and professionally managed ever since. Since then, the majority of companies have implemented CG.

1.6.2 United Kingdom (UK)

In one of the conducted studies, a comparison was made between companies founded in 1900 and those founded in 1960. At approximately the same rate, ownership becomes diffuse in both groups of firms. On this basis, it is argued that the forces that caused founding families to walk away from CG in the contemporary United Kingdom existed a century ago as well. In addition, a discussion concludes that until the late 20th century, shareholder rights in the United Kingdom were exceedingly limited, and shareholder legal protection permits diffuse possession in the UK.

The pyramids acquired prominence in the middle of the 20th century as a descriptive summary of UK CG in a more general sense. The 1948 implementation of corporate disclosure made hostile takeovers less hazardous for predators, and pyramids evolved as a line of defense against hostile acquisitions. However, they argue that British corporate executives were and are governed by higher ethical standards that prohibit the receipt of such private benefits. This made it easier to persuade British corporate insiders to sell their control units and disassemble their pyramids. Thus, the present diffuse holding of British corporations has persisted since the early 20th century.

1.6.3 Germany

Fohlin (2004) contends that Germany's major universal banks played a smaller role in its CG history than is commonly assumed. Industrial firms with financiers on BOD did not outperform those without bankers. In this era, German CG shows up to have been developed with care. The current

10   *Shariah Governance Systems of Islamic Banks*

dual board structure was established by the company law of 1870 to defend minor shareholders and the public from self-serving insiders. It also required accounting, reporting, and governance uniformity and consistency.

Thus, family controlled pyramidal organizations and businesses that appear to be broadly held but are actually under the control of middlemen from the top few banks dominate the current German economy. The majority of the shares held by the big institutions are under collective control. Due to parochial governance practices that have hampered shareholders' rights, German companies have been unable to secure capital from institutional investors in recent years on international markets (Monks and Minow, 2001).

1.6.4 *Japan*

Japan's CG history is more intricate and diverse than that of any other significant nation. Prior to 1868, Japan was an extremely isolationist and conservative nation. Priests, soldiers, peasants, and artisans were placed above business families in a hereditary caste structure. This moral inversion predictably led to stagnation. Nonetheless, the necessity of governing a densely populated nation compelled Japan's feudal shoguns to grant prominent mercantile families such as the Mistui and Sumitomo progressively more power. Japan traditionally belonged to the insider-dominated groups and possessed a "credit-based financial system" (Zysman, 1983), as its economy was characterized by intercompany shareholdings, intercompany directorships, and frequently substantial bank involvement.

In recent years, the trend has been toward a Japanese CG system dominated by the market (Cooke and Sawa, 1998). These organizations, known as *zaibatsu*, were pyramids of listed corporations controlled by families, similar to those located elsewhere in the globe. As Japan's economy soared during the 20th century, other 29 business groups, such as Nissan, a pyramidal business group with a publicly traded company at its apex, joined in. Thus, Japan's industrialization was initiated by a combination of family and state capitalism. Investors enthusiastically purchased shares, particularly in the numerous subsidiaries issued by these large business conglomerates.

1.6.5 *China*

Chinese CG in the late 19th and early 20th centuries is of interest because it corresponds with the beginning of China's industrialization and the attempted transplantation of Western norms into a non-Western economy. Thus, the industrial development of pre-communist China may provide more instructive lessons for modern emergent economies than does post-communist China herself. Moreover, pre-revolutionary capitalism provides a paradigm of "a market economy with Chinese characteristics." As a result of their inability to influence CG, portfolio investors kept away from equities. This kept the Chinese stock market opaque and susceptible to extreme cycles of prosperity and collapse. This, in turn, prevented insiders from selling their shares and diversifying, highlighting the value of their exclusive benefits.

1.7   Principles of Corporate Governance

Due to the dearth of a unified CG framework, global practice generates disparities in corporate and national practice (OECD, 2004). These differences are predominantly the result of distinct common beliefs, different ownership structures, an altered business environment, and competitive conditions (Gregory, 2000). In addition, the structure of CG is contingent upon the development of a legal and regulatory framework and an organizational environment. Various countries have published numerous reports, such as the Greenbury Report (1995), the Combined Code on CG (2003, 2006), the Cadbury Report (1992), the Combined Code (1998), and the Higgs Report (2003), to protect the rights of shareholders through CG.

In the best interests of a broad range of constituents, the King Report (2002) proposes a unified approach to effective governance. The report outlined an all-encompassing strategy for implementing core economic, social, ethical, and ecological values (Mallin, 2007). In addition, the report emphasizes that making a profit for shareholders is not the corporation's sole objective, as it must also adhere to the seven basic tenets of CG, namely discipline, accountability, equality, independence, transparency, accountability, and social obligation (Du Plessis *et al.*, 2005). In 1997, the United Nations Development Program (Graham *et al.*, 2003) identified five additional principles of effective governance: legitimacy and voice, direction, performance, fairness, and accountability. Additionally, Aboagye-Otchere *et al.* (2012) and Shrives and Brennam (2015) dealt with the transparency and disclosures of CG.

According to the OECD (2004), there is no single model of effective CG, as CG practices differ considerably from country to country and company to company. According to Gregory (2000), the distinctions originate predominantly from dissimilar cultural beliefs, ownership constructions, business conditions, and competitive environments. In addition, CG frameworks depend on the development of legal systems and the institutional and regulatory circumstances. Several international studies have examined business ethics from the standpoint of safeguarding shareholder interests. Greenbury Report (1995), Combined Code (1998), Cadbury Report (1992), Combined Code on Corporate Governance (2003, 2006), and Higgs Report (2003) are examples.

Originally released in 1994, the King Report (2002) promotes a comprehensive strategy for efficient governance that serves the needs of a wide variety of stakeholders. This report establishes in an exhaustive manner the fundamental principles of effective financial, moral, and environmental practice (Mallin, 2007). By emphasizing the tripartite bottom line (i.e., economic, environmental, and social aspects), the King Report reaffirms that generating profits for shareholders is not a company's only goal (du Plessis *et al.*, 2005). It emphasizes seven fundamental principles of corporate administration: discipline, accountability, fairness, independence, responsibility, transparency, and social responsibility.

Moreover, the UNDP in 1997 on good governance covers five principles:

(1) Performance;
(2) Legitimacy and voice;
(3) Accountability;
(4) Direction; and
(5) Fairness (Graham *et al.*, 2003).

Legitimacy and voice demand that every one of men and women participate in democratic decision-making. Whenever possible, good governance additionally mediates contending objectives to come to a broad consensus regarding what is in the group's best interest and on policies and procedures. The second concept, direction, addresses the strategic goal in which leadership and the general population have a broad and long-term perspective on efficient leadership and an awareness of what is required for the development. The third principle, achievement, refers to the production of results that satisfy the needs of stakeholders and maximize resource utilization. This includes issues like cost-effectiveness, capacity, responsiveness, the dissemination of performance-related information to the public, and tracking and assessing the performance of management. The accountability principle requires companies to be forthcoming and answerable to both institutional and public stakeholders. Processes, structures, and information ought to be accessible to those who are impacted by them, and stakeholders should be provided with sufficient monitoring data. The fifth principle, fairness, addresses equity and the rule of law and requires that all men and women have equal access to opportunities and that legislation be applied unbiasedly (Wahab and Rahman, 2013).

1.7.1 The 10 Fundamental Principles of Corporate Governance Stated in ASX

The CG standards vary from region to region and country to country. In contrast, the principles of good CG and Best Practice Recommendations of the Australian Stock Exchange (ASX) CG Committee identify 10 fundamental principles of CG. The primary components of CG, according to the South African King Report, are oversight, candor, autonomy, responsibility, accountability, fairness, and social responsibility. One might contend that these seven tenets are too broad to aid in CG. Nevertheless, the explanations provided for each of these concepts in the Report reveal that these are the real foundations for effective and consistent CG. And these values are consistent with the teachings of Islamic law (Azzam Wajeeh and Muneeza, 2012).

Governance Council's Principles of Excellent CG and Best Practice Recommendations (2003) lays a solid foundation for management surveillance, structuring the BOD to add value, encouraging accountable and ethical choices, safeguarding trustworthiness in financial reporting, making swift and balanced disclosure, respecting the rights of shareholders, identifying and managing hazards, encouraging enhanced results, remunerating fairly and responsibly, and resolving conflicts of interest. The primary focus of these principles is the essence and administration of corporations. This suggests that the basic tenets of CG vary according to the needs of the corporation and its operating environment. Therefore, CG is an adaptable and changeable mechanism (Azzam Wajeeh and Muneeza, 2012). CG for financial institutions such as banks has unique characteristics due to the opaqueness and regulatory nature of the industry (Wilson et al., 2010; Levine, 2004). According to Angelides et al. (2011), the financial crisis was caused by insufficient lending standards, inordinate borrowing, excessive leverage, and an absence of transparency. Thus, it is necessary that the banking sector be tightly controlled and that effective CG mechanisms be implemented, as such apparatus is crucial for promoting the stability of the financial system while improving the welfare of society (Grais and Pellegrini, 2006a).

1.7.2 The OECD Principles and Its Explanation

The Organization for Economic Cooperation and Development (OECD) has outlined six principles to guide the creation of CG systems in order to guarantee proper accountability and stakeholder trust. Here are some of the OECD's fundamental principles.

The first principle lays the groundwork for an effective CG structure. The CG structure should encourage open and efficient markets, be consistent with the rule of law, and make it clear who is responsible for what in terms of oversight, regulation, and enforcement.

The second guiding principle is ownership rights and critical uses. Shareholder rights should be protected and encouraged to be used within the CG framework.

Third tenet: providing equitable treatment to stockholders. All shareholders, including minorities and international investors, should be treated equally within the CG structure. Every shareholder should have a choice of efficient remedies in the event of a violation of their rights.

The fourth principle of solid CG is of significance to the stakeholders. The CG framework should acknowledge the entitlements of stakeholders as defined by law or by mutual agreements, and it should encourage companies and stakeholders to work together actively to generate wealth, create jobs, and ensure the long-term viability of profitable businesses.

Fourth tenet: be forthright and honest. Financial, performance, possession, and CG data should all be promptly and accurately disclosed within the context of good CG.

The fifth tenet: *Responsibility of the BOD*. The BOD must be held accountable to the firm and its shareholders, and the CG structure must ensure the company's strategic direction and effective supervision by the board.

And lastly, sustainability and resilience there are four guiding concepts that form the basis of the preceding principle. The mechanisms of business ethics come first, followed by those of making decisions, of providing sufficient information in a timely manner, and of balancing and closing the books. Non-members are increasingly adopting and implementing OECD guidelines because of their high quality.

1.8 Role of Corporate Governance

In accordance with early US academic research on CG, the primary function of CG is to reduce agency costs resulting from mergers and takeovers, and it then develops into additional domains, such as the role of financial institutions as businesses oversee to control supervisory shirking and maximize shareholder value (Macey, 2004). Scott (2003) agrees, defining the goal part of a CG system as a set of laws, incentives, and practices that investors may put their faith in to increase the company's profitability. The link between good CG and business success has been extensively researched and is supported by studies such as Selvaggi and Upton (2008), and Black *et al.* (2006). According to Claessens (2003), in the financial services sector, good CG is essential for a company's success because it affects the firm's ability to attract external financing, lower its cost of capital, improve its operational performance, lessen its exposure to risk, and build stronger relationships with its stakeholders. In this respect, the bank's efficiency will grow, which might result in enhanced performance, the bank will avoid unnecessary agency expenditures, and the agency issue will be addressed (Hart, 1995).

According to Wolfensohn (1999), one of the main roles of CG is to encourage transparency, justice, and responsibility inside businesses. Financial institutions need to be more open and equitable for all parties involved in order to improve CG, not just shareholders. Increasing the company's openness and accountability is a key component of good CG, which has been shown to boost growth, profitability, and reputation (Grais and Pellegrini, 2006b).

In conclusion, good CG is essential for every business to succeed in its intended pursuits. Establishing policies, a set of legal standards, and management behavior between shareholders, executives, the BOD, and various other stakeholders is the primary focus of corporate responsibility in the financial services business. The increasing sophistication and complexity of the financial services sector have given rise to a greater number of stakeholders, all of whom have a say in shaping the nature and makeup of the CG framework in financial institutions. Because of these considerations, there has to be a set of rules and regulations tailored specifically to the financial services industry that encourages good CG (Hasan, 2011b).

1.9 Key Participants of Corporate Governance in Financial Sectors

There are three major actors in CG: the upper management, the BOD, and the shareholders. A corporation's senior management is responsible for conducting daily business operations and reporting to the BOD about their status.

16   *Shariah Governance Systems of Islamic Banks*

The responsibilities of senior management include:

- Developing and, following board approval, implementing strategic objectives.
- Developing and, following board approval, operating within annual budgets and strategies.
- Maintaining an effective and suitable administrative and organizational structure.
- Establishing internal controls to ensure accurate financial reporting and providing channels for the reporting of potential malfeasance.

The BOD is ultimately responsible for overseeing the business and affairs of the corporation. The monitoring of upper management on behalf of the shareholders is one of the BOD' most essential supervision responsibilities. These responsibilities include the following:

- Selecting, determining the compensation for, and, when necessary, replacing senior management.
- Evaluating whether senior management is effectively running the corporation's business by monitoring its operations.
- Reviewing and, where applicable, authorizing senior management's proposed financial objectives and key corporate plans and actions.

In connection with these governance responsibilities, state law imposes certain duties on the BOD, including an obligation of care and a responsibility of loyalty to the company and its shareholders. The duty of care requires them to manage the corporation's funds with the same degree of care as if they were managing their own funds. Duty of loyalty means they have to constantly act in the best interests of the organization and its shareholders as a whole (i.e., when making business decisions on behalf of the corporation, they must prioritize the corporation's and shareholders' interests over their own).

It is obvious that the CG process works best when board members are actively involved, make the appropriate inquiries, work together to figure out what is going on, and approve transactions based on strong business justifications. If they do not ask the proper questions, receive the right answers, and confirm transactions with a full awareness of what is behind them, they may be held personally liable for their acts or inactions. Owners of the corporation and shareholders have a direct financial stake in how well it does financially. As a result, the BOD and senior management serve the interests of the shareholders.

Depending on the class of stock they own in the corporation, the shareholders are granted special advantages, such as the right to vote in BOD elections, the right to receive income distributions, and the right to the business's assets in the event of its dissolution. Notably, despite the fact that such plans and activities may require shareholder approval, shareholders do not normally have the capacity to begin substantial corporate initiatives and strategies on behalf of the corporation.

Other CG Players: There is a plethora of additional factors that influence CG practice and are worthy of mention. These other participants include:

- *Legislators and administrators*: As stated previously, legislators, such as the Congress, and authorities, such as the SEC and national stock exchanges, have played and will likely continue to play a substantial role in molding CG practice. Without the impetus of Congress, the SEC, and the national securities exchanges, it is evident that CG practice would not have advanced so rapidly in such a brief amount of time.
- *Proxy advisory companies*: For shareholders, including institutional shareholders like mutual funds and pension funds, casting a proxy vote is an important responsibility. Institutional shareholders increasingly rely on proxy advice firms to analyze proxy proposals and offer voting recommendations. Examples of such firms include institutional shareholders like Services and Glass, Lewis & Co. The importance of this voting rights to businesses cannot be overstated. They could prevent a management or shareholder proposal from receiving the necessary number of votes to proceed.
- *Law firms*: Various business participants, such as BOD, upper management, and shareholders, are advised on CG-related matters by lawyers who specialize in this area of law. When it comes to strategic transactions, shareholder proposals, related-party contacts, director independence assessments, or CEO compensation difficulties, CG attorneys advise corporate actors on how to comply with the "letter and spirit" of the law.

Corporate parties must adhere to legal requirements in practically every CG problem or dispute in order to accomplish their desired goals. In order for a proposal to be included in the proxy statement for a vote at an annual or special meeting of shareholders, a shareholder who owns a modest amount of a corporation's securities must abide by the procedural and substantive

18   *Shariah Governance Systems of Islamic Banks*

requirements of SEC Rules. Before pursuing a strategic transaction, management may be required to obtain board and/or shareholder approval under state corporate law or other laws, the organizational documents or regulations of the corporation, or the continued listing requirements of the national securities exchange where the corporation's securities are traded. Therefore, the role of lawyers involved in CG matters or competitions is to help corporate participants get over the relevant compliance, legal, and regulatory hurdles.

1.9.1   *The Evolving Roles of the Key Players*

CG did not exist in the form it does today until the 1990s. Senior management wouldn't use many "checks and balances" to run their businesses. The only option available to shareholders who disagreed with current developments was to sell their shares. Senior management frequently kept the BOD in the dark about their decisions. Regulatory pressures forced businesses to increase director independence and board supervision powers in response to accounting scandals and other corporate misconduct in the early 2000s (e.g., Enron, WorldCom, Tyco, Global Crossing, Adelphia, etc.). Unbiased committees of the BOD are required by such regulatory requirements, such as the Sarbanes–Oxley Act of 2002 and the CG listing guidelines of the national securities exchanges, to:

- Be in charge of the selection, supervision, and compensation of the corporation's independent registered public accounting firm;
- Manage procedures for the receipt, retention, and handling of auditing complaints;
- Hold regular meetings in executive session rooms.

In terms of the CG procedure, BOD are generally becoming more assertive. As the BOD is ultimately accountable for administering the corporation, they are increasingly requesting that management report to them prior to taking any corporate actions. The BOD meetings are now much lengthier than they were in the past because the administration is now required to devote more time to the members of the board and explain what is happening. Thus, the CG balance of power has shifted toward BOD, especially independent directors and committees, and will likely continue to shift in this direction. Similarly, the pendulum of CG appears to be swaying in favor of shareholders. Independent directors are believed to be in the best position to defend shareholders' interests, and shareholders are demanding and receiving a greater voice in their election. In 2003, when the SEC proposed the shareholder access rule, it appeared to be a turning point for this movement. The SEC decided to abandon the proposal in the face of significant opposition from business organizations such as the Business Round Table and the US Chamber of Commerce.

Shareholder activists, dissatisfied with their ineffective ability to impact director elections, set their crosshairs on the plurality voting system prevalent in the majority of US corporations. Under this system, the only ballots that count in the election of directors are those cast in favor of the nominee listed in the corporation's proxy statement. In response, activist shareholders launched a crusade to compel corporations to implement a majority voting criterion.

1.10 Corporate Governance Theories

It's been thought about for centuries, but there hasn't been any formalized or major conversation on the strategy or model of CG (Zulkifli, 2011). An important economic-based theoretical framework for the concept of CG, the agency theory, was developed as a result of a seminal study by Berle and Means (1932) that focused on the idea of corporate ownership through ownership and the dispute that ensues as a result of the separation of ownership and control. An agency relationship, described as "an arrangement that recognizes the shareholder as the company's owner and the managerial staff as an agent who has the authorization to perform operations on the proprietor's behalf" (Jensen and Meckling, 1976), is central to this concept of CG. Evidently, a conflict of agency develops between the principals and the agent when the latter prioritizes its own interests above those of the former. Management in its role as the shareholders' representative might become exploitative under such conditions.

There are many theories that have been developed to explain CG, including transaction cost theory (Williamson, 1979), legitimacy theory, political theory (Macey, 2004; Deegan *et al.*, 2022), legitimate contractual theory, managerial-class hegemony theory (Sacconi, 2006), institutional theory (Clarke, 2004), and resource-dependency theory (Clarke, 2004). As a result, the remainder of this chapter will focus on how to put these ideas into practice to better understand their foundational principles.

1.10.1 Agency Theory

As discussed by Berle and Means (1932), the establishment of corporate ownership via shareholding and the conflict that can arise over the dichotomy of ownership and corporate control produces agency theory, an essential economic-based theoretical framework for the concept of CG. American financial economists in the 1970s laid the groundwork for a CG structure based on agency theory (Lazonick and O'Sullivan, 2000).

Proponents of the agency theory, such as Jensen and Meckling (1976), define agency as a contractual arrangement between the shareholder (the principal) and the management (the agent), who are given the authority to act on the principal's behalf. The BOD and the Executive Officers are bound by legislative norms and procedures to prioritize the interests of the shareholders as part of an agency theory designed to maximize shareholder value. Mallin (2007: 12) argues that one strength of the agency theory is that it "defines an association where a single party, the person in charge, delegates obligation to a distinct party, the agent." To reduce the likelihood of problems arising from the principal–agent connection, she emphasizes that the BOD is an important mechanism for keeping tabs on things (Mallin, 2007: 13). One of the major problems with this contract is the inherent conflict of interest between the parties. This agency problem is predicated on the idea that managers will prioritize their own interests over those of the company (see, for example, Boatright, 1999; Kim and Mahoney, 2005; Ryan and Schneider, 2003). According to Demirag and Tylecote (1992) management actions that run counter to the long-term interest of increasing shareholders' wealth are said to incur opportunity costs.

By looking at the difficulties experienced by privatized businesses in developing economies, Dharwadkar *et al.* (2000) provided another look at the agency theory in a novel governance setting. They worry that this would lead to the seizure of minority rights and an increase in the already existing difficulties with an agency. According to agency theory, every member of a company's ecosystem has self-serving motivations. Each group has been shown to behave in its own self-interest. Managers are seldom seen prioritizing the interests of the firm's owners above their own (Jensen and Meckling, 1976; Fama, 1980), therefore it is safe to assume that they do not always behave in the best interests of shareholders. Establishing incentive systems and contracts for management, as well as shareholders' use of voting privileges to shape the firm's strategic direction, are examples of agency costs involved with bringing the interests of both parties into alignment (Pratt and Zeckhauser, 1985). Conversely, contracts are used to specify the rights of both parties involved (shareholders and management), including assessment of performance and pay. Two methods by which shareholders might improve the efficacy of contracts are explained by multiple scholars such as Ouchi (1978) and Eisenhardt (1989) among others. The first approach uses a system to keep tabs on the agent's actions to make sure they're in line with the contract, with the goal of reducing the agent's knowledge asymmetry issue and enforcing consequences for deviant conduct. Instead, Jensen and Meckling (1976) suggest judging managers based on how well they met goals as opposed to how well they hoped to meet goals.

1.10.2 *Stewardship Theory*

Stewardship theory takes a different stance than agency theory. The goal of governance, according to stewardship theory, is to find procedures and frameworks that encourage the most efficient collaboration among management and owners (Donaldson, 1990; Davis *et al.*, 1997). This is in contrast to agency theory, which assumes that a conflict of interest will arise if ownership is split. In addition, the individuals who work in an organization are seen as cooperative and pro-organizational rather than opportunistic, according to stewardship theory (Davis *et al.*, 1997). The stewardship theory predicts that transaction expenses will be reduced owing to the reduced need for remuneration and the oversight of conduct (Davis *et al.*, 1997).

1.10.3 *Stakeholder Theory*

Numerous academic works have criticized agency theory's focus on the BOD, shareholders, and management, arguing that it is too narrow to account for the wide range of CG regulations across institutional settings (Aguilera and Jackson, 2003; Filatotchev, *et al.*, 2008). Stakeholder theory, a framework for CG, challenges the view that shareholders are only marginally affected by corporations' actions. Stakeholder theory argues that business ethics and managerial responsibility should extend beyond the shareholders who are the focus of agency theory. Stakeholder theory (Berry and Rondinelli, 1998; Caldwell and Karri, 2005; Solomon, 2007; Collier, 2008) analyzes cases in which management prioritizes the needs of groups other than shareholders. Specifically, Freeman (1994) defines stakeholders as any collection of people who may influence or are impacted by the fulfillment of the organization's aims. Primary stakeholders include workers and customers, while secondary stakeholders include NGOs, activists, communities, and governments, as defined by Waddock *et al.* (2002).

Stakeholder theory, in its portrayal of CG, indirectly rejects agency theory's claim that maximizing shareholder wealth is the only reason for a company to exist. Management, according to Donaldson and Preston (1995), acts as the agent under stakeholder theory, choosing activities and distributing resources so as to maximize returns for all genuine stakeholders. Management's responsibility includes dealing with the various stakeholder groups in an ethical manner (Carroll and Buchholtz, 1999: 23), as well as "reconciling the disputes of interests that arise between companies and stakeholder groups." Consequently, management has a fiduciary responsibility to take into account the needs of all relevant stakeholders. To supplement agency theory in the context of CG, the theory of stakeholders has been developed (Solomon, 2007).

The theory of stakeholders has been criticized for its singular value (Jensen, 2001), for distracting the firm from its goals (Ansoff, 1987), and for causing competitive issues by facilitating the transmission of expertise to other working environments. In response to these claims, Roberts (1992) suggested that companies rank their constituents based on relevance, influence, and dependency.

1.10.4 *Transaction Cost Theory*

Similar to agency theory, transaction cost theory is an economic theory of organizational and CG that developed from the work of Coase (1937) and Williamson (1979). However, one may still see differences, such as the underlying theoretical premise that defines what a firm is. For instance, Williamson (1998) argued that the "nexus for a contracting relationship" phrase used by Jensen and Meckling (1976) implied that agency theory views a company as a function of production (as with price and output) between the principal and the agent. Anticipating aversion to risk and the possible ethical risk of the agent, agency theory bases the notion of governance on an *ex-ante* efficient motive alignment between both parties of the agreement. In contrast, transaction cost theory sees the firm as an organizational construction where efficient boundaries can be derived through the discriminatory alignment of different transactions with different organizational systems (firm or market) (Williamson, 1985, 1991b, 1998). This differentiation also highlights the separate analytical units used by agency theory and the theory of transaction costs for the individual operator and the transaction, respectively.

Key issues to be discussed include the nature of transaction costs and their connection to the underlying governance framework of transaction cost theory. Generally speaking, transaction costs include everything from bargaining and keeping tabs to actually enforcing agreements. In a market-based system, this would include calculating the appropriate pricing and any related expenses, before entering into a separate contract for each individual trade. However, Coase (1937) stated that a company forms and workers give up the freedom to contract their labor when transaction costs of executing market activities are significant. When a firm brings more of its operations in-house, it reduces certain transaction costs but incurs others, such as those associated with coordinating purchases, manufacturing activities, and personnel management. This strategy is known as vertical integration.

Based on the preceding transaction cost description, Williamson offered three general governance structures in his work (see, for example, Williamson 1975, 1979, 1981): the market, the chain of command (i.e., vertical integration), and the hybrid (a mix of the market and the hierarchy). Williamson (1975, 1985) argues that uncertainty in the contractual process and the resulting transaction costs are the results of "bounded reasoning" and "opportunism" as postulated underpinning the theoretical idea of transaction cost theory. Based on Simon's (1964) description of human action as "intendedly rational, but only limitedly so," the presumption of "bounded rationality" or contractual incompleteness describes the justification of human behavior as being limited by the capacity to process information and, thus, expose the contracting parties to certain risks. For example, if an unforeseen event renders the original governance agreement null and void, the company will need to make adjustments or face "maladaptation expenses" (Williamson, 1991a). Opportunism, on the other hand, is defined as "self-interest pursuing with falsehood" (Williamson, 1975) as a characterization of human conduct. The complexity of contracts is exacerbated by the fact that parties are wary of having their interests represented by an agent who attempts to coordinate transactions in their favor. Transaction cost theory, which assumes limited rationality and opportunism, is concerned with how *ex-ante* decisions of

24   *Shariah Governance Systems of Islamic Banks*

governance structure might mitigate *ex-post* opportunistic hazards. As a result, transaction cost theory, in line with agency theory, seeks the optimal governance structure that can rein in agents' opportunistic activity in order to maximize shareholder returns. According to Williamson (1998), the two theories of agency theory and cost of transactions are complementary from a theoretical perspective.

1.10.5 *Legitimacy Theory*

According to the legitimacy theory, businesses justify their acts by disclosing information about economic, social, and political aspects as well as the natural environment. According to Patten (2005), the theory is founded on the idea that businesses (Islamic institutions) exist in society under a social compact, and are thus regulated via the public-policy arena rather than the free market. According to Adams *et al.* (1998), businesses may justify their actions by promoting an image of being socially conscious. In other words, the corporation justifies its behavior by disclosing all CSR initiatives in the financial statement and supporting its ongoing presence in the market. According to McDonald and Rundle Thiele (2008), CSR impacts corporate profitability by building intangible assets like trust and loyalty that are essential to a company's continued success. The value of a company rises as a result of this since the company is better able to attract resources, boost performance, and create competitive advantages (Fombrun and Gardberg, 2000). Previous studies have shown that improved disclosure reporting is associated with higher profits and stock prices since it improves the company's image in the eyes of its stakeholders. According to legitimacy theory (Deegan *et al.*, 2002), businesses may be ready to share social information as a means of establishing their legitimacy in the eyes of the public. The financial repercussions of sharing personal information publicly are to blame.

According to legitimacy theory, "Organizations continually seek to make sure that they function within the constraints and customs of their various societies" (Deegan, 2002: 253). The goal is to have their actions be seen as lawful by the public. That any entity's activities are desirable, legitimate, or acceptable within a socially created system of standards, beliefs, values, and definitions is what Suchman (1995: 574) calls "legitimacy theory." According to legitimacy theory, a socially engaged corporation, like an Islamic organization, has a social agreement in which it promises to behave in ways that benefit society in return for the support of its aims, other incentives, and its continued existence. The "social contract," according to Deegan (2002), is challenging to define, but the term is used to convey the wide range of both explicit and implicit norms the community has for the company's operations. Educating and informing relevant customers about changes in company performance and activities is the first method suggested by Lindblom (1994) for legitimizing an organization's actions. Changing the perceptions of the relevant public without altering the public's actual behavior is the second. Manipulating perception by redirecting consideration to other pertinent problems through an appeal is the third. Therefore, these findings might be interpreted to show that Islamic organizations need to reveal information about their operations in order to authorize their behavior since the revelation of social information seems to be proof of this. They have an obligation to provide enough information for the public to judge the extent to which they behave ethically as a business (Maali *et al.*, 2003).

Several studies have tried to use legitimacy theory as a driver of disclosure (e.g., O'Dwyer, 2002; Deegan and Rankin, 1996; Campbell *et al.*, 2003; Ahmad and Sulaiman, 2004; Ogden and Clark, 2005; Staden, 2003; Branco and Rodrigues, 2008; De Villiers and van Staden, 2006). Legitimacy theory, according to Gray *et al.* (1995) and Deegan (2002), intersects with political economy and institutional analysis. In addition, its capacity to foretell and explain management action has been called into question (Parker, 2005), and the theory of legitimacy has been attacked for this same reason.

1.10.6 *Accountability Theory*

According to general accountability theory, "accountability" refers to the obligation of accountors (agents/directors/managers) to provide accountees (stakeholders/users/society) with an account (information/report). The accountability theory demonstrates that managers are responsible for performing a predetermined set of duties or tasks and for adhering to the rules and standards applicable to their positions in organizations (Jagadeesan *et al.*, 2009). According to Gray *et al.* (1995), managers must disclose all financial and non-financial information to their stake-holders in order to be socially accountable. In addition, emancipatory accounting includes making an entity's socioeconomic activity visible. Accounting may be viewed as having an emancipatory potential if it makes social problems visible, as providing information may facilitate

26   *Shariah Governance Systems of Islamic Banks*

a resolution. Also, the accountability between account (principal) and accountor (agent) varies based on the accountee. For instance, managers may be accountable to employees for their salary, health and safety, and all employee rights, whereas employees may be accountable for their work performance.

1.10.7 *Signaling Theory*

Signals for investors might be found in the company's yearly reports. Signals are used by investors as a factor in making decisions. Enterprises and investors benefit from signaling theory because the information given by enterprises may mitigate the effects of information asymmetry. While this analysis acknowledges that signaling theory has been used in the past to explain business disclosure choices (see, for example, Wang *et al.*, 2008), it instead relies mostly on agency theory. Many authors (e.g., Van Buskirk, 2012; Jensen and Meckling, 1976) see signaling theory as an expansion of agency theory. In an effort to bridge the gap in communication between workers and management, Spence (1973) developed the signaling theory. The information gap theory was developed to shed light on the disconnect between management and investors. If the party in possession of more knowledge were to convey that fact to the others involved, the effect of the information asymmetry may be reduced. According to Morris (1987), signaling is a common occurrence in all markets when there is an imbalance of information. Thus, this idea was used to justify the motivations of managers to provide more information in financial statements (e.g., Haniffa and Cooke, 2002). Signaling theory suggests that managers share data to show superior performance and lessen the gap between their organization and the competition. In order to reduce information asymmetry, signaling theory suggests that investors rely on the information supplied by enterprises (Abhayawansa and Abeysekera, 2009). For information signaling by businesses to be successful in decreasing information asymmetry, Morris (1987) argues that actors must incur the signaling costs so they have the incentive to signal correctly. When it comes to the capital markets, a solid business may distinguish itself from an unsuccessful business by sending an authoritative message about its quality. According to Bhattacharya and Dittmar (2004), the credibility of a signal depends on whether or not the poor business voluntarily decides to convey the same signal as the excellent firm. Full transparency, according to this hypothesis (Sheu *et al.*, 2010), denotes higher business value because of better CG and fewer agency conflicts.

For the most part, the signaling theory is used to explain the correlation between openness and business value. Full disclosure, as proposed by Sheu *et al.* (2010), suggested more efficient mechanisms of CG and fewer conflicts between agencies, both of which boost company value. Voluntary announcements in the annual report provide signals to the market that are expected to boost a company's current value and, by extension, its stock market value, as stated by Gordon *et al.* (2010). Corporate transparency affects how the market values a firm, as noted by Curado *et al.* (2011). Stock markets benefit from disclosure because of the information it reveals, as stated by Cormier *et al.* (2011). Disclosure has been shown to aid in the development of shareholder value, as shown by Gallego-Álvarez *et al.* (2010). Management, other investors, and market players may all benefit from more open communication when more information is made public. Lambert *et al.* (2007) argue that greater corporate transparency can help alleviate the asymmetry challenge and agency conflicts. However, greater transparency leads to less mispricing, higher cumulative profits, and higher firm value. The link between openness and a company's worth has been corroborated by further empirical research. Healy *et al.* (1999) discover, for instance, that companies that provide more information to investors have significant improvements in market value. By affecting managerial judgment and, by extension, the allocation of future cash flows, corporate disclosures may have a material impact on the value of a firm (Lambert *et al.*, 2007). Increases in corporate transparency may increase a company's stock price, according to research by Elzahar *et al.* (2015).

1.10.8 *Economic Theory*

Economic theory was developed by Jensen and Meckling in 1976. Prevailing economic theory is that a party's "contractual pie" portion is what motivates it to invest in acquiring knowledge. During the pre-contractual phase, a party may spend money on information gathering if it believes there is a good chance that doing so will lead to the discovery of details that will help it obtain or convey an asset that's worth (costs) exceed (fall below) what was paid (received). The investing party must incur the expenses of gathering this knowledge before the contract is formed, but they will not gain from it since the price would then represent the asset's true worth (Jensen and Meckling, 1976).

Numerous studies (e.g., Meek *et al.*, 1995; Hossain *et al.*, 1995; Haniffa and Cooke, 2002; Chen *et al.*, 2008; Hossain and Taylor, 2007) have used this theory to explain and make sense of the occurrence of voluntary disclosure in the field of accounting. One major connection between the theory of economics and modern accounting theory is the assumption that an organization's dedication to increased openness should lower the costs of capital that come from knowledge asymmetries and favorably improve the firm's value (Leuz and Verrecchia, 2000). The risk of an information gap between the corporation and its shareholders is mitigated by a commitment to increased levels of transparency. As a result, the premium paid for new capital should go down, and the cost at which existing shareholders sell their shares should shrink (Baiman and Verrecchia, 1996).

Studies use economic theory to measure how transparency impacts a company's worth. It argues that disclosure has beneficial effects on firm value, such as the following: first, investors are able to make more accurate assessments of the parameters underlying future stock returns thanks to the availability of higher-quality information, which in turn reduces non-diversifiable calculation uncertainties and risk about potential earnings and future profitability (Clarkson *et al.*, 1996). Enhanced transparency encourages investors to trade more often, which benefits both the firm's value and the liquidity of its shares (Easley and O'Hara, 2004). According to Beyer *et al.* (2010), greater levels of self-disclosure may narrow information gaps between the business and market players, leading to higher stock liquidity and firm value.

1.10.9 *Entity Theory*

The entity theory is the fundamental premise that a business's economic activity is distinct from that of its proprietors. The entity theory is predicated on the notion that a company's activities can and will be independently accounted for by those of its proprietors. The proprietors are not personally accountable for the company's loans and liabilities, according to this theory. Certain enterprises require limited liability for their proprietors in terms of business liability. In order to maintain a system that isolates owners from company liability, the entity theory establishes a baseline that enables the separation of business finances and owners. The separation of personal and professional business activities is a consistent and crucial aspect of global commerce. Entity theory is fundamental to all aspects of business.

The entity theory is an essential component of contemporary accounting. It relies on a straightforward equation:

$$Assets = Liabilities + Owners' \ Equity.$$

According to the entity theory, liabilities are equity holding distinct legal status and rights within the organization. In accounting, the entity theory separates a company's obligations, assets, revenues, expenses, and any other financial aspects from the personal finances and financial operations of its proprietors. Thus, the identity of the company is distinct from the identities of its proprietors and administrators.

Even though the entity theory has been floating since the 19th century, it has not yet attracted a large following. This is partially due to the theory's most prominent and relatively apparent criticisms. Ultimately, a company is an instrument or extension of its proprietors (and/or administrators) that is designed to generate profits. This profit is always tied to the proprietors' bank accounts. The proprietors are similarly entwined with the business in that they are likely to retain significant stakes in the company. Consequently, the proprietors expect a return on every dollar they invest in the business. Not only does investment in the company involve financial capital but also physical and intellectual capital, or the proprietors' time, perspiration, and mental resources.

1.10.10 *Proprietary Theory*

The proprietary theory that assets are possessed by the owner and liabilities are owed to him is defined in the *Dictionary of Accounting Terms*. This is the bookkeeping equation: The proprietary theory is most applicable to sole proprietorships due to the intimate relationship between the owner and the business's management. Frequently, they are the same individual. It also applies to a partnership where net revenue is added to the capital accounts of the partners each period.

1.10.11 *Resource Dependency Theory*

The principle of resource dependency suggests that boards with more members would have access to a greater depth of knowledge, improving their ability to analyze information. Collective decision-making among board

30 *Shariah Governance Systems of Islamic Banks*

members will make up for directors' individual lack of business expertise, improving the quality of managerial decisions and behaviors (Abeysekera, 2010; Ruigrok *et al.*, 2006). The effectiveness of CG has been evaluated in a number of researches (John and Senbet, 1998; Sharma, 2011). For instance, according to resource dependency theory, the BOD can help facilitate, secure, and simplify the acquisition of scarce and vital supplies (Selznick, 1949; Zald, 1969; Pennings, 1980; Pfeffer and Salancik, 1978; Boyd, 1990; Kesner and Johnson, 1990; Zahra and Pearce, 1989). The BOD is seen in this theory as the tool to reduce uncertainty about the environment (Pfeffer, 1972) that might affect resource management and strategy formulation. According to Williamson (1984), one of the BOD responsibilities is to minimize the transaction costs arising from the connections between the company and other environmental entities.

1.10.12 *Managerial-Class Hegemony Theory*

Meanwhile, managerial class hegemony theory claims that the BOD is useless because it does not actively shape the direction of the company (Mace, 1971; Lorsch and Maclver, 1989). The management oversees these functions. According to this idea (Mace, 1971; Clendenin, 1972), the role of the board of members in the strategic management of the corporation is conditional upon the firm being in crisis. Pursuant to the managerial-class dominance thesis (Scott, 1997), top executives are ultimately accountable for running and directing their companies.

1.11 Corporate Governance from an Institutional Theory Perspective

CG, as defined by Shleifer and Vishny (1997: 737), is a strategy for ensuring that investors in firms get a satisfactory return on their money. The issue of agency is central to this notion. Governance at work is more than just how a corporation interacts with its investors, according to Bradley *et al.* (1999). They point out that the way in which the organization serves and is serviced by its many stakeholders is also influenced by its CG. Relationships among the company, its workers, creditors, suppliers, consumers, and host communities are an integral part of any adequate definition of CG.

Several institutional theories of consumers place a heavy emphasis on authority and control structures. This indicates that it has the potential to significantly advance the field of CG studies. The contractarian approach has dominated the literature on CG since the 1980s (e.g., Coffee, 1984; Brudney, 1985; Eisenhardt, 1989) (i.e., the contract between the principal and the agent). However, some recent studies on CG have started to depart from this point of view in favor of a more comprehensive viewpoint that takes a configuration of interdependent elements into account, such as the relationship between stakeholders and corporations and the relationship between corporations and society (Davis and Useem, 2002). This viewpoint also emphasizes the necessity of integrating CG systems within larger institutional and legal frameworks, as Davis and Useem (2002) point out.

CG simulations, such as the Anglo-Saxon and Continental models, including both implicit and explicitly normative theories with regard to the distribution of power and the precedence or order of corporate interests, and the institutionalized approach to corporate management is predicated on this idea (Davis and Thompson, 1994). According to Fiss (2008), this means that models of governance are consistent meaning systems that symbolize the moral order by justifying the right allocation of resources. Similar to the idea of control, these models of governance reflect local hierarchies that provide people with cognitive categories through which they may make sense of their own and others' behavior (Fligstein, 2001).

CG models from an institutional viewpoint, in contrast with agent–principal practice, should be even more dynamic and culturally formed. Given the importance of power dynamics in CG, this issue must be addressed. Surrender to authority and opposition to it may both be accounted for from an institutional viewpoint (Clegg, 1919), making the contractarian conception of power unnecessary. Institutional norms in administration (Davis, 2005) provide a framework for explaining not just the creation and acceptance of new rules but also the many kinds of opposition to these rules. In contrast to the contractarian viewpoint, which sees governance models as immutable structures, the institutional perspective sees them as symbolic ordering that needs continual treatment (by human (re)enactment) to preserve (Fiss, 2008). If an organization undergoes a shift or if its existing activities have been substituted by alternate orders, the quality of its CG system may decline over time.

Fiss (2008) gave three explanations for why CG designs are less robust and more open to criticism. It is important to reproduce, socialize, or convert existing models to new members; CG models are vulnerable to technological and economic shifts that result in a disparity between the actual experience and clarification offered by the model; and CG models are

32   *Shariah Governance Systems of Islamic Banks*

unstable because the representations that form them are wide to a variety of interpretations, which may empower different actors. Another significant viewpoint on CG models and institutional theory is the connection between taken-for-grandness and deliberate agency (Colyvas and Powell, 2006). In this view, CG practice may be placed along a spectrum from those that are hotly debated to those that are just accepted without question. Symbolic orders are unstable and shouldn't be taken for assumed (Thompson, 1990); their preservation is as difficult as its transformation; the ideological task of repair and restoration is an ongoing endeavor (Scott, 1985); and even highly justified models are open to challenges. That doesn't rule out the possibility of stable CG systems. Symbolic hierarchies underpin CG systems, and they may be strengthened by formal authorities like law or politics (Fiss, 2008). However, such rules need time to show their efficacy and durability. What happens, then, is impacted by cultural and historical conceptions of authority and authority that either sustain current systems or give means for establishing novel ones (Swidler, 1986).

These CG representations are not high-level semantic frameworks. Instead, the implementation and meaning of common practices disclose the actions of the institutions they represent (Fine and Sandstrom, 1993). Understanding the role of institutions requires linking theory to actual behavior. Because the normative features of CG models are not consistently translated into corresponding practice (Fiss, 2008), focusing on practice instead opens up a promising avenue of research in the discussion of CG. Power struggles might be a sign of discontent. As a result, interested parties often try to codify and organize this authority. Auditing and monitoring systems, for example, may be influenced by social context (Covaleski *et al.*, 1993). This shows how crucial it is to pay close attention to CG procedures. After that, a literature evaluation on institutional CG practice will be presented.

1.12   Corporate Governance Systems

When looking at global CG, it's important to remember that different countries have different CG systems. Several CG models now in use across the world are discussed. The governance structure proposed by Shleifer and Vishny (1997) is based on genuine depositor protection and ownership concentration. The essential issues of CG systems, in both theory and application (Marshall, 1920; Berle and Means, 1932; Smith, 1993; Keasey *et al.*, 1997), are the separation of ownership disputes and the management decision-making process. Corporate scandals like the web fraud and deception at Bank of Credit and Trade International; the collapse of Barings and Policy Peck; and the Enron allegations in the USA (Kay and Silberston, 1995) among banks' transactions and countries prompted reforms to CG scripts, rules, and regulations.

Takeover models, block holder models, delegated monitoring and major creditor's models, board simulations, executive compensation theories, and multi-constituency models are just some of the measurable CG models that Becht and Barca (2001) cite as possible responses to the detached shareholders' collaborative dispute. The European model of CG is used by a select group of countries outside of Europe. In addition, Lewis (1999) compared and contrasted six various CG models, including the Anglo-Saxon, Germanic, Japanese, Latin, Confucian, and Islamic models. There are also not many really unique models available in certain countries. In theory, everyone supports good company governance. However, there are many different national, social, cultural, and religious opinions. The vast majority of nation-specific models declare their beginnings as a client (Anglo-Saxon) or stakeholders (Continental European) or mixed (the best of both) model in their standards of CG. A brief background of each model is provided here.

1.12.1 *The European Model*

Stakeholders' interests form the basis of the European paradigm in CG. Donaldson and Preston (1995) and Clarkson (1995) both looked at CG through the lens of the stakeholder theory. According to their argument (stated in Yamak and Suer, 2005), each stakeholder has independent self-interests that are not affected by those of any other stakeholder. Fundamentally, stakeholder theory rejects the shareholder's value model and improves the framework for CG by determining the ability of stakeholders to be involved in CG selections, where administrators are bound to protect the best interests of every stakeholder and firms' aim are geared toward enhancing the passions of all stakeholders more than shareholders' (Iqbal and Mirakhor, 2004).

Stakeholders, according to Freeman (1984), may be either members of a group with obligations to the business or individuals who make direct or indirect financial contributions to the corporation. Shareholders, employees, and labor unions are examples of internal stakeholders; customers, suppliers, creditors, and contractors are examples of operational associates;

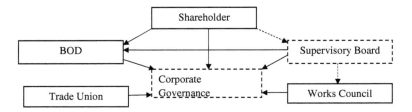

Figure 1.2: European Model of Corporate Governance.
Source: Cernat (2004).

and government agencies, organizing groups, private organizations, and civil society are examples of social community stakeholders (Pesqueux and Damak-Ayadi, 2005). The European approach has been attacked for not doing enough to solve the issue of agency (Macey and Miller, 1997). It has been shown that Separate meetings of the management board (made up of executive directors) and the supervisory board (made up of outside directors) are the norm in European CG. Figure 1.2 shows the European model of CG.

Management and oversight panels make up the backbone of the European model of CG. The management board is chosen by the staff, whereas the supervisory board is selected by the shareholders (Schilling, 2001). Shareholders, union officials, and members elected by the workers' council all make up the supervisory board (Dignam and Galanis, 2009). Management is kept in check by the supervisory board (Schilling, 2001; Hasan, 2011a). More so than shareholders, the management board is responsible for carrying out the company's economic operations in a way that takes into account the rights and concerns of all stakeholders (Hasan, 2011a; Schilling, 2001). While the European approach is cautious and avoids an explicit discussion of agency conflicts, it does a good job of protecting the rights of stakeholders.

1.12.2 The Anglo-Saxon Model

Especially in Commonwealth countries, the Anglo-Saxon model of CG that was developed in the United States and the United Kingdom has become the *de facto* standard. You may also hear this framework referred to as the finance model, the principal–agent model, the outsider model, the principal–agent and agency model, the shareholder approach, the American model,

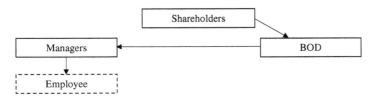

Figure 1.3: The Anglo-Saxon Corporate Governance Model.
Source: Modified from Cernat (2004).

the market-centric framework, or the equity-based framework. Managers, according to the shareholder theory (Nwanji and Howell, 2007; Daily et al., 2003; Shleifer and Vishny, 1997), have an ethical responsibility to maximize shareholder wealth since shareholders are the company's owners and bear the bulk of its risk. The board of executives has a fiduciary responsibility to look out for the best interests of shareholders. Executive and non-executive board members are both appointed and removed by shareholders at the meeting of shareholders (Denis and McConnell, 2003). Figure 1.3 highlights the Anglo-Saxon CG model.

A single-tier BOD composed mostly of non-executive directors characterizes the Anglo-Saxon style of CG. Furthermore, many single-tier boards include simultaneously executive and non-executive directors. The BOD and the stockholders are two distinct groups under this approach (Franks and Mayer, 1997). The dual character of the chief executive officer is forbidden in the US and UK but is legal and commonplace in the US (Siepel and Nightingale, 2012; Meier and Meier, 2014). Managers' abilities to adapt and free up resources might vary greatly due to the wide range of organizational structures and practices that exist today (Siepel and Nightingale, 2012). Furthermore, the Anglo-Saxon model is characterized by a high incidence of conflicts (Cernat, 2004), a low concentration of firms on a small number of persons and fellow shareholders (Akinpelu, 2012), and a trade union with a low focus and very little impact. There is a contemporary trend toward Anglo-Saxon CG practices on a global scale (Gilson, 2001; Martynova and Renneboog, 2011). This framework places limitations on how CEOs may be chosen and what they can do in their roles. In this paradigm, institutional shareholders have more say than regular shareholders do, and shareholder interests are prioritized above those of other stakeholders.

1.12.3 Germanic Corporate Governance System

Shareholders and other interested parties alike profit from the decentralized economic system fostered by Germanic CG practice. There is both a management board and a supervisory board in this setup. Banks are the key source of funding in this system (Odenius, 2008). Figure 1.4 shows the Germany's CG model.

Although there are some parallels in both the Germanic and Japanese forms of CG, the Germanic model is quite different from the Anglo-Saxon, European, and Japanese models. As in Japan, bank representatives with long-term investments in German enterprises are sought by German boards (Ewmi, 2005). In opposition to the circumstance in Japan, where bank legislatures were selected by a BOD only during times of financial difficulty, here representation is permanent.

The Germanic style of CG is distinctive due to three primary aspects. Two of them deal with how boards are put together, while the other deals with shareholders' rights. The Germanic model, first, proposes separate boards at both the supervisory (made up of workers or labor representatives and shareholder delegates) and management (made up completely of insiders, such as corporate executives) levels. A corporation's management board and supervisory board might both include the same people. Second, the number of supervisory board members is capped by law and cannot be changed by the company's shareholders. Finally, a

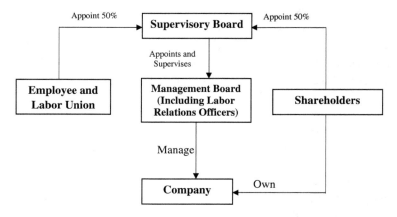

Figure 1.4: Germanic Model of Corporate Governance.
Source: Cited in Alam *et al.* (2019a). Modified from Mostepaniuk (2017).

Corporate Governance Systems of Financial Institutions 37

shareholder's voting power might be capped at a specified proportion of the company's total share capital (independent of the individual's share ownership position) in accordance with regulatory requirements (Ewmi, 2005).

1.12.4 *Latin Corporate Governance System*

The CG structure in Latin America is seen to be more flexible than older models. The BODin Latin CG may be chosen in one of two ways: either with a single ship, like the Anglo-Saxon system, or with a split board, like the Germanic model. Shareholders have a more significant role in decision-making under this structure (Aguilera, 2009). This approach is considered an insider form of corporate administration (Lewis, 1999) due to the fact that insiders, such as family members and close business associates, have a vested interest in the company's success.

The Latin approach to CG is centered on family members and the local community, therefore it looks less organized than the one used by the Anglo-Saxons and has fewer preconditions for resolution activities. The Latin model is diametrically opposed to the Anglo-Saxon model since it is based on a bottom-up mentality rather than a top-down one. As a result, the paradigm focuses on large families in which everyone has meaningful relationships and experiences mutual happiness. Additionally, younger family members look up to their elders since they are seen as wiser persons and are thus chosen for leadership roles. To this end, it is recommended that traditional structures of governance procedures and settlement structures be avoided in favor of informal methods (Ewmi, 2005). In addition, the same idea underlies the Latin paradigm at both the household and the neighborhood levels. Family members take precedence over outside investment in this setup. The members of the family run the bank and make all of the important decisions.

1.12.5 *Japanese Corporate Governance System*

The Japanese CG model is sometimes referred to as a bank-based or bank-led approach. The significance of strict state control and meddling is reflected in this banking paradigm (Okumura, 2004), as is the viewpoint of shareholders. Corporate investors, additionally referred to as investors in the market, and bank shareholders, sometimes known as stable investors, are the two main categories of stockholders in Japanese companies (Ewmi, 2005). In addition to maximizing earnings for corporate shareholders, this structure also safeguards the interests of bank shareholders by preserving the credibility of the bank's portfolio of loans (Yoshikawa and Phillip, 2005), therefore impacting the purposes of CG. The BOD acts in this arrangement as both a directors' authority and an auditors' department. As stated by Allen and Zhao (2007), the Japanese company governance framework gives banks an outsized say in management decisions.

High levels of stock ownership associated with banks and companies, a banking procedure characterized by strong, long-term relationships between bank and company, and a public and economic policy structure developed to encourage and advertise "Keiretsu" (industrial group correlated with transferring connection and cross-shareholding of both equity and debt) characterize Japan's CG structure (Ewmi, 2005). The BOD of Japanese corporations is typically made up of company insiders, with little to no representation from outside shareholders (Ewmi, 2005). This is due to the intricate processes required to carry out shareholder mandates. However, most Japanese firms are owned mostly by company insiders and their colleagues, who have considerable influence on both the companies themselves and the industry as a whole (Figure 1.5). Although the overseas ownership of Japanese equities is relatively small, it has been instrumental in helping the country develop a CG framework that is more palatable to investors from outside Japan (Ewmi, 2005).

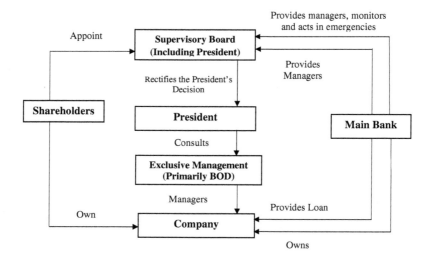

Figure 1.5: Japanese Model of Corporate Governance.
Source: Cited in Alam et al. (2019a). Modified from Mostepaniuk (2017).

In this model, institutional shareholders influence the corporations, and management is not independent in carrying out its duties. Profit maximization is the main motto of this model without more focusing on the protection of the rights of all stakeholders.

1.12.6 Chinese Corporate Governance Model

Following the Anglo-Saxon framework or market paradigm (Tam, 2000), the government exhibits the Chinese framework for CG. The Chinese government intended to recognize state-owned businesses in 1996 using a hybrid of Japanese and European CG practice called "Zhuban Yinhang" or "Main Bank" (Tam, 2000). CG in China was established by the owner, the BOD, and the top management, with input from Chinese economists and policymakers. The framework of this model guarantees the right and reliable allocation of the owner's investment to the council of directors. The BOD is the ultimate authority in a business and has the right to recruit and fire, as well as provide incentives and punishments (Wu, 1994). Figure 1.6 illustrates the Chinese CG model.

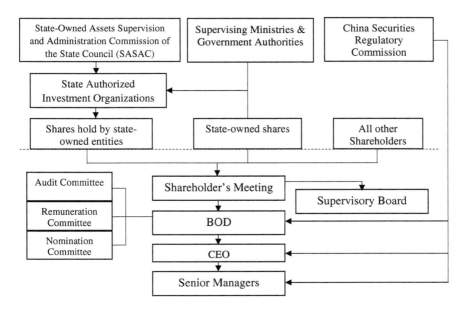

Figure 1.6: Chinese Model of Corporate Governance.
Source: Guo et al. (2013).

40   *Shariah Governance Systems of Islamic Banks*

In accordance with the Chinese model, the government exercises stringent oversight over the CG system. The BOD is the ultimate decision-making and policy-making authority for the organization.

1.12.7 *Islamic Corporate Governance Model*

Comparable to conventional banking and free-market economics, the Islamic banking system gives shareholders the opportunity to increase their wealth via investment returns. The Islamic model of CG, on the other hand, recognizes the importance of all stakeholders in ensuring the company's long-term viability and equitable distribution of resources. According to this framework, stakeholders may work closely with shareholders to look out for their own best interests (Iqbal and Mirakhor, 2004). In addition, the rule-driven incentive system that is implemented under Islamic CG guarantees social justice (Iqbal and Mirakhor, 2004), as it empowers managers to advance the interests of all stakeholders and establishes a foundation for the organization's structure to do so. The Shariah monitoring board and the Shura board, which is comprised of stakeholders, work together in Islamic CG to keep an eye on Shariah's concerns and look out for everyone's best interests. To safeguard the entire operations of Islamic banks, a Shariah Supervisory Board (SSB) monitors Shariah standards. The Islamic principles and the Islamic reputation of Islamic banks are the responsibility of a separate board.

According to the stakeholder model of Islamic CG, managers must act in the best interests of all stakeholders at all times, and stakeholders must be allowed to participate in organizational activities without fear of retaliation in order to prevent conflicts from escalating and jeopardizing their rights. Figure 1.7 outlines the CG structure for IFIs.

Furthermore, Muslims believe they will be answerable to the Almighty in this life's journey and on the final day of Verdict (as an autonomous model) based on the accepted approach to CG. The most crucial part of this framework is responsibility, since it is via this that all information can be disclosed to stakeholders and Islamic banking may continue to operate in an open and honest manner. Additionally, the organization is dedicated to keeping fiscal records that are exact, unbiased, and current. The Shariah Supervisory Council is crucial in establishing the principles of Shariah and making sure they are followed by Islamic businesses. The ultimate goal of Islamic CG is to advance social justice, and shareholders along with other participants in the community play an important part in this process (Choudhury and Malik, 1992; Choudhury and Haque, 2004).

Corporate Governance Systems of Financial Institutions

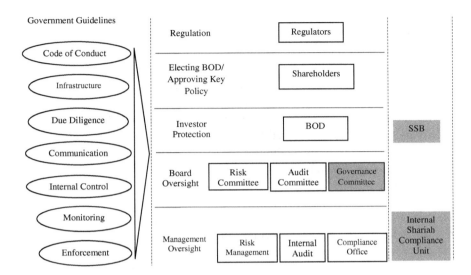

Figure 1.7: Corporate Governance Structure for IFIs.
Source: Stanley (2008). Modified from Alam et al. (2019a).

All stakeholders' rights and interests are safeguarded under the Islamic method of company governance. In addition, shareholders of IFIs have a voice in policymaking.

1.12.8 Discussion on Overall Models

This chapter compares and contrasts the practices of traditional and Islamic CG as they are used in the banking industry. The traditional financial services industry's CG structure consists of a BOD, management, administrators, shareholders, depositors, regulators, and consumers. Internal processes, such as family members, employees, and state engagement, and outside processes, such as financial institutions and public participation, dominate the forms of CG. The governments and authorities of these countries hold the notion that shareholder and stakeholder interests should be prioritized. The Shariah governing council is an extra layer of Islamic corporate oversight that oversees the application of Shariah principles in Islamic banks' day-to-day operations. CG principles were developed to protect the interests and rights of all owners and shareholders and differ widely according to the specifics of their practice, religion, conventions, cultures, and beliefs. Improvements in the legal and regulatory frameworks governing corporations are essential to their effective operation.

The purpose of this research is to contrast the Islamic CG arrangement with the more common Western one. In order to appreciate the variances in CG models applied internationally and the attempts to reform the governance structure of these countries, the research analyzes the model for CG from a conventional and Islamic viewpoint. In contrast to the Anglo-Saxon model, which exemplifies agency theory and defines the shareholder value system, the European model, which is grounded on stakeholder theory, is seen to provide remedies for the shortcomings of the shareholder model by encouraging a stakeholder focus on the values framework. While the Anglo-Saxon model places a premium on protecting the interests of shareholders, the Japanese, European, and Chinese models place a premium on protecting the interests of stakeholders or various capital players. Protecting the interests of shareholders and other stakeholders is a basic tenet of the ancient German and Latin models. Furthermore, the Islamic system of CG protects the interests of all stakeholders by embedding Shariah rules within the organizational structure. Furthermore, under the Islamic framework, stakeholders are afforded the same opportunities for active participation in the organizational framework as shareholders, with the dual goal of protecting stakeholder interests. The primary challenge with these frameworks is that the governing bodies of these countries place a premium on increasing investor and consumer trust.

Because of their varied state-by-state roots, nature and legal framework, political basis, cultural norms or culture, and economic construction (Jacoby, 2000), the Anglo-Saxon and European models have grown in influence in global practice. Muslim and non-Muslim countries alike are increasingly adopting Islamic banking, and with it, the Islamic framework of CG. Economies everywhere, Muslim and otherwise, are transitioning to Islamic principles. Applying Shariah principles within the framework of local laws and regulations, an Islamic CG structure is created to monitor and regulate Islamic financial firms. Conformity within the organizations and protection of stakeholder interests need a mix of regulators, monitoring, and lobbying for good CG practice and oversight of financial institutions. For the governance system to be effective, a concerted monitoring effort must be put in place to check the compliance of all business actors.

1.13 Issues Surrounding the Regulation in Banks

All areas of the economy are affected by the involvement of outside forces, commonly known as regulators. As was previously said, the banking industry is notoriously murky, making it probable that management will be privy to financial transactions and positions that shareholders and investors would be unaware of. Regulators often step in to enforce legal compliance forcing banks to disclose sufficient details so that investors may make educated judgments when acquiring financial products from a bank. The claim that regulators act in the public interest is bolstered by evidence from the literature, which overwhelmingly concludes that a bank's business performance significantly affects its financial health or, in the instance of a bank's failure, the demise of the economy (Levine, 2004; Ciancanelli and Gonzalez, 2001). The regulation placed on banks might be changed by government authorities like the central bank or other economic or financial institutions. The international community has seen success with global banking coordination measures including the Bank for International Settlements (BIS), the International Monetary Fund (IMF), the World Bank, and the Financial Stability Board, among others. Additional background on the Basel Committee for the Supervision of Banking and Basel II, organizations like the OECD and the Basel Committee, which advocate for specific standards for banking business procedures, are crucial. The importance of regulators is best shown by the efforts made to regulate the sector, such as the issuance of prudence guidelines and standards, and the relevance of these efforts in pressuring financial institutions to follow through and comply with these standards. The banking regulators have several tools at their disposal, including the ability to impose market limitations on banking and financial transactions, serve as a lender of last resort, facilitate deposit insurance, and formulate financial regulations. In the following section, we'll examine the literature's arguments either for or against the government's involvement in banking (Hassan, 2012).

1.13.1 *The Positive Impact of Regulation on the Corporate Governance of Banks*

Regulators' interference is one solution to the agency issue caused by the asymmetry of knowledge in the banking sector. Multiple contractual agreements seem to exist between management, shareholders, customers with deposits, creditors, and regulators, as stated above. Therefore, it may be claimed that more commercial parties than non-financial firms would be impacted by management's information privilege. Several researchers believe that external forces should step in to protect the global economy and the public interest from potential threats posed by banks due to information asymmetry and potential negative externalities such as the transmission effect caused by bank failures (Ciancanelli and Gonzalez, 2001; Levine, 2004). Regulators develop laws or ordinances to accomplish these goals, illustrating both their position as watchdogs and the role of shareholders as controllers of management. As such, regulators' participation in monitoring agents might be seen as a means of curbing agents' unethical or risky activities. Moreover, with regulators stepping in, management would have to balance the interests of shareholders and regulators via the rules that govern its operations (Hassan, 2012).

One of the primary roles of financial sector regulators is the management of systemic risk. Bank runs by depositors and its macroeconomic ramifications, such as a breakdown of the banking sector and government monetary policy, are examples of systemic risk that might spread across the whole financial system. Macey and O'Hara (2003) argue that regulators have a distinct advantage over other parties when it comes to conducting measurements, such as regulating the entry of new banks and the control of takeovers and acquisitions by existing banks. Another possible ethical risk in the banking industry may be mitigated by the market dominance of entities with the ability to dominate the system. Restricting the kind of operations in which banks participate has the potential to reduce the incentive for insiders to steal from the institution. Given that a market instrument that leads to a change in corporate control does not improve banks' poor performance, some argue that regulation through initiatives like the implementation of financial regulations might act as a "last resort" in reprimanding the management (Prowse, 1997). Lenders of last resort and deposit protection, say Ciancanelli and Gonzalez (2001), are the best regulatory instruments to limit or regulate the systemic risk of banks. They argue that shareholders no longer need to shoulder all investment risk thanks to the intervention of regulators who are concerned about the long-term health of the banking industry via market regulation.

In conclusion, financial sector interventions by authorities have varying scopes and purposes. In order to prevent banks from gaining too much economic sway, they may implement measures like needing regulatory clearance before making large purchases of bank shares. To reduce competition in the banking industry they might also restrict the ways in which banks operate and invest by prohibiting hostile takeovers or bank ownership of non-financial companies. Common financial restrictions enforced by regulators include the capital adequacy mechanism, liquidity requirements, interest rate and charge control, and the prohibition of non-lending operations and insuring of a bank's shares. There are two obvious outcomes of regulators' involvement in this sector: (1) the management of banking activities, and (2) the stifling of the healthy rivalry that occurs among non-financial companies (Hassan, 2012).

1.13.2 *The Adverse Impact of Regulation on the Corporate Governance of Banks*

Although regulators' enforcement is generally positive, the banking sector may be harmed by some of the tools imposed by the regulators. Even though it is widely acknowledged that the obstacle to market concentration in order has been created by the intervention of regulators through a market control mechanism, and in some cases, by government ownership of banks, this situation also gives rise to issues associated with the impact of market focus on administrators (Prowse, 1997; La Porta *et al.*, 2002; Ciancanelli and Gonzalez, 2001; Barth *et al.*, 2004; Macey and O'Hara, 2003). When it comes to banking operations, market discipline is essential to prevent excessive risk-taking as depositors necessitate greater profits and the possibility of release departure (Demirguc-Kunt and Huizinga, 1999; Berger, 1991), a deemed spike in the cost of sustaining due to borrowing holders' necessitate for higher yields or a decline in the value of stocks due to shareholders' threats to sell their shares. These have been turned in to the federal government as a consequence of regulatory measures taken to stabilize the sector. These results imply that the market's capacity to punish banks has diminished due to the presence of authorities in the banking sector. Deposit insurance is a contentious topic that arises when the government meddles in banking. Government efforts to protect deposits have been condemned for the harmful effects its vulnerability has on bank governance, although being successful in avoiding bank runs. Several authors, including Macey and O'Hara (2003) and Prowse (1997), argue that deposit insurance invites moral hazard by encouraging shareholders to take risks at the expense of the fund that provides deposit insurance and the taxpayers who replenish the fund. However, a recent empirical finding by Laeven and Levine (2008) indicates that the risk-taking habits produced by deposit protection are only associated with those of large holders of equity.

Meanwhile, the government's control of banks not only creates a barrier to effective bank supervision by reducing competition among bank management but also undermines the market itself. At first, the government joins the ranks of those with vested interests in keeping managers in check. However, the efficiency of supervision is called into question when an investor, such as a regulator, also becomes an ownership interest in a bank (La Porta *et al.*, 2002). Concerns have been raised about the ability of regulators to reduce moral hazard in the banking industry due to the anticipated weakness in supervision and greater disparity in information as a consequence of the regulators' assistance in the banking system (Ciancanelli and Gonzalez, 2001). Boot and Thakor (1993) found that regulators add to the confusion that exists in the regulatory supervision dilemma by participating in self-serving actions. Studies show that the conundrum has resulted in an entirely novel problem and an opportunity cost to society. Buchanan and Tullock (1965) suggested that governments develop policies that maximize their own utility rather than the public. Meanwhile, Rajan and Zingales (2003) spoke on how banks' credit flows may be affected by politics, and how financiers might capture politicians to further their own agendas. Later research by Barth *et al.* (2004) found that a negative correlation emerged between national corruption levels and overall bank development when regulators were given more power.

Studies like Levine's (2004) have expressed the need to decrease political meddling and increase the establishment of independent oversight and oversight of banks through independent regulation, such as the private-sector autonomy of a regulatory authority because the presence of effective authorities (i.e., the presence of legislators as shareholders) might threaten the regulators' freedom in their monitoring capacity. Proper CG has been linked to private regulating agency procedures in a number of studies. Exposure of data and subsequent sanctions have been linked by Barth *et al.* (2004) to the effectiveness of institutions. Private bank empowerment via the regulation of correct information exposure, as discovered by Beck *et al.* (2006), decreases corrupt interactions with bank employees in regard to loan applications. Meanwhile, Nier and Baumann (2006) shed light on how market discipline, transparency, and banks' risk-taking behavior affect the economy. Using an across-the-nation panel statistic set that covers banks from 32 different countries between 1993 and 2000, the findings suggest that banks with higher levels of uninsured liabilities and greater levels of transparency have bigger capital buffers, but that a strong government safety net reduces this impact. It was also shown that nations with high levels of interbank competition had more successful market discipline in reducing the incentives for banks to engage in risky behavior. Therefore, it seems that Nier and Baumann's (2006) results support stronger interbank competition, fewer government regulations, and greater transparency. The impact of regulations on financial institutions' ability to cut costs and maximize profits was studied by Pasiouras *et al.* (2009). Minimum capital requirements under Basel II, regulatory power, and market discipline measures were specifically addressed. Their research shows that improved market discipline may be achieved by increased regulatory power, the implementation of transparency requirements, and the provision of financial incentives. Higher capital needs have been shown to improve cost efficiency but reduce profit efficiency. Meanwhile, restrictions on banking operations reduce the effectiveness of managing costs while improving the effectiveness of managing profits. Market discipline, according to Pasiouras *et al.*'s (2009) research, is linked to complete and timely publication, which in turn allows private actors to keep an eye on public institutions. However, a robust regulator may pave the way for more timely and precise disclosure that private agents could use to keep tabs on banks and improve market discipline as a result. However, more stringent disclosure standards for organizations have been associated with reduced productivity. Costs associated with preparing formal disclosure papers, staffing investor relations departments, disclosing sensitive information to rivals, and making further disclosures were all cited as negative outcomes by Duarte *et al.* (2008).

1.14 International Regulatory Bodies

As was previously said, worldwide standard-setting agencies are also involved in the worldwide regulation of banks. These supranational organizations oversee financial institutions all around the world to ensure they adhere to prudential regulations. The importance of these factors may depend on the need to maintain liquidity in the worldwide financial system, the collapse of which might have a domino impact on the global economy. When considering the liberalization of a globalized financial system, which includes the penetration of banks into other nations (such as the establishment of faraway branches or subsidiaries), these global regulatory organizations provide an arena for international cooperation and integration between regulators in order to reach an agreement. As a result, we'll be talking about the vital part foreign regulatory agencies play in bank governance in this section.

1.14.1 The Organization for Economic Co-operation and Development

The OECD's mission is to advocate for policies that will significantly improve the social and economic well-being of people across the globe. To aid its member nations, the International Organization for Economic Cooperation and Development, commonly referred to as the OECD was established in 1961 to promote prosperity and financial sustainability. The Centre of Excellence for Co-operation alongside non-members of the OECD was set up to shape the OECD's long-term strategic direction and to monitor its implementation. The OECD has been working hard to advance the CG agenda, as indicated by its collaboration with other regulatory authorities to create transnational CG platforms and tailored roundtables that foster an effective and continuing conversation on the issue. To further help both member and non-member governments, the OECD has created prudential criteria to assess the regulatory, legal, and institutional structures needed for establishing and encouraging good CG (Ahmed Fahmi, 2012). Since its first adoption in 1999 by the 30-member nations of the OECD, the OECD principles of good corporate citizenship have been a standard reference for governments, businesses, and regulatory bodies. Stock exchanges, investors, firms, and other internationally relevant organizations that are not participants of the OECD also benefit from the organization's advice and assistance. Since then, the principles have spread over the world as the gold standard for countries improving their own legal, institutional in nature, and regulatory systems. Jesover and Kirkpatrick (2004) updated the concepts to make them applicable in a variety of legal, economic, and cultural contexts. This work was followed by that of Jamali *et al.* (2008).

According to Daniel (2003), it is important to care about good CG since it boosts economic productivity and growth, improves capital utilization, and attracts FDI. Second, it makes the economy more resistant to shocks from the outside and less likely to collapse. Thirdly, it's crucial to the credibility of a market economy. The OECD has refocused talks to include a few of the most important sections of the principles to guarantee that these criteria are considered. Taking into account new information and circumstances, the OECD started reviewing the principles in 2003; after a comprehensive examination, the organization adopted updated guidelines in April 2004. The principles of the revision take into account not just the OECD countries' experience but also the economies of emerging and developing countries. It is up to individual governments and market actors to establish their own frameworks, since the updated principles are voluntary in nature. Furthermore, it validated the principles' flexibility as a foundation in many institutional, economic, and cultural settings. How a company is led and managed is referred to as its CG. Decision-making inside a business is governed by its CG framework, which specifies the roles and duties of the BOD, the management team, the shareholders, and other stakeholders. In addition, it offers the frameworks for setting, implementing, and measuring the company's objectives (and performance) (OECD, 2004). It is now widely used as an example of effective CG throughout the world. The principles outlined in this governance framework suggestion have been used by governments, regulators, investors, firms, and stakeholders and have been approved by the Financial Stability Forum (FSF) as one of the Twelve Key Principles for Sound Financial Systems. It would seem that the OECD Principles of CG provide universal principles of CG to all firms. CG norms for banking organizations need to be adjusted to take into account the unique peculiarities of the banking sector. To aid banking supervisors in encouraging the adoption of sound CG practices by banking organizations in their respective countries, the Basel Committee on Banking Regulation published governance guidance titled *Enhancing CG for Banking Organizations* in 1999, with a revised version published in 2006. Interestingly, the OECD's established guidelines for CG serve as the basis for this guidance.

1.14.2 *The Basel Committee on Banking Supervision*

The Basel Committee for Banking Supervision (BCBS) (2006) Paper was updated from an earlier version issued in 1999 by the Bank for Global Settlements. The OECD's 1999 (2004) Fundamentals of CG served as an inspiration. The OECD Principles were updated in 2004; the BCBS Paper followed suit in 2006. The Paper's authors set out to help regulatory bodies improve their CG frameworks and adopt more consistent, high-quality CG practices by providing them with guidance.

The BCBS has made considerable strides in banking sector governance with its prescriptive, regulatory approach and rule-based capital adequacy requirement. The BIS is an international institution that acts as the bank for central banks and fosters financial and monetary cooperation across the world. BCBS is one of its committees. The BCBS was set up in 1974 to provide its member countries with a place to talk about banking supervision. All of these countries are represented here: Australia, Argentina, Belgium, Brazil, China, Canada, France, Hong Kong, Germany, India, Italy, Indonesia, Japan, Korea, Luxembourg, the Netherlands, Mexico, Russia, South Africa, Saudi Arabia, Singapore, Sweden, Spain, Switzerland, Turkey, and the United States of America. For the purpose of recommending implementation and adapting as necessary by its member countries and regulatory agencies that are not right away taking part, it takes an active role in producing cautious guidelines and standards on efficient oversight of banks, however of a broad and consultative nature. Standards Implementation Group; Policy Development Group; Accounting Task Force; and Basel Consultative Group are the four BCBS subcommittees.

In 1988, BCBS proposed the International Convergence of Capital Measurement and Capital Guidelines, also known as the Basel Capital Accord, which mandated the enactment of a credit risk evaluation arrangement with a minimum capital threshold of 8% by the end of 1992. Since its publication in June 2004, Basel II has served as a guideline that protects bank solvency via its "three pillars" rather than relying just on the ratio of capital to assets. The first pillar remains the minimum capital ratio, however, it is now determined for creditworthiness using "risk bucketing" approaches. While the second focuses on the improvement of market discipline via enhanced disclosure standards and practice, the third deals with the managing review of banks' risk control mechanisms and stipulates that major banks recognize comprehensive internal economic capital representations.

BCBS has worked hard to include stricter measures to enhance the three pillars specified in the 2004 Basel II guidelines in response to the current global economic crisis. BCBS implemented Basel III in December 2010 in response to the current global financial crisis. The three pillars of Basel II remain unchanged; however, they are updated in a variety of ways in Basel III. The percentage of total capital needed by Basel II, 8%, stays constant, but Basel III mandates that banks hold 4.5% of common stock (up from 2% under Basel II) and 6% of Tier 1 capital (up from 4% under Basel II). In addition to the mandatory capital conservation buffer of 2.5% of common equity, Basel III also introduces a freestanding countercyclical buffer of up to 2.5% of common equity that regulators can demand during times of rapid credit growth. In addition to requiring a minimum leverage ratio of 3%, Basel III also imposes two required liquidity ratios: (1) the liquidity coverage ratio, which states that a bank must have sufficient high-quality liquid assets to make up its entire net cash flow over a 30-day tension period, and (2) the net stable funding ratio, which states that a bank must have stable sustaining to address its funding requirements over a stressed one-year period. Some of the requirements of Basel III are set to go into effect in January 2013, whereas others will be phased in over the course of many years.

1.14.3 *International Accounting Standards Board*

The International Accounting Standards Board (IASB) was put forward as the first international accounting standard-setting body in 1973 by members of the Accountants Global Education, Study Group (AISG) from the United Kingdom, Canada, the United States, Germany, Australia, France, Japan, Mexico, and the Netherlands. When it was restructured in 2001 as the IASB, it took over 41 International Accounting Standards (IAS) that had been produced by the IASC. Numerous changes are the consequence of these accounting standards being updated, modified, or combined with others. These standards have been changed once more and a new set of standards, the International Financial Reporting Standards (IFRS), has been published since the IASB's foundation in 2001.

Worldwide adoption of a single set of accounting standards has been strongly advocated for by a wide range of international entities, including the World Bank, the United Nations, the International Monetary Fund (IMF), the Group of Seven finance government officials, the International Organization of Securities Commissions (IOSCO), and the BCBS. Since 1977, IASB has worked with groups like BCBS and, in the 1980s, the European Economic Community, which aimed to produce the European Economic Community Bank Accounts Directive, to harmonize the accounting behind financial reporting for banks.

1.14.4 *Regulatory Issues Pertaining to Basel II*

IFIs are subject to the same legal and regulatory standards as other financial institutions under Basel II. Some argue that Islamic banks shouldn't be committed to all of the regulatory standards set by Basel II since investment depositors share the risk of Islamic banks. On the other hand, they need to be governed by rules analogous to those that apply to corporations (Hassan and Chowdhury, 2004). There are many justifications for requiring Basel II compliance from IFIs. The majority of Islamic institutions are small to medium-sized and just getting started. International acceptance necessitates that they conform to Basel II. IFIs will be standardized by the regulatory framework if the recommendations of the AAOIFI and the IFSB are included in Basel II.

Stability in the global financial system depends on the new Basel legislative framework's success in establishing stricter market controls. It's also necessary for creating parity. According to Chapra and Khan (2000), the Islamic financial system accomplishes this goal by requiring institutions and depositors to share in the risk. As the author puts it, "Such sharing of hazards ought to motivate customers to choose their bank deliberately and to demand more candor in the bank's affairs." Basel II's third pillar proposes bolstering market discipline through more open communication and reporting. Financial performance, financial condition, risk management methods and practices, risk exposure, accounting policies, core company, leadership, and CG details are the six areas identified by Hassan and Chowdhury (2004) for financial disclosure and transparency.

Another difficulty is the interconnection of different financial institutions. Regulation of financial institutions including investment banks, commercial banks, insurance firms, and mutual funds has traditionally been handled independently. Inter-sector activities are prohibited to protect the financial security of each sector and its beneficial function in improving the soundness of the financial system (Chapra and Khan, 2000). However, there is a movement toward consolidating regulatory structures like England's Financial Services Authority in order to cover a wider variety of financial companies. Such changes need to be monitored in compliance with the Basel II rules and regulations. Including Islamic banking will broaden Basel II's usefulness and boost the standing of IFIs worldwide. Islamic financial instruments may be compared to mutual funds, leasing businesses, venture capital organizations, and risk participation organizations. According to Hassan and Dicle (2005), this innovative financial setup follows the global pattern and Basel II regulations.

1.15 Conclusion

Due to differences in projected managerial impact, attitudes toward risk, and time horizon, shareholders' interests and management tend to be at odds with one another. Important parts of CG theories based on the split between shareholder ownership and board control are summarized in this study. As was said at the opening of this chapter, the current research is grounded on three theoretical views of CG: the agency theory, the transaction cost theory, and the stakeholder theory. In this light, an economic theory of CG, such as the aforementioned three, is seen as the most useful framework for explaining the conditions under which corporations are governed and the institutions that exercise this power.

CHAPTER 2

Corporate Governance Concept from an Islamic Perspective

2.1 Introduction

In recent years, corporate governance (CG) has become more crucial in today's economy. Culture, history, and religion all play a role in shaping CG (Haniffa and Cooke, 2002, 2005; Licht *et al.*, 2005), suggesting that organizations are classified in different ways, specifically education, religion, and traditions, as a result of the operations of people from different countries, which in turn shapes their ethical viewpoints and selections (Licht *et al.*, 2005; Haniffa and Cooke, 2005). When it comes to Islamic organizations, Shariah governance (SG) is essential because of the role it plays in promoting and maintaining fairness, responsibility, and openness. It is more challenging for Islamic banks to operate in accordance with Shariah law than it is for traditional banks. It is also advised that Islamic organizations have a robust SG structure and suitable tactics that encourage the adoption of robust and efficient CG in line with the Islamic model. This chapter delves into the theoretical underpinning of SG, as well as the CG structures of both conventional and Islamic banks. Additional topics covered in this chapter include the SG process, the concept of the Shariah Supervisory Board (SSB), and the SSB's roles and obligations in the context of the global SG model.

2.2 Governance

Hawkama (legally translated, partly reached, and recognized by the Egyptian Linguistic Department, Sourial, 2004) is the Arabic and Egyptian term for administration. But "governance" originates from the Greek word "kybernan," which means to lead or direct. "Govern" comes from the Latin word "gubernare," which means "to steer" or "to govern." To govern is to "guide, steer, or direct" a society, as defined by the *Oxford English Dictionary*. Governance refers to the actions taken to manage and steer a company or other organization. The terms "governance" and "governance styles" were used by Stoker (1998) to describe the blurring of lines between the public and private sectors. Organizational, institutional, or CG is the process by which an entity is led and governed (Hasan, 2008). World Bank says good governance is "advocating equality, openness, and accountability." Governance, as defined by Stoker (1998), is the creation of governing patterns in which the lines separating the public and private sectors blur. A broad range of disciplines, including economics, politics, justice for all, and public administration, may be included in these definitions of governance. Put another way, governance is the rules and practices that regulate the leadership and management of a group, organization, or company. CG is the only focus of this study (Hasan, 2008).

The United Nations Economic and Social Commission for Asia and the Pacific (2008) defines management as "the processes of making decisions and putting those decisions into effect." Both the United Nations Development Program (UNDP) and Huther and Shah (1998) define governance as the use of a state's economic, political, and administrative authority to manage that state's resources. For it to work, society needs systems set up to help individuals and communities make their voices heard, assert their rights, meet their responsibilities, and resolve conflicts amicably. Other notable institutions define governance as:

(1) "The customs and structures through which power is exercised in a nation" (Kaufman and others).
(2) In what "A nation's economic, political, and social institutions are used to exercise power" (Download the *PRSP Handbook* from the World Bank).
(3) The responsible use of political, economic, and administrative power to oversee a nation's resources for growth. It entails the institutionalization of a framework by which individuals, institutions, groups, and organizations in a society express their interests, exercise their rights, and mediate their disagreements for the sake of the greater good (Country Governance Assessment, 2005).

Corporate Governance Concept from an Islamic Perspective 57

(4) The absolute and complete control over a country's economic, political, and governmental systems. It comprises the institutions, processes, and frameworks that enable people and groups to communicate their demands, assert their rights, fulfill their obligations, and resolve conflicts (UNDP).

(5) Citizens are understandably concerned about how attentive their government is to their requirements and how well their rights are protected. The ability of the government to create an accountable, effective, and transparent public management system that is open to citizen involvement and enhances rather than undermines a democratic system of government is generally what governance concerns are about (The Office of Democracy and Governance at USAID).

(6) Refers to the administration of any organization, including a country. It encompasses all of the procedures, frameworks, and measures employed to protect and develop assets (UNDP, 1997).

(7) The systems, practices, and guidelines are established to direct the management, accountability, and direction of an organization (City of Birmingham Council).

(8) Governance is frequently referred to as CG when used in reference to companies that conduct business.

(9) Promoting fairness, accountability, and openness (World Bank).

(10) A framework for managing and directing commercial groups (OECD).

(11) How leaders of a nation decide on how to distribute its social and economic resources for growth. A government's capacity to develop and implement laws that support social cohesion and economic expansion is referred to as institutional quality (using the term Asian Development Bank).

2.3   Why Governance Matters?

Effective governance creates a solid future for an organization by continuously pursuing a vision and ensuring that day-to-day operations are always aligned with its objectives. Governance is fundamentally about leadership. A competent board will improve the organization's financial and social outcomes and ensure that the proprietors' assets and funds are utilized appropriately. Poor governance can place organizations at risk of commercial failure, financial and legal issues for directors/trustees, or cause an organization to lose sight of its mission and responsibilities to its proprietors and those who benefit from its success. The legally based approach to governance entails that the proprietors of rights should also actively partake in determining how those rights are realized, such as through participation and increased empowerment.

The contribution of the governance viewpoint to theory does not reach the level of causal analysis. Additionally, it doesn't offer a brand-new normative framework. It is useful as a framework for organization. Based on its capacity to offer a framework for understanding evolving governing processes, the governance perspective has utility. Such conceptual frameworks give a vocabulary and reference frame through which reality may be analyzed and drive theorists to pose questions that they might not otherwise have (Judge *et al.*, 1995). If it works, it will produce brand-new insights that previous models or viewpoints might not have been able to. The attempt to bring about a paradigm shift can be represented by the usage of conceptual frameworks. These frameworks' usefulness comes from their ability to suggest study-worthy subjects.

The governance perspective is effective if it helps us identify significant concerns, although it also purports to identify a number of useful answers. It provides a reference point that challenges numerous traditional public administration assumptions. This chapter's governance discussion is organized around five propositions. Rather than making a series of declarations that can be shown to be either true or false, the purpose is to present a number of governance-related considerations. These are the five propositions:

(1) A group of institutions and players that come from the government but extend beyond it are referred to as the governance.

(2) When it comes to addressing social and economic problems, governance defines the blending of roles and duties.

(3) The power dependence presents in the interactions between institutions engaged in collective action is identified by governance.

(4) Autonomous, self-governing networks of players are important to governance.

(5) Governance acknowledges the ability to accomplish goals without relying on a government's ability to exercise authority or command. It believes that government can influence and orient using modern means and methods.

These claims are seen as complementing one another rather than being in opposition to one another or competing. Each premise is connected

Corporate Governance Concept from an Islamic Perspective 59

to a particular conundrum or pressing problem: There is a separation between the normative norms used to define and support government and the complex reality of decision-making related to governance.

- The blending of duties may result in scapegoating or the evasion of responsibility.
- For the government, power reliance makes the issue of unintended consequences worse.
- The growth of autonomous networks creates issues with accountability.
- Governmental failure may occur even when governments operate with flexibility to guide collective activity (Stoker, 1998).

2.4 Shariah Governance

A governance framework is a set of guidelines and procedures that a board of directors (BOD) uses to ensure transparency, objectivity, and responsibility in a company's interactions with all of its stakeholders (financiers, customers, management, employees, government, and the community). The structure of governance frameworks reflects the institution's interdependent interactions, contributing variables, and other impacts. The authority and governing or management obligations of an organization are defined by its governance frameworks. Additionally, governance frameworks specify, guide, and aid in the enforcement of these processes. The organization's goals, strategic directives, financial incentives, and established power structures and processes all contribute to the formation of these frameworks.

The CG approach used by Islamic institutions is founded on the safeguarding of stakeholder entitlements, the observance of Islamic law in the creation of organizational structures, and the security of property rights (Bhatti and Bhatti, 2009; Hasan, 2008). The conceptual foundation of Islamic economics is *tawhid*, which has been the subject of much discussion among Shariah scholars and Islamic economists (for example, see Mannan (1970), and Choudhury and Malik (1992)). According to Ginena and Hamid (2015), the term "SG" refers to an all-encompassing framework for ensuring that Islamic Financial Institutions (IFIs) follow Islamic law. In contrast to defining the Shariah compliance of Islamic institutions, SG is a complete set of structures that lays out the duties and duties of all stakeholders, encompassing management, the formation of SSB, and BOD (Shaharuddin, 2011). SG systems have been defined in IFSB-9 (2009) as "a set of structural procedures by which IFIs ensure Shariah compliance across all of their operational activities." Guidelines for the SSB, BOD, and Shariah auditors include internal and external Shariah audit and review of the unit, appointment of SSB according to appropriate criteria, management accountability in implementing governance framework, Shariah compliance, and Shariah review provided within the SG framework to ensure the integrity of Islamic banking operations and the growth of a trustworthy industry. The ultimate objective Shariah Governance Framework (SGF) is Maqasid al-Shariah. The inherent meaning of Maqasid al-Shariah is an effective reaction of people and organizations to justice and social welfare by implementing Shariah principles in their entirety as opposed to in part. Alam *et al.* (2021a) outlined the SG as a process of ensuring Shariah compliance in the overall functions of Islamic banks, while Shariah denotes some rules, regulations, guidelines, objectives, and directions to enhance accurate functions and activities, which are solely based on Shariah principles.

Nevertheless, Shariah compliance is a unique aspect of the SGF, and SSB is necessary in conjunction with the BOD to ensure the Shariah compliance of Islamic institutions. The SSB should be nominated by shareholders in their general meeting and suggested by the BOD or respective Islamic banks in order to monitor, guide, review, evaluate, and supervise banking activities on an *ex-ante* and *post-ante* basis (Abdullah *et al.*, 2017; Nathan and Ribière, 2007). The primary purpose of SG is to enhance the integrity of Shariah principles implemented by all Islamic institutions. To implement Shariah principles, it is essential to have sound and standardized Shariah guidelines that Islamic institutions can use to ensure and apply Shariah principles while being monitored and controlled by the BOD, SSB, management, and regulatory body (Alam *et al.* 2021a, 2021b).

2.5 Shariah Governance in IFIs

One example of an Islamic CG structure is presented by Rahman (1998), who presents a framework based on Shariah and Islamic moral principles and places a focus on the governing bodies of *shura*, *hisbah*, and religious audit. The effectiveness of every corporate decision that may influence the company may be ensured by the establishment of Shura, which consists of oversight, BOD, shareholders, workers, customers, and other interested parties. The governing body of *hisbah* and the religious auditor perform a role in overseeing company operations with regard to both regulatory and moral issues, while the SSB is responsible for making legal decisions and giving Shariah advising and supervision services.

A more comprehensive Islamic business governance system is shown by Choudhury and Hoque (2004). The philosophical frameworks of Tawhid and Shura serves as the basis for the definition of the proper degree of authority for each organization, as well as its respective responsibilities, functions, aims, and legal frameworks. By highlighting the regulatory structures of Islamic law in addition to ordinary banking law and regulations, Nienhaus (2007) presented an additional instance of the Islamic CG structure. Banaga *et al.* (1994) proposed a holistic structure that includes an Islamic business atmosphere and a system of Islamic governance. As a whole, scholars such as Choudhury and Hoque (2004), Banaga *et al.* (1994), and Rahman (1998) agree that a theoretical foundation of Islamic CG must account for the Shuratic process, Tawhid's epistemology, the concept of vicegerency (*khalifah*), accountability (*taklf*), regulatory aspects of Islamic law, social justice (*al-adlwalihsn*), and the despite the availability of a sound theoretical foundation, it is difficult to put all of the previously mentioned ideas and Islamic rules into practice inside the business. Actually, as mentioned by Banaga *et al.* (1994), an Islamic business organization's adoption of Shariah, upright, and ethical norms does not guarantee superior financial results.

The nature of Islamic corporate governance (ICG), according to Lewis (2005), is shaped by two factors. The first component is Shariah. The ICG model is founded on the Tawhidic epistemological paradigm, in which the functional role of an organization conforms to the Shariah (Hamid *et al.*, 2011). Good CG involves the development of mechanisms and practices that assure the accountability of corporate management and enhance firm performance (Maliah *et al.*, 2015; Brammer *et al.*, 2007). Therefore, Shariah-based CG is more involved than conventional CG, as the BOD, SSB, depositors and account holders, investors, and regulators have direct interests in the business operations and performances of IFIs. Therefore, it is intriguing to determine whether this is true in practice, particularly given that the IFIs must operate with conventional infrastructure.

In addition to being mandated by law to have a CG framework, Islamic banks must also adhere to SG. In the absence of such a framework, violations may occur that result in economic and non-economic repercussions. The most significant of these is the harm to the image of Islamic institutions and the loss of consumer confidence (Zada *et al.*, 2017). Governance is also of the utmost importance in the case of Islamic banks due to the nature of some of their unique products, which resemble equity but are not ideal equity. A conflict between management and the SSB of an Islamic bank may lead to Shariah and CG issues. The SSB of the bank was anticipated to assess the bank's compliance through Shariah review, Shariah audit, Shariah research, and Shariah risk management, according to Zada *et al.* (2017).

2.5.1 *Definition and Objectives of Shariah*

Maqasid al-Shariah is the five pillars of Islamic law that include belief, life, knowledge, ancestry, and inheritance (Kamali, 2008). As a rule of law or religious restraining orders that guides the conduct of human beings on an individual and collective level, Shariah is often associated with Islamic law. Many areas of Muslim life, such as those dealing with *muamalat*, or interpersonal connections, have included the idea of Maqasid al-Shariah. Several academic works, including Borham (2013), Kamali (2000), Kahf (2006), and Siddiqi (2004), have put forward that modern Islamic organizations' operations are motivated by a desire to meet Maqasid al-Shariah. According to Borham (2013), contemporary Islamic banking seeks to maintain the application of Shariah principles, legislation, and traditions in the banking and financial sector. Many researchers have drawn the conclusion that Islamic banking activities help build a Sharia-compliant financial system (for example, Iqbal (1997) and Zaher and Hassan (2001)). Shariah, often known as Islamic law, is the guiding principle for all of Islam and all of Muslim society. By admitting that there is indeed no God apart from Allah and recognizing that the Prophet Muhammad (PBUH) is the messenger of Allah, Muslims demonstrate their belief in Tawhid. Shariah's ultimate or basic sources of divine law, the Quran and Sunnah (the practices of the Prophet Muhammad PBUH), is essentially textual. In contrast, Muslim jurists use *ijtihad*, also known as legal reasoning, to interpret Shariah by creating a rule of law based on facts from the Qur'an and the Sunnah. Islamic legal reasoning founded on the spirit of knowledge and justice and *furu'* (branch cases) rulings that are not defined in the Qur'an and Sunnah are formed from this reasoning. As a result, this shows how crucial secondary sources are for *ijtihad* as Islamic divine knowledge secondary to the Quran and Sunnah in the development of Islamic legal theory. *Qiyas* (analogical reasoning), *Istihsan* (judicial preference), *maslahahmursalah* (unrestricted public welfare), and *urf* (customary practice) are all examples of secondary Shariah sources (Hassan, 2012).

Corporate Governance Concept from an Islamic Perspective   63

According to Faruki (1962), quoted by Bakar (2008: 28), "the distinction between Islamic law and Fiqh refers to the almighty law as it is as well as the divine law as humans understand it." This statement provides insight into how the concepts of Shariah and *fiqh* are viewed by Muslims. The examination of the foundations and guiding principles of Islamic law is referred to as *usul al-fiqh*. Thus, *usul al-fiqh* is Islamic jurisprudence's technique, with the goal of providing a sound basis and supporting data for Islamic legal judgments. *Wajib* refers to that which is obligatory in Islam, whereas *sunnah* to that which is permissible, *haram* to that which is forbidden, *makruh* to that which is disapproved, and *harus* to that which is permitted. The middle-8th century saw the establishment of many Islamic legal organizations known as *madzahib*. These institutions of higher learning closely parallel the various methods of practicing Islamic law; however, they often base their rulings on technicalities rather than broad concepts of Shariah application (Kamali, 2008). These controversies, known as *khilaf*, arise from different understandings of the Qur'an and Sunnah in light of local customary law rather than any debates over the divine sources of Islamic knowledge. The current *madzahib* are called for their founder scholars: Maliki, Hanafi, Shafii, and Hanbali. It would seem that *khilaf*, or conflicts among Shariah experts, are unavoidable given the centrality of *ijtihad* in the development of *fiqh*. The next part will examine the occurrence of *khilaf* in the context of *muamalat*, one of the several branches of Shariah (Hassan, 2012).

Islamic finance differs from its conventional equivalent by claiming to follow Shariah guidelines. Contemporary literature also emphasizes how Islamic finance differs greatly from conventional finance, not only in terms of the framework in which it examines corporate performance but also in terms of the way that noble values govern Islamic finance's entire methodology and attitude. The principles of the Shariah are conveyed not only in the particulars of its transactions but also in the scope of its involvement in putting into practice the Maqasid al-Shariah (objectives of Shariah) (Soualhi, 2008). Fundamentally, Maqasid al-Shariah discloses the proper interpretation of Islam that must be followed in full, not in part, as Islam is an absolute and integrated pattern of life whose goal embraces all of life, both private and public, in this world and the Hereafter (Kamali, 1998). Therefore, a thorough grasp of Maqasid al-Shariah includes substantial obligations on the side of every person and organization for justice and social welfare. A society where each person (or group) cooperates rather than competes would be the outcome of such a profound understanding, as the proper goal of this life is to achieve ultimate joy (*falah*) (see Kamali, 2008). Therefore, in a Muslim society, profit maximization cannot be the only driving force. At all levels of human contact (*mu'amalah*), profit maximization must be supported by initiatives to advance human health, justice, and fair play.

All economic actions, including the fundamental rules governing contracts in general, must be governed by the Shariah. Accordingly, the contract's intended goals should be in line with Shariah principles, and its subject matter should be legal. It should also be free of interest (*riba*), gambling (*maysir*), fraud, coercion, and a high degree of uncertainty (*gharar*), and its participants should agree to actively cooperate for the benefit of their community. Each participant also makes a donation to aid those in need, and the consignor should. As a result, the ways in which Shariah goals are actually implemented vary according to the sectors that the open codes cover (Ullah *et al.*, 2016).

2.5.2 The Sources of Shariah

The Shariah is derived primarily from the Quran, the Sunnah, Ijma', and Qiyaa'. Ijma (Consensus) and Qiyas (Analogy) are considered subsidiary sources of Islamic law that are developed from the first two (El-Gamal, 2006; Vogel and Hayes, 1998). For Muslims, the Quran and the Prophet Muhammad's (PBUH) outstanding, divinely inspired style of living, and the Sunnah, serve as the basis for a corpus of laws and regulations known as Shariah (Islamic law; Akram, 2008). Rules and regulations given by Allah SWT, such as those found in the Quran and Sunnah, constitute the foundation of Islamic law. There is no need for an intellectual reason for the authority and binding power of the evidence revealed in the form of Al-Quran, Sunnah, and Ijmaa'. In addition to the Quran, Sunnah, and Ijma', *qiyaas* is logical evidence since its truthfulness is founded on an established *hukm*. It has been shown that in Qiyaas, whether or not the *illah* is shared is a question of *ijtihad* and personal reflection (Hassan, 2012).

2.5.3 Muamalat (Human Relations)

The revelation of the Quran to Prophet Muhammad (S.A.W.) occurred in stages, with the first revelation focusing on the aspect of *aqidah* (belief), complied with by the descriptions of two broad sets of guidelines: *ibadat* (i.e., worship) and *muamalat* (i.e., human relations) (Kamali, 2003: 20).

Corporate Governance Concept from an Islamic Perspective 65

Anything that is not specifically authorized by the Shariah is judged and banned according to the basic Shariah principles controlling the judgments of *ibadat*, but the opposite is true for *muamalat*, where everything is acceptable with the possible exception of those specifically prohibited by the Shariah. Determining the Shariah judgment on *muamalat* by the use of *ijtihad* (legal reasoning) is a crucial part of *fiqh al-muamalat*. This is because the events of human life are endless in nature, whereas the wisdom given by God (the Quran and the Sunnah) is limited in text. Nonetheless, the process of making a new decision needs an understanding of the effective cause (*illah*) and logic (*hikmah*) of the previous judgments and assessment of *maslahah* (benefits) on different changing conditions (Kamali, 2000: 78).

It is generally agreed that *ijtihad* was crucial to the development of contemporary Islamic banking and finance (IBF). For instance, Kamali (2000: 69–71) argued that all Islamic economic rules should be approved on the basis of permissibility (*ibahah*) so long as they do not contradict Shariah's tenets. Current Islamic financial products like futures and options should be built on this principle. By allowing for *ijtihad*, the Shariah allows the Islamic economic system to adapt to the changing needs of Muslims in the global economy. SSB's *ijtihad* led to the redesign of the traditional Shariah financial contract.

2.5.4 *Accountability from the Islamic Perspective*

Muslim leaders and subordinates within an Islamic institution should present themselves as the *khalifah* (i.e., viceroy) of Allah, signifying that they are ultimately accountable to Allah for all their actions (Rahman, 1998), establishing the Tawhid concept (submission to the oneness of God) mentioned earlier. Shariah restraining orders indicate that every party involved within the company and its operation must uphold and promote essential Islamic values like trustworthiness, justice, and openness when the responsibility and *khalifah* structure of Islam is incorporated into the behavior of corporations. As an added bonus, the Islamic principles of *adalah* (social harmony) and *ihsan* (benevolence) give a justification for organizations (like an Islamic bank) to advocate for a socially and ethically responsible approach to banking. Some scholars (such as Rahman (1998)) believe that these firms should not prioritize profit maximization because of these funding principles. Rahman (1998) and Iqbal and Mirakhor (2004) all agree that societal optimization is an essential goal as well. The necessity to create profits for the different stakeholders has been superseded in certain cases by the IFI's (like Islamic banks) mandated corporate social responsibility function (Dusuki, 2008).

In light of the above, the *tawhid, adalah,* and *ihsan* ideas must be reflected in the responsibility spectrum and in the fiduciary obligation that the management of an Islamic organization due to its owners and all other stakeholders. Therefore, businesses like Islamic banks need to take on the risks and obligations associated with pursuing the goals that flow from the constitutional possession of the shareholders while also protecting the best interests of all of their stakeholders. In addition, Islamic institutions have a transcendental responsibility to God and should act in accordance with the ethical ideals and precepts provided in Islam (Rahman, 1998; Iqbal and Mirakhor, 2004). Therefore, it is essential that all parties engaged in the day-to-day operations of an Islamic bank be realistic and aware of their roles and duties. It is widely held that the success of Islamic businesses (including Islamic institutions) is directly related to the realization of *maqasid* as Shariah (Shariah goals).

It appears logical to conclude that Islam favors a stakeholder-focused governing organization, given the ethical aims of Islamic banks and the importance of stakeholders underlined in the Islamic attribution framework. Stakeholders in conventional banks and Islamic banks have similar interests and needs, but Islamic bank stakeholders put a higher value on the bank's adherence to Islamic Shariah. Stakeholders who have an interest in seeing that Islamic banks perform in accordance with Shariah are expected to exert some pressure in this regard.

2.5.5 *The Principles of Islamic Finance*

Although Islamic institutions have grown rapidly in the Muslim world in recent years, they still only account for a tiny fraction of the world's financial system as a whole. In this part, we lay forth the framework of Islamic banking that allows for the inclusion/understanding of the problems addressed in our study. The Islamic bank was set apart from its mainstream competitors by its adherence to sacred ideals. In accordance with Khan and Mirakhor (1986), Muslims are expected to follow certain guidelines when it comes to money and business. Iqbal (1997) and Zaher and Hassan (2001) explain that the Islamic economic system is based on Islamic Shariah principles such as risk communication, individual rights and duties, ownership rights, and the veracity of contracts. The prohibition of *riba* is the fundamental tenet of the Islamic economic system and falls under the purview of Islamic Shariah finance (Iqbal, 1997). A distinguishing feature of the Islamic financial system may be the formation of Islamic banks as financial entities that offer Muslims worldwide financing according to contracts drawn from Shariah. According to many sources (Haron and Wan Azmi, 2009), the term "Islamic banking system" is used to describe a financial institution that adheres to Islamic law. As an alternative to the Western financial system, Islamic banks work to foster and maintain social and economic institutions (Khan and Mirakhor, 1986; Haniffa and Hudaib, 2007). Furthermore, Shariah concepts such as risk sharing, rights of individuals, ownership, and contract integrity control the Islamic financial sector (Iqbal, 1997; Zaher and Hassan, 2001). In their definition of IBF, El Hawary *et al.* (2004) listed four guiding principles: (1) significance or value to the economy; (3) no abuse, in which neither side nor the transaction itself should be exploited; (4) no support of sinful activities forbidden by the Quran (such as alcohol, pork products, gambling, etc.). However, it's important to note that the underlying philosophy of Islamic banking aims to do more than just maximize profits; it also attempts to perform social commitments. The Islamic banking sector, according to many studies (Hasan, 2010; Dusuki, 2008), is built on Maqasid al-Shariah whereas the traditional banking system is founded on the social contract. One may argue that the differences between Islamic banking and traditional banking extend beyond the methods used by each (Haridan, 2016) due to the Maqasid al-Shariah's emphasis on monetary and social justice.

Interest, uncertainty, gambling, and investments in unlawful businesses including the selling of alcoholic drinks, illegal drugs, and illegal guns are all prohibited under Shariah law. Another basic element of Shariah is a profit-sharing risk, which is employed as a substitute for interest-based banking. These tenets are what set Islamic banks apart from their conventional counterparts (Othman, 2016). One distinguishing feature of the Islamic banking system is the total restriction on interest payments and receipts as reported by Ghayad (2008). Muslims are forbidden by Islam to take or provide interest (*riba*), irrespective of the nature of the loan or the rate at which it is charged. Interest and usury have been distinguished from one another, and loans for consumption and production have been treated differently. No *riba* occurs when interest is assessed on productive loans, and it has been suggested that *riba* relates to usury performed by private moneylenders rather than the interest levied by contemporary banks. There are some Muslim scholars who disagree, but the vast majority holds that *riba* and interest are synonymous terms. These two phrases will be used interchangeably from here on out. Even if interest is forbidden in Islam, it doesn't mean investment in an Islamic economy doesn't cost anything. While capital is acknowledged in Islam as a component of production, it is forbidden to have a fixed or arbitrary claim on the excess produced. Therefore, under an Islamic context, the question of what would replace the interest rate process emerges. There is the possibility of profit sharing, as indicated by Kahf (1982a, 1982b). Owners of capital are allowed to share in an entrepreneur's earnings under Islamic law. The fact that only the profit-sharing ratio, and not the amount of return itself, is fixed makes profit-sharing acceptable in Islam but interest is not. Islam does not disagree with the idea that compensation should be given for the use of capital in production. Capitalists are allowed under Islam to share in an amorphous excess. Put together, Islamic investors are not entitled to a guaranteed return on their money. No party is entitled to a rise in the principal amount if it does not bear a proportionate share of the risks. The primary difference between conventional banking and Islamic banking is that the latter claims to adhere to Shariah regulations, also known as Fiqh al-Muamalat (Islamic rules on trades). The tenets of Islamic banking include mutual benefit and the elimination of *riba* (interest). Islamic banking often employs Mudharabah (profit sharing), Musharakah (joint venture), Murabahah (cost plus), and Ijarah (lease) (Ghayad, 2008). In accordance with the sacred rules, IBF avoids engaging in interest-based activities, trading in forbidden things (including pig production, trading and delivery of alcoholic beverages, and betting organizations), too much unpredictability, implementing gain without carrying out effort or accepting liability, and advocates for the equitable distribution of the hazards and responsibilities (Khir *et al.*, 2008).

Riba, which is usually misinterpreted as interest, is forbidden under Shariah rules, which form the basis of IBF (Pryor, 2007). In medieval Islamic civilization, free loans (Qard Al-Hasan) were actively promoted. Interestingly, Islamic law permits a product's price to be different from its present worth if payment is postponed, recognizing the temporal value of money. Contrary to what is often believed, Sharia law does not prohibit interest-only loans. Islamic banks seldom employ Sukuk bonds to support lending, instead relying on customer deposits and internal equity. Transactions from the Middle Ages, as recorded in Fiqh al-Muamalat, served as a model for the development of modern Islamic finance. One major category is debt-based financing, in which the lender first acquires the underlying assets (either directly or via a third party), and then sells back them to the customer at a profit. Payment for the purchase would be delayed and made in a few installments. Lenders provide lease-based finance, whereby they create or buy the underlying assets and then rent them out to the lessee. The customer would become the only or primary owner at the end of the rental term (or based on the number of rentals). Third, profit-sharing loan and bond financing (PSLB) positions the lender as the client's partner and allocates the achieved profit or loss according to the predetermined terms of the loan and bond (Khan and Ahmed, 2001). "Non-PSLB" contracts refer to the first two types of Islamic financing. The Sharia has several more restrictions that must be followed in addition to the limits on Riba.

For instance, Shariah requires that all contracts be without "Gharar," which may be translated as "excessive uncertainty." Financial derivatives, also and other sorts of contracts (including different insurance policies) are not permitted for use by IFIs, as was previously stated. Furthermore, IFIs are not allowed to invest in enterprises that produce or distribute *haram* goods or services, such as alcoholic beverages, gambling, non-Islamic monetary services, pornographic material, tobacco products, or firearms. Since many large corporations (including hotel chains and alcohol retailers) derive a small portion of their income from such prohibited activities, contemporary Sharia scholars tend to allow investment in organizations with tolerable dimensions of revenues from *haram*-prohibited operations. As a result, investors must give up a percentage of their payouts from these firms to nonprofits in order to purge their money off the taint of criminal activity (Hoepner *et al.*, 2011). SSBs, made up of both upper-level management and Islamic experts, are in place at all Islamic banks in order to monitor Shariah compliance. A number of authors (Dar and Presley, 2000; Abedifar *et al.*, 2013; Sundararajan and Errico, 2002) have argued that Sharia-based financing contracts are more complicated than traditional contracts. Murabaha is a kind of lease finance in which IFIs act as the buyer and subsequently the lessor to the customer. The customer acts as the bank's agent in making purchases and putting projects into action while dealing with IFIs. Such a framework is more intricate than standard loan arrangements. The specific risks of using some non-PSLB methods, such as Salam and Ijara, are described by Sundararajan and Errico (2002). The former exposes Islamic banks to credit and price of commodities risks, while the latter, in contrast to ordinary lease arrangements, leaves Islamic banks exposed to all liabilities until the conclusion of the lease period since ownership cannot be transferred. Default penalties are another point of disagreement. Banks use rebates as a substitute for such sanctions in certain countries on the grounds that they are contrary to Sharia (Khan and Ahmed, 2001).

One of the most fundamental tenets of Islamic finance is that there must be a one-to-one relationship between funding and real market transactions. As a result, whether they include an exchange, a share, or an agency contract, all forms of Islamic finance are asset-based. Other principles include not taking advantage of others in business dealings, making sure that illegal activities like tobacco, booze, arms, and pornography aren't funded, and acknowledging the connection between possession and profit entitlement. Maintaining these principles, assuring stakeholders that they are being adhered to, and reducing the risks resulting from non-compliance with Shariah all need SG. The SSB is crucial for this kind of governance since it evaluates and monitors operations to guarantee Shariah compliance (AAOIFI, 2010). It is identified as a separate component of corporate responsibility for IFIs (Magalha es and Al-Saad, 2013) and has a "social well-being function" (Choudhury and Hoque, 2006).

The financing arrangement's markup comprises not just the banks' return but also a default penalty. The refund will be given to the customer if they make their loan payments on schedule. Some Islamic banks recover the fee for late payments across the full financing term, although in conventional banking the default interest payment is normally computed for the duration of the delay. The use of derivatives and collateral may also be limited for Islamic banks; for example, they cannot utilize interest-bearing assets like money markets or bonds as collateral. Traditional banks not only lend money but also put some of their money to work on the stock market. Bonds and other securities with varying maturities are common examples of such investments due to their ability to diversify risk and provide a steady stream of income. Islamic institutions are restricted in their ability to invest due to a prohibition on the purchase of interest-bearing products. They might also put their money into Sukuk provided by the International Islamic Liquidity Management Corporation (IILM; for further information, see Archer and Karim, 2014). Although the asset class is currently relatively undeveloped (similar to Islamic short-term in nature money markets), Haraam purification and the growth of different Islamic financing tools have gradually eased constraints on Islamic investment by banks options. In a hybrid system, interest rates (and "PSLB rates" in a fully Islamic system) are normally set by the central bank. PSLB rates, which normally follow market rates, are used to set interbank rates for "wakalah" (agency) contracts. Furthermore, Chapra (1992) stressed the significance of stakeholder engagement (Shura) in the business of the company, either directly or via representatives. The SSB interprets and oversees the application of Islamic law (Shariah) in financial services on behalf of Shura in the framework of governance. To protect the rights of all parties to a contract and encourage social harmony among investors, IFIs should be put into place (Warde, 2010).

2.5.6 Shariah Compliance of IFIs

As was noted before, the main contrast between Islamic banks and traditional banks is that Islamic banks are required to follow Islamic Shariah in their day-to-day operations. This stipulation paves the way for Islamic institutions to be run in accordance with Islamic principles and values (Sharia), as outlined in the Quran and the Hadith (Ahmad, 1984; Siddiqi, 1983; Khan and Mirakhor, 1986). Furthermore, it has been suggested that if an Islamic bank's activities were proven to be incompatible with Shariah, the integrity of the bank and the faith of its stakeholders might be damaged. Thus, the management of an Islamic bank has to ensure that Islamic financial principles are applied consistently. It might be argued that the Islamic accountability system has close ties to this duty on the side of the Islamic bank's management.

The shareholders and owners of an Islamic bank would likely put pressure on the bank to engage in Shariah-compliant financial operations since this is the major reason for forming an Islamic bank. For example, the confidence that the bank's operations and earnings are in line with Shariah law is said to have a role in the investment choices of the shareholders. Furthermore, institutional investors, who typically hold a sizable portion of a company's stock, could use their right to vote to choose the rules and operations of the company that would give them a positive return on their money while still upholding the moral component of the Islamic banking functioning. Meanwhile, the BOD would keep an eye on management and demand that it reports to them that the bank's actions are Shariah-compliant in order to maintain the bank's reputation in line with the expectations of these shareholders. Shariah academics and *fiqh-al-muamalat* experts make up the external and impartial SSB that is tasked with carrying out these duties. Shariah compliance at the bank is evaluated by the BOD, who gets advice on Shariah-related matters from the SSB. An annual Shariah report is released with the bank's financial statements, including the SSB's findings based on the outcomes of the Shariah compliance examination. As discussed in numerous academic works (Tomkins and Karim, 1987; Karim, 1990a, 1990b; Briston and El-Ashker, 1986; Banaga *et al.*, 1994; Ghayad, 2008; Rammal, 2006; Laldin, 2008), the SSBs of Islamic banks are crucial to the institutions' credibility and the trust of their shareholders and other stakeholders. Others contend the Board of Shariah Supervisors has an unspoken duty to keep an eye on the actions of Islamic bank management in order to safeguard the bank's standing in the community (for more on this, see Ghayad, 2008). Others besides these also deal with the issue of complying with Shariah in the Islamic banking sector. The government, for instance, ensures legislation by, say, enacting laws and pronouncing regulations and instructions for the functioning of Islamic organizations. These rules are in place to protect the financial sector and keep the required level of oversight in place. The Islamic banking system also benefits greatly from the work of various international regulatory groups that create and enforce standards for the industry. Although adoption of the standards developed by the AAOIFI and the IFSB is optional, both organizations are actively involved in the creation of standards and recommendations for use in IFI. One such rating agency that serves as a standard against which IFI-issued capital instruments and other financial products are measured is the Islamic International Rating Agency (IIRA). The AAOIFI's Shariah criteria, as well as those of other organizations, are met by the IIRA benchmarks. A market and worldwide standardizing organization, the International Islamic Financial Market (IIFM) encourages self-regulation of Islamic capital and money markets. Guidelines, best practices, standardized financial contracts, market suggestions, and infrastructure development are all areas of focus as they relate to the standardizing and documentation of Islamic financial products. Another organization helping Islamic banks and financial companies be Shariah-compliant is the Liquidity Management Centre (LMC). The LMC helps IFIs manage their short-term cash flow by investing in high-quality, Shariah-compliant both short- and medium-term debt and equity instruments.

Shariah compliance has been underlined as crucial to the success of the Islamic banking business in the previous paragraphs. Furthermore, the idea of Shariah compliance in Islamic banks covers a wide range, including everything from the profitability of the banks to the morality and ethics of their workers to the Islamic legality of the goods and services supplied by Islamic banks. Establishing regulatory organizations that act as the industry's major drivers of growth and survival is just one example of the many governance structures in place to safeguard the sector's credibility. Therefore, it is crucial to recognize that SG is essential for the Islamic banking business and that it is superior to the CG generally contested in regard to other organizations (Hassan, 2012).

2.6 Role of Shariah Governance in IFIs

The closure of Ihlas Finance House in Turkey, the Islamic Bank of South Africa, and the Islamic Investment Businesses of Egypt, as well as the corporate challenges of Dubai Islamic Bank and Bank Islam Malaysia Berhad, highlights the importance of an effective and efficient governance system for IFIs. These occurrences show that IFIs are vulnerable to crises and failures associated with governance.

Governance of corporate entities in IFIs serves a similar purpose to that which it does in other organizations. The goal of CG may be summed up as to increase corporate fairness, openness, and accountability. Good CG is necessary to safeguard the interests of all stakeholders. This is why there is so much focus on CG these days, particularly among banks (Macey and O'Hara, 2003). The framework of CG in IFIs goes beyond the traditional four pillars of shareholder, BOD, management, and stakeholder engagement to incorporate spiritual well-being. As such, IFIs need the supplementary Shariah framework to safeguard not only their connection with God but also their interactions with one another and the natural world.

Grais and Pellegrini (2006a) claim that IFIs have two distinct roles in CG. At the outset, all parties involved need to be confident that their operations are fully compliant with Shariah law. Second, IFIs need to prove to stakeholders that they are committed to maintaining and expanding economic development. Harmonizing Shariah regulations with the corporation's natural purpose of maximizing its profits without compromising the liberties and desires of stakeholders is a primary duty of CG.

Governance risk mitigation is only one kind of risk that may be helped by good CG in IFIs. For example, Iqbal and Mirakhor (2007: 227–250) describe governance risk as "the risk that results from failure to govern the organization, carelessness in conducting company operations and meeting obligations under contracts, and a weak both within and outside the environment." As an addendum, Iqbal and Mirakhor (2007) classify governance risk as either "operational," "fiduciary," "transparency,"

74 *Shariah Governance Systems of Islamic Banks*

"Shariah," or "reputation" risk. Risks in IFIs are more complicated and have more distinctive features than those in traditional financial institutions, hence it is essential that they have a robust and effective CG mechanism in place to manage them.

A specific style of governance is required to ensure that IFIs adhere to Shariah rules and values in everything that they do. IFIs are required to operate in accordance with Islamic morality or the Islamic code of ethics, which includes refraining from engaging in illicit operations and avoiding *riba* (interest), *gharar* (uncertainty), speculation, and *maysir* (gambling). To ensure that their goods, operations, and activities are in accordance with Shariah norms and principles, IFIs must practice Islamic CG Hasan (2011a). This will help them develop and acquire the trust of their stakeholders.

2.7 Objectives of the Shariah Governance

The goal of CG in the banking and finance sector is to set up organizational mechanisms that guarantee corporate integrity, openness in information sharing, and responsibility for actions. In his article, Hasan (2009: 279) said, "the eventual goal of good CG is to guarantee justice not just for shareholders, but additionally to all stakeholders, which can be accomplished via more openness and accountability." The final purpose of CG is to guarantee that all IFI practices are in accordance with Shariah principles, also known as Maqasid al-Shariah. The transparency, probity, and dependability of IFIs may be bolstered by adopting a Shariah-compliant governance structure. SG standards are issued by AAOIFI and implemented by IFSB to fulfill the needs of the Islamic financial sector (Kasim *et al.*, 2013). Strategic benefits accrue to IFIs, the Islamic finance sector, and stakeholders engaged in banking and finance operations in accordance with Shariah when proper governance is in place. One of the most significant components of the IFIs governance structure is its SSBs. The results indicate that the establishment of IFIs for the express aim of upholding Islamic values according to Islamic teachings and rules is the ultimate objective of the Shariah administration. All IFI actions should be in line with Shariah principles, which is why SG exists (Sori, 2015).

Shariah compliance, which is at the heart of the SG system, is the system's overarching purpose. It necessitates the involvement of several IFI governance entities and their attendant costs. Despite the additional cost, time, and effort involved, IFIs continue to support SG even after the formation of the SSB. This begs yet another important issue about the nature of SG structures for international financial institutions. To solve this problem, it's best to have an understanding of the goals and instrumental duties of SG in IFIs, such as ensuring the product's legitimacy, encouraging caution and justice in financial operations, gaining the trust of stakeholders, and incorporating risk management tools that are specific to IFIs. Legality and conformity with the Shariah are prerequisites for Islamic financial products. To this end, IFIs need the guidance of Shariah experts, particularly those versed in *fiqh al muamalat* and *usul al fiqh*, to ascertain whether or not a certain Islamic financial product complies with Islamic law. The SG system is essential for preserving the SSB's credibility and guaranteeing the legitimacy of the products in light of the many issues involved, such as the Board's independence, credentials, submitting structure, accountability, and openness.

All of these major events highlight the need for the SG system as a tool for risk management in order to reduce the possibility of non-compliance with Shariah principles. Shariah risk is harder to control compared to other types of risk such as credit, investment in the equity market, liquidity, and return rate. In addition, IFIs face a risk of Shariah violation for which there is currently no risk management mechanism. Shariah risk is an operational risk that may be controlled with a competent and adequate SGF, according to the IFSB Guiding Principles on Risk Management (IFSB-1). The SG system would help international financial institutions (IFIs) reduce the risk of Shariah non-compliance, which might lead to catastrophic losses and damage their reputation (Hasan, 2011b).

2.8 The Importance of Shariah Governance

Literature highlighting various corporate controversies that have stigmatized the business world provides ample evidence for the necessity of a proper CG framework. In addition to being mandated by law to have a CG framework, Islamic banks must also adhere to SG. SGF is important for Islamic banks to implement Shariah principles, confirm Shariah compliance, and monitor the functions of the banks. Besides, it is needed for a well, efficient, effective, profitable business, and higher performance and, finally, to eliminate the confusion among the management, executives, conventional bankers, and banks (Alam *et al.*, 2021a). In the absence of such a framework, violations may occur that result in economic and non-economic repercussions. The most significant of these is the harm to the image of Islamic institutions and the loss of consumer confidence.

As a procedure, SG ensures Shariah compliance in the whole operations of IBs (Alam *et al.*, 2021a, 2021b, 2021c, 2021d). SGF is necessary for IBs to adopt Shariah principles, confirm Shariah compliance, and supervise the banks' operations (Alam *et al.*, 2019b, 2021a, 2021b). Governance is also of the utmost importance in the case of Islamic banks due to the nature of some of their unique products, which resemble equity but are not ideal equity. This has generated considerable discussion in the pertinent literature. In Malaysia, the SGF (SGF, 2011) is a response to the need for a distinctive governance structure for Islamic institutions. Due to a conflict between the management and the SSB of an Islamic bank, a case study of one subsidiary Islamic bank provides significant insights into Shariah and CG issues that may arise.

The SSB of this bank was required by its charter to assess the bank's compliance through Shariah review, Shariah audit, Shariah research, and Shariah risk management. On one occasion, a credit card facility based in Bay al-nah was to be inaugurated, and the management made the necessary preparations. However, due to numerous unresolved Shariah issues, the SSB concluded after extensive deliberation that the product does not comply with Shariah. The bank management was dissatisfied with the decision and brought the matter to the board's attention. The management argued that since two other Islamic banks had authorized a similar facility, the SSB should have approved the product. A second meeting of the SSB was convened to review the previous decision. In it, the earlier decision was reversed under certain conditions, the most significant of which was that the legal documentation guarantees the complete independence of the two contracts comprising Bay al-nah. Although the legal documents presented to the SSB did not meet the requirements of bay al-nah as stipulated by the regulator, the committee was falsely assured that the documentation provided for the independence of the two contracts. This case illustrates potential flaws in the SG mechanism of Islamic institutions. It demonstrates the potential for direct conflict between managers and SSB members and indirect conflict between these members and the board. In addition to raising questions regarding the Shariah-compliance claims of such institutions, such conflicts may also result in significant losses for the Islamic bank. The following anecdotes demonstrate how governance flaws can result in substantial losses. In November 2015, Bank Negara Malaysia (BNM) fined a subsidiary Islamic bank in Malaysia RM 53.7 million for violating Sections 234 and 245 of the IFSA. Although the case's specifics have not been made public, it is suggestive of possible governance flaws within the subsidiary Islamic bank. In addition to the sanction, the bank agreed with the central bank to implement a four-year program to attain market best practices, allocating an average of 25 million ringgit per year for investments in systems, infrastructure, and training. It also took corrective measures to mitigate the issues, stating that it has strengthened its compliance function and increased staff training and awareness programs. It may be too soon to draw firm conclusions on whether SG is more successful in full-fledged Islamic banks or subsidiary Islamic banks based on the few examples listed previously. It will take more time to form a valid opinion on this issue. However, as we will discuss further, the image of a "true blue" Islamic bank may have a positive effect on the governance framework of fully fledged Islamic banks in that the employees of such banks may feel a greater sense of responsibility as a result of the public perception they bear (Zada, 2017).

The IBF has grown rapidly during the last three decades in every part of the world. It has already reached over 100 nations, including traditionally non-Muslim cities like London, Tokyo, Beijing, Shanghai, Seoul, Singapore, Berlin, and Hong Kong. The internationalization of Islamic finance has bolstered Islamic mysticism, and as a result, all commercial endeavors that showcase this progress and include the public interest must be supervised by a code of conduct. For Islamic finance to grow, it's important that IFIs be regulated by rules that can flag any Shariah violations. The privacy of IBF consumers of IFIs must be protected, as must the interests of investors and other players in the Islamic financial system, all of which need adherence to SG norms. Shariah regulatory challenges must be addressed by Islamic financial institution authorities using a legal and robust SG model in accordance with Islam's real principles for the industry as a whole to attain a particular degree of maturity (Minhas, 2012). The SGF is a collection of institutional structures that ensures the BOD, upper management, and SSB of an Islamic financial institution are subject to effective supervision, responsibility, and accountability. The framework serves as a manual for keeping the working environment Shariah-compliant at all times. Complete compliance with the principles of Shariah will inspire public and financial market trust in the truthfulness of Islamic finance transactions and provide the foundation for the practice of Islamic finance by adhering to the beliefs, conditions, and principles preached by Islam.

With a well-defined institutional structure inside IFIs that are under the Bank's control, the Bank of Malaysia has created the basic mechanism for the Islamic finance industry to function in Malaysia in line with Shariah Muamalah principles. An overarching Shariah advisory body is in place at

78   *Shariah Governance Systems of Islamic Banks*

the Bank, and a supervisory SSB is in place at every Islamic financial organization.

- IBF rely heavily on Shariah conformity. It gives legitimacy to the practices of Islamic banking and finance.
- Shareholders and the general public may be certain that the company is always operating in accordance with Shariah law. The existence of non-Shariah-compliant elements would not just affect the confidence of the public in IBF.
- Risks, such as fiduciary and reputational dangers, might be posed to IFIs. Compliance with the Shariah principles will be achieved by having a proper SGF.
- Unquestionably, SG is significant in IFIs.
- To enable the SAC/adequate SSB's advising and oversight duties, the appropriate methods and framework must be established.
- To create an environment that is favorable for greater SG, integration between the SAC and SSB of Islamic FIs should be facilitated.
- Both micro and macro IFI-related considerations should be taken into account while providing advice and providing oversight.

Shariah compliance principles provide a set of rights and responsibilities that allow Islamic banks to acquire credibility and integrity as ethical and religiously based providers of financial services. Indeed, nearly 45 years after the first initiative, which initially provided *halal* financial alternatives and profitable ethical investment instruments, this initiative was created to promote partnership-based financing and community empowerment. Theoretically, an Islamic financial institution (IFI) provides an asset-backed financing system founded on an interest-free contract, with Islamic law serving as its guiding principle. Customers of IFI are referred to contractually as investment account holders (IAH), so any profits and losses are subject to be shared proportionally based on a predetermined rate of return. Therefore, optimal CG in IFIs as a whole and Islamic bank in particular should combine Shariah compliance principles with internalized stakeholder value (Grais and Pellegrini, 2006a). It should provide participation rights to all stakeholders, including IAH, with a strong fiduciary obligation to both stakeholders and SSB, so that they can accomplish their goal of complying with Shariah principles and providing outstanding service to the entire community. Eventually, an intriguing inquiry emerges. Where does the value of the partnership go? Do they demonstrate a spirit of community service? Or is a distinct course of action dictated by the logic of commercial profit? Islamic institutions are founded on the principle of sharing profits and losses, in accordance with the Islamic principle that "profit belongs to the risk-taker." Interest is rejected by Islamic institutions as a cost associated with the use of money and loans as investment vehicles. The purpose of the statement is to promote the efficient use of economic resources by IFIs and to require accountability for their management.

Transparency, information sharing, and a dedication to the letter of Sharia law are all highly valued by Islamic financial principles. The SGF is a collection of institutional structures that ensures the BOD, upper management, and SSB of an Islamic financial institution are subject to effective supervision, responsibility, and accountability. The framework serves as a manual for keeping the working environment Shariah-compliant at all times. The major goal of the framework is to improve Shariah-based governance by bolstering decision-making, accountability, and autonomy. If Islamic finance activities were fully compliant with Shariah principles, consumer and financial market trust in them would increase. Internal Shariah evaluation and audit requirements, supported by a proper risk management methodology and research capability, will be developed to bolster Shariah compliance operations. By promoting Shariah compliance across the board, it is hoped that the framework's application would aid in the establishment of a more solid SG structure inside IFIs. The BOD will be answerable to the framework for ensuring that IFIs are properly supervised in accordance with Shariah law and that the Shariah administration structure, policies, and procedures are effectively implemented (Adan, 2014).

With the help of the BOD and the SSB, the top executives of an Islamic financial institution are tasked with establishing and maintaining a company-wide culture of Shariah consciousness and compliance. This includes ensuring that all business operations adhere to the highest standards of SG. Every submission to the committee on Shariah must be well-researched and backed up by a thorough study of Shariah concerns, product structure, and supporting documentation. Effectively providing and conducting research would need the establishment of in-house Shariah research skills backed by sufficient expertise and materials.

In addition to safeguarding the interests of capitalists and other stakeholders in the Islamic financial system, SG rules are necessary to preserve the faith of IBF customers in IFIs. Shariah regulatory challenges must be addressed by Islamic financial institution authorities using a legal and solid SG model in accordance with Islam's real principles for the industry as a whole to attain a particular degree of maturity. Values and institutions of good CG, openness in sharing information, and strict adherence to Sharia law are highly valued in the concepts of Islamic finance. Public trust in the goods' legality and validity may suffer if there is no oversight mechanism in place (Chapra and Ahmed, 2002).

Transparency, information sharing, and a dedication to the letter of Sharia law are all highly valued by the Islamic financial principles. The framework serves as a manual for keeping the working environment Shariah-compliant at all times. The major goal of the framework is to improve Shariah-based governance by bolstering decision-making, accountability, and autonomy. Internal Shariah review and audit requirements, supported by a proper risk management methodology and research capability, will be developed to bolster Shariah compliance operations. The application of the framework is expected to promote Shariah compliance across IFIs by contributing to the establishment of a stronger and more stable SG structure. Shariah oversight of IFIs and the effective functioning of the SGF, policies, and processes would fall within the purview of the board under the proposed framework (Adan, 2014).

To be sure, the board must acknowledge the SSB's autonomy and defend the committee's decisions addressing Shariah-related parts of the institution's commercial operations. The framework does not necessitate the appointment of a Shariah expert to the BOD of an Islamic financial institution; nonetheless, the board is strongly urged to explore co-opting board members with strong Shariah understanding to act as a "bridge" between the board and the Shariah panel. The board must also provide SSB members with a fair compensation that reflects the seriousness of the committee's oversight role. The SSB's position and obligations are now more accountable and less consultative. Decisions and recommendations from the SSB must be followed by the whole Islamic financial organization.

2.9 Internal Governance Mechanism in Islamic Financial Institutions

To provide Muslims with financial services consistent with their religious beliefs, Islamic institutions are established. In this regard, shareholders and other stakeholders anticipate that Islamic banks will pursue their mission by ensuring that all transactions and business activities adhere to Shariah law. Several studies (Van Greuning and Iqbal, 2008; Chapra and Ahmed, 2002) contend that effective management would increase the level of trust and confidence among equity holders, investors, and others in the Islamic banking industry. Several stakeholders within Islamic institutions hold crucial SG responsibilities in ensuring Shariah compliance. For example, the BOD is responsible for implementing the advice provided by the SSBs and monitoring and supervising the management to ensure that all business activities not only meet the expectations of shareholders and other stakeholders but also adhere to the Shariah (AAOIFI, 2010; BNM, 2019, 2013; IFSB, 2006; Alam, 2022). In addition, the BODs may require the management to provide them with a report on the activities of Islamic banks, including all Shariah compliance-related matters (BNM, 2019; IFSB, 2006; Alam, 2022).

Shariah officers are pivotal to SG mechanism for Islamic institutions. Shariah officers are viewed as an essential component of the governance of SSBs in providing Shariah compliance assurance for Islamic bank operations (Zaidi, 2008; Alam *et al.*, 2022). Shariah officers play a crucial role in assisting the SSB with *ex-post* Shariah compliance duties (BNM, 2019; IFSB, 2009). Monitoring the internal Shariah control system of Islamic banks by ensuring that all transactions and operations are conducted in accordance with the Shariah advice provided by the SSBs is one of the most important responsibilities of these Shariah officers. Shariah officers are essentially subject to the same requirements as SSBs in that they must possess a Shariah qualification background (BNM, 2019; IFSB, 2009; Alam, 2022). In addition to educational qualifications, Shariah officers are expected to demonstrate high levels of integrity and impartiality when carrying out their duties (BNM, 2019; IFSB, 2009).

According to studies, Islamic institutions face formidable obstacles in the area of *ex-post* Shariah compliance procedures, where their internal governance mechanisms are held accountable. Hassan (2012) conducted one of the empirical studies in this field, in which he identified deficiencies in the implementation of Shariah compliance review involving multiple stakeholders within Malaysian Islamic institutions. Hassan (2012) revealed, among other things, that the SSB had doubts about the authenticity of the Shariah compliance review procedure conducted by various stakeholders within the management of Islamic institutions. Hassan (2012) also reported instances in which the upper management of Islamic institutions dictated operational issues despite objections from the SSB. Hassan (2012) proposed, in light of these findings, that the SSB should focus on their advisory role, while the responsibility of Shariah compliance review and the issuance of the relevant Shariah compliance report should be assigned to an External Shariah Auditor in order to improve the quality of Shariah compliance assurance. The BOD may introduce external Shariah audit and review committee to ensure Shariah compliance (Alam *et al.*, 2022a). Shariah officers are essentially subject to the same requirements as SSBs in that they must possess a Shariah qualification background (BNM, 2019; IFSB, 2009). In addition to educational qualifications, Shariah officers are expected to demonstrate high levels of integrity and impartiality when carrying out their duties (BNM, 2019; IFSB, 2009).

According to studies, Islamic institutions face formidable obstacles in the area of *ex-post* Shariah compliance procedures, where their internal governance mechanisms are held accountable. Hassan (2012) conducted one of the empirical studies in this field, in which he identified deficiencies in the implementation of Shariah compliance review involving multiple stakeholders within Malaysian Islamic institutions. Hassan (2012) revealed, among other things, that the SSB had doubts about the authenticity of the Shariah compliance review procedure conducted by various stakeholders within the management of Islamic institutions. Hassan (2012) also reported instances in which the upper management of Islamic institutions dictated operational issues despite objections from the SSB. In light of these findings, Hassan (2012) proposed that the SSB should focus on their advisory role, while the responsibility of Shariah compliance review and the issuance of the relevant Shariah compliance report should be delegated to an External Shariah Auditor in order to improve the quality of Shariah compliance assurance. The results of Shariah audits will then be reported at least annually to SSBs. According to studies, establishing a Shariah audit framework and an effective Shariah audit program in Islamic banks may reduce the risk of Shariah non-compliance and facilitate the harmonization of Shariah practice across Islamic banks (Uddin *et al.*, 2013; Shahwan *et al.*, 2010; Alam *et al.*, 2021c, 2021d, 2023a; Tumewang *et al.*, 2023).

Despite the importance of Shariah auditing discussed previously, according to Rahman (2008), only a small number of Islamic banks perform the crucial task of reviewing and examining transactions after the completion of contracts. This could be due to the absence of Shariah auditing framework regulations and experts to perform this task. It is therefore not surprising that Yahya and Mahzan (2012) disclosed that Malaysian Islamic banks used conventional auditing frameworks when conducting the Shariah audit, despite the argument that such use of

International Standards on Auditing (IAS) was inappropriate because IAS did not take Shariah-related matters into account (Haniffa, 2010). Studies have also revealed that the majority of Shariah officers who conduct the Shariah compliance review and audit in Islamic institutions lack Shariah expertise (see, for example, Kasim *et al.*, 2009; Yahya and Mahzan, 2012; Alam and Thakur, 2022; Tabash *et al.*, 2022; Alam *et al.*, 2019b; 2022a, 2022b, 2022c, 2022d).

In the meantime, Kasim *et al.* (2009) found a discrepancy between the "desirable" and "current" practice in the Malaysian Islamic banking industries through an explanatory analysis. According to their research, the effectiveness of the Shariah audit function will depend on four crucial aspects of Shariah compliance structures: the framework, the scope, the qualifications, and independence issues. Shafii *et al.* (2013) conducted an exploratory study on the impact of Shariah audit functions on the role of SSBs following the implementation of the SGF, a new governance regime for the Malaysian Islamic banking industry. Their study concluded that effective communication between Shariah audit and SSBs will ensure the efficacy of Islamic institutions' internal control systems. Nevertheless, this conclusion was based on an evaluation that was limited to the function and qualifications of parties responsible for the Shariah audit task. Consequently, the study has not analyzed how key governance mechanisms such as SSBs, Shariah Officers, and Internal Auditors collaborate to ensure Shariah compliance in Islamic banking operations.

The significance of internal SG mechanisms was also addressed in the regulations' standards and guidelines. The IFSB, for instance, stipulates that Islamic institutions must appoint Shariah officers to assist SSBs with the Shariah compliance review function (IFSB, 2006: 23). The IFSB also outlined that the Shariah officer must be adequately trained and possess the necessary expertise to ensure that the Shariah review functions are carried out appropriately. In addition, the regulatory body emphasized that Shariah officers may require management to rectify Shariah compliance-related issues (IFSB, 2009).

2.10   Foundational Dimension of Shariah Governance

Several academic works have sought to create an Islamic framework for CG in light of the discrepancies between Islamic fundamentals and the Western paradigm. Islamic CG is based on the Tawhid philosophy and the embedded Shariah rules and principles, with the Tawhid philosophy referring to the

84   *Shariah Governance Systems of Islamic Banks*

principle of discussion where all stakeholders share the same goal of Tawhid, or the oneness of Allah, and the Shariah rules and principles referring to the observance of Islamic law (Choudhury and Hoque, 2004, 2006). Secular humanism is where the Western concept of CG originated. According to the literature, the Islamic CG model is supported by the four fundamental principles of *tawhid, shura*, property ownership, and contractual obligation. These concepts also govern the economic and social behavior of individuals, groups, societies, and states (Zulkifli, 2011a).

2.10.1   *Tawhid and Shura-Based Model*

Muslim jurists and Islamic economists both agree that Tawhid is a central tenet of Islamic economics, although there is surprisingly little literature on the Tawhid epistemological dimension of Islamic business governance. Choudhury and Hoque (2004, 2006) provide an introduction to the fundamental Islamic philosophy of Tawhid in the context of Islamic business governance.

Similar to how Tawhid underpins the Islamic religion (Al-Faruqi, 1982), it underpins the Islamic CG system. Men who glorify Allah whether they are standing, sitting, or lying down on their sides, and who reflect on the (wonders of) existence in the sky and the earth, (thinking): "Our Lord! What you've made is not for nothing. Praise be to You! Save us from the penalty of fire (verse 19). The Tawhid paradigm is shown by Allah's commendation of the believers who, whether standing, reclining, or resting, appreciate the wonders of creation. In another verse (51:56), God reinforces Islam's Tawhid principle by saying, "I have only created Jinns and humans to serve Me." In a roundabout way, these two passages lay forth the bedrock ideas of governance: everything Allah creates serves a purpose, and humans are made to be God's representatives on Earth, seeking out God's unity. Allah, who is everywhere and knows everything, actively participates in human affairs by using mankind as a vicegerent (Chapra, 1992). In al-Qur'an, Allah states, "O my son! (said Luqman), if there were (only) the weight of a mustard seed and it was (hidden) in a solid substance, or (anywhere) in the heavens or on earth, Allah could send it forth: for Allah understands the finer mysteries and is well acquainted with them." Given that everyone ultimately answers to Allah, the Tawhid paradigm broadens a corporation's responsibility and accountability beyond its shareholder base. It also represents the Islamic principle of *taklf*, or personal responsibility, which holds each individual responsible before God for their own deeds.

Therefore, *taklf*, which originates from Tawhid, should be the foundation of Islamic CG. Firms and business organizations have a duty of care to promote the concept of distributive justice via the Shuratic process, in line with the Tawhid paradigm, which acknowledges stakeholders as vicegerents. Every human being is obligated, according to several passages in the al-Qur'an and the al-Sunnah, to use the concept of *shura* in all decisions big and small. In al-Qur'an 3:159, Allah instructs believers to overlook others' sins, ask for forgiveness on their behalf, and seek their advice on issues of consequence. Then, after you've made up your mind, put your faith in Allah. Because Allah loves those who trust in Him. Chapra (1992: 234) uses this passage to argue that *shura* is mandated rather than optional. When it comes to CG, *shura* allows for the greatest possible representation of shareholders and other interested parties. All members of the *shura* — shareholders, management, the BOD, workers, and communities — have a hand in making sure the corporation's operations are in line with Shariah principles and further the firm's aims. In this sense, the various governing bodies all perform important functions. Management and the BOD, for instance, play an active role in setting policy and making decisions. Rather than making choices based on profit maximization for shareholders alone, consideration is given to the interests of all stakeholders, both direct and indirect. Mutual collaboration and the promotion of the corporation's social well-being function are the responsibilities of the other stakeholders, such as the community.

Choudhury and Hoque (2004) outline their model of Tawhid and the Shuratic process, which they used to deconstruct the underlying paradigm of SGF, by referring to the four principles and musical instruments governing SGF: the principle of unity of knowledge; the principle of justice; the principle of productive engagement of resources in social; the principle of economic endeavor and recursive intention. Shariah norms established in the Qur'an and Sunnah make the Islamic firm market-oriented while respecting the values of social justice (Choudhury and Hoque, 2004), and these are the cornerstones of SGF. When discussing how decisions in business and other activities might correspond to Islamic moral norms, Lewis (2005: 16–18) seems to corroborate this position by stressing the importance of Tawhid and the formation of a Shuratic decision-making process. He claims that Allah is the source of all good, that He is the source of all wealth, and that man is nothing more than a trustee who must answer to Allah. The maintenance of the Tawhid principle must be the ultimate objective of business and economic activity as well as the goals of the business

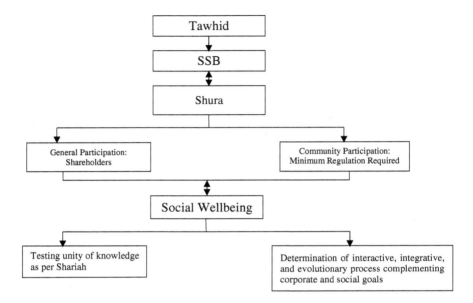

Figure 2.1: Tawhid and Shura Based Corporate Governance Model.
Source: Modified from Choudhury and Hoque (2004: 86).

organization. Choudhury and Hoque's (2004: 86) concept of CG from an Islamic viewpoint is summarized in Figure 2.1.

Figure 2.1 reveals that the Tawhid epistemological paradigm is the bedrock of the Islamic method to CG, which places Shariah law at the center of the corporation's operational obligations. Vicegerency (*khilfah*) and fairness (*al-adlwal ihsn*) are two important concepts that emerge from the Tawhid principle. Stakeholders, in their capacities as representatives of Allah, have a fiduciary responsibility to respect the principles of distributive justice as articulated in the Shuratic process. According to Chapra (1992: 234), *shura* is a necessary aspect of any decision-making procedure and its constituent represents the widest possible representation of interested parties.

In the Islamic model of CG, the SSB, BOD and the organizations that make up the Shura play significant roles. The SSB steps in to determine what areas of business must comply with Shariah and plays a critical role in making sure that happens. Furthermore, owners have a duty as active participants and responsible stakeholders in the process of decision-making and policy structure, where they should prioritize the interests of all stakeholders, both direct and indirect, above their personal profit maximization. The community and other interested parties have an obligation to work together for the common good, protecting everyone's interests and bolstering the social welfare system. Islamic CG seeks to balance individual and community interests via the application of the idea of equitable distribution (Choudhury and Hoque, 2004).

Islamic banks do not follow complete Shariah principles in all aspects of SG nor violate them fully in their overall functions due to less accountability, which contradicts the concept of the Tawhidi epistemological process of Islamic CG. Islamic banks announce that they are following AAOIFI guidelines, but in practice, they do not follow the instructions accurately because all of the standards and policies of AAOIFI and the IFSB are not applicable in Bangladesh due to its cultural, legal, and regulatory structures. It is found that Islamic banks in Bangladesh have a lower practice of *maqasid* as Shariah and Tawhidic approach and Shuratic process (Alam *et al.*, 2021, 2023a, 2023b; Alam and Miah, 2021).

The epistemological basis of business administration is the Tawhid and Shura approaches. The existing CG structure does not provide a clear and unambiguous framework for adopting and implementing such a plan. According to research (Zulkifli, 2011b), the trend also shows that major firms, especially IFIs, often use the present business governance model, which rests on the episteme of rationalism and reason. This calls for further practical, rather than theoretical, research into how this Tawhid- and Shura-based method functions in practice.

2.10.2 *Stakeholder-Oriented Approach*

The rights of all stakeholders, even those who do not possess equity, must be protected, according to Chapra and Ahmed (2002). This seems to support the model put forth by Iqbal and Mirakhor (2004), who contend that the Islamic economic system's CG model is a stakeholder-centered simulation in which the governance technique and structures safeguard the rights and interests of every stakeholder instead of the shareholders every single time (Iqbal and Mirakhor, 2004; Iqbal, 2007). The foundation for Iqbal and Mirakhor's key arguments in Islamic law is the notion of property rights and the observance of both explicit and implicit binding agreements that regulate the financial and sociological behavior of individuals, organizations, corporations, societies, and states. These two principles offer strong support for the claim that the stakeholder-oriented model accurately captures Islamic CG.

The Islamic notion of property rights offers a structure for determining and safeguarding the rights and interests of all parties involved. Usufructs (*manafi'*) and rights (*huquq*) were generally agreed upon by jurists to be considered property and so worthy of protection. All property rights, including ownership, acquisition, use, and disposal, are safeguarded in modern Islam, whether they be *manafi'* or *huquq*. According to Islamic teachings, all property ultimately belongs to Allah and any person who is entrusted with it as Amanah (trust) is only a trustee and custodian who is granted permission to utilize and manage the property in accordance with Shariah. "Believe in Allah and the Messenger of Allah and spend (in charity) from what He has made you heirs of" is only one of many verses in the al-Qur'an that speak to the importance of respecting the rights of others to their property.

Stakeholder theorists disagree with the three main tenets of the shareholder system and instead advocate for the following: (1) the right of all stakeholders to participate in corporate decisions that affect them; (2) the fiduciary duty of managers to serve the interests of all stakeholder groups; and (3) the promotion of the desires of all stakeholders, not just shareholders, should be the firm's objective. Customers, vendors, providers of supplementary services and goods, distributors, and workers are all considered stakeholders in this view, which is also known as the stakeholder's paradigm of CG. For this reason, stakeholder theory argues that businesses should be run in a way that benefits all of those involved.

Any entity with a direct or indirect interest in the corporation is considered a stakeholder, regardless of whether they are investors or owners. How to create an efficient CG framework for an Islamic financial institution is a concern given the Western model of CG. It may be inferred from the consideration of the two models, Tawhid and Shura-based and Stakeholder-based, that Tawhid serves as the epistemological basis for Islamic CG. The stakeholder value model, with its governance approach focused on protecting all stakeholders, is another factor that tends to influence CG's goal. By taking into account an Islamic viewpoint, the term "stakeholders" is expanded to include Islam itself in addition to people who participate in the governance of the organization. As a result, with the other stakeholder entities, the CG model based on Shariah views Islam as the most significant stakeholder. The SSB was established as a component of the CG institutions as a result of the concept of Islam as a sovereign stakeholder, which establishes Shariah as the law that governs all company transactions.

Azid *et al.* (2007) claim that under Islamic law, everyone has "the right to possess private property and financial assets in order to make a profit, to create employment, to encourage investments, and to increase prosperity." This requires recognizing the existence of separate ownership interests among shareholders of a company. Shariah principles give guidance for addressing property ownership, and Islam recognizes the right of individuals and businesses to possess property. Shariah mandates a fair distribution of benefits between private property owners and the public good. Islam's acknowledgment of this property rights issue is an indication that the company must take into account the needs of more than just its shareholders while making decisions. There are three pillars upon which the Islamic concept of property rights rests: (1) the right is subject to Shariah; (2) enjoyment of the right is balanced with the rights of society and the state; (3) people, society, and the state are stakeholders whose liberties are recognized under Islamic law. The contractual structure in Islam is likewise distinct.

With this contractual structure in place, the term "stakeholders" may now include both active and passive participants in the company, as opposed to only stockholders. Iqbal and Mirakhor (2004) propose two tests to determine if an individual is a stakeholder: first, whether the person or organization has any explicit and implicit contractual obligations; and second, whether the individual's intellectual property rights are at risk due to the business exposure of the corporation. This means that anybody who is in any way touched by the firm's activities has a stake in the company and should be treated as such. In this context, shareholders contribute money, management runs the show, workers do their jobs, and regulators uphold the law by making sure contracts are enforceable. All of these duties are established by the agreement between the parties and show how the Islamic model of CG prioritizes the interests of its stakeholders.

CG with a stakeholder perspective on values is preoccupied by the two core Shariah notions of property rights and contractual responsibility. Any business operated by Muslims must follow the rules of Shariah. It places a focus on protecting the legal rights and financial interests of all parties. It is interesting to note that the SSB, which is charged with supervising the Shariah-related parts of an Islamic firm, is acknowledged as a distinct institutional arrangement in CG by the stakeholder-based governance structure. The managers have a fiduciary obligation to govern the firm, while the BOD, on behalf of the owners, is responsible for monitoring and supervising all corporate activity. Employees, depositors, and clients, among others, have legal responsibilities that must be met. The regulatory and supervisory authorities are an external stakeholder group that helps ensure rules and legislation are promulgated and a suitable regulatory environment is provided.

The bulk of the arguments supported the model of stakeholder engagement and recognized the rights of the stakeholders, but failed to indicate how these rights would be maintained, as stated by Chapra (2004) in his analysis of Iqbal and Mirakhor's arguments. It seems to be difficult to establish that the claim that behavioral standards assure the internalization of shareholder rights is correct. According to Chapra (2004) Islamic standards were internalized within classical Muslim culture, but this is not the situation in modern Muslim society. The broad adoption of Islamic beliefs, the makeup of communities, and the economic situation all played roles in the phenomena of internalization of stakeholders' rights (Chapra, 2007). To internalize stakeholder rights, Chapra argues that additional conditions, such as competitive markets and an effective legal framework for safeguarding the interests of stakeholders, are required. There is also the controversial view that Islamic governments should be the ones to develop a CG structure. The regulations and legislation that outline the proper business governance structure are the purview of the Islamic government. Some of the questions that this argument brings up concern the CG structure of Islamic firms in countries where Muslims are a minority. The corporate goal of Islamic firms is a delicate balancing act between the maximization of profit and the obligation to uphold social justice by safeguarding the rights, passions, and welfare of all stakeholders, as evidenced by the arguments for the value of stakeholders' orientation as the ideal model of corporate responsibility in the Islamic economic system. It has been noticed that the maximization of shareholder profit is the major goal of many organizations, even those that declare themselves Islamic. This indicating that contrary to the stakeholder value orientation, many Islamic firms actually use the shareholder form of CG. Researches and academics are faced with the issue of developing not only the theoretical underpinnings of ICG but also empirical data and pertinent case studies about the actual practice of CG and its possible reform (Zulkifli, 2011b).

Each party is responsible for carrying out his duties under the contract with respect to CG in line with its terms. Despite the fact that Islam protects the right to contract within the bounds of Shariah, the participants of any transaction are nevertheless required to uphold their end of the bargain. The managers have a fiduciary obligation to govern the firm, while the BOD, on behalf of the owners, is responsible for monitoring and supervising all corporate activity. Employees, depositors, and clients, among others, have legal responsibilities that must be met. Regulatory and supervisory bodies are an external element that helps promulgate rules and legislation and create a conducive regulatory environment (Hasan, 2011b).

The protection of all parties' interests is at the heart of Islamic financial enterprise, which places a premium on good CG within an Islamic framework. Stakeholder interest extends beyond maximizing profits or financial return in an Islamic setting to include adherence to Islamic law (Shariah) and the Tawhid principle (Allah's oneness, in other words). Both the business model based on the principle of consultation, in which all stakeholders share the same goal of Tawhid (the oneness of Allah), and the model of adopting the stakeholders' principles with modifications have been discussed by Muslim scholars as major examples of Islamic CG (Zulkifli, 2008). Islamic CG, as described by Zamir Iqbal and Abbas Mirakhor, is very similar in structure to the stakeholder model. According to Safieddine's (2009) CG analysis, IFIs confront more severe agency difficulties than traditional banks do. Abdullah *et al.* (2015) highlight many reasons why good CG is especially crucial for Islamic organizations.

2.10.3 *Conventional Corporate Governance vs Shariah Governance*

SG and conventional CG are distinct due to their distinct purposes. SG closes the distance between these models by incorporating the religious aspects of company activities and concluding the CG system within the organization. In addition to dealing with jurisdictional and national laws, Islamic banks also implement Shariah law in their business cycles. SG guarantees strict adherence to Islamic law and principles (Rahajeng, 2012). Islamic CG demands consideration of spiritual standards and religious principles, in contrast to traditional CG, which places emphasis on the firm's financial performance. IFIs must also follow state laws and regulations as well as Shariah standards. Last but not least, the SSB is a further crucial player in IFIs whose main duty is to make sure that IFI functions adhere to Shariah standards (Obid and Naysary, 2014). Since IFIs and markets are required to function in line with the Shariah concept and principles, this is the main difference between conventional and Islamic finance (Kasim *et al.*, 2013). A SSB should also be constituted in the case of an Islamic bank to ensure Shariah compliance in the bank's activities. One of the most important distinctions between the CG structures of conventional financial institutions and IFIs is the existence of the SSB and the Shariah review unit (Grais and Pellegrini, 2006b).

CHAPTER 3

Theoretical Explanation of Shariah Governance

3.1 Introduction

Shariah governance (SG) is an essential part of the Islamic banking industry's corporate governance (CG), although it has received little attention in the existing literature. Research on the management of faith-based businesses, such as Islamic organizations, becomes especially important in light of the complexity of Islamic CG compared to more traditional CG systems. Islamic banks are worthless and doomed if their governance procedures are ineffective since they cannot satisfy the stakeholders' need for religious and ethical legitimacy. As a result, the International Financial Services Board (IFSB) proposed a model for a Shariah Governance Framework (SGF) that mandates Islamic banks (IBs) to adopt suitable organizational frameworks and procedures to ensure their practices are consistent with Islamic principles. To legitimize operations and assure a wide variety of stakeholders, IBs must establish governance structures (for examples, see Tomkins and Karim, 1987; Iqbal and Mirakhor, 2004; Grais and Pellegrini, 2006a; Ullah *et al.*, 2016; Karbhari *et al.*, 2018) that ensure the organization's actions are consistent with the values and norms of the society it serves.

Intuitively, an efficient SGF for IBs would have strong structural governance structures that safeguard the BOD, management, and SSB's ability to supervise and be held accountable by the Shariah. Abu-Tapanjeh (2009) argues that a complete governance system will be produced by any procedure that does not have an acceptable ethical and moral foundation.

Islamic business teachings differ from the Western perspective in that they emphasize both spiritual and temporal concerns (Archer and Karim, 2007; Tinker, 2004; Karim, 2001), however, their governance implications are little understood. Kamla (2009) is true that if Islam is performed exclusively and without unnecessary laxity, it would fulfill its stated socioeconomic aims within an Islamic environment. The SSB is responsible for advising, monitoring, and overseeing Islamic banking operations to guarantee their conformance with Shariah principles and a good reputation (Ghayad, 2008). Contemporary business systems are firmly rooted in the Western Enlightenment movement and positivist thought, which saw the secular separated from the sacred and the "normative" eliminated from the "discourse" (Hamid *et al.*, 1993; Gambling *et al.*, 1991; Tinker, 2004; Carmona and Ezzamel, 2006). This raises important questions when examining the influence of religion on business.

Since Shariah compliance is what sets IBs apart from their conventional counterparts, improving their public profile is essential (Belal *et al.*, 2015; Mallin *et al.*, 2014). There are many normative (Islamic spiritual philosophies and values) and critical reviews of the uniqueness of Islamic governance structures (Choudhury and Hoque, 2006; Kamla *et al.*, 2006; Abu-Tapanjeh, 2009; Williams and Zinkin, 2010) because the concepts and principles prescribed by the Islamic faith are very different from the systems adopted in traditional CG. Different from the traditional CG's concentration on profit and institutional performance, the implementation of SGF is entirely concerned with adhering to Islamic values. Also, Carpenter and Feroz (2001) argued that successful governments and institutions are those that gain legitimacy in the social order by caving in to demands and using legitimization tactics to prove their social and financial acceptability.

According to Western scholars (Choudhury and Alam, 2013; Hasan, 2009; Nathan and Ribière, 2007; Grassa, 2013; Platonova *et al.*, 2018), CG may be distinguished from SG by its epistemological emphasis. Muslims and Islamic institutions are responsible before God and must follow a rigid set of rules. Furthermore, Islamic accountability implies a duty to society at large to combat poverty and promote equity or social justice (Maali *et al.*, 2009; Napier, 2006). According to the literature on CSR (Baydoun and Willetts, 2000; Gambling and Karim, 1986; Lewis, 2001), Islamic organizations are obligated to provide any information requested by their stakeholders. Responsibility may also be determined by the nature of the contractual connection between the parties involved (Grey *et al.*, 1995).

Previous literature has advocated three theories to explain SG in relation to managerial structures (see, for example, Obid and Naysary, 2014; Al-Nasser Mohammed and Muhammed, 2017): agency theory (Jensen and Meckling, 1976), the theory of stewardship (Donaldson and Davis, 1991), and stakeholder theory (Freeman, 1984). However, the analysis of these divergent views has shown a handful of limiting ideas about SG, such as accountability, impartiality, openness, disclosure, expertise, and confidentiality. Regarding the impact of institutional theory (IT) on religious organizations, DiMaggio (1998) provided elaboration on the ideas of procedural, figurative understanding, and cultural validity. In contrast to traditional corporate organizations, which tend to regard coherent actors and a reputation oriented on profit maximization, he argued that technological innovation is relevant to the goals of religious organizations. The corporate community development practice of Islamic banks in Bangladesh (Hossain and Yahya, 2017) and the impact of governance processes on the efficiency of the global Islamic insurance industry (Karbhari *et al.*, 2018) have all been the subject of previous IT research. IT indicates a missing link in how Islamic institutions impact society regulation, which is something that is not addressed by the predominant ideas of SG. The theory offers a framework for understanding how prevalent practices and standards across businesses with comparable structures impact the understanding and application of the regulation (in this case, SG) in IFIs. In this light, Kalbers and Fogarty (1998) state that "organizational frameworks have evolved into symbolic representations of compliance and social responsibility." A desire to satisfy legitimacy may also motivate a number of governance successes and structures, such as Islamic institutions and the intricate role of SSBs.

The study's overarching goal is to learn about the several theoretical frameworks (e.g., agency, stewardship, stakeholders, and organizational theories) and choose the one that seems most suitable for the creation of an SGF in IFIs. Karbhari *et al.* (2020) took the SGF idea to the realm of IT, analyzing it for its usefulness in the context of establishing a clearly articulated set of rules for governance. Karbhari *et al.* (2020) carried out the SGF from an IT perspective, providing critical insights into why this theory is of greater importance than other organizational theories concerning the establishment and discharge of roles, powers, and operations of various bodies including regulators, institutions, BOD, management, and SSBs. This is in contrast to the traditional studies which provide useful background information on organizational regulations and emphasize issues related to ownership and control. Second, while previous studies have looked at and discussed the various theoretical frameworks (e.g., agency, stewardship, stakeholder, resource dependency theory, transaction cost economics, political theory, legitimacy, and social contract theory) regarding the formation of board structures (e.g., Hasan, 2011b; Iqbal and Mirakhor, 2004; Obid and Naysary, 2014; Haridan *et al.*, 2018; Al-Nasser Mohammed and Muhammed, 2017), these studies outlined the organizational framework and guiding principles of SG but ignored the critical concerns of openness, disclosure, and accountability.

Since IT best highlights operational rules and processes for organizations, Karbhari *et al.* (2020) and Alam *et al.* (2021e) are particularly compelled to see it as the main theoretical foundation. The following are the fundamental tenets of our argument (Karbhari *et al.*, 2020; Alam *et al.*, 2021e). When it comes to strengthening organizational structures and performance, Karbhari *et al.* (2020) and Alam *et al.* (2021e) believe that IT may play a crucial role by harmonizing the role of stakeholders (including regulators, institutions, and SSBs involved in an SGF). Because IT may provide substantial insight into operational rules and processes for organizations, particularly religious institutions, Karbhari *et al.* (2020) hypothesize that it offers a more acceptable basis for considering an SGF for Islamic banks. Thirdly, IT promotes the idea that in order for businesses to thrive they should adopt culturally acceptable organizational structures, systems, and procedures. Therefore, Karbhari *et al.* (2020) and Alam *et al.* (2021e) draw the conclusion that the regulatory, normative, and coercive pressure has an equal effect on Islamic institutions.

Organizational effectiveness is argued by IT to be influenced not just by resource dependencies and mechanical demands but also by rational mythical creatures, perceived knowledge established over the enlightened framework and by the occupations, a commonality belief, and the control (Zucker, 1977; Meyer and Rowan, 1977; DiMaggio and Powel, 1978). Furthermore, practice and structures inside institutions are seen as reactions to externally generated policies, attitudes, and resolutions (Scott, 1987). IT is also acknowledged as a theoretical viewpoint that displays rational myths, isomorphism, and legitimacy (Scott, 2008), showing "how" corporations are responsible for their social commitments and practice of these qualities (Feldman and Rafaeli, 2002; He *et al.*, 2007).

Make use of the "acquiesce," "compromise," "avoid," "defy," and "manipulate" tactics when faced with mimetic pressures in the workplace. Organizational isomorphism (DiMaggio and Powell, 1983), organizational reliance (Pfeffer and Salancik, 1978), and organizational credibility

(Ashforth and Gibbs, 1990; Scott, 1995) all provide context for why SG has been adopted as a management technique.

3.2 Theory Used in Shariah Governance

In the Islamic model of CG, the SSB steps in to determine what areas of business must comply with Shariah and plays a critical role in making sure that happens. In addition, stockholders have a duty as engaged and responsible stakeholders in the policy framework and decision-making procedure, where they must prioritize the interests of all stakeholders, both direct and indirect, above their own financial gain. The community and other interested parties have a duty to work together for the common good, protecting everyone's interests and bolstering the social welfare system.

Stakeholder theory, which takes into account a wider set of stakeholders, and agency theory, which emphasizes the interaction between managers and shareholders, have been the most significant ideas in the development of CG (Mallin, 2007). The two most common CG models are the shareholder benefit system and the stakeholder value orientation, both of which may be traced back to these ideas. A second aspect in which Islamic and Western views of CG diverge is in the epistemic orientation of the former (Choudhury and Hoque, 2004); IFIs must follow the norms and principles of Shariah, including *tawhid*, *shura*, rights pertaining to property, and the commitment to fulfill a contractual duty.

The shareholders' delegation of decision-making power to the management as an agent produces information asymmetry, in which the manager has an advantage over the shareholders while the shareholders have a disadvantage (Jensen and Meckling, 1976). Managers may act in their own best interests rather than that of the owner when there is an information asymmetry. When the agent's interests diverge from those of the principal, a conflict of agency exists between the parties to the contract. Management, in its role as the shareholders' representative, might become exploitative under such conditions. Furthermore, the agency issue may cause shareholders and management to have unequal access to information (Heath and Norman, 2004).

Despite its central role in the field of CG research, agency theory has been criticized for its flawed assumptions about human conduct and motivation (Perrow, 1986; Eisenhardt, 1989; Donaldson, 1990). Stewardship theory was developed by Donaldson and Davis (1991) to account for people's emotions and motivations. According to this theory, a steward's utility function is maximized when he or she safeguards and increases the assets of shareholders via the performance of the business (Davis et al., 1997). Arthurs and Busenitz (2003) state that the principle of stewardship suggests that a steward's actions are more likely to win over the principal by improving the organization's efficiency. When compared to agency theory, stewardship theory holds that the goal of governance is to find processes and structures that promote the most effective coordination between management and owners and that there is no conflict of interest that results from the separation of ownership (Donaldson, 1990; Davis et al., 1997). The stewardship theory predicts that transaction expenses will be lowered because of the elimination of the need for incentives and the close monitoring of conduct (Davis et al., 1997).

According to Freeman's (1984) stakeholder theory, businesses have an obligation to look out for the interests of all the people and groups inside the social system in which they participate (Donaldson and Preston, 1995; Rowley, 1997). According to this view, the link between executives and their stakeholders is even more important than that between owners, managers, and workers (Elena, 2012). The stakeholder and the business have equal sway over one another and may exert influence via a number of channels, making this relationship very important (Freeman, 1994).

Stakeholder theory, on the other hand, considers the wider interests of organizations that may be impacted by a company's actions. Stakeholders are described by Carroll (1993) as "those groups or individuals whose decisions, policies, or objectives are directly or indirectly affected by the organization." Management now considers not just the interests of shareholders but also those of other stakeholders when making decisions (Solomon, 2007; Berry and Rondinelli, 1998; Collier, 2008) thanks to stakeholder theory's expansion of the idea of CG. The agency hypothesis, which holds that a corporation exists only to maximize its stockholders' income, is clearly at odds with the stakeholder view. In fact, Carroll and Buchholtz (1999) stated that management responsibilities involve addressing organizational conflicts of interest in addition to dealing with numerous stakeholders. That's why it's expected that management would act as a fiduciary and look out for everyone's interests (Haridan, 2016). According to Carroll and Buchholtz (1999), managers are responsible for addressing internal conflicts of interest and communicating with a wide range of stakeholders. Islamic CG seeks to balance private and societal goals by enforcing the concept of distributive justice (Choudhury and Hoque, 2004), and all of these steps lead to that end.

SG is seen as a crucial tool for IFIs to fulfill this obligation, especially with respect to Shariah concerns, in line with the notions of stakeholder theory, which calls for accountability toward stakeholders (Grais and Pellegrini, 2006a). Information and openness on Shariah compliance are increasingly desired by many stakeholders in society, including the Muslim Ummah, as shown by multiple studies (Grais and Pellegrini, 2006b; Abu-Tapanjeh, 2009; Bhatti and Bhatti, 2009; Kasim *et al.*, 2013).

For example, Jensen (2001) argues that stakeholders only care about one thing — profit — while Ansoff (1987) argues that the theory creates competitive problems by allowing information to leak between offices. In response to these claims, Roberts (1992) suggested that companies rank their constituents based on relevance, influence, and dependency.

By digging further into these connections, we found that some important ideas in these theories are connected to Shariah administration. Accountability, openness and candor, expertise, privacy, and impartiality also fall under this category. The IFSB (2009), and the work of numerous scholars like Kasim and Shamsir (2012), Hamza (2013), Ullah (2013), Hasan (2011a), Grais and Pellegrini (2006a), and Minhas (2012), all agree that these five principles are essential for ensuring the quality of SG in IFIs.

3.3 Agency Theory and SGF

It is generally accepted that agency theory emphasizes the predetermined or controlling relationship between the principal and agent. The theory concentrates on concepts and solutions such as (1) the agent–principal conflict of interest, (2) information asymmetry, and (3) risk aversion concerns (Jensen and Meckling, 1976). According to the application of agency theory in CG, "the primary role of the board is to reduce the potential divergence of interest between shareholders and management by minimizing agency costs and protecting shareholders' investments" (Hendry and Kiel, 2004). Additionally, agency theory describes how committees superintend the activities of management. However, it does not define the strategies regarding the external organizational environment that can be used to modify the directors' abilities and control the organizations. Information asymmetry (Jensen and Meckling, 1976) refers to the fact that management's policymaking authority, as an emissary of the owner, generates an informational advantage for them but is a deficiency for the owners. In essence, managers serve as agents chosen by shareholders.

The agency problem may result in information asymmetries between managers and proprietors (Agrawal and Knoeber, 1996; Heath and Norman, 2004).

The issue of CG and its numerous approaches are associated with specific perspectives on the environment and objectives of a corporation (Zollo and Freeman, 2010; Rajan and Zingales, 2001). Critics of this theory and its implementations to the matters of CG highlight issues such as impractical premises regarding managers' motivations and activities, inappropriate commendations inferred from the theory, and uncertain authorized explanations of CG being completed on its basis. Other researchers have also expressed uncertainty regarding the presentation of shareholder–manager relationships based on agency theory. Focusing on studies on the disclosure of CG and agency theory, some researchers concluded that their findings supported the theoretical components regarding corporations disclosing CG information to reduce information asymmetry and agency costs (see, for instance, Bauwhede and Willekens, 2008; Henry, 2010; Kent and Stewart, 2008). According to Aljifri (2008) and Ferrer and Ferrer (2011), the influence of success on the phases of disclosure is insignificant. Consequently, when utilizing the same theory, there are three extremely diverse perspectives. Prior conventional banking literature has revealed that the application of agency theory tends to limit operational activities of a bank to the responsibility of only its investors. Due to its ethical foundational ethos, heritage, and integrity, a suitable social and political culture, and Shariah compliance, this expands in an Islamic context (Archer et al., 1998; Chapra and Ahmed, 2002; Beekun and Badawi, 2005; Safieddine, 2009; Belal et al., 2015; Ullah et al., 2016). Nonetheless, the fundamental profit and loss allocation principle implemented by Islamic banks permits the transmission of multiple categories of operational risk to its depositors (Siddiqui, 2001). This concept does not permit depositors to participate in decision-making procedures, which creates a culture in which management achieves self-interest by having depositors bear the cost (Iqbal and Llewellyn, 2002). In light of agency theory (Hill and Jones, 1992), the isolation between ownership and monitoring process in Islamic institutions (Safieddine, 2009) is deemed an agency problem (Hill and Jones, 1992). In addition, the contract structure of the Mudaraba (profit sharing) implemented by Islamic banks to mobilize and execute depositors' funds can be viewed as a hidden agency problem (Archer and Karim, 1997). In fact, this problem becomes more complicated for Islamic banks compared to their counterparts, in which profit and loss along with risk are allocated to depositors, whereas conventional bank investors have certainty regarding their returns (Siddiqui, 2001). Consequently, in Islamic institutions, the agency problem can be seen to prolong currency flow and control, thereby making the issue more complex (Safieddine, 2009). Due to this unique "agency" issue, information reporting is deemed to be even more crucial in the context of Islamic institutions (Archer and Karim, 2009).

According to Kamla *et al.* (2006) and Abu-Tapanjeh (2009), managers in Islamic banks are also responsible to God and social goals in addition to the company or stockholders, which is the opposite of the self-opportunistic viewpoint advocated by agency theory. Given that Islamic laws have been applied to property and contractual rights, it does not explain why Shariah disregards the owner's interest (Bhatti and Bhatti, 2010). As a result, the authenticity of the report and adherence to all Shariah principles increases the public's trust and confidence as well as that of depositors, agents, and stockholders, thereby reducing information asymmetry between management and other related parties regarding the institution's operational functions (Grais and Pellegrini, 2006a; Archer and Karim, 2007; Vinnicombe, 2010). Additionally, owners and depositors must have access to accurate information, therefore IFIs must be open about religious topics (Haniffa and Hudaib, 2007).

3.4   Stewardship Theory and SGF

In contrast to agency theory (directors' and managers' opportunism), stewardship theory holds that both directors and managers have the same interests as shareholders. This is the case information as compared to other companies based on studies conducted (see, for example, Aerts *et al.* (2007) and Cormier *et al.* (2009)). Here, the proprietors believe they have the primary authority to regulate and control the corporations. In contrast, the agent believes that because they are designated to supervise the firms' activities, they have the authority to make any decisions regarding the firms' efficacy. Due to the limitations of agency theory regarding human behavior, this perspective creates agency problems between management and proprietors (Perrow, 1986; Eisenhardt, 1989; Donaldson, 1990). Donaldson and Davis (1991) devised the stewardship theory, which encompasses the psychological behavior of individuals. The theory demonstrates that a custodian protects and maximizes the owner's wealth over organizational performance, in contrast to agency theory. Essentially, the theory indicates that the separation of stewardship and ownership does not generate any conflict, thereby promoting the most effective harmonization between them (Donaldson, 1990; Davis *et al.*, 1977). In Islam, however, the perception of ownership derives from the view of stewardship (Khilafah), which suggests that God is the sole owner of all assets and that man is merely a representative and steward of that property (Iqbal and Mirakhor, 2004). Consequently, in Islamic CG, the actions of custodians to enhance the success of the institution may be motivated by factors other than the need for self-esteem.

This prompted researchers such as Lewis (2005) and Bhatti and Bhatti (2009) to assert that ICG is similar to the concept of stewardship, in which stewards are regarded as important players within the corporation and are encouraged to fulfill their responsibilities in accordance with the guidelines of Islamic principles within the spirit of partnership. Turnbull (2000) argues that this theory necessitates the recruitment of qualified and competent stewards within the organization. Numerous influential executives of large corporations concur that the demand for an independent board within a corporation is increasing with the addition of senior directors. In this regard, Islam emphasizes "Shuratic (collective) decision-making" (Lewis, 2005) in accordance with the explicit directives of the Holy Quran.

For these reasons, Islamic banks are required to staff and the SSB with qualified and experienced Shariah scholars in Islamic law (Fiqh Muamalah) and Islamic finance. The SSB is tasked with guiding, revising, and monitoring the activities of IFIs in order to ensure Shariah compliance (IFSB, 2009). Among other responsibilities, SSB members must ensure the application of Shuratic (or consensus-based) decision-making (Lahsasna, 2011). Therefore, the knowledge and proficiency of SSB members are significant, as DeLorenzo (2012) notes that without certification of commercial products as Shariah-compliant by a knowledgeable Shariah advisor, the legitimacy of such products and services remains questionable.

3.5 Stakeholder Theory and SGF

While stakeholder theory (Freeman, 1984) posits that corporations are the combination of various entities within a societal structure wherever they operate, Donaldson and Preston (1995) and Rowley (1997) argue that corporations are responsible for the safety and security of such concerned groups. Broadly speaking, stakeholder theory demonstrates that management not only pursues shareholder benefits but also plays a crucial role in protecting the interests of other stakeholders (Berry and Rondinelli, 1998; Solomon, 2007; Collier, 2008). This theory denies the assumptions implied by agency theory because, according to stakeholder theory, the company's objectives are not limited to maximizing shareholder assets, as agency theory suggests. In addition, Carroll and Buchholtz (1999) argued that management duties include not only interacting with the institution's numerous stakeholders but also resolving any conflicts of interest that may arise. Therefore, management is expected to fulfill their fiduciary duties by safeguarding the interests of all stakeholders. In accordance with Choudhury and Hoque (2004), all of these procedures are geared toward achieving the ultimate objective of Islamic CG, which is to support isolated and social objectives by upholding the principles of social justice.

On the basis of the prescribed concept of the stakeholder theory (which signifies the management's accountability to the various stakeholders), SG is regarded as an important mechanism for IFIs to achieve this account-ability (Grais and Pellegrini, 2006a). Regarding this aspect, prior literature (Grais and Pellegrini, 2006a; Abu-Tapanjeh, 2009; Bhatti and Bhatti, 2009; Kasim *et al.*, 2013) suggests that information and transparency regarding Shariah compliance are increasingly desired by a variety of stakeholders and society at large. Numerous researchers have emphasized the importance of stakeholder theory in the field of ICG (Iqbal and Mirakhor, 2004; Azid *et al.*, 2007; Chapra, 2007; Bhatti and Bhatti, 2009; Bhatti and Bhatti, 2010; Hasan, 2009). In addition, Asutay (2007) suggested that the transition to a social banking structure would help bridge the divide between the objectives of Islamic economics and its current banking position. In addition, he emphasizes that the viability of Islamic banking is extremely reliant on the relationships with the Muslim population as a whole. Moreover, Hasan (2009) explains the four major key components of ICG and conventional CG, including epistemology, firm objectives, characteristics of the board and management, and finally the capital connected to the structure of ownership, where the principles of Tawhid in Islamic epistemology indicate that Allah Almighty has created all things and that the ultimate accountability must be to him. This view establishes the Maqasid al-Shariah as the goals of businesses where the interests and welfare of all members of society must be protected. The characteristics of the board and management can be observed in the principles of Shuratic decision-making procedures, in which the SSB is responsible for supervising and monitoring banking activities and confirming Shariah compliance in

104 Shariah Governance Systems of Islamic Banks

accordance with Islamic principles. Indeed, Carroll and Buchholtz (1999) argue that the duties of management are to deal with various stakeholders and to resolve any organizational conflicts of interest. Thus, management is anticipated to exercise their fiduciary responsibilities with regard to the best interests of all stakeholders. All of these procedures are geared toward achieving the ultimate objective of ICG, which is to obtain personal and social objectives by preserving social well-being and equity principles (Choudhury and Hoque, 2004).

Regarding ownership, Islam regards both IAHs and shareholders as merchants, as opposed to passive shareholders. According to Iqbal and Mirakhor (2004), the evolution of the stakeholder model can be viewed through the lens of property rights and contractual obligations. In addition, Bhatti and Bhatti (2009) assert that SG is a crucial mechanism of ICG by which IFIs corroborate the observance of Shariah principles and moral values, as well as acts as an instrument for boosting stakeholder confidence in IFIs. The authors also note that ICG is comparable to the stakeholder model of CG as it emphasizes moral principles, accountability, and transparency, which is consistent with the OECD's prescribed CG principles.

3.6 Institutional Theory Framework

The term "institution" is used to describe a collection of norms that businesses and people are expected to follow. These norms can include formal rule sets (North, 1990), *ex-ante* commitments, informally shared communication sequences (Jepperson, 1991), and assumed truths (Meyer and Rowan, 1991). Pressures to conform may be found in many different areas of society and culture, including regulatory frameworks, government agencies, regulations, tribunals, professions, procedures, and many others (DiMaggio and Powell, 1983, 1991).

According to Scott (1995), the term "IT" refers to the basic and malleable features of social organization. Regulatory, normative, and sociocultural cognitive frameworks are also taken into account since they are often recognized as commanding methods for social conduct. IT's rise to prominence may be attributed to its ubiquitous delineation of best practices for consumers and companies alike (Scott, 2005). In addition, it's a policymaking framework that places a focus on what makes government organizations legitimate and effective (Kraft and Furlong, 2007). IT was additionally attacked for focusing too much on showing the parallels and dissimilarities across occurrences. Meyer and Rowan (1977) and Zucker (1977) also created a new institutional predictor technique that places a focus on people's impressions and understandings of institutions. Meyer and Rowan (1977) argued that remodeling is important because it helps to provide a rationale for the adoption of new rules. They discussed how organizational policies and procedures serve as myths that provide organizations credibility, cohesion, and a fighting chance. According to Meyer and Rowan (1977), this indicates that the capacity of institutions to adapt applications and procedures to improve their legitimacy and survival is driven by the rational conceptions of companies.

DiMaggio and Powell (1991: 12) pointed out several key distinctions between old and new institutionalism, including the fact that the former places more emphasis on the relationship between isomorphism and legitimacy and the power of rarely explicitly articulated common understandings, while the latter places more emphasis on the vesting of desires within organizations as a result of political trade-offs and alliances. Meyer and Rowan (1977) highlight the importance of legitimacy to the continued existence of organizations as a key difference between old and modern institutionalism. However, traditional institutionalism emphasizes the political in its understanding of group disputes and organizational methods (Powell and DiMaggio, 1991). For instance, whereas "conflict of interest" played a major role in traditional institutionalism, it plays a much smaller one in modern institutionalism.

The formal organizational structural demands that brought about this new approach to institutional philosophy, called "neo-institutionalism," led to isomorphism. Meyer and Rowan (1977) explored isomorphism at the macro-societal level; DiMaggio and Powell (1983) did the same at the microlevel of the organizational field in explaining the institutional isomorphism.

To paraphrase Hawley (1968: 149), the selection is "a constraining procedure that forces one unit in an organism to share characteristics with other units facing the same set of environmental conditions." He highlighted three isomorphic processes: (1) coercive for legitimacy, (2) mimetic to avoid ambiguity, and (3) normative, which is primarily the result of professionalization. DiMaggio and Powell (1983) looked to the new institutionalism to explain the long-term viability of successful organizations. Furthermore, Tolbert and Zucker (1983) ignored logic and emphasized legitimacy over efficiency. These three isomorphic processes will be explored in further depth in the following paragraphs.

In order to understand how institutions generate and affect organizational structures, it is crucial for this study to adopt a new institutionalism perspective. Knowing what may affect the course of action of phenomena (like CG) and how it could shape the theory's evolution is also crucial. So far, it has been apparent that institutional theory incorporates many different theoretical approaches. Scott's (1994) subsequent set of concepts takes a similar tack toward institutional isomorphism as a result of this. The "institutional pillars" that make up this set of guidelines are the legal, social, and cultural ones, respectively. He said that they are the cornerstones of every functional institutional framework.

The New Institutional Structure (NIS) provides an explanation for why businesses have commonalities (Scapens, 2006). It delves into the influences of government, society, and the economy on businesses. In this view, organizations and organizations try to gain credibility by playing by the rules laid down by society. The major process through which NIS organizations adopt identical practices is an institutional isomorphism, which may take the form of coercive, mimetic, or normative isomorphisms (DiMaggio and Powell, 1983). Organizations compete for a variety of factors, including resources, legitimacy, and political stability. It has been stated that the NIS method, rather than focusing on differences, explains similarities and shifts in organizational structures (Greenwood and Hinsdale, 1996).

Institutional theory, as described by Scott (2008), is "a widely accepted theoretical posture that emphasizes rational myths, isomorphism, and legitimacy," and researchers who have built upon this viewpoint have emphasized the importance of imitation as a central insight of institutional theory. Institutional theory is grounded on the most basic and adaptable parts of social structure, as defined by Kraft's Public Policy (2007) as "Policymaking that emphasizes the formal and legally binding elements of government structures." Normative, cultural, cognitive, and regulatory frameworks are explored as they are used to define rules for acceptable social conduct. Individual and organizational behavior are increasingly being explained by institutional theory (Scott, 2005), which has gained recognition as an important and popular explanation. This hypothesis has been compared to many others and is considered dynamic (Dacin et al., 2002). Despite its undeniable expansion, institutional theory has been challenged for being utilized largely to explain the permanence and resemblance of occurrences.

Institutional isomorphism, additionally structural and administrative in nature will earn an organization's legitimacy (Dacin, 1997; Deephouse, 1996; Suchman, 1995), as stated by Scott (1995), and this is necessary for the organization to survive in its environment (DiMaggio and Powell, 1983; Meyer and Rowan, 1977). Isomorphism (coercive, normative, and cognitive), rationalized myths, connecting macro and microstructures, and institutional logic are all given more weight in institutional theory, a theory of derivational systems. It also explains "how" their products or services contribute to the greater good of society. Organizational and personal viewpoints may be brought closer together with the help of the institutional logic approach.

Organizations shift in line with these norms, beliefs, and assumptions to increase their influence, longevity, and legitimacy (Scott, 1987). The concept of institutional isomorphism is new to this theory. Organizations that function in the same environment tend to be similar to one another (in their methods of operation and their goals) (see DiMaggio and Powell, 1983). Organizations become isomorphic to gain legitimacy and influence since everyone shares the same environment and they must conform to its norms and values (DiMaggio and Powell, 1983; Carruthers, 1995). Coercive, mimetic, and normative institutional isomorphism are the three categories identified by DiMaggio and Powell (1983). External pressure from dependent organizations or broader cultural standards might lead to coercive isomorphism (DiMaggio and Powell, 1983; Carruthers, 1995). Additional pressure comes from lobbying organizations, investors, regulators, accounting standard setters, and stock exchanges. In times of ambiguity, it is common practice to respond with mimicry (DiMaggio and Powell, 1983: 151). Organizations tend to adopt the structures and systems of comparable and more successful organizations when there is a lack of understanding of internal structures, processes, and procedures; when goals are unclear; and when the external environment is unpredictable. (DiMaggio and Powell, 1983; Carruthers, 1995). Mimetic isomorphism develops when a company is forced to adopt standards in the face of uncertainty. Last but not least, the term "normative isomorphism" describes the ways in which people in the same profession do the same tasks across different companies (DiMaggio and Powell, 1983; Carruthers, 1995).

In the 1970s, Meyer and Rowan (1977) and Zucker (1977) presented a new method of institutional analysis that placed more emphasis on the roles played by culture and the human mind. Meyer and Rowan (1977) argued that modernity plays a crucial role in legitimizing previously held beliefs on a macro level. The authors point out that "institutional rules constitute myths that organizations embrace in order to gain legitimacy, materials, stability, and greater probabilities of survival" (p. 340). This indicates that organizations are motivated to improve their legitimacy and survival by adopting new practices and processes based on logical ideas of institutions (Meyer and Rowan, 1977).

To begin, governmental power, both formal and informal, is the root source of coercive isomorphism. Dependence on other organizations and cultural norms provides the foundation for this authority (DiMaggio and Powell, 1983). Oliver (1991) notes that one crucial part of characterizing organizational reactions to the environment is the variety in organizations' capacities to exercise control over external influences. Organizations may adjust their procedures in reaction to a regulatory shift, but they may also do so for more legitimate reasons, such as to accommodate society's preferences (Oliver, 1991). Organizations may keep their funds, power, and initiative by always doing what the people want them to do.

Second, ambiguity, which is a powerful incentive for imitation, leads to mimetic isomorphism (DiMaggio and Powell, 1983). When businesses face symbolic ambiguity, hazy goals, or a general lack of knowledge, they may try to fill the void by emulating the acquisition, diversification, tactics, and other procedures of similar businesses. Taking cues from the organizational structures of other businesses increase the likelihood of developing "variously, more modern and appropriate, or professional" motifs (Scott, 1987: 504). DiMaggio and Powell also point out that there aren't too many organizations that might be used as models, hence most organizations have similar structures. DiMaggio and Powell (1983) describe how the impacts of cognition might be seen as mimetic isomorphism via the lens of 'ambiguous' action in response to cultural rationalization. However, Suchman (1995) contends that businesses might ensure their cognitive validity by adhering to popular "heuristics" even in the absence of a formalized model.

Third, professionalization pressures cause normative isomorphism because professionals use normative procedures to create and maintain cultural norms that are congruent with their aims and values (Scott, 1987). Particularly interesting are two features of normative isomorphism that DiMaggio and Powell present: (1) the legitimization of formal education in a cognitive base generated by university specialists, and (2) the expansion of professional ties that allow for the rapid emergence of new activities and practice across organizations. Inspiring the creation of norms and values for the professions, universities play a pivotal role in promoting normative standards that create professionals. Accountants, lawyers, and doctors, among others, have extensive ties to the governing organizations that establish ethical guidelines for their professions (Greenwood *et al.*, 2002).

Meanwhile, early sociological studies on legitimacy were informed by the work of philosophers (Parsons, 1956, 1960; Weber, 1978). As can be seen from the literature, scholars in this discipline are primarily concerned with two different facets of legitimacy (Suchman, 1995). Prior to the institutional method (e.g., DiMaggio and Powell, 1983; Zucker, 1987; Meyer and Rowan, 1991), the strategic approach (e.g., Pfeffer, 1981; Ashforth and Gibbs, 1990) was used. The tactical approach proposes that businesses arrange and use emotive signals instrumentally to tap into cultural resources. The institutional approach, on the other hand, contends that cultural forces emerge as a result of structuration processes and are thus beyond the influence of any one organization. According to Scott (1995), "legitimacy is not a commodity to be possessed or exchanged, but rather an attribute reflecting cultural alignment, norm support, or compliance with pertinent rules and laws."

Additionally, IT enables research into the omnidirectional interactions between firms and their surroundings. (Ruef and Scott, 1998). IT is often linked to businesses since it aids in the improvement of internal operations and procedures (Scott, 2008). IT must also account for the fact that many institutions find the same results when subjected to the same economic, social, and political stresses (Scapens, 2006). In this approach, firms place an emphasis on being seen as legitimate rather than strictly adhering to their own set of internal rules and regulations. According to the already mentioned coercive, mimetic, and normative isomorphisms (DiMaggio and Powell, 1983), organizational isomorphism is the key component of IT in which institutions perform comparable procedures. So, according to Greenwood and Hinings (1996), IT strategy, rather than accentuating the discovery, depicts the parallels and changes in organizational structure. Organizational legitimacy is achieved through structural and procedural isomorphism (Dacin *et al.*, 2002; Suchman, 1995; Deephouse, 1996), as demonstrated by Scott (1995), and thus institutions can only survive if they conform to the norms and belief systems of their environment.

IT is essentially a derivation structure theory with an emphasis on isomorphism (i.e., coercive, normative, and cognitive; rationalized mythology, linking macro and micro arrangement and organizational logic). Coercive isomorphism, however, results from pressures from significant parties, investors, organizations that set accounting standards, regulators, stock exchanges, and general cultural norms, in addition to pressures from these external factors (DiMaggio and Powell, 1983; Carruthers, 1995). Uncertainty also generates mimetic pressures that compel institutions to adopt and carry out the strategies of more successful organizations (Carruthers, 1995). DiMaggio and Powell (1983) add this uncertainty to their list of factors that contribute to mimetic pressures, which also includes the absence of clear objectives, a lack of diversity in institutions, a dearth of appropriate models, an ambiguous environment, and improper structures, systems, and procedures. While professions rely on normative procedures and make an effort to create cultural conventions that are relevant to their goals and values, normative isomorphism shows how a group of members from similar professions perform their activities in varied organizations (Carruthers, 1995). Three more pillars are also suggested by the research: the regulative, the normative, and the cultural-cognitive (Scott, 2014). The normative pillar emphasizes the prescriptive, evaluative, and obligatory components of social structure, while the regulative pillar focuses on legal and regulatory procedures (North, 1990). The cultural-cognitive pillar contends that the common philosophies that define social realism's nature also define the parameters within which social realism operates. These three pillars were additionally theorized along three dimensions: obligation (the area that businesses must follow), precision (the region of conduct guidelines that must be followed), and delegation (the extent to which third parties are authorized to implement rules). It is projected that the regulatory structure will exhibit high requirements in certain areas while the normative will exhibit low standards.

Institutional coercion is additionally characterized by organizational dependence. Many perspectives on organizational novelty assume an environmental impetus (Ulrich and Barney, 1984). An organizational dependency perspective hypothesizes the environment in terms of other institutions with which the primary institution interacts (Thompson, 1967; Pfeffer and Salancic, 1978). In addition, the resource dependence perspective enables a greater comprehension of how resource dependencies establish precise governance mechanisms regarding sound governance structures and the activities of the BOD and management (see Table 3.1). Huse (2005) and Lynall *et al.* (2003), advocates of the resource dependence perspective, regard the BOD as a key organizational mechanism that

Theoretical Explanation of Shariah Governance

Table 3.1: An Overview of the New Institutional Theory Framework.

	Pillars		
	Regulative	**Normative**	**Cultural-Cognitive**
Basis of compliance	Experience	Social obligation	Taken for Grantedness Shared understandings
Basis of order	Regulative Rules	Binding Expectations	Consultative schema
Mechanisms	Coercive	Normative	Mimetic
Logic	Instrumentally	Appropriateness	Orthodox
Indicators	Rules	Certification	Common beliefs
	Laws Sanctions	Accreditation	Shared logic of action Isomorphism
Affect	Fear Guilt/Innocence	Shame/honor	Certainty/confusion
Basis of legitimacy	Legally sanctioned	Morally governed	Comprehensible Recognizable Culturally supportive

Source: Modified from Scott (2014).

can provide the company with prospective resources to protect it from environmental uncertainties and reduce the costs of conducting business with external parties. External directors, in particular, play an important role in providing: (1) specific resources otherwise unavailable to management (e.g., financial funds, evidence); (2) access to external organizations and influential institutions (e.g., regulatory authorities, consulting firms, and international firms); (3) legitimacy; and (4) expert knowledge and instruction (Hillman *et al.*, 2000; Lynall *et al.*, 2003; Pfeffer and Salancik, 1978).

In the preceding section, the components of IT have been described in order to develop an organizational framework and comprehend the procedures and practices associated with its components. In the section that follows, Karbhari *et al.* (2020) and Alam *et al.* (2021e) discuss the applicability of IT to SGFs as well as IT's contributions to Islamic institutions.

3.7 Application of Institutional Theory to SGF

There is a growing emphasis on ensuring that IFIs adhere to Shariah law and other Shariah activities (Grassa, 2013; Nathan and Ribière, 2007), which promote qualities including openness, faith, moral conduct, trustworthiness, ideals, and beliefs. Strong SG standards and structures, openness, disclosure, and rigorous adherence to Shariah standards are all areas where Islamic financial concepts have had a considerable impact. Public trust in the validity and effectiveness of the goods may decline without a control tool or governance method (Chapra and Ahmed, 2002). The SGF of Islamic institutions is based on the principles of Shariah and the SSB. However, the SSB is tasked with ensuring that all Islamic banking operations are conducted in conformity with Shariah law. Thus, SG serves a similar purpose to CG, which is also used to analyze the compliance of the entire operations to check that Shariah principles are strictly adhered to, from the standpoint of the stakeholders. In accordance with the Shariah compliance guidelines of Islamic banking practice in relation to Shariah regulations, SG is governed by a full set of SGFs which establish an extensive framework of roles and responsibilities for every party involved (management establishment, and affairs of the SSB).

Instead of focusing just on profit, shareholders should have a voice in setting the company's policies and overall strategic direction to ensure that everyone's needs are met. In addition, other societal actors should carry out their duties so as to promote social cohesion, safeguard the best interests of all parties involved, and inspire the community assistance function for the common good. Managers have a critical role as SG's control mechanism, enforcing Shariah standards and keeping tabs on banking operations to safeguard stakeholders' interests. As a default idea developed from the self-interest notion mandated by agency theory, IFI managers are responsible not only to shareholders and the firm but also to God, with the ultimate objective of well-being and prosperity for mankind (Abu-Tapanjeh, 2009). To verify Shariah compliance throughout Islamic banks and to compile a Shariah report that may be influential in terms of owners, other stakeholders, and environment are, thus, the goals of the observing procedure used by SG (Grais and Pellegrini, 2006a). An organization is not only involved in the internal workings of a single institution but also in the internal workings of multiple institutions that collaborate toward a common goal, such as the dissemination of good SG practices or the articulation and implementation of accounting standards.

Shareholders, management, investors, society as a whole, and other stakeholders (regulators, accounting standards groups, and the general public) all have a vested interest in a company's operations, and this information asymmetry may be mitigated by the effective dissemination of relevant data. Shariah-related concerns need a considerable level of openness in IFIs (Haniff and Hudaib, 2007) since shareholders and investors have a right to obtain genuine and correct information. Additionally,

Chapra and Ahmed (2002) pointed out that the agency issue may influence the credibility and interest of investors in Islamic organizations. The SG is a controlling tool inside IFIs for addressing the agency problem with regard to Shariah concerns, as per the principles of agency theory. In addition, decreasing information asymmetry and boosting public and investor confidence is possible via the publication of transparent and genuine data on the extent to which an Islamic financial institution (IFI) complies with Shariah norms and regulations in its operations as a whole.

IT, on the other hand, is the capacity of different countries and organizations to apply the same (SG) structures and procedures (DiMaggio and Powell, 1983). Organizational marking, as Carpenter and Feroz (2001) call it, is a common practice that, contrary to popular belief, does nothing to improve the efficiency of formal organizations. Carruthers (1995) adds that the social and political significance of the institutional process is far more than its just functional significance. Thus, special SG exercises may be implemented by governments and organizations not only for performance improvement or monetary growth but also for social legitimacy. Legitimacy in modern cultures is awarded to political parties that deliver services in line with the accepted cultural values and norms (Covaleski and Dirsmith, 1988). Furthermore, according to Deegan (2002), a government or institution's "agreements" for presence are effectively revoked by culture if societal expectations on their legitimacy are not revised. Achieving legitimacy and belief are also essential survival tactics; effectiveness alone is not enough.

Covaleski and Dirsmith (1988), Carruthers (1995), Brignall and Modell (2000), and Khadaroo (2005) all provide helpful frameworks for thinking about the social, economic, legal, and strategic effects of IT on countries and institutions. It also implies that myths about proper social and economic practice were the primary source for the components of suitable structures, methods, and processes (DiMaggio and Powell, 1983). Here, SGF supplies Islamic institutions with overarching principles, approaches, and methods for managing their operations. Mythologies are culturally entrenched and legitimate sets of assumptions about how things ought to be (Meyer and Rowan, 1977).

From an ICG vantage point, Bhatti and Bhatti (2010) state that spiritually sanctioned CG would stimulate choice and clarity, as well as encourage the growth of capital, the replacement of healthy markets, and the creation of incentives to participate in an activity that maximizes

114 *Shariah Governance Systems of Islamic Banks*

value. In addition, Abu-Tapanjeh (2009) believes that an inappropriate governance structure would not be created in the absence of a good ethical framework. Therefore, it seems that Islamic institutions may have a positive impact on the development of SG practice. Another indicator of SG's epistemological leanings is its deviation from Western modes of reasoning. Companies headquartered in Islamic nations have the choice, but not the need, to follow Shariah-based legislation in regard to legal and financial concerns so long as it is not in conflict with the CG code. All stakeholders who place significance on the cognitive and normative cultural elements of IT (Zucker, 1987; Schur *et al.*, 2005) should accept the idea that IFIs are committed to delivering banking and financial operations based on Islamic principles. Islamic institutions must follow a specific set of laws derived from the Holy Quran and the Sunnah (Khan and Bhatti, 2008) that emphasize social fairness and accountability in accordance with Shariah principles. Institutional and personal levels form a relationship characterized by soft power (Zucker, 1987). Normative pressures have an effect as well, whether they come from the BOD, the Supervisory Board, regulatory agencies, or the government (Tsai *et al.*, 2013; Farrington and Farrington, 2005). These normative constraints motivate the adoption of policies and procedures established by the organization's higher management.

According to Islamic principles, the governance structure encourages the law, Shariah compliance, and *zakah* management (Mittal *et al.*, 2008). The SG structure also explains how boards interact with one another, how they delegate authority, how they handle management, and how they share information (Zahra and Pearce, 1989, 1990; Ayuso and Argandoña, 2009). More fundamental features of institution formation, maintenance, alteration, and postponement, as well as the restrictions of IFIs on human conduct, as reflected in their practice, i.e., guidelines, procedures, and standards, are the focus of IT. There are many institutional and personal organizational logics provided, and all parties engaged in these logics recognize the biased autonomy of institutions and people. In addition, relationships between persons and institutional structures account for accomplishments, assessments, and consequences. IT examines how many of an organization's social systems — including its policies, norms, and practices — are accepted as supreme guides for workplace conduct (Scott, 2004). To this end, Islamic banks operate in accordance with the tenets of Shariah law.

To offset the effect of outside forces on their organizations, corporate leaders are encouraged to participate in inter-organizational relationships

Theoretical Explanation of Shariah Governance 115

due to a lack of internal resources (Pfeffer and Salancik, 1978). The SSB, in conjunction with the BOD and management, functions as an inner mechanism of the SG of an Islamic bank, boosting the credibility of the institutions in the eyes of shareholders, stakeholders, i.e., depositors, investors, and customers, and reinforcing their Islamic documents of identification (Rammal, 2006; Greuning and Iqbal, 2008). Simply said, SSB makes sure that all Islamic organizations follow Islamic law. The SSB often works in tandem with upper management to discover whether the given goods and services are in accordance with the requirements of Islamic law. Furthermore, the SSB verifies the transparency and responsibility of the Shariah system (Majeed *et al.*, 2015) and guarantees that all operations of Islamic banks are conducted in accordance with Shariah ethical and moral standards (Grassa, 2016). In a nutshell, the SSB is a part of the institution's internal governance framework and plays the role of a watchdog. However, IFIs' reputations, both internally and externally, might be at jeopardy if they don't confirm Shariah principles (Grais and Pellegrini, 2006a; Besar *et al.*, 2009).

3.8 Application of Institutional Theory in Islamic Banks and SGF

The early political scientists who studied information technology (Burgess, 1902; Wilson, 1889; Willoughby, 1896) underlined the management schedules and legal structures that makeup governance frameworks. By highlighting procedural, figurative understanding, and cultural validity, DiMaggio (1998) widened the IT paradigm to include religious organizations. He added that whereas traditional commercial organizations tend to prioritize cohesive components and image-oriented profit maximization, Islamic institutions may benefit from IT since it is relevant and consistent with their goals. IT has been shown to provide important contributions to the study of religious organizations by focusing on questions of procedural in nature symbolic, and cultural authority (DiMaggio, 1998). He remarked that symbolic rituals have a role in the creation of Islamic organizations (DiMaggio, 1998). The "corporate image" of Islamic organizations may be analyzed in this setting from two angles thanks to IT: the performative image and the institutional image (Handelman and Arnold, 1999). Islamic banks may project an image of being trustworthy, reliable, and secure while also being seen as kind, honest, visually pleasing, inventive, and devoted to their customers. The authors also found that Shariah is the key reason Muslims select Islamic banks and that institutional reputation is the primary priority of Islamic banks, which manage their financial business in line with Shariah standards. Furthermore, Yeo and Yusuf (2010) looked at the management, public relations, and finances of Saudi Arabian Islamic institutions to determine how they project to the public. In addition, the client's choice of bank is affected by the bank's reputation, the level of privacy it provides, the recommendations of relatives and close friends, and the ease with which the bank's quality services may be accessed (Mettawa and AlMossawi, 1998). Accordingly, the compliance measurement was shown to be the most important measurement within Islamic bank clients in Malaysia (Parasuraman *et al.*, 1985). In the end, Islamic banking is an established sector whose mission is to safeguard the rights of all parties involved by providing financial services in line with Islamic Shariah. A person's religiosity, according to Delener (1994), will affect their actions and choices. This is an example of an organizational culture that places a premium on the social and ethical implications of IT (Schur *et al.*, 2005; Zucker, 1987).

Nonetheless, the SGF, BOD, SSB, shareholders, and proprietors have an impact on the performance of Islamic institutions and on ensuring Shariah compliance. In addition, previous research indicates that proprietorship concentration has a positive impact on the performance of Shariah-compliant firms (Shahrier *et al.*, 2018; Gaur *et al.*, 2015). In addition, the higher education level of board members has a significant impact on company performance (Shahrier *et al.*, 2018; Darmadi, 2013). In addition, BOD members with superior knowledge and skills will affirm compliance with Islamic principles based on their practical experience (Shahrier *et al.*, 2018). In essence, the institutional procedure of SG establishes the SSB as the structure's primary pillar, and this construction has become a crucial component of the SGF of IFIs (Hasan, 2011a). Mollah and Zaman (2015) conclude that, from an SSB perspective, the supervisory role and structure of SSB have positive effects on the performance of Islamic institutions. In addition, empirical evidence outlines on CG and corporate performance demonstrates an association between governance and corporation achievement, such that weaker governance instruments have better agency problems resulting in minor corporate achievement (Hart, 1995; Hirschey *et al.*, 2009; John and Senbet, 1998; Ozkan, 2007); larger stockholder rights have a positive effect on corporate achievement (Hirschey *et al.*, 2009); and independent boards motivate to greater corporate achievement (John and Senbet, 1998). Karbhari *et al.* (2020) transmit this statement that governance currently drives corporation success from the conventional CG to the SG domain.

Although companies may react in a number of ways to institutional constraints, some of the more common responses are shown below (Greenwood and Hinings 1996; Oliver 1991, 1997). Organizations, according to Oliver (1991), may either "acquiesce," "compromise," "avoid," or "defy" when faced with organizational constraints. In the "acquiesce" strategy, institutions are advocated for accepting and complying with organizational constraints by adapting their unique processes and structures in order to adopt generally recognized practices and procedures. In such a scenario, IFIs adhere to national guidelines or follow the practice of dominant trade groups (Khadaroo and Shaikh, 2007). The "compromise" strategy is used in political negotiations to strike a balance between the competing interests of various institutions and parties. Institutions might "escape" the need to conform to organizational constraints by, for example, hiding the fact that they are not in line with Shariah or by drastically altering the way they operate. Institutions that "defy" established norms and suitable standards and procedures by discharging or fostering activity in opposition to them or by claiming that they are unnecessary do so at their own risk. However, there are always others who will try to influence or even control the laws and standards that govern society. In conclusion, IT argues that organizations improve their chances of existence by adopting structures, procedures, and practices that are widely seen as legitimate in the target culture. Relationship between the resources available in a number of different countries. In addition, customers of IFIs are well-versed in the different products available to them, including *musharakah*, *mudarabah*, and *murabaha* (Okumuş and Genc, 2013). Employees continually deploy a range of reactions (acquiesce, compromise, avoid, defy, and manipulate) in response to different influences (coercive, normative, and mimetic) in their organizational environments (Karbhari *et al.*, 2020).

3.9 Conceptual Framework for Shariah Governance Using IT

Based on the pioneering research of (Meyer and Rowan, 1977; Zucker, 1977; DiMaggio and Powell, 1983; Scott, 1987), Karbhari *et al.* (2020) embrace IT for the study of SGF in Islamic institutions. The fact that attention is political and mimics the comparative control of structured benefits (Tolbert, 1988; DiMaggio and Powell, 1991) is irrelevant (Covaleski *et al.*, 1996).

Examining the relationships between IT and an SGF with reference to IT and the concept of isomorphic behavior, this paper seeks to develop a theoretical representation of the structure of SG. The adoption of SGF as a management tool can therefore be explained by the concept of the coercive, mimetic, and normative aspects of organizational isomorphism (DiMaggio and Powell, 1983), organizational dependency (Pfeffer and Salancik, 1978), and organizational legitimacy (Ashforth and Gibbs, 1990; Scott, 1995).

The following diagram depicts the institutional influences on organizational isomorphism, dependency, and legitimacy in SG practice, Shariah compliance quality, and the structure and process of an SG system. Organizational reliance is an additional characteristic of institutional pressure, and perspectives on organizational novelty assume an environmental inspiration (Ulrich and Barney, 1984). After all, the organizational dependency concept hypothesizes the environment in relation to other institutions in which the primary institution exchanges relations (Thompson, 1967; Pfeffer and Salancik, 1978). The resource dependence perspective also allows for a better understanding of how resource dependencies reveal particular governance mechanisms pertaining to appropriate governance structures and management activities (Huse, 2005; Lynall *et al.*, 2003). The advocatory perspective of resource dependence identifies directors as a key institutional authority that can support efficient resources for the corporation, minimize transaction costs in managing external relationships, and protect firms from environmental uncertainties. Outside directors also play an important role in providing access to external and powerful institutions (such as regulators, consulting institutions, and international standard-setting organizations), as well as in providing legitimacy, expert knowledge, and direction (Hillman *et al.*, 2000; Lynall *et al.*, 2003; Pfeffer and Salancik, 1978). In addition, the lack of resources motivates directors to engage in interdependent institutional relationships in an effort to mitigate the effects of external pressures on their corporations (Pfeffer and Salancik, 1978).

Additionally, the directive role is embedded in resource dependence (Hillman *et al.*, 2000; Daily and Dalton, 1994a, 1994b; Gales and Kesner, 1994; Boyd, 1990; Pfeffer, 1972; Pfeffer and Salancik, 1978) and stakeholder behaviors (Hillman *et al.*, 2001; Johnson and Greening, 1999; Luoma and Goodstein, 1999) and recommends that directors should perform a role that centers on guiding the management and improving policy construction. Significantly necessary to an institution's operation are both its external environment and its interior management structure. Nonetheless, individuals would have a negligible effect on the institution's outcomes, compared to the institution's perspective. There are numerous opportunities for corporate management and administration. In Islamic banking, the SSB is an independent entity that, along with the BOD and management, is responsible for directing, monitoring, revising, and supervising the overall function. The SSB collaborates with management to ensure that the offered products and services comply with the Shariah and to ensure process transparency. The SSB's role is integrated with the organization's internal governance structure, and its functions are viewed as an integral element of the internal control mechanism within institutions. Inevitably, this functional setting increases the IFIs' credibility in the minds of their shareholders and clients, thereby strengthening their Shariah identities.

Literature reveals that the resource dependency theory emphasizes an institution's need to utilize the resources of another actor in the setting and defines how inadequate resources can force institutions to adopt new systems that employ alternative resources (Pfeffer and Salancik, 1978; Sherer and Lee, 2002). Nonetheless, this theory also has implications for the divisional composition of institutions, the employment of directors and executives, manufacturing policies, agreement structure, external corporeal connections, and other institutional tactics-related perspectives. In general, the theory suggests that corporations rely on internal resources and that a larger BOD necessitates additional competencies intended to enhance director capabilities. The BOD will reduce individual board member limitations in terms of corporate expertise through a group policy-making system, thereby enhancing the quality of tactical resolutions and functions (Ruigrok *et al.*, 2006). On this basis, it can be expected that the effectiveness of an SG system would be indicative of Shariah compliance of a high standard. In fact, resource dependency has been defined as an institution's susceptibility to external influences to the extent that it is dependent on the resources controlled or provided by an external institution (Scott, 1987).

Contextually, an SGF's structural process includes many interrelated internal and external components (such as the BOD, SSB, Central Shariah Supervisory Board (CSSB), management, external and internal Shariah review officers, Shariah department officers, and regulators). In formulating the theoretical framework, Karbhari *et al.* (2020) and Alam *et al.* (2021e) take into account the internal mechanisms' dependence on resources, which is related to the implementation of SG guidelines. To comprehend and develop the SG structure, the Centralized Shariah Governance Framework (CSGF), and Shariah compliance of Islamic institutions, the duties

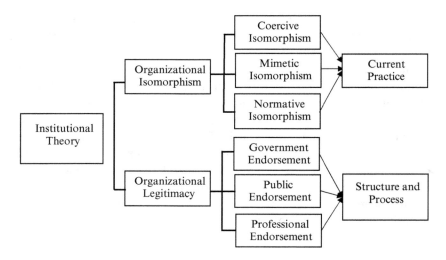

Figure 3.1: A Conceptual Paradigm for Examining SGF Using IT.
Source: Alam (2019), Alam et al. (2021e).

and responsibilities of shareholders, the BOD, the SSB, management, regulators, government policy, and national laws and regulations are deemed essential. In addition, review officers, religious auditors, depositors, and Investment Account Holders (IAHs) are essential SGF members. In the end, the duties and responsibilities of these organizations have combined efforts to implement Shariah regulations in Islamic banking activities. From this perspective, empirical evidence demonstrates that proprietorship concentration benefits Shariah-compliant firms (Shahrier et al., 2018; Gaur et al., 2015). In addition, board competency (in terms of higher education) significantly improves a company's performance (Alam et al., 2022d; Darmadi, 2013). Practically, board members with greater knowledge and skills will confirm Shariah compliance (Shahrier et al., 2018), and corporations with larger boards exhibit positive performance due to the corporations' ability to budget more effectively, access external capital, and tap into societal influence (Pfeffer and Salancik, 2003). Figure 3.1 illustrates a conceptual paradigm of SGF by using IT.

Mollah and Zaman (2015) discovered that the supervisory role and structure of SSB have positive effects on the performance of Islamic institutions. Almutairi and Quttainah (2017) also find that the magnitude of SSB, its composition, education, qualifications, and knowledge of Islamic jurisprudence, conventional finance, and Islamic finance are all positively correlated with IFIs' performance. In addition, Islamic banks engaged with reputable SSB members can adhere strictly to the guidelines of religious principles, accounting disclosure, and corporate social responsibility disclosure in their annual reports. Such SSB can also play a more effective role in supervising and controlling bank activities and advising management, thereby enhancing the quality of SG, operational functions, performance, and disclosure of banks (Rahman and Bukair, 2013; Grassa, 2016; Ajili and Bouri, 2018). In addition, existing literature on CG and firm performance indicate a relationship between governance and institutional achievement, i.e., weaker governance instruments have more agency problems, which leads to lower firm performance (Hart, 1995; John and Senbet, 1998; Ozkan, 2007); better shareholder privileges have a positive effect on firm performance (Bhagat and Bolton, 2008); and independent directors lead to better firm performance. Important for the establishment of IFIs is a robust and solid SG that ensures the sector's robust growth.

The organizational legitimacy component of IT stipulates that Islamic institutions must attain legitimacy in order to survive (DiMaggio and Powell, 1983). Legitimacy refers to the application of deemed appropriate, sound practices. External authorization is another definition of organizational legitimacy (Pfeffer and Salancik, 1978; Ashforth and Gibbs, 1990). Organizational legitimacy can be summarized as the acceptance of an institution by its external oversight bodies and other authorities (Meyer and Rowan, 1977; Meyer and Scott, 1983; DiMaggio and Powell, 1983), where the identity of these authorities is significant. This legitimacy is a key idea in NIT, serving as the fulcrum of a greatly expanded hypothetical instrument (Suchman, 1995). A company is genuine if its standards and conduct are consistent with certain qualities. Organizational legitimacy is the accreditation of a corporation by external groups, assuming of course that the identities of these groups are meaningful and that the accreditation is by external groups. Public prosecutors grant this endorsement in their capacity as a regulatory body (Pfeffer and Salancik, 1978; Ashforth and Gibbs, 1990), such as a government or government agency (i.e., a regulator), that has control over the organization, the general public through public opinion, setting and upholding standards of sufficiency, and the professionals over the systems and upholding the principles of professional competency and responsibility (Meyer and Rowan, 1977; Meyer and Scott, 1982). By stating that effective organizations and governments are those that use legitimacy rituals to create societal and financial stability, Carpenter and Feroz (2001) contributed to the conversation. As a result, earning credibility and faith

122 *Shariah Governance Systems of Islamic Banks*

is just as important as being proficient as a survival tactic for Islamic institutions. Currently, there are numerous governmental and regulatory constraints on the Islamic banking sector.

3.10 Background of the Legitimacy

Social theorists from the beginning (Weber, 1978; Parsons, 1956, 1960) used the term "legitimacy" to describe the foundational principles of society. Weber is often credited with introducing the concept of legitimacy to sociological theory and, consequently, organization studies (Johnson *et al.*, 2006; Suchman, 1995; Ruef and Scott, 1998). Many scholars of the organizational theory are acquainted with Weber's examination of the justifications for different kinds of authority. Conformity with official regulations and general social norms may lead to legitimacy, according to Weber's writings (Weber, 1978). According to Parsons' (1956, 1960) application of Weberian theory, a group is legitimate if and only if it abides by established social norms and ideals. Czarniawska-Joerges (1989), Pfeffer and Salancik (1978), and Dowling and Pfeffer (1975) are only a few of the later organization theorists who agreed with this statement. Weber's notion was received more warmly by the initial institutionalist discourse than his formulation. For example, Meyer and Scott (1983) said that it was "unfortunate, given Weber's lack of clarity on the subject" that Weber was so often cited as the definitive explanation of legitimacy.

The legitimacy idea has its origins in studies of institutions and political science more generally. According to Scott (1995), legitimacy is not an object to be possessed or transferred, but rather a condition demonstrating cultural alignment, ethical support, or compliance with relevant regulations and regulations. Legitimacy, according to Suchman (1995), is the general perception or assumption that an entity's actions are acceptable, appropriate, or desirable within a socially established framework of norms, values, beliefs, and jurisdictions. Parsons (1956), an early theorist on the topic, defines legitimacy as "society's appraisal of the organization's usefulness and its output," and from this, he extrapolates that the company would take steps to ensure its legitimacy. Maurer (1971) provides supporting evidence for this view by defining legitimacy as the method by which a company explains its existence to a system that is either on par with or above it. Two studies (Dowling and Pfeffer, 1975; Parsons, 1960) outlined that to be legitimate, an organization's social ideals must align with the accepted behavioral standards of society as a whole. Meyer and Scott (1983) and Scott (1991) argued that an organization's legitimacy stems from the degree to which it is consistent with the surrounding culture.

Legitimacy comprises beliefs about what is right or appropriate, as well as acts that are designed to win over others. As an ideological effort to reify/depersonalize/incorporate certain social conventions and principles (Meyer and Scott, 1983; Scott, 1995), this research analyzes how legitimacy originates from inside the workings of an organization. Whether with internal or external stakeholders, legitimacy is created when social actors consciously participate in certain practices that might lead to obtaining or destroying credibility (e.g., Lawrence *et al.*, 2011). Conscious activities that increase legitimacy are an example of legitimacy transformation (e.g., Lawrence and Suddaby, 2006).

Zelditch (2001) claims that legitimacy construction is a key social process because of its role in creating and reproducing structure in contexts involving tangible action. Research on the process of legitimacy generation in new initiatives shows that internal and external legitimacy, as well as their respective settings and structures, are interrelated. An organization that depends on internal legitimacy for its survival develops new cultural schemas and configurations around "how things are done." These schemas tend to acquire their inertial features after being accepted and legitimized, while the organization's authority structure stays constant (Zelditch and Walker, 1984). However, as Johnson *et al.* (2006) point out, methods for establishing legitimacy are subject to the dynamics of the surrounding environment, particularly for new organizations involved in contentious processes meant to affect normative, professional, and regulatory requirements. A four-stage model of the legitimation process is created by Johnson *et al.* (2006). The first is the emergence of social innovations developed by actors in response to a need to address certain social situations that give them legitimacy. Second, local social actors who support the suggested legitimation activities on the basis of the dominant cultural domain bestow legitimacy on social innovations. Thirdly, after gaining local acceptance, the social invention spreads to new contexts with the implicit endorsement of numerous social players who see it as a valid social truth. A societal consensus develops when social innovation is supported, disseminated, and accepted in various contexts. The isomorphic identification of IFIs and their SG system requires the construction of an extra organizational legitimacy mechanism, which we suggest. The persistence of this procedure is backed by approval and support. As a result, even if an organization's members have different standards, values, and views, their actions nonetheless uphold

124   *Shariah Governance Systems of Islamic Banks*

the established social order (Zelditch, 2001). IFIs and their roles are nonetheless certified by the internal system of SG as a whole, which also produces a report in the annual report.

Lastly, it is not only the perception and evaluation of external or internal legitimacy, but also the legitimacy's pertinent contextual factors, such as product development, auditing, reviewing functions, supervising roles, preparing guidelines and manuals, and providing suggestions. These responsibilities are carried out by the Shariah departments and their officers.

3.11   The Construction of Legitimacy

There are two main sources of authority that scholars in this field draw upon (Suchman, 1995). The institutional method (e.g., Zucker, 1987; DiMaggio and Powell, 1983; Meyer and Rowan, 1991) and the strategy-based approach (e.g., Pfeffer, 1981; Ashforth, and Gibbs, 1990) are two examples. The strategic method suggests that businesses use emotionally charged symbols in an effort to win over the public. The validity of an organization may be seen from a variety of angles. Some have argued, for instance (Guthrie and Parker, 1989; Dowling and Pfeffer, 1975; Parsons, 1956, 1960) that firms have a social mandate that may be withdrawn if they engage in unethical practice. Suchman (1995) breaks down legitimacy into its mental, practical, and ethical components. Cognitive accounts are those that are accepted without question, provide no value judgments, and are always seen as having some kind of external validity (Tost, 2011). Self-interest, both on the part of the legitimating body and the people that make up that authority, is a necessary condition for pragmatic legitimacy (Bitektine, 2011; Suchman, 1995).

Researchers, on the other hand, have created categories for the many forms of legitimacy. By focusing on earlier publications, Suchman (1995: 579) uses Aldrich and Fiol's (1994) concept of moral legitimacy to give a favorable normative appraisal of the organization as well as its operations. The concept of moral legitimacy (Rindova *et al.*, 2006; Greenwood *et al.*, 2002; Suchman, 1995) focuses on how an institution is seen by its constituents or broader environment. Only pragmatic and moral legitimacy is relevant to the process and articulation of internal authenticity (Tost, 2011) due to the role of motives in shaping the legitimacy process at the individual level of analysis. Shariah officers and their responsibilities are crucial in Islamic SG systems, much as the SSB is in other systems.

They provide assistance to the SSB while they carry out their duties. The SSB provides its assessment of *ex-post* Shariah compliance efforts based on the Shariah officer's report (BNM, 2019; IFSB, 2009). In the same way, as SSB officials are required to have a Shariah foundation qualification (BNM, 2019; IFSB, 2009), so do Shariah officers. Therefore, the SG system includes any agreement, written or verbal, that governs, directs, or controls the SSB to ensure it complies with Shariah (Alam, 2021a). This means that the search for social facts that need to be legitimized or delegitimized drives the contestation, construction, and deconstruction of legitimation processes (Greenwood *et al.*, 2002). Getting official approval is important for many different reasons. Both (a) maintaining credibility and consistency and (b) rallying support has been seen as important (Suchman, 1995).

Furthermore, Suchman (1995: 579–581) distinguished between four types of moral authority:

There are four types of legitimacy: personal, structural, procedural, and consequential. Organizations should be assessed in terms of their consequential legitimacy by looking at their achievements and how satisfied their customers are with their products or services. Organizations may establish their credibility in the eyes of the law by using methods that are generally accepted by the public. A similar point of view may be found in large corporations. What we call SG has some similarities to formal legitimacy. Separate and distinct responsibilities for shareholders, management, and boards of directors (SG), SSB, etc. When an organization has structural legitimacy, it is seen as important and worthy of support by its constituents because it falls into a morally valued taxonomic category. Executives' reputations as a whole rest on their personal charm. However, corporations may be held accountable to their local partners as foreigners due to legitimacy restrictions caused by institutional distances, such as variations in law, norms, and cognition across countries and/or regions (Martinez and Dacin, 1999; Scott, 2008). Market legitimacy, relational legitimacy, legitimacy in society, investment credibility, and alliance legitimacy are the five types of legitimacy that Dacin *et al.* (2007) conceptualize as necessary to reduce these institutional risks. In this regard, the IFIs follow Shariah rules and regulations, the SSB is responsible for ensuring that the banks' operations do not involve forbidden industries (such as interest-based funding companies, drugs and pork-based products, and the manufacture and sale of weapons), and the banks follow egalitarian and just principles (such as limiting profit-making in favor of equitable communication; quite holding workers in the highest regard). IFIs achieve higher legitimacy than traditional banks because they communicate their viewpoints and arrange talks with other IFIs; in addition, CEOs are subject to personal moral evaluations (Alam, 2021).

In contrast, the institutional perspective stresses that cultural factors emerge from the processes of structuration that are outside the organization's control. There are six pillars upon which an organization's legitimacy rests. The identity of the organization, including its mission and desired place in the world, is crucial to establishing its credibility with stakeholders and the public. The technical validity of a group is based on its members' skills and expertise. The moral validity of an organization comes from the ideals it maintains, which are what give it character and set it apart from others. Any document — a charter, a statute, or a regulation — that establishes the organization's rights, privileges, and duties is evidence of its legal validity. The views of the many stakeholders are what constitute "perceptual legitimacy," and they have a major bearing on the legitimacy as a whole. As a group develops and builds upon the pillars of legitimacy upon which it depends as a whole, a new dimension of legitimacy emerges: institutional legitimacy.

However, legitimacy may be broken down into two main categories: internal and external. External stakeholders may bestow it on an organization if they see value in its vision or aims and believe it has the ability to work effectively toward achieving those goals (Zimmerman and Zeitz, 2002). The accumulation of finances and the attraction of consumers, consumers, and investors who are seen as genuine members of an organization's community are often the results of exogenously determined legitimacy, or the acceptance and validation by external stakeholders (Shane and Stuart, 2002; Zucker, 1987). Internal and outside legitimacy are studied and a process model is presented by Drori and Honig (2013). We are concentrating on the legitimacy through internal authority, the acceptability that the internal mechanism of SG, namely the SSB and Shariah the department executives, can legitimate the corporation in addition to the prevalent external parties because previous research has not clearly illustrated this. Internal legitimacy, as defined by Drori and Honig (2013), is the acceptance or normative validation of an organization's strategy by its participants; it serves as a tool that solidifies organizational practice and mobilizes members around a shared trustworthy, strategic, or ideological vision. From Weber's definition of legitimacy as the deliberate acceptance of specific actions and convictions by social actors (Johnson *et al.*, 2006; Courpasson,

2000; Weber, 1978 [1924]), this perspective on legitimacy highlights the importance of authority and governance. Furthermore, internal legitimacy allows for the autonomous development of internal practice and logic, allowing it to function through philosophical or preference processes (Alam, 2021; Tabash *et al.*, 2022). Here, the SSB plays an autonomous role by creating SG rules and policies to monitor IFIs' Shariah compliance (AAOIFI, 2005; IFSB, 2009).

Internal legitimacy in the task environment is developed by actors and may complement externally granted legitimacy (Kostova and Zaheer, 1999; Kostova and Roth, 2002). Building strong links with external constituencies and receiving support from prominent external collective actors is what gives an organization external legitimacy (Stinchcombe, 1968). Because it is an honor bestowed upon an entity, maintaining its legitimacy is usually the responsibility of parties external to that entity (Pfeffer and Salancic, 1978). Consistency between social ideals and organizational behavior (Dowling and Pfeffer, 1975; Meyer and Rowan, 1977) is a necessary condition for this phenomenon to occur.

3.12   SG-System, Internal Legitimacy and Social Acceptance

The fundamental element in any country's development of Islamic finance is likely to be political or official backing. But for SG to flourish, we need a regulatory and supervision system that works for it. Examples of nations that have been instrumental in the growth of the Islamic finance sector include Malaysia and Bahrain. A functioning Islamic banking system and marketplace are impossible to ensure in the absence of the SG, which is why it is not inaccurate to call it the heart of the Islamic financial sector. The process of SG is the most crucial part of the method. Within the internal governance framework of CG in IFIs, the SG process symbolizes the instrumental functions of the SSB (Hasan, 2011b; Grais and Pellegrini, 2006a). The SSB is usually set up by the bank in an effort to reassure its constituents (Grais and Pellegrini, 2006a). If IFIs fail to adhere to Islamic finance principles, it might damage their reputations as well as the image of the Islamic finance sector as a whole (Grais and Pellegrini, 2006a; Besar *et al.*, 2009). Loss of customers and other stakeholders might have an effect on the bank's market share, liquidity, and earnings (IFSB, 2005). The success of the investment banking business depends on gaining and keeping the public's trust and confidence (Leventis *et al.*, 2013). Particularly important to IFIs is maintaining their credibility in the eyes of the public through their observance of Shariah in everything that they do (Archer and Haron, 2007). Given the complexity of this process and the importance of the SSB's reputation and the validity of the goods at stake, the SG system is essential. This is because of concerns such as the SSB's independence, credentials, reporting framework, accountability, and transparency.

In contrast, under the dispersed or individual SGF, the compliance of proposed goods is determined not by the Central Bank but by the SSB of each individual IB. The SSB of each organization decides whether or not agreements and Shariah-compliant financial services are legal. In this model, SSB may be implemented in two ways: for individuals and for the community as a whole. Ghayad (2008) The SSB is responsible for guiding, assessing, and monitoring Islamic banking operations to ensure they adhere to Islamic Shariah norms. Among the many Shariah responsibilities of the SSB are the following: advising on and designing operational procedures (Banaga *et al.*, 1994; Briston and El-Ashker, 1986; Ahmed, 2006); advising on and designing corporate strategic issues (Alhabshi and Bakar, 2008); and monitoring and ensuring good organizational image and reputation (Ghayad, 2008). When the sector was first introduced to the Muslim community, the SSB was credited for establishing the legitimacy of IFIs (Siddiqi, 2006). The SSB at the micro level performs a variety of duties, including taking part in product development and organizing activities, examining and approving matters related to Shariah, issuing the *fatwa*, Shariah auditing, and issuing an annual authorization of Shariah compliance in order to ensure the Shariah compliance of IFIs' investments in shares, equities, *sukuk*, and other business avenues. Shariah experts serve as the IFIs' gatekeepers and guarantors.

Only with good Shariah coordination and a dedicated internal Shariah review unit can the SSB ensure the validity of the products and amenities (Hasan, 2011b). The Shariah coordinator acts as an officer of liaison or coordinator for the SG process from the creation of the product through the yearly Shariah review. When comparing IFIs to their counterparts (i.e., traditional banks), the SSB and the Centralized SSB stand out as the clear governing mechanism. One of the CG's several arms, the SSB is well recognized for its vital contributions to Shariah oversight. Shariah-related provides within the organization, compliance with Shariah laws and governance, Shariah-related difficulties, and a compliance report on the overall operations to protect the Shariah structure, the stakeholders and shareholders of the IB, and their customers fall under the purview of the

SSB (Gintzburger and Saïdi, 2010). Existing Islamic Banks (IB) will quickly lose a significant amount of their market share, as pointed out by Iqbal *et al.* (1998) if the Islamic banking system is not viewed as Islamic. Truth be told, it's only via fully autonomous mission performance that the SB can keep its honor. The IB's reputation among the general public, investors, and businesses is bolstered by its ability to operate independently, making it a crucial component of good governance. Therefore, SG encourages open communication and honesty. The credibility of IFIs and the services they provide is bolstered when their membership rosters are made public (Hasan, 2011). In the context of SG, this term refers to the SSB's duty to issue the annual Shariah report on its activities, data pertaining to duties and products and services, Shariah pronouncements, fatwa release, and declaration of Shariah legal compliance which increases the trustworthiness of IFIs and SG procedures (Banaga *et al.*, 1994).

3.13 Legitimacy of Islamic Financial Institutions SGF and Social Acceptance

Several writers (Suchman, 1995; Hybels, 1995; Ashforth and Gibbs, 1990), among others, have argued that an organization's legitimacy is crucial to its success. Pfeffer and Salancik (1978) and Ashforth and Gibbons (1990) both use the term "externally conferred status" to describe what this means. According to the works of Pfeffer and Salancik (1978) and Deephouse (1996), an organization is legitimate if its beliefs and activities are consistent with those of the external party. Identifying the groups or individuals who provide an organization's external legitimacy is essential. Institutional theories of legitimacy hold that for an organization to thrive, it must adhere to generally accepted standards of conduct set by other groups with an interest in its success (Deephouse, 1996; Meyer and Rowan, 1977; Scott, 1995; Covaleski and Dirsmith, 1995). Here, the government or government agency exerts influence on businesses, the general public, and the professions by setting and enforcing norms for appropriate behavior, expert knowledge, and responsibility (Baum and Oliver, 1991; Meyer and Scott, 1983; Elsbach, 1994). This complements normative isomorphism and allows for the establishment of appropriate accounting practices by businesses. According to Milne *et al.* (1975) and Patten (2002), companies will benchmark against competitors to align with valid symbols, ideals, and practices. The SSB and Shariah executive officers have been recognized as internal SG mechanisms with agreed-upon roles and actions for providing

130 *Shariah Governance Systems of Islamic Banks*

practical monitoring, advising, and supervisory tasks, complementing those of external organizations. They may be more concerned with what we call "internal legitimacy" or "legitimacy conferred by within the parties" in this context. Islamic governance might offer incentives for more engagement, according to the new legitimization idea drawn from the legitimation/moral approach.

In contrast, myths are "widespread but mistaken convictions about generally accepted norms that have become institutionalized and legitimate" (Meyer and Rowan, 1977). In order to gain public trust, most organizations try to play by the social norms and legal frameworks already in place (Scapens, 2006). When seeking legitimacy and influence, organizations often adopt an isomorphic structure (Carruthers, 1995; DiMaggio and Powell, 1983) because they must conform to the norms and values of their environment. Firms require legitimacy and the ability to mobilize social, economic, and political assets in order to adapt to specific institutional settings in order to improve their profitability. In order to achieve social acceptance from many legitimating groups without sacrificing efficiency, businesses commonly use techniques like isomorphism, decoupling, and ceremonial acceptance. Legitimacy allows enterprises to operate freely and build mutually beneficial connections with customers in a market with unique institutional features. Elsbach and Sutton (1992) and Oliver (1991) argue that, in contrast to Meyer and Rowan's work, legitimacy in this context is achieved not through a logic of trust and cooperation but rather through determined, manipulative, or even deceitful behaviors that conceal independence while displaying complying to external observers. The underutilization of CG practice has been studied fruitfully from this vantage point.

It's possible that certain nations and organizations utilize CG practice not because they improve performance or promote economic growth, but rather because doing so will provide them credibility with the general public. Political institutions in modern nations earn legitimacy when they are seen to reflect the values and beliefs of the populace as a whole (Covaleski and Dirsmith, 1988). If an authority or organization fails to live up to the public's expectations for its legitimacy, Deegan (2002) argues that its "contracts for existence" will be terminated. Carpenter and Feroz (2001: 569–579) argue that popular governments and organizations win public trust and acceptance by caving in to pressure and performing "legitimacy rituals that demonstrate their economic and social fitness." This means that success relies on more than just efficiency; legitimacy and trust are equally essential. Conformity with society's values and acts, as well as the justification and context supplied by the relevant norms and regulations, contribute to legitimacy (Scott, 1995). Therefore, competence isn't the only way for IFIs to make it; establishing credibility and trustworthiness is also essential. The Islamic banking sector is now facing several regulatory and policy challenges. The SSB of the Islamic bank, working in compliance with relevant legal or quasilegal standards, is seen as providing legitimacy, therefore conformity is based on practical considerations (Scott, 1995).

In a study, Van Gruening and Iqbal (2008), outlined that the SSB is trusted by stakeholders like investors and depositors to deploy their funds in accordance with Shariah principles. The board's principal responsibility is to guarantee that the Islamic bank adheres to Islamic values and principles in all aspects of its business (Grassa, 2016). Shariah experts are considered as an integral part of Islamic banks as well as considered as an staff. This board, which is part of the institution's internal leadership structure, acts as an internal control body, bolstering the institution's credibility in the eyes of consumers, shareholders, and so on (Rammal, 2006). However, SSB is a shareholder in the Islamic bank, and their choices are discussed at the board of management and internal auditing levels, with the nature of those decisions potentially influencing the approval of a particular service over another. As the industry has expanded, religious scholars have started conducting audits to ensure that IFIs are adhering to Islamic principles in all aspects of their business (Karim, 1990a, 1990b). This means that the amount of banking activity may rise or fall depending on whether or not the SSB-approved certification is obtained. Furthermore, the Shariah report is essential as a stamp of approval of an IFI's compliance with Shariah principles and is seen as a significant mechanism by which the general public as well as interested parties may discover to what degree the IFI's services and products satisfy Shariah criteria (Hasan, 2011b).

Institutional theory, according to Beasley *et al.* (2009), shows that many governance systems are largely symbolic/ceremonial; their legitimacy is crucial, but formal procedures are only loosely tied with real monitoring. Kalbers and Fogarty (1998) also support this idea. According to this idea, the SSB and other similar organizational systems exist for no other reason than to please the public. In reality, IFIs must follow the advice of the SSB. Adopting an approach that has been successfully applied by other businesses may also boost a company's credibility. Over time, this trend toward copycatting amongst companies may lead to a leveling out of CG standards (Lee, 2012; Braiotta and Zhou, 2006). But the SG structure shows how the boards interact with one another, how they establish and fill committees, how they handle management, and how they share information (Ayuso and Argandoa, 2007; Zahra and Pearce, 1989; Zahra and Pearce, 1990). Here, Shariah law is used as the basis for governing how IFIs do business. The inclusion of a Shariah Supervision Board (SSB) made up of religious experts is what sets Islamic banking apart. Since the Shariah is the fundamental governing concept for all Islamic banks, IFIs are considered Islamic by adherents of the faith (Ahmad, 1984; Siddiqi, 1983; Siddiqi, 1985; Khan and Mirakhor, 1986; Siddiqui, 2001; Ahmad, 2000). Compliance with Shariah law ensures the legitimacy and trustworthiness of a company and inspires confidence between shareholders and other stakeholders (Tomkins and Karim, 1987; Briston and El-Ashry, 1986; Karim, 2002). According to the research of Naser *et al.* (1999), Ahmad and Haron (2002), Metawa and Almossawi (1998), Rashid *et al.* (2014), and Archer and Karim (2002), religious affiliation is the most influential factor in choosing Islamic banks. The core principles of Islamic leadership and ethics in IFIs have been the subject of many recent qualitative research (Ullah *et al.*, 2018). According to Ragatz and Duska (2010), for instance, a code of ethics may be used to gain the trust of the general public, strengthen bonds within a profession, and provide a foundation for the resolution of legal issues. For example, Haniffa and Hudaib (2007) found that Islamic institutions disclose additional information regarding SSBs as a means of establishing an ethically and socially responsible identity. Ullah *et al.* (2014) have reported comparable findings regarding Shariah departments and socially responsible investments.

Nonetheless, organizations are valid if they are comprehensible and desirable. By responding genuinely to the demands of the audience, the audience perceives the organization as legitimate and supports its activities. In contrast, Palazzo and Scherer (2006) note that corporate legitimacy focuses on "the appropriate role of corporations in society." The social recognition of actions or institutions is one definition of legitimacy. It is subjectively perceived and assigned to organizations during social construction processes (Ashforth and Gibbs, 1990; Berger and Luckmann, 1966). Thus, legitimacy is a crucial resource for the continued survival of businesses in competitive environments. Globalization processes, however, have made it more difficult for organizations to maintain their legitimacy (Palazzo and Scherer, 2006; Vaara and Tienari, 2008). In this instance, countries implemented the international Shariah standards provided by the

AAOIFI and IFSB to enhance the local Shariah standard and ordered or advised IFIs to adhere to their guidelines and standards to maintain international quality standards. The Islamic banking and finance sector was recognized in order to provide Islamic Shariah-based banking, and this information should be communicated to all relevant parties. This type of organizational culture emphasizes cultural-cognitive and normative factors (Zucker, 1987; Schur *et al.*, 2005). Governance Structure ensures "fairness" for all stakeholders through increased transparency and accountability (Majeed *et al.*, 2015), while promoting Islamic values such as justice, Shariah compliance, and *zakah* obligations (Mittal *et al.*, 2008). Governance structure describes the organization of the board, including the number and types of committees, their members, management, and information transfer between them (Zahra and Pearce, 1989; Ayuso and Argandoa, 2007). Abu-Tapanjeh (2009) argued that if a system lacks an appropriate ethical and moral structure, it is unlikely to produce an effective system of government. It appears that religious institutions have some influence on the evolution of CG practice. In this regard, the institutional structure of Singapore positions the SSB as the system's linchpin. The formation of the SSB has become an integral element of the SG system in IFIs.

3.14 SG and Accountability Theory

Muslims as well as Islamic institutions are both answerable to Allah for their worship of Him and observance of Shariah, according to Islamic belief. Accountability may be established by the nature of the contractual connection between the different parties, as suggested by Gray *et al.* (1995). On the other side, there are professors who take a more nuanced view of what it means to be accountable. "Accountability is not merely about holding accountability and judging behavior; nor does it presuppose a simple agency-principal connection; rather, it appears to correspond to the capacity to render accounting conducive to wellbeing," write Gallhofer and Haslam (1994).

Accountability in Islam is first and foremost duty to Allah, then to society as well as other stakeholders. Therefore, the accountability theory is relevant to this research because it broadens the idea of responsibility beyond the investors and owners of Islamic banks. In Islam, Allah, as creator, has complete control over all things. Since humans are the only trustees in this world, they have a responsibility to uphold God's (Allah's) will by protecting themselves, one another, and all of God's other creatures from harm until the final Day of Judgement (AlQiyamah). Baydoun and Willett (2000) claimed that organizations, including Islamic institutions, should publish all information necessary for their customers and the community in order to complete their role in providing CSR information, which is a requirement of accountability in Islam.

CHAPTER 4

Historical Development of *Shariah* Governance and International Standard-Setting Agencies

4.1 Introduction

This chapter outlines the historical development of Islamic Financial Institutions (IFIs), international standard-setting authorities, and other regulatory bodies.

4.2 The Development of Corporate Governance in IFIs

By tracing the development of banks and other financial organizations from the earliest days of Islam to the current day, this section gives a short overview of corporate responsibility in IFIs. A thriving economy can't grow without a sophisticated and reliable banking system. It helps increase the pace of growth by guaranteeing an unbroken supply of financial resources to persons engaged in a wide range of economic activities by, among other things, facilitating the movement of financial assets from surplus assets to deficit units. The extraordinary rise of the global economy over the last three decades may likely be attributed in large part to the rising availability of loanable capital among institutional investors. Banking serves a similar purpose as the artery system in the body of a human being. Business owners and entrepreneurs, who are often at the forefront of economic development efforts, may get short-, medium-, and long-term loans from commercial banks and other financing organizations for development. This is thanks to the system of financial intermediation, which allows traditional banks to collect small savings from the public at a fixed interest rate and then advance loanable amounts from the savings that are deposited to enterprising consumers charging relatively higher interest rates. The bank makes money on the spread between these two rates. Banks also charge service fees for the many supplementary services they provide their customers.

Despite significant contributions, traditional (interest-based) banking has been criticized by both historical and modern economists. Some economists believe that interest's role in the traditional banking system is a major cause of economic cycles (Minsky, 1982). The failure of interest rates to act as a stabilizing factor during the period known as the Great Depression is especially notable. Government intervention, as proposed by Keynesians became necessary as a result. In a *Newsweek* piece on the former US Secretary of State Henry Kissinger, a similar worry was voiced. The volatility and unpredictability have continued, to put it another way. High tangible interest rates and risky exchange currency changes have exacerbated the global economic downturn and a record-breaking jobless rate that followed years of painfully high inflation. Allais (1993) cites Nobel laureate Maurice Allais's warnings about the global financial system's vulnerability and Allais's subsequent urge for a quick reform of the World Economic Order. While some support the use of interest rates as a tool for economic stabilization, others are strongly opposed to this idea. Because of this, an entirely novel banking system had to develop that could deal with the complex issues now plaguing the financial sector of the global economy. There was a clear split in opinion about money in the second decade of the 20th century, but it wasn't all due to need. Islamic finance, additionally referred to as Profit-Loss Sharing Banking (PLS), is a new financial system that emerged as a result of this practice becoming formalized at the conclusion of the third quarter. More than 50 nations, both Muslim and non-Muslim, are now home to IFIs numbering in the hundreds.

For both spiritual and material reasons, PLS banking has developed as an alternative to conventional banking. Supporters of the PLS system claim that the Quran's ban on "Riba" served as the impetus for the creation of Islamic Shariah-compliant organizations. To avoid violating Shariah principles and to engage in financial transactions free of Riba, Muslims set out to recognize their monetary activity, leading to the creation of Islamic banks (IBs). According to these writers, the Riba mentioned in the Quran [2:275; 30:39] is equivalent to the standard interest rate. Interest, as Chapra (1985) points out, "inevitably entails an element of Gharar," or uncertainty, since the outcome of the constructive attempt is unknown. As a result, proponents of the PLS system strongly advise the Islamic community to steer clear of dealing with any financial institutions that charge interest.

The fact that interest reduces wealth rather than increases it lends credence to the economic argument from the Quran that motivated the development of an interest-free financial system. The goal of Islam is to create a system of economic justice that is free from all types of exploitation (Chapra, 1985). The Quran has such a strong stance against interest because of this. Furthermore, Muslim economists argue that the interest-based financial system of the capitalist world often results in depression and stagflation. As a result, Islamic banking was developed to meet the spiritual and material needs of its adherents. Economic urgency sheds light on how banking may foster investment/productive activities, affect income distribution, and contribute to economic stability, yet religious exigency necessitates avoiding any transaction that is based on interest. This means that Islamic banking is superior to conventional banking in every way.

Islamic banking as a concept has really been around for quite some time. The first effort to create an Islamic financial organization was made in the late 1950s in Pakistan when a small Islamic bank opened in a rural location. The venture was launched by a band of religious business owners who pooled their resources and provided loans to farmers and ranchers at zero interest. A small fee was levied to fund the bank's overhead, but the borrower did not have to pay interest on the money that was loaned to them. The charge was far lower than the rate of interest. Despite the positive outcomes, there were two key reasons why this experiment failed. First, the depositors' landlords saw the payments as an isolated event. The growing number of creditors exacerbated a massive gap between supply and demand for credit. Second, the bank's employees did not have total control over the institution's policies and procedures, since depositors were concerned about the safety of their money.

The Mit Ghamr Savings Bank was founded in a rural region of the Nile Delta in Egypt between 1963 and 1967 as the second pioneering venture in implementing the principles of Islamic financial services and banking. In this project, German savings bank ideas were fused with Islamic concepts of rural banking (Ahmed, 1992). Neither customers nor creditors faced interest as part of the bank's core Islamic principles. The borrower

138   *Shariah Governance Systems of Islamic Banks*

was obliged to have bank deposits when compared to the Pakistani bank where collateral was not needed. Additional branches were established in different parts of the country, and the total amount of deposits went up, thus the experiment was quickly declared a success. As a result, a single bank eventually spawned a whole system of community-based credit unions. A change in the political atmosphere caused the initiative to stall, despite its promising beginnings and early successes. Nasser Social Bank was the name given to the revived program in 1971. Cairo was the site of the world's first urban Islamic bank. The bank operates independently due to its position as a government agency. Its principal goal was to support social causes, such as helping low-income students pay for college and providing interest-free loans for small enterprises based on a profit-and-loss model. Nasser Social Bank was initially excluded from the Banking and Credit Act of 1957 because of the social services it provided. While the Ministry of Treasury was responsible for founding the bank, it is presently run by the Department of Social Welfare and Security. It is capitalized by allocations from the state budget, payments from the Ministry of Awqaf, and cash allotted by the executive branch from extrabudgetary resources (Ahmed, 1992). Naser Social Bank's guiding principles are quite similar to those of Mit Ghamr Savings Bank. The latter, however, offers not only the full gamut of traditional banking services but also access to a wide variety of investment opportunities through participation in equity.

Even though it was only a complete achievement, the initial IBs have been the subject of much scholarly discussion, notably in regard to how they operate, what they do, how well they do it, what kinds of financing options they provide, and what kinds of social and legal challenges they face. The issue of corporate governance (CG), however, has not received the kind of focus that it merits, and there is no dedicated dialogue or effort in this area. This is due to the fact that all IFIs started out as social banks or cooperatives. Financing options were relatively limited and targeted mainly toward meeting social and local needs. CG is, however, less crucial for this kind of firm structure.

4.2.1   *Tabung Hajji: Achieving One's Goals*

Islamic banking originated in Malaysia, which took a totally different approach from Egypt at the time. It was a bank set up specifically to serve the needs of Malaysian tourists. These organizations were set up because many Malaysian Muslims believe that "Riba"-tainted money should not be used for pilgrimages. It was unable to do so using typical banking services, hence a specialized financial institution was necessary. Following the formation of the Pilgrims Preservation Corporation in 1969 the Pilgrims Administration Fund Board (Tabung Hajji) was founded.

The Islamic Development Bank was established in Jeddah, Saudi Arabia (KSA) in 1975. The Islamic Development Bank is a multilateral organization that provides funding for projects in its member countries. Its stated goal is to promote the social and economic development of its member nations in accordance with Shariah law. Islamic Development Bank has grown to become the industry leader in Islamic financing. Al-Rajhi Banking and Investment Corporation is the biggest Islamic bank in the world. The Islamic Development Bank, the world's first commercial Islamic bank, was established in the same year as Dubai Islamic Bank.

The Islamic banking industry expanded most rapidly between 1975 and 1990. Dubai Islamic Bank, Faisal Islamic Bank, Kuwait Finance House, and the Islamic Development Bank in Jeddah are just a few examples of IFIs that have been formed as companies and hence need their own unique CG structure. In reality, certain international infrastructure organizations were formed to help the Islamic financial sector improve and reinforce its corporate responsibility framework in response to a number of corporate failures and challenges experienced by IFIs in the 1990s and 2000s. A few examples include the International Islamic Financial Market (IIFM), the Association of Accounting and Auditing Association for IFIs (AAOIFI), the International Islamic Rating Authority (IIRA) in Bahrain, the Genera Islamic Rating Agency (GIRA), and GIRA. CG challenges in IFIs are addressed by the AAOIFI and the Islamic Financial Services Board (IFSB) via the publication of guidelines on governance and best practice recommendations, while the other institutions offer infrastructural assistance for the introduction of Islamic finance. In addition, the Dubai-based Institute for CG, Hawkamah, set out on its own to study and develop best practices for CG in the Middle East and North Africa by forming a task force and establishing a committee on corporate administration for IBs and financial institutions. Seven governance standards have been issued by the AAOIFI so far. These include the standard on Islamic law Supervisory Board: Appointment, Composition, and Report; the Shariah Review; the Internal Shariah Review; the Standards for the Audit and Governance Committee for IFIs; the Declaration of Independence of the SSB; the Statement on Governance Fundamentals for IFIs; and the corporation's social responsibility standard. Similarly, the IFSB has announced 28 standards on administration, disclosure, and supervision review procedures for IFIs.

4.3 Frameworks for Islamic Banking General

The creation of a unified framework for IB would be categorized as a teleological theory of change whose ultimate objective is focused endorsement and social construction. This development is necessitated by the increase in competition and scarcity of resources. The implementation of this framework will depend on the unit of change, which comprises the interaction of organizations within an industry and environment, and the mode of change, which is sanctioned by deterministic laws and produces first-order change (Huber and Glick, 1993). The greatest obstacle in this transition from a conventional to an Islamic financial framework has been acceptability, or more specifically, the industry's adoption of the strategic application of innovation to produce returns (Weick and Quinn, 1999). Largely due to their interest-based economies, Muslim countries initially appeared incompatible with Islamic finance. Nonetheless, changes in government priorities and public sensibilities, especially in the last two decades, have permitted IB to progressively acquire legitimacy (Cader, 2007). In nearly every Muslim nation, the government has taken the initiative to introduce and expand IB (Ibrahim *et al.*, 2010).

In some Muslim and non-Muslim countries, comprehensive regulatory frameworks for IB do not yet exist (Archer and Karim, 1997). These prudential and regulatory frameworks were initially devised as a first step toward a comprehensive framework designed specifically for IFIs. When Islamic financing gained momentum in the 1990s, Bahrain was the first nation to develop and implement a regulatory framework. AAOIFI was founded in 1991 as a non-profit organization. Its primary functions include the preparation of auditing, accounting, and CG standards for the Islamic financial services industry based on Shariah principles (Chapra and Ahmed, 2002; Karim, 2001). Syria, Qatar, Sudan, Jordan, the United Arab Emirates, Bahrain, and Lebanon, to name a few, provided AAOIFI with positive feedback regarding the adoption of their standards in recent years. Countries such as South Africa, Pakistan, Indonesia, Australia, Malaysia, and Pakistan are attempting to issue guidelines based on AAOIFI's proclamations and standards. Nonetheless, AAOIFI continues to face significant obstacles in its efforts to build consensus and implement its standards for the global Islamic financial services industry.

4.4 Need for Good Corporate Governance in the Muslim World

The growth of the Islamic market necessitates sound CG in line with the tenets of Shariah law and the true spirit of Islam. It has a lot of weight in the Islamic business world and Islamic financial world. Recent growth in Islamic investment and the number of Islamic firms has far outpaced regulators' capacity to define or agree on a single, definitive model of Islamic governance for corporations. Islamic CG, in addition to being in accordance with Shariah law, must also be attractive to and compatible with world norms. Due to the strict nature of Shariah law, it is challenging for Islamic organizations to implement an efficient CG framework. However, a Shariah oversight committee is essential for two reasons. First, if the management of an Islamic bank continued to break Shariah law, the majority of the bank's investors and customers would lose trust in the institution. Second, Muslims are thought to be less likely to engage in immoral activities because of Shariah's focus on ethics.

Conformity with Shariah is a defining trait of IBs and is crucial to preserving their credibility. The IFSB has stressed that IBs should put in place a system to obtain and apply decisions from Shariah scholars and to keep track of Shariah compliance. As per IFSB guidelines, IBs should have both an internal Shariah review process, carried out by an independent department, and an SSB made up of competent scholars selected by shareholders as well as reporting to the board of executives, with the task of approving goods and services and carrying out reviews to ensure Shariah compliance (among other responsibilities). An important choice must be made about the creation of a centralized SSB (in addition to SSBs at the bank level) to oversee the SG structure in IBs. By standardizing Shariah judgments, a Centralized SSB may cut down on compliance and Shariah-related expenses for IBs. In secular states where substantive law bans regulator engagement in Shariah concerns, a central SSB might be formed by the regulator, or IBs could be urged to establish such a body collectively.

The custom of creating an SSB differs from one nation to the next. Differences in how different countries address Shariah concerns, limitations on the regional accessibility of competent scholars, and the IB's incomplete condition all contribute to the lack of consistency in the implementation of SG requirements. Most Shariah-compliant states mandate that IBs have a Shariah Board, and in other cases, this board's duties have been reinforced by the creation of a Centralized Shariah Supervision Board (CSSB).

142 Shariah Governance Systems of Islamic Banks

The CSSB is housed within the central bank in some countries (including Afghanistan, Malaysia, Bahrain, Pakistan, and Palestine) while in others (including Sudan, Turkey, and the United Arab Emirates) it is an independent public institution.

Responsibilities and reporting lines of the SSB to IB boards of directors are not standardized. While some of the SSBs the central bank has set up have the power to legislate and adjudicate on Shariah matters, others are just advised on changes to the rules and regulations. Concerning accountability, it is difficult to tell whether SSB members report to the IBs' BOD or not. The bulk of SSB–IB relationships seems to be consultative in nature, with the BOD of the bank ultimately bearing responsibility for Shariah compliance. While this is in line with IFSB SG requirements, there is a need for improvement in terms of making clear the SSBs' mission, responsibility, and independence in order to mitigate ethical and legal risks associated with Shariah compliance (Song and Oosthuizen, 2014).

4.5 The Development of Standards and Regulatory Guidance in the World

The safe growth of Islamic banks (IBs) depends on a solid legal framework. To establish a legal foundation for the supervision of IBs, general banking laws (or particular legislation relevant to IBs, if present) must clarify the nature of IBs and how they collaborate with the Federal Reserve and conventional banks. Different jurisdictions have taken different approaches when developing the legal framework that permits the operation of IBs because IBs operate within nations with vastly different constitutional environments that reflect different legal frameworks and divergent perspectives on the Shariah as a foundation of law (Song and Oosthuizen, 2014). The laws and regulations that apply to Islamic organizations are not universal. Islamic banking regulations have been implemented in Iran, Indonesia, Malaysia, Pakistan, Turkey, Sudan, the United Arab Emirates, and Yemen. In contrast to the *mudarabah* contract used by IBs elsewhere, Iranian IBs accept consumer investments on the basis of the *wikala* contract, an agency contract. IBs are not governed by legislation in other majority-Muslim countries such as Bangladesh, Saudi Arabia, or Egypt. As a result, they follow the same rules as other types of establishments. The Ministry of Commerce, not the Central Bank, oversees Kuwait's one and only foreign financial institution (El-Hawary and Grais, 2004), which is authorized as a finance house rather than a bank.

Codes of CG of various types have been adopted in several countries to deal with problems in the CG framework of organizations. The consequences of both economic downturns and financial crises are expected to be lessened by improved CG measures and improved transparency. The CG frameworks and transparency of Islamic organizations have been improved through the establishment of a number of rules and norms. Authorities at all levels have promised to create comprehensive regulations for Islamic organizations to follow. To better assist governments and regulatory bodies in understanding Islamic banking and providing standards and best-practice recommendations for this business, a number of global organizations have been set up in recent years.

The Islamic banking industry expanded most rapidly between 1975 and 1990. The Dubai Islamic Bank, Faisal Islamic Bank, Kuwait Finance House, and Islamic Development Bank in Jeddah are all examples of IBs established in the form of companies, which required the development of a unique CG framework (Hasan, 2011b). In reality, various international infrastructure organizations were formed to help the Islamic financial industry improve and enhance its CG regime in response to a number of corporate failures and challenges of IFIs in the 1990s and 2000s. Among them are the IIFM, the IFSB in Malaysia, and the Accounting and Auditing Organization for IFIs (AAOIFI). There are more such organizations besides the IMF such as the Bank for International Settlements, also known as BIS, and the Arab Monetary Fund (AMF).

Late in 2010, a second international regulatory agency, the International Islamic Infrastructure Management Corporation (IILM), was founded, having a profound effect on the commercial operations of financial institutions worldwide. IILM is hosted by Malaysia and welcomes participation from governments, central banks, and international organizations. The Islamic Development Bank is also a member of IILM along with the central banks and financial agencies of Kuwait, Indonesia, Luxembourg, Mauritius, Malaysia, Nigeria, Turkey, Qatar, the United Arab Emirates, and Qatar. The IILM is an international organization with the mission of providing and issuing Shariah-compliant short-term financial instruments to promote efficient international in nature Islamic liquidity management, international links, and monetary stability.

Bank Indonesia (BI), Bank Negara Malaysia (BNM), the Central Bank of Bahrain (CBB), the State Bank of Pakistan (SBP), the Regional Bank of Sudan (CBS), and other Gulf Cooperation Council (GCC) countries are just a few of the central banks that have established governance

144   *Shariah Governance Systems of Islamic Banks*

and auditing standards to boost customer trust in financial statements. The plan's secondary objective is to get people to use IBs for their savings, investments, and other financial needs. There are now several governance and disclosure roles due to the fact that these laws are not uniform.

Most Islamic organizations have a dedicated Shariah Monitoring Board, and some go so far as to create their own Shariah review section or department to help the board do its job. This is encouraging news for the future of Islamic organizations governed by Shariah law. Whether or if nations that embrace a larger role for regulatory bodies are more common and more amenable to future adoption is still up for debate (Hasan, 2011b). However, the researcher disputes this claim and maintains that Islamic banking must be regulated owing to a variety of unavoidable dangers. From a regulatory perspective, Hasan (2009, 2011b) outlined five distinct types of SG: the reactive, passive, minimalist, proactive, and interventionist models.

4.6   Current Legal and Regulatory Framework Practice

The establishment of the IILM as a second global regulatory agency at the end of 2010 had a significant impact on the business operations of financial institutions. IILM is headquartered in Malaysia and is open to membership from central banks, monetary authorities, and multilateral organizations. The present membership of IILM includes the central banks and monetary authorities of Indonesia, Kuwait, Luxembourg, Malaysia, Mauritius, Nigeria, Qatar, Turkey, the United Arab Emirates, and the Islamic Development Bank. The IILM is an international organization with the mission of facilitating effective cross-border Islamic liquidity management, global connectivity, and financial stability through the provision and issuance of Shariah-compliant short-term financial instruments. As a pioneer in credit-rating services for the Malaysian capital market, RAM Rating Service Berhad (RAM ratings) offers investors the impartial credit opinion they need regarding the portfolios of firms, including Islamic institutions. A favorable influence on IBs' portfolios and increased confidence from capital sources could result from the credibility of IBs in providing Islamic financial products and good management (Hassan *et al.*, 2017).

Additional guidelines/standards are provided by the Central Bank of Bahrain, State Bank of Pakistan (SBP), Bank Negara Malaysia (BNM), and Bank Indonesia in addition to the AAOIFI and IFSB. Bahrain-Oman governmental standards and guidelines have been produced by Pakistan, Malaysia, and Indonesia. To complete the governance system, it is necessary to incorporate further guiding principles in order to implement the accountability and transparency notion of governance. These additional rules for the governance system are the internal Shariah audit rules, the Shariah parameter reference rules, and rules for audit and risk management in IFI. Guidelines for risk management are outside the purview of AAOIFI because it concentrate on accounting, auditing, Shariah, governance, and ethical standards. The IFSB, in contrast, won't create a Shariah parameter reference, an IFI auditing standard, or an internal Shariah audit. The auditing, risk management, and Shariah parameter standards are made available to all central banks involved in the review process, even if some of them are the same as standard guidelines and weren't created exclusively for IFI. However, the absence of internal Shariah audit guidelines is the biggest problem. A crucial component of the IFI's governance and Shariah compliance certification process is this standard.

Examining the accounting rules used by the two central banks in Asia and the MENA area, which have significantly influenced the growth of the Islamic financial sector, is also fascinating. While Bank Indonesia and BNM are developing their accounting standards to conform with IFRS, SBP and CBB have fully accepted the AAOIFI accounting standards. The readiness and initiatives of three regulators, Oman, Bahrain, and Pakistan, to encourage and promote the implementation of AAOIFI, IFSB, and Basel standards and guidelines are also among the most noteworthy features of this comparison of standards. This is regarded as essential since collaborating internationally on standards is an important stage in the harmonization process. With regard to resolving Shariah compliance principles, each regulatory framework has its own strategy, goal, and character (Hidayah, 2014).

The laws and regulations that apply to Islamic organizations are not universal. Islamic banking regulations have been implemented in Malaysia, Indonesia, Iran, Pakistan, Sudan, Turkey, the United Arab Emirates, and Yemen. However, it's possible that Islamic banking's unique features aren't always accounted for in these statutes. The Islamic organizations in other Muslim countries like Saudi Arabia and Egypt are not governed by any legislation. As a result, they follow the same rules as other types of establishments. In Kuwait, there is just one IFI, and it is regulated not by the Central Bank but by the Ministry of Commerce.

146 *Shariah Governance Systems of Islamic Banks*

There has been a heightened interest in the regulatory and supervisory structures that control IFI since the early 1990s. Considerable implications for the reporting of financial information and accounting have been recognized due to the differences between the balance sheet architecture of conventional and Islamic organizations and the peculiarities of Islamic financial transactions. One of the first groups of researchers to bring up the topic of IFI control and supervision was Archer and Karim (1997), followed by Archer *et al.* (1998). These findings suggest that accounting standards and transparency need to play a larger role in the regulatory environment. Errico and Farabakash (1998) suggest a regulatory framework based on the norms and best practices established by the Basle Committee, as well as a prudential framework based on the CAMEL system that is specific to Islamic finance. The recommendations of Errico and Sundarajan (2002), who advocate for a regulatory framework analogous to the CAMEL concept and the implementation of a disclosure system modeled after the SEC, lend credence to this idea. To account for the differences between conventional deposit accounts and Islamic investment accounts, AAOIFI has released an announcement on the Purpose and Measurements of Capital Adequacy Ratio (CAR) for IBs. The principles of capital adequacy established by the Basel Committee are elaborated upon in this declaration. Specific accounting, governance of companies, and prudential requirements are needed for Islamic finance due to the features. They discuss the work done by the AAOIFI to develop accounting and auditing rules, standardize Shariah conclusions, and set capital adequacy measures for IFI, all of which are relevant to the question of whether or not the IAS applies to IFI.

4.7 International Standard-Setting Agencies

The Islamic banking and insurance industry has expanded greatly during the last three decades. IFIs have been actively competing with traditional banks over the last several decades. The latter, however, has not been able to meet the unique needs of Islamic organizations. Many international organizations have been set up to ensure the continued expansion of the Islamic financial sector, and work has started on this front.

Several programs have been launched to improve the Islamic financial system. Under the guidance of the Islamic Development Bank and with the enthusiastic backing of the World Bank, the IMF, and the Basel Committee, a number of worldwide IFIs have been founded. Also, while IFIs have access to many of the same payment, trading, and information systems used in conventional finance, the operational modalities of these systems have typically been adapted to better suit the needs of Islamic financial educational institutions (Hassan and Lewis, 2007).

The nascent Islamic financial infrastructure undoubtedly has to be strengthened, however, there are two additional immediate requirements. One of these challenges is avoiding unnecessary repetition of effort by new institutions by unifying the emerging structure and synchronizing their efforts. The second is the need to retain the distinctiveness of Islamic financial architecture while incorporating it into the international institutional framework. As such, it's important to think about and deal with the ways in which the present trend of globalization and technological improvements are changing the foundations of financial institutions.

The IFSB Islamic Development Bank (IDB), IIFM, AAOIFI, International Islamic Rating Agency (IIRA), International Islamic Centre for Reconciliation and Commercial Arbitration, and General Council of Islamic Banks and Financial Institutions (GCIBFI) are all mentioned as examples of IFIs. A closer look indicates that the vast majority of those involved in these groups are from Muslim-dominated countries. There is some functional overlap between these organizations despite the fact that they are not all under the same jurisdiction; all are committed to the expansion of Islamic banking.

Despite the best efforts of numerous international standard-setting bodies like the AAOIFI and IFSB to put the Islamic finance industry back on solid ground, the industry's future prospects appear to be less than promising. Despite the best efforts of AAOIFI and IFSB, no globally acknowledged norms or standards exist for auditing, accounting, legal, administration, or Shariah concerns. In their place are the OECD Principles and the BCBS Paper, two globally known criteria of good CG that aim to take into account the particularities of Islamic institutions.

Self-regulation is favored by certain jurisdictions, even as they seek economic integration with the global financial sector (Oseni *et al.*, 2016). The relevant authorities should communicate with the industry's local interlocutors to promote the free flow of knowledge and concepts (Sole, 2007). However, there were voids since standards set by the Bank for International Settlements (BIS) did not fully cover the needs of Islamic banking operations and transactions.

IFIs have both difficulties and possibilities as a result of the coming effect of Basel III rules. IFIs will need to make substantial investments to meet the new international criteria. Capital treatment and risk connected

148 *Shariah Governance Systems of Islamic Banks*

with the different kinds of Islamic financial agreements must, therefore, take these changes into account to appropriately represent their features (Beseiso, 2014).

An all-encompassing legal framework is necessary for the growth and advancement of Islamic banking. Understanding the Islamic banking legal frameworks is crucial to their successful implementation. Sharia and any other applicable substantive or procedural laws must be followed by Islamic financial organizations. The legal framework of any financial system consists of both administrative and legislative frameworks. These models work together to provide a workable, equitable, and fair system. Since Shariah law is the basis for the incorporation of Islamic principles into every sphere of life, it must be taken into account while thinking about Islamic law and its potential application to a preexisting financial system. The elimination of interest, the backbone of all traditional monetary transactions, is another hurdle that has to be overcome by this framework. These issues are fundamental to the growing discussion on how Islamic banking may function inside existing systems (Rafay and Sadiq, 2015).

The safe growth of IB depends on a well-established legal framework. To establish a legal foundation for the supervision of IBs, general banking laws (or particular legislation relevant to IBs, if present) must clarify the nature of IBs and how they collaborate with the central bank and traditional financial institutions. Because IBs function in countries with widely varying legal systems, which in turn reflect different legal traditions and viewpoints on the Shariah as a source of law, various jurisdictions have taken various routes to establish the legal framework that allows for the functioning of IBs (Song and Oosthuizen, 2014). More specifically:

- Although efforts have been made to provide uniform Shariah requirements for IB across countries with a Shariah incorporation model, deviations reflecting local rules remain. Therefore, the types of organizations that are allowed to engage in IB vary among various countries. Some countries prohibit the use of Islamic windows or the transformation of a conventional bank into an Islamic bank, such as Iraq, Kuwait, and Jordan.
- To provide an equal opportunity for Islamic financial products, purely secular countries have sought to amend legislation without necessarily introducing Shariah features into the fundamental laws of the state. Countries like Singapore (which amended its banking and tax regulations in the early 2000s), the United Kingdom (which amended its Financial

Services and Markets Act in 2000 to permit the establishment of IBs), France (which amended its tax code in 2008 and its civil code in 2009), Japan (which amended its Asset Securitization Law in 2012), Hong Kong (which amended its tax law in 2013), and so on are all good examples.

Jurisdictions that allow IBs must make the important choice of whether or not to retain a uniform core set of banking laws and regulations for IBs and CBs. For reasons that likely have to do with the need to increase transparency and compensate for a lack of experience, some relatively new IB jurisdictions (such as the countries of Lebanon, Morocco, and Oman) appear to have selected issuing distinguish laws and regulations. Meanwhile, some mature markets (such as Malaysia) have maintained the separation for development purposes. Most nations, however, have standardized on a core set of banking rules and regulations that are applicable to both international and domestic banks. This has the positive effect of reducing the likelihood that IBs and CBs may be subject to conflicting legal and regulatory requirements (Song and Oosthuizen, 2014).

The IB business model has particular governance issues, such as defining the role of Shariah-compliance governance and protecting the interests of investment account holders. The governance structure of the bank must take into account the various interests of investors and stockholders, as has already been established. In light of this, the IFSB recommended in 2006 that IBs set up an internal board-level administration committee with the authority to oversee the governance policy system, including the protection of the interests of the holders of investment accounts, and to disclose their policies and performance with regard to investment accounts in order to enable adequate monitoring by their holders. It is challenging for IBs to provide investment account owners with all the information required to make them aware of the risks facing the bank because the governance committee answers directly to the bank board, which means any conflict of interest between shareholders and investment account holders will likely be disclosed *ex-post*, if disclosed at all. One solution to this problem would be to mandate that a specific number of bank directors be responsible for defending the accounts of investors.

4.7.1 *Accounting and Auditing Organization for Islamic Financial Institutions*

Financial institutions must address issues of openness and corporate responsibility if they want to earn their customers' confidence. Financial statements must be created in a fashion that offers adequate and comparable information for shareholders, investors, and lenders to assess the health of the organization. The regulations and processes for disclosure are typically established by central banks; however, Islamic institutions have unique requirements and hence need a different approach. Financial statement comparisons between these institutions would be more objective if they all adopted the same standards.

There aren't many robust regulatory systems for IBs, both in Muslim and non-Muslim countries (for references see Archer and Karim (1997)). The original intention behind these macroeconomic and regulatory frameworks was to serve as a stepping stone toward the development of a more complete framework tailored to IFIs. During the 1990s, when Islamic finance became popular, Bahrain was the first country to create and execute a framework for regulation. In 1991, a group of accountants and auditors came together to form the Accounting, Bookkeeping, and AAOIFI. As stated by Chapra and Ahmed (2002) and Karim (2001), the organization's principal role is to develop Shariah-compliant auditing, accounting and finance, and CG guidelines for the Islamic financial services sector. Sudan, Syria, Qatar, Jordan, Bahrain, the United Arab Emirates, and Lebanon are just some of the countries that have shown interest in adopting AAOIFI's criteria in recent years (Nadzri, 2009). Many nations are making an effort to create regulations in conformity with AAOIFI's pronouncements and standards, including Pakistan, South Africa, Indonesia, Australia, Malaysia, and Pakistan. There are still substantial challenges that AAOIFI must overcome before it can achieve agreement and execute its rules for the worldwide Islamic financial services sector (Khan, 2007; Rafay and Sadiq, 2015). The AAOIFI norms are strongly supported by the Central Bank of Bangladesh.

Numerous studies have looked at both the AAOIFI compliance with standards (Abuhmaira, 2006; Al-Baluchi, 2006; Sarea, 2012) and the Islamic Financial Reporting Standards (IFRS) (Al-Mehmadi, 2004; Hasan, 2011b; Hameed, 2009; Hameed *et al.*, 2004). For the most part, researchers in this area rely on either a survey (Hasan, 2011; Al-Mehmadi, 2004; Sarea, 2012) or an information disclosure index (Al-Baluchi, 2006; Hameed *et al.*, 2004). The AAOIFI was founded in Bahrain with the goal of standardizing and spreading best practices in areas like accounting, auditing, morality, Shariah, and CG. When it comes to harmonizing practices that are important to IFIs, AAOIFI is the standard-setting and consultative body (Ahmed, 2002; Venardos, 2005).

To avoid having accounting rules imposed on their business, IBs regulate their financial reporting (Karim, 1990). Concerned that the regulatory body would release accounting standards and rules that are incompatible with their operations, IBs encouraged the formation of AAOIFI to set accounting requirements for IFIs. However, AAOIFI cannot mandate that its criteria be followed. IFIs are subject to the regulations of the jurisdiction in which they are chartered or listed. Therefore, AAOIFI must convince national regulatory and monetary authorities to adopt AAOIFI norms (Abuhmaira, 2006). International Accounting Standards (IAS)/International Financial Reporting Standards (IFRS) are followed by Islamic organizations in the vast majority of countries. However, AAOIFI-adopting IFIs are still required to follow IFRS in their financial reporting. Where the IAS/IFRS does not address the accounting procedure for Islamic financial instruments, the AAOIFI rules are used. The 31 accounting standards, 57 Shariah standards, 8 governance standards, 6 auditing standards, and 2 codes of conduct are only some of the 104 standards released by the AAOIFI to date (AAOIFI, 2018). The AAOIFI guidelines cover how Islamic financing is recorded in the books generally. To further define the SSB's function and mandate, the AAOIFI has set three standards (AAOIFI, 2009). Among them is GSIFI, the Governance Guidelines for IFIs. GSIFI 2: Shariah Review; GSIFI 5: SSB Independence; GSIFI 1: SSB Appointment, The Structure, and Report (with a sample report).

4.7.2 *International Financial Service Board (IFSB)*

With its headquarters in Kuala Lumpur, Malaysia, the International Financial Service Board (IFSB) is a standard-setting body of regulators and regulatory agencies working to improve the framework for IFIs. Stakeholders are the foundation upon which the IFSB's guiding principles for the organization, operation, and best practices of IFIs are built. Thus, regulatory bodies may use the guiding principles to assess the openness of CG frameworks in place in IBs. The IFSB creates prudential standards and guiding principles for the efficient supervision and regulation of the banking, financial markets, and insurance sectors that make up Islamic finance. The fundamental goal is to provide the groundwork for Shariah-compliant monetary, capital, and banking instruments (Merton, 1995; Mawdudi, 1986). In light of modern difficulties, the IFSB works to establish an open and robust Islamic financial services market in accordance with Shariah principles. According to many studies (Chami *et al.*, 2003; Rammal and Parker, 2013; Rafay and Sadiq,

2015), the Islamic financial system may be most successfully implemented in countries with a favorable legal environment. A total of 28 standards, comprising 19 governing tenets, 8 guide notes, and 5 technical notes, have been produced by the IFSB since the organization's founding (IFSB, 2023).

Organizations and market players on a global, regional, and national scale that share IFSB's aims make up the organization's membership. The International Food Safety Board welcomes organizations that want to participate and offer their skills, resources, and information. The IFSB welcomes Full, Associate, and Spectator members. Membership is open to international intergovernmental organizations with a mandate to promote Islamic finance, as well as the regulatory bodies of independent nations that recognize Islamic financial services, either through legislation, regulation, or established practice, in the areas of banking, securities, and/or insurance/ *Takaful*. Any institution that does not meet the criteria for or seek to become an IFSB Full member, such as a central bank, monetary positions of power, financial supervisory or regulating organization, or international organization, is welcome to apply for Associate membership with the IFSB. Every professional or industry group, Islamic financial institution, and firm or organization that offers professional services like legal, accounting, rating, research, and training to these institutions are welcome to join as observers, regardless of their location. However, the IFSB Council has the discretion to approve any application for membership in any category of membership it sees fit.

Since its inception, the IFSB has issued seven standards, fundamental values, and a technical note for the Islamic financial services industry, covering topics such as risk management, capital adequacy, CG, the supervisory review process, transparency, and market discipline, the acknowledgment of ratings on Shariah-compliant instruments of finance, and the growth of Islamic money markets. The IFSB is also working on new regulations and principles in the following areas: Capital Adequacy; Investment Fund Governance; *Takaful* Operations; SG; Business Conduct and Ethics.

4.7.3 *Islamic Development Bank (IDB)*

The Conference of Finance Secretaries of Muslim Nations released the Jeddah Declaration of Intent in December 1973, which led to the formation of the Islamic Development Bank, an international financial organization for development. The Bank's stated purpose is to aid the Muslim world financially so that Muslim countries and communities may flourish in accordance with Islamic law. The IDB is made up of a diverse group of countries including Malaysia, Kazakhstan, Saudi Kuwait, Arabia, Iran, Egypt, United Arab Emirates, Morocco, Turkey, Bangladesh, Guinea, Indonesia, Libya, Guinea Bissau, Mauritania, Pakistan, Senegal, Sierra Leone, and Sudan. To join the IDB, a nation must be an associate member of the Organization of Islamic Cooperation (OIC), make a capital contribution, and agree to abide by the rules and regulations set out by the IDB Board of Governors.

To help member countries and non-Muslim groups with project finance, the IDB creates and maintains dedicated funds for such objectives. The bank invests in equity capital and funds productive ventures via loans, in addition to providing different types of financial aid for the development of the economy and society to member nations. The Bank is able to take deposits and raise capital thanks to its adherence to Sharia law. It also provides educational opportunities for employees involved in development initiatives in Muslim nations to comply with Islamic law, and it encourages international trade, especially in capital items, among its member countries.

There is a Board of Governors that oversees the IDB. A nation may join the IDB by making a monetary contribution to its capital and agreeing to the terms and conditions set by the IDB's Board of Governors. Financial operations, such as regular operations (which comprise project financing and assistance with technology activities, Waqf Fund processes, and trade financing operations), are the primary means by which the IDB offers development assistance. Financing is provided by loans without interest, equity participation, installment sales, and leasing, all of which are considered to be Islamic modalities of finance.

4.7.4 *International Islamic Financial Market (IIFM)*

Standardizing Islamic contractual arrangements and product blueprints for the money and capital markets, corporate finance, and trade finance sectors of the Islamic financial services industry is the primary focus of the IIFM, a standard-setting organization. The challenges faced by the Islamic banking sector necessitated the creation of this organization, including the need for innovative products to meet investors' requirements in a rapidly shifting market environment, the development of an assistance infrastructure that tackles the pressing requirement for liquidity management among IFIs, and the standardization and codification of laws and market practice. In light of the above, Muslim nations' financial authorities saw a need for a coordinating body, and thus the IIFM was founded to provide it. Members include the Ministry of Finance of Brunei Darussalam, the Central Bank of Sudan, the Central Bank of Indonesia, the Islamic Development Bank, and the Bahrain Monetary Agency.

The IIFM is governed by its Articles of Association, which state the organization's mission as "the unification of the Islamic financial market," with a focus on the standardization of Islamic Capital and Money market products. To increase the extraterritorial adoption of Islamic financial products and to improve cooperation among Muslim countries, IIFM went live in 2002 with the main goal of allowing worldwide secondary market trading of Islamic financial instruments (Hassan and Lewis, 2007). The IIFM's first operations plan was severely lacking. However, it has recently been more proactive, and the following are the means by which it plans to achieve its aims:

1. Amended Islamic financial instrument issuance guidelines;
2. Findings from studies on the expansion of Islamic financial markets encouraging product development and trading of instruments on the secondary market; and
3. Strengthening cooperation among market participants in order to create a market for the autonomous sharia enhancement of existing or fresh Islamic financial instruments.

4.7.5 *International Islamic Rating Agency (IIRA)*

The importance of external rating mechanisms and accounting standards cannot be overstated due to the benefits they provide to investors, banks, and regulators. A bank with a solid reputation may easily get funding from other banks and investors. Due to their expansion, IFIs may increasingly be found operating in nations where the local financial institutions and regulatory bodies may lack a thorough understanding of Islamic finance's unique characteristics and risk profile. This is because IBs don't follow the same procedures as their Western counterparts. Both borrowers and the instruments they create must be given risk ratings on these exchanges. In order to compete on a global scale, IBs need to improve their standing.

An Islamic rating agency was badly needed since conventional rating processes prioritize financial stability above Sharia compliance. As a result, in 2002, Bahrain became home to the International Islamic Classification Agency. IIRA's major role is to independently evaluate the institution's or its instruments' adherence to sharia by conducting analysis, research, and rating of responsibilities, dues, commitments, and other securities. In order to provide unbiased ratings for IBs and IDB member countries, the Islamic Investment Rating Agency (IIRA) was established. With approval from the Central Bank of Bahrain, IIRA may now call itself an External Credit Assessment Institution (ECAI). The Islamic Development Bank recognizes IIRA as a credit rating agency.

4.7.6 *International Islamic Centre for Reconciliation and Commercial Arbitration*

Because of their distinctive character, Islamic financial organizations may lack a clear foundation in the common law of any given nation. This might lead to legal problems that are difficult to settle. The IBFI General Council and the IDB acted in response by establishing a place where disputes could be settled amicably. Because of this need, the Islamic banking industry welcomed the establishment of the International Islamic Centre for Reconciliation and Commercial Arbitration in 2005. Banks and IFIs make up its Board of Trustees. The Center's foundational legislation is the Constitution and Arbitration and Reconciliation Rules and Regulations, which details the Center's mandate, jurisdiction, and location (the United Arab Emirates). It specifies the expenses of arbitration and the reconciliation processes. Its goal is to mediate conflicts in the commercial and financial sectors between organizations that adhere to Sharia law. Disputes involving other individuals are also often settled via arbitration and reconciliation (Hassan and Lewis, 2007).

4.7.7 *General Council of Islamic Banks and Financial Institutions (GCIBFI)*

Throughout the globe, IFIs are represented by the International Council of Islamic Banks and Financial Organizations, which is an autonomous, non-profit organization. According to its Articles of Association, Islamic financial organizations, and Islamic organizations will make up the general council of IFIs. It is said that Bahrain will serve as the company's main office. It also describes the Council's goals, which include expanding access to Islamic banking on a global scale, increasing awareness of Islamic banking organizations, and spreading applicable ideas, regulations, and requirements. With the goal of bolstering and advancing the Islamic banking and insurance sector, it acts as an umbrella body for IFIs. A few of the services it provides to the corporate sector include media, information, R&D, consulting, and HR training. It aims to advance and enhance the perception of the Islamic financial sector by, among other things, enhancing and supporting the growth of IFIs by offering them the necessary advisory and consultancy services, supplying the IFIs with the information they require for their development and growth, contributing to the growth of IFIs by offering research and development services, helping to amass the necessary personnel to deal with global challenges, and providing the IFIs with the information they require.

4.8 Legal Instruments

4.8.1 *Basel I*

Banks failed often in the 1980s owing to their risky lending, leading to "savings and lending crisis" headlines as nations' foreign debt expanded at unmanageable rates. As a result, the insufficient security of multinational banks raised the probability of their failure. To stave off this risk, the central banks and regulatory agencies of 10 nations got together in 1987 in Basel, Switzerland to form the Basel Committee on Banking Supervision. A paper outlining global bank capital requirements was developed by the group. With the goal of reducing competitive disparity among international banks, the Basel I Accord was established in 1988 to bolster the stability of the global financial system and to develop a fair and consistent worldwide banking system. Basel I's key contributions are the definition of bank capital and the establishment of the bank capital ratio. The Islamic banking systems were left out of the agreement's provisions for traditional banks. Thus, it was timely to adopt Basel II, since it included measures beneficial to IFIs.

4.8.2 *Basel II*

The Basel Committee for the Supervision of Banking put in a lot of work before 1999 to publish the Basel II Accord, which sets the capital adequacy criteria for banks and takes into account developments in the organization and operation of markets for securities and financial institutions. Banks' inability to manage banking risks, as well as insufficient external and internal monitoring, were identified as the most major contributing factors to banking crises by the Committee before the Basel II Accord was issued. As a result, the new Accord aimed to address these concerns in order to guarantee institutional stability.

The goal of Basel II was to institute market discipline that would ensure the safety of the global financial system. The second pillar of Basel II is the promotion of market discipline via improved openness and disclosure. Financial performance, financial condition, risk management methods and practice, risk exposure, accounting policies, and core company leadership and organizational governance information are the six areas suggested by Hassan and Chowdhury (2004) for financial disclosure and openness.

Basel II applications have been strengthened by the incorporation of Islamic banking, and Islamic institutions have gained prominence on a global scale as a result. Mutual funds, leasing businesses, entrepreneurship firms, and risk participation businesses are only a few of the Islamic financial instruments that are similar in nature to their Western counterparts. This novel banking setup is in line with global tendencies and Basel II (Hassan and Dicle, 2005).

A novel approach to measuring credit risk was presented at the Basel II convention. Basel II does not specifically address IBs; however, the new credit risk assessment models may be implemented without issue.

4.8.3 *Basel III*

Banking supervision throughout the world has been improved because of the implementation of the Basel III framework (Harzi, 2012). The global banking system's stability has been improved by the measures introduced as part of Basel III to tighten global liquidity and capital standards. The goals of Basel III are to increase the importance of common stock in the definition of regulatory capital and to tighten the eligibility criteria for other capital vehicles in order to enhance the quality of capital maintained by banking institutions.

In addition, Basel III has implemented measures to increase capital requirements for counterparty credit risk exposures originating from derivatives, which are repo, and securities financing operations, as well as trading book and complicated securitization exposures. To lessen the impact of excessive deleveraging on the financial sector during difficult times, Basel III includes a Leverage Ratio as part of its efforts to tighten risk-based standards and restrict leverage growth.

Capital requirements under Basel III are more relaxed than those of IBs. Islamic commercial institutions' profit-sharing accounts for investments were not eligible for inclusion in Basel III as a type of capital because of their risk-absorbing capabilities. And as banks are mandated to build up capital buffers during times of economic expansion to weather losses during periods of economic contraction, IBs are unable to adopt distribution programs that are compatible with good capital conservation principles. Basel III is different from Basel I and Basel II because it combines micro- and macro-prudential changes to deal with risks on several scales, not only inside individual institutions. New macro-prudential criteria are part of the reforms, and they push for the creation of emergency reserves of capital.

The Basel Committee did not factor in the unique features of Profit Sharing Investment Accounts (PSIA), hence the Basel Accord does not differentiate between traditional and IFIs in terms of capital requirements. PSIA assets do not put IBs in danger of losing money (Errico and Farahbaksh, 1998). This is because the risk is shared by the account holders. Basel authorities, on the other hand, do not consider PSIA holdings to be equity capital (Errico and Farahbaksh, 1998).

Counterparty credit risk without prescription derivatives and banks' accounts for trading are two areas that benefit from Basel III's expanded risk coverage. Since trading book activity and short selling are forbidden in Islamic banking, according to Harzi (2012), an Islamic bank needs much smaller Risk-Weighted Assets than traditional financial institutions do under Basel III. Despite the growing popularity of Islamic banking throughout the globe, Basel III does not differentiate between conventional banking institutions and Islamic financial organizations. The Islamic banking industry has been less affected by Basel III than traditional financial institutions. This is due to the fact that Islamic organizations have a more traditional approach to doing business than their Western counterparts (Fischel, 1992). As a result, Islamic institutions can't adopt Basel III as-is, since it doesn't work for them.

The Islamic Development Bank recognized the need for ongoing improvements to the infrastructure supporting the Islamic financial industry, so it launched a number of initiatives, including the creation of specialized institutions like the AAOIFI, the IFSB, an Islamic market for financial services, and an Islamic rating agency. The intrinsic qualities of Islamic finance and the existence of these institutions have contributed

Historical Development of Shariah Governance 159

to increased financial stability across the world, especially in the banking sector.

These Islamic organizations on a global scale have often functioned autonomously. Consolidation of the aforementioned institutions' activities, however, has become obvious as a means to accelerate the growth of the Islamic financial industry. For instance, the AAOIFI criteria and the international special risk requirements adopted by the IFSB are mandatory for all institutions. For instance, the Islamic Rating Agency is obligated to operate in accordance with IFSB and AAOIFI guidelines. Consolidating all of these organizations into one will eliminate duplicative efforts and inconsistencies in regulation, both of which are necessary for the Islamic financial infrastructure to be effective.

4.9 The AAOIFI Governance Standards

The AAOIFI has reportedly issued 100 guidelines and standards which are already implemented by 45 countries in the development of Islamic banking and finance. When there were no established CG regulations for IFIs in the late 1990s, the AAOIFI stepped in to fill the void with its own set of Shariah-based governance norms (Nos. 1–5). It's important to remember that these five guidelines are meant to be read together (Hasan, 2011). The AAOIFI has established seven core guidelines for the governance of IFIs. Audit and Administration Committee for IFIs; Shariah Review; Internal Shariah Review; Independence of SSBs; Statement on Administration Fundamentals for IFIs; Corporate Social Responsibility Guidelines for Conduct and Disclosure by IFIs; and (1) Appointment, Composition, and Report of the SSB.

(i) *Governance Standard for IFIs No. 1: SSB: Appointment, Composition and Report*: At its No. 13 meeting, held on June 15–16, 1997 (AAOIFI, 2005), the Accounting and Auditing Standard Board (AASB) approved Governance Standard No. 1. It's broken down into eight different parts: preamble; definition; appointment; composition; selection and dismissal; fundamental aspects of reports; publishing of reports; publication of Shariah decisions and guidelines; and effective date. Section 2 of Governance Standard No. 1 is the most crucial part of the document. There are three components that together make up the SSB. To begin, a Shariah oversight committee is a group of impartial jurists who have expertise in *fiqh al malt*. In accordance with this provision, the SSB may include non-*fiqh al muamalat* specialists in Islamic finance. Second, it establishes the SSB's role in guiding, assessing, and overseeing IFIs to guarantee adherence to Shariah principles. Finally, it represents the Shariah Monitoring Board's legal jurisdiction over IFIs.

The appointment and compensation of the SSB are outlined in Sections 3–6. AAOIFI prefers those shareholders, acting on the proposal of the BOD, to nominate and remove members of the Supervisory Board of the Shariah at the annual meeting. The market circumstances may make AAOIFI's suggestion to appoint the board of the SSB inappropriate in certain cases. The study's authors think the BOD may also make appointments to the board, provided that appropriate safeguards are in place to maintain the members' independence and to handle potential disputes of interest, such as making the appointments and removals of members subject to regulatory approval. Appointment terms must be approved by the SSB and recorded officially. The BOD, with the backing of the shareholders, may decide how much to pay the SSB. The AAOIFI requires that there be a minimum of three members on any SSB. Regardless of their credentials, directors or large owners of IFIs are ineligible for appointment to the Shariah Advisory Board.

4.9.1 *Shariah Supervisory Board: Appointment, Composition, and Report*

An autonomous organization of specialist jurists in *fiqh al muamalat* (Islamic business law), as described by the AAOIFI. A non-specialist in *fiqh muamalat*, but a specialist in IFIs, may serve on the SSB. Their principal role is to steer the Islamic financial institution and keep an eye on its operations. The goal is to make IFIs more faithful to Islamic law.

The BOD has recommended that shareholders nominate Shariah supervisory members at the next annual general meeting. The shareholders might give the BOD the authority to set the salary of the SSB. Proof that the IFIs are willing to work with the Shariah board should be included in the appointment letter. At least three people are needed on the commission, it has been recommended. Consultants with experience in business, economics, law, accounting, and other relevant professions may be hired by the board. Members of the board should not be shareholders or own a disproportionate number of shares to ensure the board's impartiality. To remove a member from the board, the board must vote to do so and the shareholders must approve the action in a special or annual meeting.

Historical Development of Shariah Governance 161

SSB members need to provide the report which should include at least seven elements as follows.

- The report needs a suitable title, so be sure to include it.
- The report must be handled correctly in accordance with the facts and applicable laws and regulations.
- We are obligated to provide the following report in accordance with the terms of our participation, which should be stated in the introductory paragraph.
- Scope paragraph describing the nature of the work performed.
- A paragraph labeled "Opinion" expresses the author's view on whether or not the Islamic bank in question abides with Sharia law.
- Date of report.
- Signature of the members (Kasim *et al.*, 2013).

4.9.2   *Governance Standard for IFIs No. 2: Shariah Review*

At its 15th meeting, held on June 21–22, 1998, the AASB approved Governance Standard No. 2. There are 8 main portions and 18 sub-sections in total. In Section 3, "Shariah review" is described as "an evaluation of the IFIs' adherence to Shariah principles." Provision 5 lays compliance on the management, while this provision further establishes the Shariah Monitoring Board's jurisdiction to obtain any information essential for Shariah assessment. The only function of the Supervisory Board of Shariah is to create and express views on the level of Shariah compliance. Planning, designing, implementing, preparing, and evaluating are all covered in detail in Sections 7–13. At least once a year, there must be a public presentation of the Shariah review report.

4.9.2.1   *Shariah review*

Shariah review is defined by the AAOIFI as "an investigation into the extent to which an IFI's operations are compliant with Shariah." Documents such as articles of incorporation, financial accounts, audit reports (especially from the central bank), and contracts are reviewed. The goal of this analysis is to guarantee that no Shariah infractions are being committed by the IFI in question. SSB members are accountable for providing an assessment of an IFI's level of Shariah compliance. However, compliance is the management's duty. Management still has to make sure all transactions are lawful under Shariah after a review, however.

AAOIFI further lists down Shariah review procedures and stages. They are:

- It is important to organize the Shariah review processes in advance to ensure that they are carried out in an efficient and effective manner. The plan's complexity and the quantity of transactions should inform the size and number of samples chosen, and both should be recorded.
- To carry out Shariah review processes and prepare and review working papers, one may (1) learn about the level of knowledge and dedication among management, and (2) go over existing legal documents. (3) Verifying if the year's transactions included Shariah-compliant items; (4) carefully evaluating further data and reports; and (5) debating the results with the IFI's administration.
- Adequate quality control rules and processes should be put in place by the SSB to guarantee that the evaluation is completed in line with this requirement. All work documents may be reviewed as part of quality control processes.

In addition to the Shariah review, AAOIFI suggests doing an internal Shariah evaluation. The goal of this audit is to verify that IFI management is meeting its obligations with respect to the application of Shariah principles and standards, as established by the IFI's Shariah oversight board. Since Shariah review is an essential part of the boards of directors of IFIs, it must become ingrained in organizational culture. Either the internal audit or internal control divisions may carry out the Shariah review.

The position of the internal Shariah review should not be lower than that of the internal audit or internal control departments, according to AAOIFI's recommendations for ensuring the independence and impartiality of the internal Shariah review. In addition, they need the full backing of the company's upper echelons. There are no limits on who may see the papers, reports, etc., nor on their extent. The head of Shariah review inside the company reports directly to the BOD.

Employees conducting the internal Shariah review must be qualified in their fields and have the necessary experience and education to carry out the evaluation properly. The process of overseeing an internal Shariah review begins with the planning stage and continues until the end. The AAOIFI-issued Code of Conduct for Accountants and the auditors of IFIs must be followed in the internal Shariah examination. In addition, they need to keep their technical skills sharp by attending classes and seminars often.

The quality of performance in carrying out assigned obligations and the efficacy of the internal Shariah oversight process are both to be evaluated as part of the internal Shariah review. Efficient and effective achievement of the IFI's compliance goals with Shariah laws and principles is the primary motivation for conducting an analysis of the system of internal Shariah control in place.

The planned material for the internal Shariah review work should at the least mention the sources and references listed as follows:

- Background information on the activities that will be examined, including addresses, items, services, branches, etc.
- *Fatwas*, rules, directives, and the outcomes of the prior year's internal and external Shariah reviews from the SSB. All levels of individuals who need to be informed about the internal Shariah review should receive this information.
- Documentation confirming approval from the relevant authorities, such as the IFIs' Shariah supervisory bodies.

Examining and evaluating information regarding internal Shariah review, they must acquire, analyze, interpret, and document information to support internal review reports. Examining documentation, conducting analytic evaluations, conducting inquiries, conversing with management, and making observations must all be a part of the information collection process. In addition, the information must be trustworthy, sufficient, pertinent, and beneficial in order to provide a solid foundation for internal Shariah review. However, the report's findings should be followed up on to ensure that appropriate action is taken. The management is also responsible for the correction of non-compliance and the prevention of its recurrence (Kasim *et al.*, 2013).

4.9.3 *Governance Standard for IFIs No. 3: Internal Shariah Review*

At its 17th meeting, held on June 13–14, 1999 (AAOIFI, 2005), the AASB approved Governance Standard No. 3. It adds to Governance Standard No. 2 with 11 parts and 30 subsections. The third norm's purpose is to provide parameters for conducting an internal Shariah assessment. Due to their responsibility for Shariah compliance, IFI management must put in place an effective internal Shariah review procedure. The AAOIFI mandates that IFIs do an internal Shariah assessment, but does not mandate the creation of a dedicated internal Shariah audit division. The internal Shariah evaluation might be conducted by the auditing department or a separate, independent department.

According to the IFI Accountants and Auditors Code of Ethics and the AAOIFI, an impartial third party must do the internal Shariah examination. The internal Shariah evaluators need the full backing of management and the BOD. The head of the in-house Shariah evaluation team reports directly to the BOD. The internal Shariah reviewer must be knowledgeable and have the required academic background and training important to Shariah review, including Shariah and *fiqh al muamalat* competence, since the internal Shariah review is distinct from the usual auditing method. According to the established reporting structure, the head of the internal Shariah review must present the results to management and send the final report to the BOD through the SSB and the executive team. In the event of a dispute between management and internal Shariah reviewers, the SSB should mediate in the SG functions.

4.9.4 *Governance Standard for IFIs No. 4: Audit and Governance Committee*

Governance Standard No. 4 was approved by the AASB at its 21st meeting in May 2001 (AAOIFI, 2005). To supplement the CG framework for IFIs, the AAOIFI recommends strongly the creation of an Audit and Governance Committee (AGC) at the board level. At least three of the institution's non-executives and non-executive directors who are also knowledgeable in Shariah norms and principles should be assigned to the AGC by the BOD.

The AGC, along with the Supervisory Board of the Shariah and the BOD, is responsible for protecting the truthfulness of financial reports and processes, looking out for the best interests of stakeholders, bolstering trust in the data's reliability, and acting as a go-between for management and other interested parties. The AAOIFI Code of Ethics for Accountants and Auditors of IFIs mandates that the AGC perform audits of the organization's internal controls, accounting procedures, audit strategies, interim and annual accounts, financial reports, Shariah compliance, and the use of restricted investment account funds. The AGC's report must then be sent to the BOD (with a duplicate to the Chief Executive Officer).

4.9.4.1 *Audit and Governance Committee (AGC) for IFIs*

This group, also known as the Committee of Auditing, is crucial to the success of IFIs because of the work it does to ensure that Shariah principles and norms are followed and that the public may have faith in the IFIs. This committee ought to be in charge of things like:

- Preserving the integrity of the financial reporting process.
- Safeguarding the interests of shareholders, investors, and other corporate stakeholders.
- Providing additional assurance on the reliability of financial information presented to the BOD.
- Acting as an independent link between the IFIs' management and its stakeholders.

Regarding internal control, AGC is responsible for ensuring that the IFI has the appropriate controls in place and monitoring the implementation of management's strategy. However, the AGC must have sufficient knowledge of the IFI's business and control environment in order to ask germane questions about the system of internal control. Specific responsibilities associated with internal control review include the following:

- Recognizing the main risks to which the company is subjected. Keeping track of management's awareness of control, particularly as it relates to the importance placed on managing the IFI's policies, practices, and techniques.
- Reviewing the available tools and expertise, the range of duties, the overall work schedule, and the internal audit reporting lines.
- Reviewing the management replies to the results of central bank inspection and other regulatory agencies as well as the findings of those bodies, and ensuring that the necessary steps have been taken to satisfy the demands of the central bank inspector.
- Examining the IFI code of ethics and how well it is being applied.

Examining financial transactions and projects is part of reviewing accounting procedures and the audit plan. Specific duties related to this role

166   *Shariah Governance Systems of Islamic Banks*

include:

- Understanding areas in which the IFIs are vulnerable to high degrees of risk and uncertainty, with special reference to judgment areas involving estimations, contingent liabilities, and large claims.
- Maintaining the independence and professional integrity of auditors, as well as coordinating the work of internal and external auditors.
- Examining any concerns pertaining to the appointment, resignation, or termination of the chief internal auditor and members of the SSB.
- Examining nominations for new SSB members and for external or internal auditors.

The committee should assess all of the aforementioned reports to make sure that they are thorough, accurate, and unbiased in the case of analyzing the interim and annual accounts and financial reports (including matters originating from the audit). Prior to submission to the IFIs' BOD, the committee must also analyze these reports (interim and annual accounts as well as financial reports). This function has the following specific responsibilities:

- Ensuring adherence to legal and regulatory obligations as well as Shariah.
- Examining how major areas of judgment and accounting estimations have been handled Examining substantial alterations made as a result of the audit.
- Presenting a fair and understandable analysis of the company's situation in relation to the committee's duties.

The committee is responsible for upholding ethical standards and practices and making sure that other IFIs do the same. Faith-based behavior, technical standards, technical conduct, objectivity, religious legitimacy, and professional skill and diligence are all examples of this. The committee is accountable for examining the use of controlled and unconstrained savings account money as well as the internal Shariah evaluation reports. In accordance with Shariah regulations and tenets, IBs and account holders agree to review these accounts periodically to ensure that the funds have been invested as agreed upon and that the proceeds have been distributed as specified. The composition of the committee might change based on the country's laws and the policies of international financial institutions. The committee will be legally established by the BOD, but all of its members must be independent of management. The committee is responsible for reporting its findings to the board of governors and the CEO.

4.9.5 Governance Standard for IFIs No. 5: Independence of Shariah Supervisory Board

The AASB approved Governance Standard No. 5 during its No. 29 meeting, held on June 7–8, 2005. Its stated goal is to serve as a set of rules by which its independence may be maintained and conflicts over independence can be settled (AAOIFI, 2005d). There are nine chapters and an annex with a sample problem with diminished independence. Increasing public trust in Shariah compliance is dependent on the SSB's ability to maintain its position of independence. According to Article 3, the SSB is not allowed to defer to the decisions of outside parties in matters of Shariah supervision. Employees of the same IFIs or those with administrative or operational duties should not make up the SSB. The SSB must do regular reviews of IFIs and take corrective action to restore their autonomy if any problems are found (Hassan, 2011).

- Record the problem.
- Examine the problem internally among the members of the SSB.
- The member with the independence impairment issue must resign and the General Assembly of the IFI must be informed if the problem persists after the internal examination by the SSB members.
- Local rules and regulations must be taken into account if any resolution is necessary (Kasim *et al.*, 2013).

4.10 The IFSB Guiding Principles

The IFSB is an international institution whose mission is to establish and promote universal standards for the Islamic financial services sector. Since the IFSB's role is separate from that of internal and external SSBs and since the IFSB does not issue fatwas or judgments pertaining to Islamic banking and finance, the IFSB is not equipped with its own SSB. A few of the goals of the International Food Safety Board are the creation and promotion of various standards, the provision of supervisory and regulatory instructions, the promotion of cooperation among its members, the facilitation of training and development, the conducting of research, and the creation of databases of industry participants.

The IFSB has produced 10 guidelines for IFIs, including two on capital adequacy criteria, on risk management, and on governance, disclosure, and supervisory review. IFIs have to develop appropriate policies and institutional structures to manage operational risks, particularly

Shariah-compliance risks, and define the mechanism for the supervisory review process, so the need for an SG mechanism has been addressed previously in IFSB-1 and IFSB-5. In addition, IFSB3, IFSB6, and IFSB8 provide guidelines for the management of IFIs, ICICS, and Takaful, respectively. There hasn't been any prior guidance that particularly addresses the SG problem, merely the overarching framework of CG. The IFSB then launched IFSB-10 to particularly address SG in IFIs. The IFSB-10 is based on four tenets with the overarching goal of promoting SG best practices.

The IFSB-10 SGF makes allusions to the essential parts of a strong SG system in an effort to encompass the broad strokes of compliance with Shariah processes. As a highly noteworthy SG system guiding concept, the IFSB-10 is currently in the hands of regulatory bodies to decide on implementation. However, there is a gap that has to be bridged within the IFSB-10 and the AAOIFI governance criteria. It is possible that the IFSB-10 is not applicable in certain jurisdictions, such as Bahrain, the United Arab Emirates, and the nation of Qatar, since these countries have previously approved the AAOIFI governance requirements while others have been quiet. The IFSB-10 also does not seem to provide a suitable structure for a Shariah advising business. Having suitable standards and guiding principles for Shariah advice businesses is of the utmost importance in light of the likely growth in the number of such firms in the future (Table 4.1).

To provide effective autonomous Shariah compliance monitoring of the subsequent structures and procedures, an Islamic financial institution must implement an SG system, as defined by the IFSB.

Table 4.1: Key Elements of Shariah Governance in the IFSB-10.

Key Element	Principle	Operational Framework
Competence	Fit and proper criteria Professional training Formal assessment	*Ex-ante*: Screening process *Ex-post*: Review and assessment
Independence	Adequate capability to exercise objective judgment Complete, adequate, and timely information	*Ex-ante*: Appointment, disclosure, and full mandate *Ex-post*: Review and assessment
Confidentiality	Strictly observe confidentiality	*Ex-ante*: Undertaking secrecy *Ex-post*: Review and assessment
Consistency	Fully understanding the legal and regulatory framework strictly observes the said framework	There must be consistency in all *ex-ante* and *ex-post* SG processes

Source: IFSB (2009). Modified by Hasan (2011b).

(i) Pronouncement or adoption of a relevant Shariah resolution. An Islamic financial institution's SSB may deliver a legal ruling on any question of Shariah compliance.
(ii) Communicating such Shariah rulings or decisions to IFI operational staff who are responsible for ensuring their implementation across all levels of business and in every transaction. However, this is often handled by the organization's Shariah compliance team.
(iii) According to an internal Shariah compliance assessment or audit, all instances of non-compliance should be noted, addressed, and corrected. IFSB-3 states that the Shariah decision made by the SSBs should be scrupulously followed in this regard.
(iv) Annual compliance with Shariah review or audit to ensure that the SSBs have taken notice of the results of the internal Shariah compliance assessment or audit and acted accordingly.

IFSB explains in further detail how the Shariah system of governance enhances the IFIS's preexisting capabilities in these areas. From a governance standpoint, IFIs should have both a BOD and an SSB. Internal and external Shariah assessment units, in addition to the standard internal and external auditors, should be used by IFIs as part of the control system. When it comes to rules and regulations, IFIs must also follow Sharia law. However, depending on the types of structures established by IFIs and allowed by the competent authorities, the exact extent may vary from one region to the next in practice. IFSB also has five sets of guidelines. Competency, independence, secrecy, and consistency are all covered, in addition to the overarching approach of the SG system.

4.11   Bank Negara Malaysia (BNM) Shariah Governance Framework

Bank Negara Malaysia (BNM) has issued an SGF with the following goals: (1) to establish the bank's desires on an IFI's SG structures, processes, and arrangements; (2) to provide an in-depth manual to the SSB, and management of the IFI in discharging their obligations in matters relating to Shariah; and (3) to outline the functions related to Shariah compliance for the IFI. Typically, there are six distinct parts to a discussion of the framework: the basic need; monitoring; accountability and responsibility; independence; competence; secrecy and Shariah compliance; and the research role. While the BNM does anticipate conformity from every institution's SSB, it does not conduct Shariah compliance inspections at this time.

Key organs in the SG system include the board, Shariah, the committee, management, and Shariah compliance and study duties, all of which are required by Shariah law. IFIs are tasked with developing a robust SG structure in accordance with the BNM SG structure, with special attention paid to the roles of the framework's major functionality. When it comes to the supervision, accountability, and duty of the SG structure, IFIs need to spell out the roles and responsibilities of every key player. IFIS must guarantee the quality of Shariah decisions and highlight the role of the BOD in respecting the committee's independence in order to safeguard its autonomy.

In addition, the SSB must always be free from outside influence so that it may make fair and balanced judgments. Anyone at an IFI tasked with carrying out duties outlined in the Shariah framework for governance should be well-versed in the Shariah and up-to-date on the latest trends in Islamic finance. Members of the SSB are expected to keep any sensitive or proprietary information they may get in the course of their obligations to the organization secret and to not utilize such knowledge in any inappropriate way. Professional integrity, good judgment, and uniformity are essential for Shariah compliance.

The framework suggests establishing an internal research capacity and a Shariah compliance department that includes review and auditing operations and is backed by a risk management control mechanism. The goal of Shariah review is to ensure that IFIs are operating in accordance with Shariah principles by having certified Shariah officers do frequent audits. Objectives, scope, requirements for reporting, and next steps must all be thought out as part of the review process. In addition, the outcomes of the evaluation must be communicated to the Shariah board and upper management, as well as documented. Finally, in order to avoid other cases of Shariah disobedience, it is crucial to correct any existing ones.

To evaluate its worth and increase the degree of compliance with regard to the IFI's commercial operation, a Shariah audit is done on a quarterly basis to give an independent review and objective assurance. An audit of the IFI's financial statements, a review of the adequacy of the IFI's SG process, and an audit of the IFI's organizational structure, people, processes, and IT application system are all part of the Shariah audit.

To mitigate the potential for Shariah non-compliance events, it is recommended that Shariah risk management include a component that systematically identifies, measures, monitors, and manages Shariah non-compliance risks. The pre-product approval process, research, issue evaluation, and administrative matters pertaining to the SSB shall be carried out by an internal entity comprising licensed Shariah officers in addition to the aforementioned departments (Kasim *et al.*, 2013).

4.12   Importance of International Standard

All of the guidelines fall short of providing sufficient detail. For instance, the IFSB specifies SG, while AAOIFI and BNM do not. When BNM speaks on the Shariah risk management and research roles, the other two guidelines remain mute. Thus, we would like to propose that we have a single standardized and exhaustive guideline or framework so that it can serve as a convenient resource for industry participants, regulators, and investors.

In addition, a comparative analysis of the guidelines is currently being developed. Financial institutions' Shariah non-compliance function should be emphasized and the research function should be thoroughly covered by the guidelines. Regarding the approach, we believe that, when implementing the CG code, the respective regulators should adopt a prescriptive approach similar to the first approach taken by the United Kingdom. This is because SG is relatively new compared to CG; therefore, it should be obligatory for industry participants to comply. In addition, Shariah compliance is the ultimate goal of the Islamic finance industry; therefore, rigorously instructing industry participants to adhere to SG guidelines will presumably achieve this objective. It is anticipated that the focus of this research will be on the interests of regulators and industrial actors in the future development of the aforementioned guidelines (Kasim *et al.*, 2013).

The IFI has expanded rapidly in a brief period of time, and regulators and international organizations have established the necessary rules and regulations for the IFI to ensure that the objective, Maqasid Shariah, is met. Since this industry offers conventionally comparable products while adhering to Shariah, industrial actors, and Shariah scholars are scrambling to develop products that are both Shariah-compliant and conventionally compatible. Consequently, this industry is replete with numerous complex and sophisticated products. Consequently, it has become difficult for all involved parties, including financiers, accountants, auditors, policymakers, marketing officers, and Shariah advisors, to keep track of these transactions. In addition, the rapidly expanding market must be

172　　　*Shariah Governance Systems of Islamic Banks*

reviewed and revised frequently to ensure Shariah compliance and satisfy market demands.

Concerns regarding Shariah compliance have introduced a new governance dimension that falls under the CG framework. The Islamic system of financial administration is somewhat unique in this regard. SG's primary function is to ensure that the operations of Islamic finance activities comply with the Shariah and do not violate the rights of the parties involved. Due to the relative novelty of the subject, the literature on SG is still limited. Regarding SG regulations, Bank Negara Malaysia (BNM) has issued them. According to Kasim *et al.* (2013), the standards for SG have been supplied by the top international organizations in the field of Islamic finance, such as the IFSB and the AAOIFI.

Table 4.2 shows some of the common institutional arrangements for CG frameworks between IFIs and traditional financial institutions. These are most evident in the areas of governance, management, and compliance. The main distinguishing feature of CG in IFIs is the institutional architecture for their SG process. A Shariah Oversight Board, an external or internal Shariah review, and an organizational Shariah compliance unit are all necessary for IFIs to achieve the religious requirement of Shariah adherence in all areas of their commercial transactions and activities.

The SG system provides an additional layer of CG framework. The SSB and either external or internal Shariah supervision are additional entities responsible for ensuring Shariah compliance, which just depicts the unique CG framework for typical IFIs. According to the AAOIFI governance guidelines, the SSB should have the same status as the BOD and be directly accountable to the shareholders. The IFSB-10 method, on the other hand, places the SSB in a subordinate or parallel role to the BOD. However, the Supervisory Board of Shariah must be separate from the BOD and

Table 4.2:　Institutional Arrangement in the Shariah Governance System.

Functions	Typical Financial Institutions	Exclusive to IFIs
Governance	BOD	Shariah Supervisory Board
Control	Internal Auditor/External Auditor	Internal Shariah Review Unit/External Shariah Review
Compliance	Regulatory and Financial Compliance Officers/Unit/Department	Internal Shariah Compliance Unit

Source: Modified from IFSB (2009: 4).

Historical Development of Shariah Governance

accountable to all stakeholders, not only shareholders, according to the AAOIFI and the IFSB.

4.13 Resolution Framework

Resolution is a procedure that guarantees the orderly liquidation/ restructuring of a bank through the use of resolution instruments by a resolution authority. Its purpose is to ensure the continuity of its essential functions and prevent the failure of a particular bank from escalating into a systemic banking crisis. An effective resolution regime should be built in such a way that it can detect the problem, act in a timely manner, and choose the most suitable instrument to address the issue. Although there are no universal criteria that define what makes an effective resolution regime, such a regime should be constructed in such a way that it can achieve these three goals. This may include the authority to transfer or merge the business of a troubled bank with another bank, to establish an interim bridge bank to operate its critical functions, to segregate its good and poor assets, and to transform failing banks' debt into shares or write it down bail-in.

In 2014, the International Monetary Fund (IMF) surveyed the resolution framework for IBs in a number of countries where IBs operate. With the exception of Yemen and Jordan, the framework for Islamic bank distress resolution does not differ from that of conventional banks in the majority of cases, as determined by the survey. With the single exception of Afghanistan, there are no significant distinctions between Islamic and conventional banks in terms of the regulatory framework for enforcement, remedial actions, and procedures. Regarding the seizure of a problematic bank by the respective regulatory agency, the regulatory authority can assume the administration of a troubled bank in order to administer a proper resolution process. Palestine is the only exception to this rule. Very few countries have comprehensively addressed the issue of bank resolution in the context of Islamic banking (Song and Oosthuizen, 2014).

In contrast to the absence of a resolution framework for IBs, conventional banks in many countries have well-established resolution frameworks that have been tested repeatedly, particularly during the global financial crisis. Consequently, enormous alterations are occurring in areas that require them. A resolution framework for Islamic institutions is still in its infancy, and Islamic subsidiaries present additional potential complexities.

Generally speaking, subsidiaries are typically smaller than full-fledged Islamic institutions. According to Wilson (2004), lesser institutions are more susceptible to run-on deposits due to a loss of consumer confidence. In a similar vein, the parent company of the subsidiary could have its headquarters in a country other than the one in which the subsidiary is physically located. Researchers have cautioned against the additional repercussions that might be brought about by such circumstances. For example, the IMF (1998) emphasized that cross-border expansion can present a number of difficulties for regulators. This is especially true for emergent market nations that are still developing their legal and accounting systems and have limited supervisory resources. These obstacles include:

- First, to escape regulation and effective supervision, a variety of corporate structures can be created across international borders.
- Second, domestic prudential regulations can be easily circumvented due to the growing ability of banks to shift their activities to tax havens in offshore jurisdictions.
- Third, if disclosure laws and accounting practices are relatively unsophisticated, cross-border transactions may be resorted to in order to conceal problems at the level of local financial institutions by way of booking troubled assets with subsidiaries or other offshore entities.
- Fourth, offshore transactions could also be used to facilitate outright fraud.

On the basis of these concerns, it appears that the resolution of Islamic subsidiaries, particularly when the parent is an external entity, will present additional challenges for regulators.

Due to the recent development of IBs and the varying levels of development between various jurisdictions in which they operate, the issue of liquidating an Islamic bank remains unresolved, and numerous challenges lie ahead (Song and Oosthuizen, 2014). Wilson (2004) identified a significant challenge: if a bank operates in more than one country, the central bank of its native country will perform the primary supervisory role. Other host nation central banks will rely on it to demonstrate efficient supervision. However, the most difficult situation would arise in the event that the home nation has Islamized its financial system while the host country has not. This will create difficulties in terms of the compatibility of rules and regulations. Similarly, designing a resolution framework for jurisdictions with both conventional and IBs operating concurrently presents a unique challenge. Islamic banking operations may take the form of full-fledged IBs, Islamic banking windows, or subsidiary IBs in accordance with the legal and regulatory framework. If any of these things happen, and Islamic banking activities are carried out in conjunction with conventional banking practices, then the resolution framework will need to be altered in such a way that takes into account the interaction between conventional banks and Islamic banking practices.

The preceding discussion has made it abundantly clear that the problem of establishing a resolution framework that is applicable to IBs is a complex one. In this regard, there is much work to be done, and Islamic banking subsidiaries will present additional obstacles. This is also true because subsidiaries may be located overseas, which presents a unique challenge. From a regulatory standpoint, the resolution of a regime consisting of only full-fledged Islamic institutions seems preferable in this scenario (Zada, 2017).

There are three instances that, taken together, may indicate potential flaws in the CG of IIFs. The first is not making sure everyone's religious preferences are taken into account. The other two incidents show how the long-term viability and stability of the Islamic financial system throughout its entirety can be impacted by weak CG structures, both internally and externally. This is especially true for the relatively vulnerable investors who hold UIAs. The CG of an Islamic bank must be consistent with Shariah law. Typically, an institution would either set up an SSB or hire Shariah advisers to guarantee the Shariah compliance of its financial operations in order to reassure its constituents. However, the amount of activity, the availability of monitoring tools, the intricacy of financial transactions, and the level of independence may all limit the ability of the SSB or Shariah advisers to carry out their tasks. Multiple IIFS were engaged in the collapse of Bank of Credit and Commerce International (BCCI), and these factors may have played a role in its demise. Five IFIs placed significant deposits with BCCI, a leading CFS organization, with the expectation that the money would be invested in commodities contracts compliant with Shariah law. After BCCI's collapse, the bank's auditor, Price Waterhouse, said, "there is not any proof to suggest that the financial institution actually entered into commodity agreements." The revelation was particularly important because of how widespread the IIFS's vulnerability was in the BCCI. A study indicates that one of the IIFS in question placed 25% of its assets with the BCCI. The severity of the risk points to a lack of evidence supporting

Shariah compliance due diligence. The situation is representative of the greater difficulties an SSB may face while attempting to do its purpose. Inadequate internal and external controls led to the 2001 collapse of Turkey's Ihlas Finance House (IFH), which is a prime example of the impacts of capture by special interests.

CHAPTER 5

Shariah Governance Framework in Islamic Banks

5.1 Introduction

The economic sector is crucial to the expansion of a nation's economy, and the relevant government is crucial to the creation of a clear Shariah Governance Framework (SGF) to oversee the overall operations of the Islamic finance (IF) sector. By using the underlying Shariah principles to implement the present corporate governance (CG) of Islamic banks (IB), SGF is different from the traditional CG structure. In this situation, the Shariah Supervisory Board (SSB) is crucial to the implementation of the laws and regulations of Shariah as well as the central and decentralized supervision of IBs' Shariah-related matters.

5.2 Shariah Governance Framework in Islamic Banks

A framework is a physical or conceptual roadmap intended to guide, support, and expand a structure into something useful. Governance framework refers to the set of rules and practices by which a board of directors (BOD) assures accountability, impartiality, and transparency in a company's relationships with all of its stakeholders (financiers, customers, management, employees, government, and the community). The governance framework reflects the institution's interdependent relationships, factors, and other influences through its structure. It outlines an organization's authority and governing or management responsibilities. In addition, the governance framework defines, directs, and facilitates the enforcement of these processes. These frameworks are formed by the organization's objectives, strategic mandates, financial incentives, and established power structures and processes.

One example of the Islamic CG structure is presented by Rahman (1998). This framework incorporates Shariah and Islamic moral principles with a focus on the organizations of *shura, hisbah*, and religious audit. The effectiveness of every corporate decision that may influence the company is ensured by the establishment of *shura*, which consists of the administration, BOD, shareholders, employees, customers, and other interested parties. While the SSB is focused on making legal judgments and providing Shariah advising and supervisory services, the *hisbah* and the religious auditors are responsible for monitoring the ethical and legal compliance of businesses.

Choudhury and Hoque (2004) provide an example of a more comprehensive Islamic CG system. They established the structure and suitable levels of each organization, as well as its responsibilities and activities, aims and purposes, and governing rules, depending on the epistemologies of Tawhid and Shura. By highlighting the regulatory structures of Islamic law in addition to ordinary banking law and regulations, Nienhaus (2007) presented an additional instance of the Islamic CG structure. An Islamic business culture and governance framework was conceptualized by Banaga *et al.* (1994). In general, scholars such as Choudhury and Hoque (2004), Nienhaus (2007), Banaga *et al.* (1994), and Rahman (1998) agree that a conceptual framework of Islamic CG must account for the epistemology of Tawhid, the Shuratic process the concept of vicegerency (*khalifah*), social justice (*al-adlwalihsn*), responsibilities (*taklf*), and regulatory aspects of Islamic law. Although the groundwork has been laid conceptually, it is difficult to put all of the previously mentioned ideas and Islamic rules into practice inside the business. Actually, as mentioned by Banaga *et al.* (1994), an Islamic business organization's adoption of Shariah, moral, and ethical standards does not guarantee superior financial results. Alam *et al.* (2021d) illustrated that IBs in Bangladesh are neither following the Shariah principles in all of the segments of Shariah governance (SG) nor violating them completely as a result of lower accountability, which contradicts the concept of the Tawhidi epistemological process of Islamic CG. It is found that IBs in Bangladesh have a lower practice of *maqasid* as Shariah and Tawhidic approach and Shuratic process.

IBs must follow SG in addition to the requirements of any applicable CG framework. Without such a structure in place, there is a greater chance that infractions will occur with negative financial and social consequences.

The biggest of them is the decline in public trust in Islamic institutions and businesses (Zada *et al.*, 2017). Due to the nature of certain IBs' unique products, which resemble property but are not perfect equity, governance is also of the highest significance in the case of IBs. When there is tension between the bank's management and its SSB, IBs may provide light on important questions of Shariah and CG. According to Zada *et al.* (2017), the bank's SSB is supposed to evaluate the institution's conformity through Shariah review, Shariah audit, Shariah research, and Shariah risk management. Alam *et al.* (2021b) outlined that the IBs expect the SSB members to provide opinions on Shariah issues, guidelines, and decisions regarding modern banking, practices, and delivery of *fatwas* on the contemporary issues offered by the management to fulfill the demand of the numerous stakeholders. In addition, they can also develop SG policies and implement those guidelines, approve and develop new products, observe and monitor banking functions, identify problems, and outline solutions as well as ensure Shariah principles and compliance. The SSB members perform roles and functions in monitoring and reviewing overall banking activities and functions such as reviewing products, services, and contracts, preparing SG guidelines, ensuring Shariah principles and compliance, providing opinions on existing SG practices, and finally, delivering Shariah resolutions on the overall functions (Alam *et al.*, 2021b). According to the basic approach of the SG system, good governance practice comprises both *ex-ante* and *ex-post* processes. Shariah resolutions and compliance checks are examples of *ex-ante* procedures that must take place before a product can be sold to customers (Kasim *et al.*, 2013).

5.3   Shariah Governance Mechanism in Islamic Banks

The roles and responsibilities of investors and depositors, the BOD, management, and the SSB must be explored in order to fully understand and appreciate the SGF and compliance with Shariah in Islamic institutions. In contrast to their conventional counterparts, IBs include a wider range of stakeholders in their CG, including the SSB of Directors, religious auditing firms, and customers who deposit money, notably investment account holders (IAHs). Management and supervision, Shariah advice, Shariah compliance and review, and openness and disclosure are the four pillars of Minhas's (2012) complete SG system. The primary CG actors in Islamic institutions are shown in Table 5.1, along with a short description of their roles and duties.

Shariah Governance Systems of Islamic Banks

Table 5.1: The Key Participants in CG in IBs.

Key Participants	Participants	Roles
Regulatory Authority	Economic stability	Set a regulatory framework for sound and proper corporate governance
Supervisory Authority	Compliance with the laws and regulations	To supervise and monitor the effectiveness of corporate governance and to check compliance with regulations
Shareholders	Profit maximization; satisfactory earnings per share; dividends; above-average return on investment; and excellent continuous growth	Appoint fit and proper boards, management auditors, and Shariah Supervisory Board
IAHs	Repayment of deposits at maturity on the agreed terms; protection of their interests and profit	To monitor the investment performance
SSB	Compliance with Shariah and fulfilling *maqasid* Shariah	To ensure Shariah compliance and protect the rights and interests of depositors and other stakeholders Set Shariah-related rules and principles Provide a clearance of Shariah compatibility of all products Oversee compliance and its verdict to create confidence with respect to compatibility with Sharia
BOD	Monetary and non-monetary compensation; managing the company efficiently, effectively, and with high integrity; outstanding corporate reputation and brand	To set the IBs' direction and policies Monitor progress toward corporate objectives Ensure accountability of the management Protect Shareholders' and Investment depositors' rights
Management	Monetary and non-monetary compensation; and commitment to claims of the contract	To implement policies set by the BOD

Source: Modified from Hasan (2011b); Chapra and Ahmed (2002).

By outlining the rules and regulations and legal environment, the regulatory body plays a significant role in CG as an external instrument of governance. Its other duties include drafting rules for IBs, creating risk management and transparency benchmarks, and keeping an eye on how the industry as a whole is run. To ensure that these requirements are being followed, the supervisory body must also oversee and monitor the CG structure (Hasan, 2011b).

The shareholders must choose qualified individuals for the BOD, the Board of Management Auditors, and the SSB. Islamic bank shareholders, unlike those of conventional banks, are obligated to elect an SSB. The AAOIFI Governance Standards affirm this by requiring the shareholders to elect members of the SSB. What distinguishes IBs from conventional banks is that shareholders vote on who will serve on the SSB and who will be nominated to the board. The Shariah oversight committee may therefore advise and oversee the company without fear of retaliation from the BOD, making this role essential.

The BOD is accountable for carrying out the recommendations of the SSB and supervising and monitoring the management to guarantee that all business operations are compliant with Shariah principles (Alam, 2022; AAOIFI, 2010; BNM, 2019; IFSB, 2006). The BOD is responsible for establishing the vision, mission, core values, and standards of behavior for the company (Chapra and Ahmed, 2002; Alam, 2022). The BOD must have the necessary experience to comprehend and value *maqasid* Shariah and have at least a basic understanding of the principles and regulations of Shariah in order to fulfill their CG responsibilities. In addition to maximizing profits for shareholders, the company's management is also concerned with the well-being of its employees, suppliers, customers, and the community at large (IFSB, 2006: 3–4). The BOD must oversee the creation of a governance framework for policies in accordance with the principles of IFSB-3. By adhering to these principles, the BOD will ensure that the company's profit-driven business plan is balanced with the interests and rights of all stakeholders, including depositors, workers, and consumers (Alam, 2022).

Furthermore, the BODs may demand that management report on the operations of IBs, including all issues of Shariah compliance (BNM, 2019; IFSB, 2006). According to many researches, this would improve the trust and confidence between shareholders and others in the Islamic banking business (Alam, 2021, 2022, 2021; Alam *et al.*, 2020a, 2020b, 2020c, 2020d,

2022; Van Greuning and Iqbal, 2008; Chapra and Ahmed, 2002). When it comes to carrying out the BOD's policies and programs, management has a more direct fiduciary role than the BOD itself. Management acts as a trustee for the BOD, shareholders, and other interested parties. In light of this, it is crucial that management always act in an honest and frugal manner. Management must have an in-depth familiarity with the *maqasid* Shariah doctrine and other Islamic principles in order to protect the interests of all parties involved in their duties. Since management is responsible for running day-to-day IFIs, the IFSB-3 considers it a vital entity for ensuring that the direction and all business transactions conform with Shariah standards and are aligned with the interests of all stakeholders (IFSB, 2006: 16).

It is generally agreed that the SSB is a crucial participant in Islamic CG (Alam, 2022). The SSB is a unique part of the corporate structure of Islamic businesses. For the purpose of supervising and monitoring the execution of the governance policy framework in partnership with management and the audit committee, each IFI is required by Principle 13 of the IFSB-3 (IFSB, 2006: 3) to form a Shariah board with at least three members. The SSB is widely recognized as an integral part of the CG structures responsible for Shariah regulation. The primary roles are advisory and supervisory, and they include providing guidance to IFIs on how to run their businesses, studying and analyzing the Shariah implications of any banking or financing activity, and keeping tabs on how strictly such activities adhere to Islamic law (Alam *et al.*, 2022b).

Shariah officers are a significant SG mechanism for Islamic institutions. Shariah officers are viewed as an essential component of the governance of SSBs in providing Shariah compliance assurance for IB operations (Zaidi, 2008). As a result of this, the Shariah officers play an important part in aiding the SSB in the field of *ex-post* Shariah compliance responsibilities (BNM, 2019; IFSB, 2009). Monitoring the internal Shariah control system of IBs by ensuring that all transactions and operations are conducted in accordance with the Shariah advice provided by the SSBs is one of the most important responsibilities of these Shariah officers. Shariah officers are essentially subject to the same requirements as SSBs in that they must possess a Shariah qualification background (BNM, 2019; IFSB, 2009). In addition to educational qualifications, Shariah officers are expected to demonstrate high levels of integrity and impartiality when carrying out their duties (BNM, 2019; IFSB, 2009).

According to studies, IFIs face formidable obstacles in the area of *ex-post* Shariah compliance procedures, where their internal governance mechanisms are held accountable. Hassan (2012) conducted one of the empirical studies in this field, in which he identified deficiencies in the implementation of Shariah compliance review involving multiple stakeholders within Malaysian Islamic institutions. Hassan (2012) revealed, among other things, that the SSB had doubts about the authenticity of the Shariah compliance review procedure conducted by various stakeholders within the management of Islamic institutions. Hassan (2012) also reported instances in which the upper management of Islamic institutions dictated operational issues despite objections from the SSB. Alam *et al.* (2020d) outlined that management and BOD influence the activities of SSB and their decision-making as well as SG activities. Moreover, Alam *et al.* (2023b) and Alam and Miah (2021) outlined that SSB and Shariah department officers are not independent in the SG functions, decision-making, and Shariah implementations. Hassan (2012) proposed, in light of these findings, that the SSB should focus on its advisory role, while the responsibility of Shariah compliance review and the issuance of the relevant Shariah compliance report should be assigned to an External Shariah Auditor in order to improve the quality of Shariah compliance assurance. Moreover, Alam *et al.* (2022a) outlined the formation of an external Shariah Audit and Review Committee to better ensure Shariah compliance along with internal Shariah audit and review. Establishing a Shariah audit framework and an effective Shariah audit program in IBs, according to studies (Alam *et al.*, 2023a; Uddin *et al.*, 2013; Shafii *et al.*, 2010), may reduce the Shariah non-compliance risk and facilitate the harmonization of Shariah practice across IBs.

The significance of internal SG mechanisms was also addressed in the standards and guidelines of the regulations. The Islamic Financial Services Board (IFSB, for instance, stipulates that Islamic institutions must appoint Shariah officers to assist SSBs with the Shariah compliance review function (IFSB, 2006: 23). The IFSB also outlined that the Shariah officer must be adequately trained and possess the necessary expertise to ensure that the Shariah review functions are carried out in an appropriate manner. Moreover, Tabash *et al.* (2022) found that IBs are not properly following SG functions and are negatively legitimized due to Shariah violations. In addition, the regulatory body emphasized that Shariah officers may require management to rectify Shariah compliance-related issues (IFSB, 2009: 3; Haridan, 2016).

In conclusion, Islamic CG adds value to the existing governance structure by emphasizing faith, ethics, and Shariah principles. A distinctive

184 *Shariah Governance Systems of Islamic Banks*

aspect of the Islamic CG model necessitates an additional layer of governance structure to accomplish all of these elements. In this regard, IBs require a specific organizational structure as part of their CG framework to ensure Shariah compliance and independent supervision of Shariah-related issues (Tabash *et al.*, 2022; Alam *et al.*, 2022b).

5.4 Conceptual Framework of Shariah Governance Systems

SG guidelines or recommendations have been produced for Islamic financial organizations by a number of nations (including Malaysia) and organizations (including the AAOIFI and the IFSB). The problem is that these laws or norms cannot be approved and implemented universally by all Islamic organizations because, first, they aren't applicable to Islamic companies in general, and second, they aren't enforceable around the world. Now that domestic and regional Shariah CG has been established, supporters and financiers of IF should realize that it is time to give SG the flavor of globalization by applying a Code consistent to all Islamic business entities, regardless of location (Muneeza and Hassan, 2014). It is not even defined in detail in AAOIFI Governance Standard No. 1–5. Therefore, it is essential to understand what is meant by the phrase "SG system" and to have a clear definition of the word. The IFSB-10's definition of Shariah-compliant governance may be the most precise currently available. The SG system is defined by the IFSB-10 as "a set of institutional and organizational arrangements through which IFIs maintain that there exists an efficient independent oversight of compliance with Shariah all through the issuance of relevant Shariah pronouncements, propagation of information, and an internal Shariah compliance review" (IFSB, 2009: 2). Alam *et al.* (2021a) defined SG as a system of ensuring Shariah compliance in the overall functions of the IBs, while Shariah denotes some rules, regulations, guidelines, objectives, and directions to enhance accurate functions and activities. There are three main parts to this definition that are necessary for a full understanding:

(i) *The set of institutional and organizational arrangements*: This refers to the SSB and its related institutions, such as an internal audit department and Shariah division.
(ii) *Effective independent oversight of Shariah compliance*: This indicates the aims and objectives of the SG system to provide efficient mechanisms for the purpose of Shariah compliance.

(iii) *Shariah pronouncements, dissemination of information, and an internal Shariah compliance review*: This involves the overall SG processes that cover both *ex-ante* and *ex-post* aspects of the Shariah compliance framework.

According to this interpretation, the SSB has the ultimate authority in determining whether or not an IFI is Shariah-compliant, making it a crucial part of the SG structure. According to AAOIFI (2005: 4), "An independent body assigned with the duty of managing, reviewing, and overseeing the activities of IFIs for the objective of complying with Shariah and issuing rulings on legal issues pertaining to Islamic banking and financing." The IFSB-10 uses a similar description, calling it "a body consisting of a panel of Islamic scholars who provide Shariah knowledge and act as special consultants to the institutions" (IFSB, 2009: 1). In order to fulfill its role effectively, the SSB needs a unique structure and framework that guarantees its independence, the binding power of its judgments, its impartiality, and the breadth of its mission. The SG system, thus, includes any mechanism for the direction, administration, administration, and control of the Shariah oversight board for Shariah compliance, whether official or informal.

SG is unique from other forms of financial architectural governance because it prioritizes religious considerations in all IFI endeavors (Hasan, 2011b). To demonstrate the reasoning of the SG system inside the existing CG paradigm in IFIs, Table 5.2 provides examples of how SG compliments the current framework.

Table 5.2 shows some of the common institutional arrangements for CG frameworks between IFIs and traditional financial institutions. These are most evident in the areas of governance, management, and compliance. The main distinguishing feature of CG in IFIs is the institutional architecture for their SG process. SSB, an external or internal Shariah review, and an organizational Shariah compliance unit are all necessary for IFIs to

Table 5.2: Institutional Arrangement in the SG System.

Functions	Typical Financial Institutions	Exclusive to IBs
Governance	BOD	SSB
Control	Internal Auditor/External Auditor	Internal Shariah Review Unit/ External Shariah Review
Compliance	Regulatory and Financial Compliance Officers/Unit/ Department	Internal Shariah Compliance Unit

Source: Modified from IFSB (2009: 4).

achieve the religious requirement of Shariah compliance in all areas of their commercial transactions and activities.

The SG system adds another layer of governance to the already established CG framework. Addition to the Board of Shariah Advisors, traditional IBs also have internal and external Shariah reviews to ensure Shariah observance. According to the AAOIFI governance guidelines, the SSB should have the same status as the BOD and be directly accountable to the shareholders. The IFSB-10 method, on the other hand, places the SSB in a subordinate or parallel role to the BOD. However, the SSB must be separate from the BOD and accountable to all stakeholders, not only shareholders, according to the AAOIFI and the IFSB.

The SG structure covers both the up-front, like the issuing of Shariah judgments and the distribution of Shariah-related information, and the back-end, such as the periodic and yearly internal Shariah review process.

It is seen in Figure 5.1 how far-reaching SG systems inside IFIs really are. There is a certain process that must be followed, and many

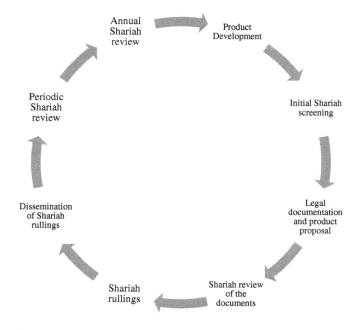

Figure 5.1: Scope of the SGF.
Source: Dar (2009): Cited in Hasan (2011b). (Modified).

different organizations must be involved. Phase 1, procedures 1–6, represent *ex-ante* Shariah compliance considerations such as product proposal, legal paperwork, Shariah assessment, and the acquisition and distribution of Shariah judgments. *Ex-post* procedures, such as semiannual and annual Shariah reviews, are shown in the processes 7–8 diagram of Phase 2. Only with effective Shariah coordination and a capable internal Shariah review unit can the SSB fulfill its responsibility of assuring the legality of the goods and services. The Shariah coordinator is responsible for coordinating the SG process from the initial conception of the product through the yearly Shariah review insert process.

5.5 Central Banks' Role in Islamic Banking Governance

How can we build a new and strong foundation for a new system of Islamic banking governance and surveillance that can strengthen our capacity for more financial sector development input into the sustained development and the sector's capacity to prevent crises and advance countries' shared goals of stability by adopting the proposed conceptual and pragmatic approach? We should acknowledge the innovative contributions and pioneering roles of the business people and institutions that started the investment in Islamic banking, as well as the regional and global financial institutions, including international Islamic banking, that have played a pioneering role in laying the institutional foundation for the growth of the Islamic banking sector while achieving a successful takeoff and supporting their growth. We also value the contributions made by regional and other international institutions, research and training facilities, and other organizations. All of these entities have helped Islamic banking operate and develop in accordance with established standards and best practices that are similar to those of other countries. A number of multinational entities have just lately been created to help governments and regulatory bodies understand Islamic banking and issue standards and best-practice guidelines for this sector. These organizations include the Islamic Development Bank (ISDB), the AAOIFI (Annexes 1 and 2), and the IFSB. These organizations exist in addition to the International Monetary Fund (IMF), the Arab Monetary Fund (AMF), and other institutions like the Bank for International Settlements (BIS). The relevant authorities should hold discussions with the local stakeholders in this sector to encourage an open and free exchange of ideas and information (Sole, 2007). To this purpose, the IFSB was created in 2002 as an organization that develops global standards for prudential regulation and oversight of IFIs. The IFSB has made progress in formulating prudential standards for risk management frameworks and capital sufficiency in this regard. The IFSB has also been developing guidelines for CG. In order to achieve secure banking activities, some countries have embraced Basel 2 and the most recent 3 Accord standards in their regulatory and supervisory framework for their Islamic banking business, particularly for capital sufficiency in connection to asset management risks. These guidelines, which were created by BIS, have inadequacies since they did not adequately address the requirements of Islamic banking operations and transactions (Beseiso, 2014).

5.6 Four Basic Pillars of a Shariah Governance Model

Political support is believed to be the primary factor behind the promotion of Islamic finance in any country. Nonetheless, an accommodating regulatory and oversight framework for effective SG is essential for its development. To describe SG as the industry's conscience would not be inaccurate. It offers a thorough framework to guarantee adherence to Islamic business principles. If SG is disregarded, it is impossible to ensure the existence of a functioning Islamic financial system and markets. Thus, Minhas (2012) outlined that a comprehensive SG system is founded on the four pillars listed in Figure 5.2.

5.6.1 *Management and Supervision*

When it comes to management, the BOD takes center stage in SG. The BOD, upper management, and organizational framework all provide insight into the company's underlying values and practices. The ability of any organization, but especially an IFI, to succeed hinges on its leadership's desire to embrace and institutionalize Islamic ideals. For a firm to be legitimate and acceptable under Shariah administration, it is the exclusive obligation of management to provide sufficient resources, system processes, infrastructure, and a code of ethics. Just having the right rules and mechanisms in place isn't enough without proper management and oversight. The following are some of the bare minimum standards for management that may be imposed by authorities in an effort to enhance outcomes:

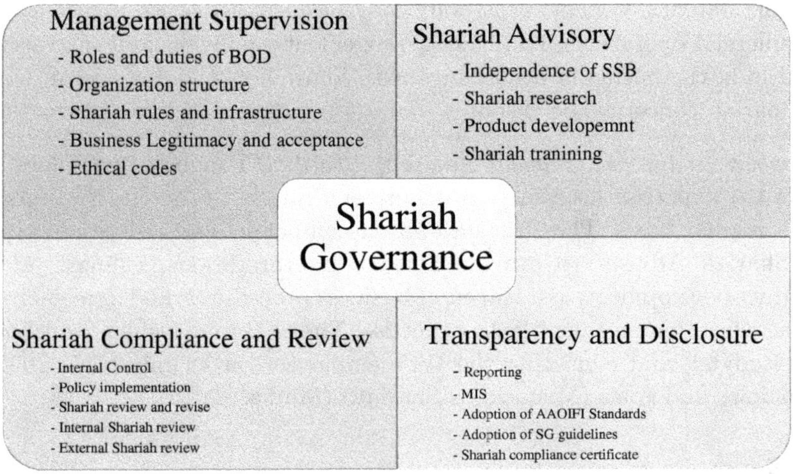

Figure 5.2: Four Pillars of SG System.
Source: Modified from Minhas (2012).

- Appropriateness standards for the BOD and executive leadership;
- Shariah risk-management strategies that take a methodical approach to assessing, mitigating, and reporting on the potential for Shariah-related non-compliance;
- The Shariah Advisory Board's responsibilities and duties;
- IFI activities are Halal and free from Riba, Qimar, and Gharar thanks to the introduction of finance agreements and Shariah compliance system;
- The purification of income and the administration of charitable giving;
- The screening procedure for investments in stocks and securities (Minhas, 2012).

5.6.2 *Shariah Advisory Board*

An impartial Shariah advisory council or Shariah advisor is the model's second fundamental component. The Shariah Advisory Body at the regulatory level and the in-house advisor/board inside the IFI are the two ideal tiers of the SSB. Both advisory panels' functions will be explained in more detail as follows.

The Shariah Council of America: This is the top Shariah advisory body in the nation, responsible for outlining the basic framework of the

190   *Shariah Governance Systems of Islamic Banks*

Islamic banking system. This body may be responsible for approving the commercial operations, financing arrangements, policies, and instructions of IFIs in the nation in accordance with Shariah as the decisive authority in Shariah concerns and disputes.

Members of the IFI Shariah Advisory Board: IFI management does not have the expertise necessary to understand Shariah concerns that emerge on a regular basis. The IFI must hire a competent and independent SSB or Shariah Advisor to provide Shariah interpretations, rulings, *fatwas*, product development, assessment of business procedures, and agreements in areas where management lacks expertise. The SSB may also be responsible for studying and educating the IFI's employees on Islamic law's guiding principles and goals (Maqasid as-Shariah) (Minhas, 2012).

5.6.3 *Shariah Compliance and Review*

Shariah compliance and review is the third fundamental pillar of the SG model. Shariah compliance includes regular Shariah assessment and evaluation of the efficacy of internal controls. To accomplish these objectives and to promote an atmosphere of Shariah non-compliance risk consciousness across the business, a Shariah audit department will be set up and report to the Board's internal audit committee. For several reasons, the public does not consider the internal audit to be an adequate and trustworthy tool. Independent external Shariah audits of IFIs are to be done by statutory auditors, who are obliged to build their capability by engaging competent Shariah auditors, in order to instill more trust among IFIs' stakeholders. Until audit firms establish a trustworthy Shariah audit system, IFIs may utilize an in-house SSB or advisor to assess their operations and transactions from a Shariah perspective (Minhas, 2012).

5.6.4 *Transparency and Disclosure*

The fourth pillar of the SGF is transparency and disclosure. Capital costs, brand value, investor confidence, and stock value are all significantly impacted by a company's willingness to be transparent and provide relevant information. Stakeholders, shareholders, and the general population are constantly interested in up-to-date and accurate information about a firm, especially when making investment choices. Information may be broken down into two broad classes: financial and non-financial. Insightful reporting on the organization's activities raises its profile, which in turn facilitates the acquisition of low-cost funding from the general public and financial institutions (Minhas, 2012).

The executive level also requires a well-thought-out management information system. Management can make better judgments about the company's future, profitability, competitiveness, and growth if they have access to timely and reliable information.

Major areas of disclosure:

- Details about the IFI, its business strategy, market trends, significant business plans, significant shareholdings, ownership, and voting rights.
- Information on the management, such as the number of directors on the board, the names of the top executives, and their salaries.
- Information on the governance system, including best practices, power transfers, risk areas, regulations, and key performance metrics.
- Information about the company's financial situation, major financial indicators, and significant concerns affecting the company's stakeholders, including workers.
- Predicted risk variables.
- A valid certificate of Shariah compliance from the External Auditor, SSB, or Advisor (Minhas, 2012).

5.7 Shariah Governance Framework Model

IBs must follow SG in addition to the requirements of any applicable CG framework. The biggest ones are the loss of confidence among customers and the damage to the reputation of Islamic organizations. Due to the nature of certain IBs' unique products, which approach equity but are not perfect equity, governance is also of the highest significance in the context of IBs. In order to augment their current CG structure, Islamic organizations have implemented an SG system. IBs are distinguished from their conventional counterparts by their unique CG structure, which is based on the SG system. One of the most important features of Islamic bank CG is the SSB. It oversees the observance of Shariah, conducts audits, and issues judicial judgments. An SSB ensures that Islamic financial organizations are adhering to Shariah regulations, such as the *zakat* duty, in their daily operations.

The SSB is crucial for ensuring that Islamic organizations adhere to the Shariah's standards for good administration. The Shariah framework of government is more centralized in Malaysia, Sudan, and Pakistan than it is in Bangladesh. The IB employs SSBs that are separate from the Central

Bank (CB) in line with this approach. Each Islamic bank in Bangladesh has its own SSB responsible for ensuring the bank abides by Islamic law. In a CSGF system, all IB products and operations are subject to regulation by a single SB that is formally associated with the CB. Every IB needs its own SSB, but it must follow the rules set down by the governing SSB. As long as the CB does not try to force its own viewpoints on the SSB, but rather explains the perspectives via open discussion, the establishment of an SSB inside the CB will diminish discrepancies in interpretation (Alam, 2022; Chapra and Khan, 2000).

In the long-term interest of IB, Iqbal *et al.* (1998) advocated creating an autonomous SB to monitor the application of Shariah law. If the Islamic banking system is not seen as Islamic, existing IB will lose a significant chunk of their business, as argued by these writers. The need of the BOD is to understand the function of SG and accept SSB's autonomy. Any interference from above would taint the Shariah judgment and undermine the integrity of the governing process. Truth be told, it's only via fully autonomous mission performance that the SSB can keep its honor. Because of its autonomy, the IB is more credible in the eyes of the public, investors, and businesses. This autonomy is a vital component of responsible leadership. The nomination and remuneration of the SSB should be conducted by an independent body, not the government or CB, to maintain its impartiality. In addition to ensuring data privacy, the SSB's autonomy also ensures it acts without outside influence. Members of the SSB from various IBs are obligated to keep all paperwork and records related to contracts, activities, and activities secret. Another potential conflict of interest arises if the SSB members use this knowledge to their advantage when dealing with management and the BOD. Therefore, an IB should have administrative mechanisms in place to protect its interests if confidentiality is breached.

5.7.1 *Decentralized Shariah Governance Model*

In this setup, IFIs operate under their own SSBs rather than the CB. Each IB in the GCC/Middle Eastern and other nations has a separate SSB, which is responsible for ensuring that the items it offers are compliant with local regulations. CBs in the GCC do not have effective national SSBs. Every Islamic bank in Bangladesh reports to its own SSB, much as they do in the GCC. At the IB level, there are separate SSBs for each individual. Contracts and Shariah-compliant financial products are approved or disapproved by

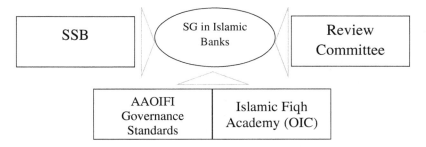

Figure 5.3: SG in GCC.
Source: Modified from Hamza (2013).

the SSBs of these organizations. We see that the bulk of IB SSBs in GCC nations are influenced by AAOIFI board standards and views. When it comes to Sharia compliance, the Central Bank of Bahrain's national SSB solely provides and reviews its own goods. Members of the national SSB are not limited in their ability to work with numerous financial institutions. In line with AAOIFI's Governance Standards, the IB must form an SSB to oversee Sharia compliance and evaluate Sharia-compliant offerings. The SSB is obligated to provide the IB's shareholders with an annual report and assessment of the IB's operations and activities. The aim of the AAOIFI's SSB Harmonization Committee is to ensure that all members of the committee are using the same terminology and principles. Its goal is to help in the development of new goods and to ensure consistency across the SSBs of different organizations. Figure 5.3 illustrates the SG in GCC.

The AAOIFI Governance Standards require the IB to set up an SSB to ensure Shariah-compliant goods. An annual report and evaluation of the IB's operations and activities must be submitted to the shareholders by the SSB. The AAOIFI was established to ensure that the various IB SSBs were using the same terminology and principles in their deliberations. Its goal is to help in the development of new goods and to ensure consistency across the SSBs of different institutions. It has been argued that this paradigm invites conflicts of interest by permitting a Shariah expert to sit on more than one SSB at once. The SC and the bank's staff are not validated under this approach, and there are no clear criteria for reporting Shariah non-compliance instances to the CB. The independence of the audit report would be jeopardized if the SC were given permission to undertake an external audit.

5.7.2 Centralized Shariah Governance Model

Shariah government has several forms in different parts of the world (Arshad and Wardhany, 2012). When it comes to matters of centralization, every single CB and government in the world has an SSB. The concept of centralization may be broken down into either a one- or two-tiered system. The banking operations in this sector are regulated and overseen by a single SSB under a Centralized format. In the "Centralized model" as used in Morocco, *fatwa* is Centralized in a single committee. However, how feasible this framework would be given the high volume of inquiries an IFI would get on a daily basis is still up in the air. In Morocco, the *fatwa* development at the institutional level is prioritized within a one-tier CSGF. This is helpful in the commencement of any country's journey toward Islamic banking, as it allows for the creation of *fatwas*, laws, and regulations for the growth of IBs. There is still a lot of mystery around the queries and implementations of this paradigm from the perspective of regular labor (Soualhi, 2016). In addition, a one-tier model may function during the organization's inauguration but not afterward (Soualhi, 2016), since it has been decided that an individual SSB is essential to monitor the Islamic bank's operations on a daily basis in the operation of IBs.

Some countries, like Malaysia and Sudan, use a "two-tier Centralized model" that consists of a Shariah Advisory Council (SAC) at the CB and an SSB (SC) at individual IFIs to increase Shariah compliance at the tier-2 level. However, the Sudanese framework has not yet reached the level of Malaysia in terms of comprehensiveness, structure, and applicability. Shariah law is used as the basis for the government of Malaysia, Pakistan, and Sudan. SSBs exist at the national level in Bahrain, Malaysia, Sudan, Indonesia, the United Arab Emirates (UAE), Pakistan, Brunei, and Oman. The Bangladeshi SSB is an autonomous body established by the country's Islamic institutions. It's a consultancy firm. The CB failed to incorporate it into its design and thus does not have the power to regulate financial institutions. Self-regulation seems to be the norm in Western countries like Luxembourg, the United Kingdom, and the United States.

Each Islamic bank will have its own SSB in addition to the Centralized SAC or CSSB at the CB. The two-tiered or Centralized method relies on a single, CB-affiliated SSB to ensure that all IB goods and operations are in line with the law. Every IB needs its own SSB, but it must follow the rules set down by the governing SSB (Alam, 2022). As long as the CB does not try to force its own viewpoints on the SSB, but rather explains the

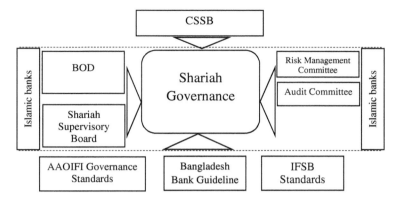

Figure 5.4: Shariah Governance Standards for Centralized Framework.
Source: Modified from Hasan (2007). Cited in Hamza (2013).

perspectives via open discussion, the establishment of an SSB inside the CB will diminish discrepancies in interpretation (Chapra and Khan, 2000). Each IFI has both an SSB and an apex Shariah advisory body at the CB, creating a two-tiered SG structure. Figure 5.4 illustrates SG standards for a CSGF.

To assist the SSB, the IB conducts audits and assessments of Shariah compliance. All questions on Shariah compliance and the validation of Islamic banking products to ensure Shariah compliance fall within the purview of the Shariah Advisory Council. When making decisions on Shariah-related issues, the SSB will go to the SAC for guidance. When it comes to questions of Islamic banking and the application of Shariah principles, the SAC is the final authority. The goal is to enhance the regulatory framework and support good governance in the Islamic financial industry, as well as to guarantee consistency and harmony in Shariah interpretations. Apart from the central SAC, the SSB at the IB level is the most critical governance tool for ensuring Shariah compliance. Before assigning any Shariah experts to the SSB, the IB must get approval from the financial authorities. The Shariah Advisory Committee of the CB and the SSB have both issued regulations on Shariah issues and the administration of IB activities. Shariah compliance and governance are monitored by the authorities to protect the Shariah framework, the IB's owners and stakeholders, and the customers of the IBs (Gintzburger and Saïdi, 2010).

The SSB of IB is responsible for enforcing this *fatwa* in connection to the provided contracts, and it can only be issued by the Shariah Board of Bank Negara and the Securities Commission. Board members of IFIs cannot serve on the SSBs of Bank Negara or the Securities Commission, and *vice versa*. Members of the SSB are restricted to working at a single financial institution within their sector (Islamic banking and *takaful* are treated as different businesses) to protect the secrecy of the industry's standards. Like Malaysia, Pakistan's Central Bank has an SSB with the ability to issue *fatwas* on areas pertaining to Islamic banking. Furthermore, it required each IB to hire a Shariah advisor. Shariah compliance in IFIs was given extensive rules and instructions by the State Bank of Pakistan in 2008. The guidelines provide that the SSB or advisors must be selected by the BOD of a local bank or by the management of a foreign bank having branches in Pakistan. An SSB member at the State Bank of Pakistan may only advise a single financial institution on Shariah matters. Disputes between Shariah consultants must be brought to the attention of the State Bank of Pakistan's SSB, the ultimate authority whose rulings are enforceable. The government of Sudan has consistently advanced IF since 1978, when it established the first Sharia-compliant bank, the Faisal Islamic Bank. In 1984, Shariah-compliant practices were implemented in the banking and financial sectors. In 1992, Central American governments adopted SSBs similar to Malaysia's. Alam (2022) proposed a CSGF for IBs. In this CSGF, the CSSB is envisaged as the final authority for Shariah resolutions in the planned CSGF, and as such, it will be in charge of overseeing and ensuring conformity with the principles of Shariah throughout all implementations (AAOIFI, 2017). To address any Shariah-related issues, resolve disputes, create a Shariah audit process, and report, each individual SSB will contact the central authority. The SSB and management's accountability to the CSSB for Shariah-related matters would improve the standard of Shariah applications and compliance. In addition to having the vested power and authority to enable them to make decisions free from interferences, influences, and prejudices; and to take appropriate action against any Shariah violations, the CSSB should be impartial, completely devoted, and composed of practicing Muslims. To guarantee that the SG guidelines and principles are properly applied, they will be permitted to undertake the Shariah audit and inspections of the individual banks through the executives of the CB. If they discover any infractions and misleading practices, they must take the necessary procedures and may recommend to the CB how to resolve the situation (AAOIFI, 2017). The CB can establish a Shariah audit and Shariah inspection committees to oversee the IBs generally in connection with the CSGF, together with four departments and the CSSB. Furthermore, each body associated with the CSGF should have its authority, functions, and responsibilities disclosed by the CB. For the IBs in Bangladesh, Bangladesh Bank (BB), the CB of the country, BODs, SSBs, board committees, management, Shariah executives, and IBs' executives, the study has a variety of unique practical implications that will help them to reduce misconceptions, improve SG practices, and improve the standard of Shariah compliance as well as IBs' reputation.

The proposed CSGF (shown in Figure 5.5) seeks to decrease varied practices and promote the uniformity of SG processes and resolutions (Alam, 2022). It is anticipated that the two-tier monitoring by the CB and CSSB through proposed departments and institutional SSB will raise the application of SG principles and improve the standard of Shariah compliance. When necessary, due to changes in the IB business, the CB may suggest minor amendments to this framework. It would be better for the development of the IB industry if the CB could implement a CSGF.

Thus, at the central level, both CSGF and CSSB are necessary. It is anticipated that the CB will be able to provide greater responsibility, independence, and openness in the roles of IBs and SSBs by implementing such a CSGF. This framework will reduce the shortcomings of current procedures and increase the trust of many stakeholders. The report recommends the establishment of Islamic chartered accounting firms and Shariah rating organizations to carry out the CB's external audit duties concurrently with those of conventional external audits. It also proposes giving the appropriate rating based on the level of compliance. Last but not least, the four-tier CSGF will strengthen the application of Shariah principles, safeguard the independence of the SSB and Shariah department executives, increase the standard of Shariah compliance, and improve the reputation of IBs.

5.8   The Problem of SGF in the World

Due to the unique characteristics of each country, the regulatory framework varies, and various approaches have been adopted by countries in establishing regulatory frameworks for Shariah compliance. Some have taken a very lenient stance, whereas others have taken a strict regulatory stance. Despite the fact that a lenient approach is insufficient to ensure Shariah

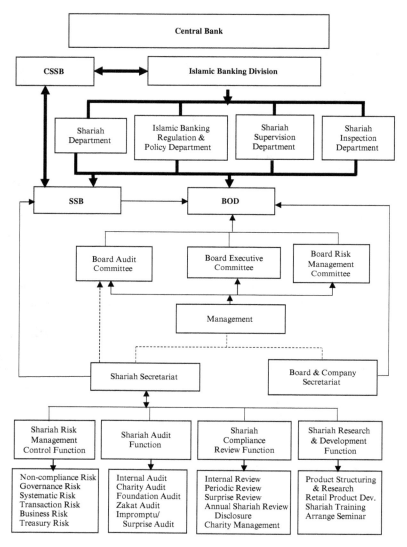

Figure 5.5: Proposed Centralized SGF.
Source: Modified from Alam (2022).

compliance, the query now is: How effectively and efficiently are regulatory-based, comprehensive approaches such as Malaysia and Pakistan operating? Obviously, their strategy is producing the desired outcomes, but not to the fullest extent because the current system is not fully functional. It should be noted that Islamic institutions currently operate under fewer than two jurisdiction-specific general situations.

In some instances, IBs coexist with interest-based banks, whereas in others, IBs operate under an Islamic banking system in its entirety. Islamic banking and finance are governed by the divine Islamic law (Shariah), whereas conventional banking and finance are governed by the laws of a nation (that is, legislation passed by the state). Islamic jurisprudence provides its own framework for the implementation of commercial and financial contracts, and banking and company laws suitable for the enforcement of Islamic banking and financial contracts do not exist in a great number of nations around the globe. Also, it is commonly supposed that two distinct systems within the same organism would result in certain conflicts. The obstruction begins here. The existence of such mixed legal systems necessitates that all transactions, contracts, and other operational matters comply with Shariah on the one hand and other prevalent laws in the country, which may in some cases directly conflict with Shariah. This may not be a problem in countries where the legal framework is based on Shariah, but it may be in the majority of countries. In Malaysia, which has a hybrid legal system, the High Court once ruled that Bai Bithaman Ajil (BBA), which constitutes 80% of Malaysia's total financing, is unlawful and illegitimate. The judges could have referred this matter to the SAC before issuing the rule (Hasan, 2010). Another issue is the divergence of opinion among scholars of Shariah. There is diversity among scholars; consequently, an SSB-approved product may not be acceptable to another Board. This is best illustrated by Islamic credit cards. Researchers outlined that Bangladesh has been lacking in comprehensive SG guidelines as well as its proper implementation (Alam *et al.*, 2020a, 2020b, 2020c, 2020d; 2021d; 2022a; Alam and Thakur, 2022).

Hasan (2014) discovered divergent opinions among respondents on a range of topics and indicated that the current governance structure has serious flaws and needs to be improved and developed. Lack of standardized practices, the inability of management to differentiate between traditional CG and SG, difficulties understanding Shariah-based laws, and incorrect interpretation of rules are some of them (Chowdhury and Shaker, 2015). In the event of non-compliance with Shariah principles, the majority of depositors in IFIs would withdraw their funds, according to Chapra and Ahmed's findings from 2002. The growth of the IF industry also appears to be accelerating in emerging markets like Southeast Asia and the Middle

East, where the governance structure is very different from other markets and where high capital ownership and family business are distinguishing characteristics. As a result, there is less protection offered to IFIs' IAHs and minority shareholders in these markets (Darmadi, 2013; Claessens, 2006). Perhaps these capital markets have many more agency problems than established markets, such as monitoring costs and information asymmetry (Sori *et al.*, 2015).

Choudhury and Hoque (2006) examined the mentality of Islamic economics and finance organizations to demonstrate that capitalist globalization is at the core of their mission. Consequently, a strict (Fiqhi) interpretation of the Shariah is followed, while the Tawhidi essence is disregarded. The religious principles implemented in Islamic nations are not universal. In the absence of a universally recognized central religious authority, Islamic institutions have founded their own religious committees as a source of guidance. Each new financial instrument must be approved by the religious committees or Shariah advisors of Islamic institutions. Different schools of thought may interpret Islamic principles differently, causing identical financial instruments to be rejected by one board but accepted by another. Consequently, the same instrument may not be accepted in all nations. Defining cohesive rules and accelerating the process of introducing new products can be accomplished by forming a unified council comprising various schools of thought to address this issue. Kayed and Mohammed (2009) argued that implementing A1 Shariah-compliant guidelines and procedures derived from the principle of IF would be an effective tool for controlling risks such as systemic risks (the possibility of a financial system or institution failing), credit risks (bad loans), and market risks (currency fluctuations) of Islamic modes of finance.

The executive role held by SSB members has resulted in a conflict of interests inside the SSB, as well as conflicts of interest between the SSB and the BOD and other parties, according to research by Garas (2012). The governance framework for IBs now in place needs additional standardization and refinement, according to Grassa and Matoussi's (2014) analysis of the governance practices and governance structure of IBs in the Gulf Cooperation Council and Southeast Asian countries. When Kasim *et al.* (2013) compared the SG criteria published by the AAOIFI, IFSB, and BNM, they found that there were several differences among them. According to Ahmed *et al.* (2016), a lack of transparency, especially for CG, may make Islamic instruments' innate dangers worse. Significant SG difficulties, such as rejecting a *fatwa*, shopping for a *fatwa*, enticing or influencing the SSB's decision, and varying interpretations of current Shariah decisions, have the potential to harm IF's credibility and reputation (Grais and Pellegrini, 2006a; Ullah and Lee, 2012). Alam *et al.* (2020d) outlined that BOD and management directly and indirectly influence the functions of SSB and implement the process of SG guidelines.

Zada *et al.* (2017) demonstrated the potential for direct conflict between managers and SSB members and indirect conflict between these members and the board. In addition to raising questions regarding the Shariah-compliance claims of such institutions, such conflicts may also result in significant losses for the Islamic bank. The following anecdotes demonstrate how governance flaws can result in substantial losses. In November 2015, Bank Negara Malaysia (BNM) fined a subsidiary Islamic bank in Malaysia a substantial amount of RM 53.7 million under Sections 234 and 245 of the IFSA (Zada *et al.*, 2017). As the measuring cup for Shariah CG, local perceptions would be disregarded and the Islamic worldview would be followed. Undoubtedly, an SG Code is required to impose a minimum standard of Shariah CG on all Islamic corporations, regardless of their location (Muneez and Hassan, 2014).

5.9 Need for a Special Shariah Governance Code

Images of corporations with the Islamic prefix should be evaluated using the same standards. This would make it simple for all parties involved to determine whether or not the SG Code has been followed. This would also help Islamic investors from across the world find Shariah-compliant businesses to invest in. If a universal SG Code were to be put into place, multinational firms would be able to compete on a level playing field in terms of Shariah compliance. Since the Islamic worldview is used as the yardstick for Shariah business governance, local perspectives are neglected. All Islamic organizations, no matter their location, need to adhere to a uniform level of Shariah CG, hence an SG Code is necessary (Muneez and Hassan, 2014).

In addition to working to develop governance standards unique to IFIs, regulatory and academic bodies and IFIs are attempting to ensure that their governance principles conform to international standards for conventional institutions. This includes adopting Basel III and OECD standards. While nations and institutions have labored to agree on Islamic-specific governance standards, all nations and institutions have essentially adopted the OECD and Basel III principles. This has resulted in a degree of uniformity among industry governance practices (Chapra and Habib, 2002).

The proper framework should be put in place to ensure optimal SG of IFIs:

> There is a critical need for a proper framework and procedures regarding the appointment of SAC and SSB members, the relationship between the two bodies, membership, procedures, etc. on the scope of advice and supervision, which should be a holistic approach, looking at the operations of Islamic FI as a whole, covering before, during, and after the execution of all products and structures on the internal and external Shariah compliance review/audit.

Constant enhancement of the framework is necessary to ensure optimal SG in Islamic finance.

5.10 Recommendation: Envisioned Model Shariah Governance Code

Propositions for better SG:

- The necessity of implementing the best SG standards for the IFI.
- There is no absolute standard or one model that applies to everyone.
- Depending on the stage and rate of growth of IF, it may differ from one nation to the next.
- Notably, the Islamic financial services sector is still in its infancy.
- Therefore, any rigorous, rule-based strategy adopted in a hurry to improve industry governance may endanger and impede the industry's potential and healthy growth.
- To help enable the construction and optimization of a healthy and viable environment for SG while not limiting the industry's further expansion, several common components that constitute good governance and best practices may be identified.

In a model, SG code which is applicable to all Islamic corporations, the following components shall be common, irrespective of their geographical location or localities:

Every Islamic company shall have an independent SSB. The need for an independent SSB to oversee the activities and management of an Islamic corporation arises from the fact that these scholars would be in a better position to advise on the questionable activities occurring in the company due to the vagaries of the economy. This body would be responsible for providing objective guidance and oversight over all company activities, as well as advising the Chief Executive Officer (CEO) on the Islamic nature of the company's affairs.

This SSB can be defined similarly to what AAOIFI standards have defined SSB used for the purpose of IBs:

> [...] an independent body of specialist jurists in *fiqh muamalat* (Islamic commercial jurisprudence), which is entrusted with the duty of directing, reviewing, and overseeing the activities of the Islamic financial institution in order to guarantee compliance with Islamic shariah regulations and tenets through *fatwas*, and rulings.

Expertise in both Islamic law and Islamic business law, as well as relevant practical experience, is desirable for the SSB's Shariah scholars. That way, only well-considered choices may be made without prejudice.

Having a separate SSB is beneficial for three main reasons. From a Shariah viewpoint, first, the SSB is tasked with ensuring that Muslims profit from the corporation's contracts, deals, and transactions. Second, economically, the SSB promotes the shift from *riba* or usury-based economy, which is unfair and exploitative, to Islamic economics. In order to carry out monetary transactions that are in accordance with Islamic law, the SSB issues *fatwas* and makes recommendations. Finally, from a sociological point of view, the SSB is able to sustain the corporation's social duties, including paying *zakat* or alms and making investments in accordance with Shariah law.

The SSB member also has to be objective. They shouldn't worry about being treated unfairly by the company's BOD or its shareholders. There shouldn't be any room for a conflict of interest to arise. They serve God, not the people who pay them or give them access to supernatural possibilities. To do this, the SSB's proper standing under relevant domestic law must be clearly stated in the Corporation's Memorandum and Articles of Association. If the SSB is not a subcommittee of the BOD, it is not doing its job. The SSB should not report to or take orders from the company's management. Further, academics who oversee a single company's SSB shouldn't simultaneously oversee many Boards, since this might lead to conflicts of interest. It is also inappropriate for a firm director to serve as the SSB's supervisor due to the potential for a conflict of interest.

The SSB should have at least one meeting every month, and everyone should be expected to show up. At these gatherings, the BOD and the board of management of the company may ask for Shariah-related advice. In and out of the company, the SSB should act as a Muhtasib. The Arabic term for "Ombudsman" is "Muhtasib." This would give the SSB the power to investigate any allegations of wrongdoing under Islamic law, whether they come from inside or outside the institution. The SSB has the ability to examine any allegations of Shariah non-compliance or problematic (*shubhah*) activities brought up by any employee of the organization via this process. Additionally, any member of the public may register a complaint with the SSB, prompting the SSB to investigate the matter further. The SSB also has the authority to prevent workers from participating in activities that are forbidden by Shariah on its own initiative and without Board agreement. But the SSB shouldn't have any say in anything but Islamic law.

Importantly, the attributes or credentials, appointment, rights and duties, compensation, hierarchy, and dismissal and resignation of those who make up the SSB must be specified in the Article and Memorandum of Association of the corporation in order to legally establish and enforce the duties of the SSB in different countries around the world. In the absence of such recognition by national legislation, the idea of forming a self-governing SSB inside the business is both impractical and unnecessary.

In addition, without binding authority over the BOD, the SSB is a toothless tiger. The BOD is influencing and tries *fatwa* shopping (Alam *et al.*, 2023b). In reality, the CEO or the BOD may or may not follow the SSB's recommendations, thus making the SSB a waste of time and misleading the public by pretending to monitor the company's actions and advise the CEO appropriately. As a consequence, having such an SSB would be pointless, and safeguarding Islamic values would take a back seat. As a result, the line between standard and SG would be blurred. Almost all nations with SG guidelines (like Malaysia's SG Guidelines for IFIs released by Bank Negara) lack this provision.

All choices must originate from the process of *shura*, or consultation and consensus-seeking. In an Islamic company, decisions should be made via a process of *shura*, or consultation, and consensus-seeking. The two passages below, both taken from the Holy Quran, the basic source of Islamic law, provide adequate evidence. Islam advocates for *shura* because of its positive effects on society. By sharing their own concerns, individuals who will be most directly impacted by a decision are given a voice in the process via *shura*. Also, unlike under current democratic systems, where the majority always wins and the minority's viewpoint is ignored by the authorities, this would never be an issue under *shura*. It is God's intention for the person in power to seek input from others when making collective choices (Mawdadi, 1974), and decision-making is not entirely in the hands of the person in charge. In this manner, the choice wouldn't be the result of a single person's preferences, thus it would be binding on everyone, and everyone could be happy with the outcome. This is important for creating a "win–win" situation.

The SSB must have subcommittees in every division. The main SSB wouldn't need to depend on verbal or written reports from department heads if they formed subcommittees of SSB inside the different divisions of the business. This would solve two problems at once: (1) the disruption caused by the SSB's members serving as non-executive directors and holding meetings only when the directors or BOD demand one, and (2) the problem of the SSB's members serving as non-executive directors and holding meetings only when the directors or BOD request one. The quality of a judgment suffers when Shariah experts are invited for a one-time event but are not actively engaged in the day-to-day operations of the business.

Annually, the company must perform a Shariah audit and disclose the results in the annual report. Auditors are very important in both traditional and Shariah forms of company governance. The job of the auditor is to check the books and make sure everything adds up. Auditors are the "keepers of the financial integrity of the business," as Krishnan (2010) puts it. To enable them in their mission to uncover instances of improper management action, auditors have broad discretionary powers. They need to be able to report on the firm objectively and independently. Auditing practices in accordance with Shariah law are obligatory. People are so used to conventional or prudential assessments that they forget about, or are just unaware of, Shariah audits, thus they neglect to include this component.

Both a prudential audit and a Shariah audit, as required by SG, must be included in the annual report. Prudential parts of the company would be audited by licensed accountants and legal advisors. The organization's SSB would undertake the audit of Shariah compliance.

Shareholders are not the only parties with a vested interest in an Islamic business. An Islamic corporation's responsibility of care and accountability extends beyond its shareholders to include all of the company's stakeholders. Shareholders who care about the safety of their investment and the possibility of a better return are welcome in an Islamic business. Depositors who want their money to be safe and accessible whenever they need it (known as "demand depositors"), government agencies with jurisdiction over IFIs (known as "regulators"), and financial market authorities (known as "financial market authorities") who establish minimum standards for clarity and transparency in the financial markets Islamic companies are required by Shariah to consider all of these parties and their interests, and to act accordingly.

The ability to file a negligence lawsuit against the SSB. One way to ensure the SSB fulfills its responsibility to those to whom it owes a duty of care is to allow such parties to sue the SSB if it is proven that the SSB was negligent. This would be at odds with the present norm, which shields SSB from any negligence claims made by customers or other stakeholders. The vast majority of Shariah experts and academics would disagree with this, considering it to be completely illogical. Stakeholders and society at large depend significantly on the SSB, but if the SSB is negligent and causes a third party's rights to be infringed, there is nothing stopping that party from filing a lawsuit against the SSB. The SSB and its members should lose their immunity only in extreme instances, such as those involved in intentional wrongdoing or recklessness.

For the SG guidelines to be effective, it must adhere to all of the aforementioned principles. Only then will the full potential of Islamic firms to advance SG become clear, to the benefit of people everywhere. This would certainly aid in the Islamization of the international financial system as a whole.

This justifies the need for an SG Code, which provides guidelines for the operation of Islamic businesses in accordance with Islamic law. Since Islamic law cannot be changed, a codified system of SG will surely benefit Muslims and non-Muslims alike who seek to invest in or otherwise take advantage of Islamic businesses. In an Islamic company, the SSB, BOD, administration, and auditors all have distinct but interdependent functions that must be spelled out in detail by the specific Code. All of these components of Islamic businesses must do their work in a way that honors God and satisfies all of their customers. Accountability, openness, disclosure, and clarity would all be enhanced by the adoption of a unique code. This approach is far more in accordance with the core principles of Islam, and it may be used to set up and manage systems of governance and social responsibility. More research is needed to determine the possible critical success roots of this occurrence (Muneeza and Hassan, 2014).

CHAPTER 6

Shariah Governance System

6.1 Introduction

The SG is defined as the legal framework that controls and supervises Islamic Financial Institutions (IFIs) to ensure that the laws of the sacred Shariah are upheld throughout all of the Islamic banks (IBs) and IFIs' operations (Alam *et al.*, 2021a; Elasrag, 2014). The primary objective of SG is to support IBs and IFIs in implementing all religious requirements. Adopting thorough Shariah regulations, it seeks to ensure that the IFIs' activities are run ethically and that the Shariah compliance aspects of the business are upheld as required, at the same time safeguarding the interests of shareholders, customers, depositors, and all other relevant IFIs' parties. All IFIs must therefore adhere to Shariah governance (SG) standards for them to be supervised by the SSB and the Central Bank and to follow those rules (Alam *et al.*, 2021b). As a procedure, SG verifies Shariah compliance in the whole operations of IBs (Alam *et al.*, 2021a, 2021b, 2021c, 2021d). Shariah Governance Framework (SGF) is necessary for IBs to adopt Shariah principles, confirm Shariah compliance, and supervise the banks' operations (Alam *et al.* 2021a, 2021b).

6.2 The Shariah Governance Model from a Regulatory Perspective

The SG system is a collection of institutional and organizational procedures to oversee Shariah compliance elements in IFIs, as defined by the IFSB Exposure Draft of the Guidelines on SG System of IFIs 2009 (IFSB-10). To this end, the great majority of IFIs have formed their own SSB, with some going so far as to create a dedicated Shariah review unit or department inside the organization. This bodes well for the implementation of Shariah principles in international financial institutions. The regulatory structure of the SG system in different nations is worth investigating because of the wide variety of SGFs and styles seen in different legal settings and banking models.

There is a wide range of SG system practices and models seen in the existing framework of Islamic finance across different countries. There are certain countries that want a smaller role for regulatory bodies, while others choose the reverse. Whether the former is more common and adaptable than the latter is still up for debate. Five distinct SG models are identified within the framework of a regulatory viewpoint in this research (Hasan, 2009).

6.2.1 Reactive Approach

Countries with non-Islamic systems of law, like the United Kingdom and Turkey, are more likely to follow this paradigm. Although some IFIs have been granted Islamic banking licenses, the regulatory authority's position on the SG structure remains unclear. Like other types of financial institutions, IFIs must follow the rules and regulations already in place. In addition, IFIs must guarantee that their services and goods are in accordance with Shariah. No regulations or laws exist that set down SG standards for IFIs. Until there is a major problem impacting the financial industry, authorities will not act or interfere in SG problems. SSBs of IFIs, according to the UK Financial Services Authority, for instance, are seen as having an advising and supervisory role rather than an executive one (Hasan, 2009).

6.2.2 Passive Approach

Only the Saudi Arabian Shariah paradigm of government uses this methodology. International financial institutions are accorded the same status as domestic banks by the Saudi Authority Monetary Agency (SAMA). Neither Islamic finance nor SG system rules have been provided by SAMA as of yet. Neither a national Shariah advisory committee nor any other agency is the final arbiter in matters of Islamic finance (Hasan, 2009). Self-initiative, rather than legal requirements or regulator guidance, led to the implementation of the SG structure now being applied by IFIs in the Kingdom.

6.2.3 Minimalist Approach

All, except Oman and Saudi Arabia, members of the GCC follow this paradigm. Minimalist models, in contrast to reactive ones, allow for less interference from regulators. Although they do not lay out the specifics, regulatory authorities presume that IFIs would have a Shariah-compliant governance framework. There are no limits on how many institutions may each have a member of the SSB. Bahrain, Dubai, and Qatar are just a few of the GCC countries that support the implementation of the AAOIFI Governance Standards. Minimalists (Hasan, 2009) would rather see the market create its own SG structure than see authorities become more involved in the industry.

6.2.4 Proactive Approach

The Malaysian government has given its stamp of approval to this system. The proponent of this paradigm places a priority on the use of regulations to strengthen the SG system. The Malaysian government has instituted an SG structure for both regulated and unregulated sectors as a result of this drive. Parliament enacted and revised a number of financial and banking regulations between 1983 and 1993, including the Islamic Banking Act, the Takaful Act, the Banking and Financial Institutions Act, and the Securities Commission Act. The National Shariah Advisory Council (SAC) is recognized as the ultimate authority in Islamic finance under the Central Bank of Malaysia Act 1958 (Amendment, 2009). Furthermore, BNM/GPS1 Regulations on the Governance of the Committee on Shariah for IFIs have been released by the Bank Negara Malaysia (BNM). Guidelines for the registration of Shariah advisers in the capital market sector were also released by the Securities and Exchanges Commission of Malaysia in 2009 (Hasan, 2009).

6.2.5 Interventionist Approach

While Saudi Arabia is the only country to take such a passive stance, Pakistan's Shariah style of government is actively participative. Islamic financial choices pertaining to Shariah may be made by independent entities under the interventionist model but the Shariah Federal Court is the supreme authority in Islamic finance in Pakistan (Hasan, 2009), despite the State Bank of Pakistan establishing the SSB.

Based on this, it may be said that different nations take different routes to enacting Shariah-compliant legal codes. Some have taken a regulatory-based position, while others have taken a far more permissive approach.

The question today is, given that a lax approach is inadequate to guarantee Shariah conformity, how efficient and successful are regulatory-based, all-encompassing systems like those of Malaysia and Pakistan? Their plan is obviously working, but clearly not perfectly, since the existing system is not optimal. It's important to emphasize that there are now two different contexts in which Islamic organizations may function, depending on their location. Islamic banks may function side by side with interest-based banks or exclusively under an Islamic financial system. Unlike conventional banking and finance, which are subject to a country's laws (i.e., legislation approved by the state), Islamic banking and finance are controlled by the divine Islamic law (Shariah). Many countries lack banking and business regulations that are amenable to the implementation of Islamic banking and financial contracts, whereas Islamic jurisprudence offers its own framework for the fulfillment of commercial and financial transactions. It's also generally assumed that the presence of two distinctly different systems inside the same organization will lead to some kind of conflict. This is the first point of impediment. Shariah, on the one hand, and other popular laws in the nation, which may in some circumstances directly clash with Shariah, on the other hand require that all transactions, agreements, and other operational concerns conform with both sets of laws. It's possible that this won't be an issue in nations where the legal system is founded on Shariah, but it probably will in the vast majority of nations. Bai Bithaman Ajil (BBA), which accounts for 80% of Malaysia's overall finance, has been declared illegal and illegitimate by the High Court of Malaysia, a country with a mixed legal system. Before adopting the ruling, the judges had the opportunity to consult with the SAC (Hasan, 2010).

6.3   Shariah Governance Process

When it comes to Shariah law, this is the most crucial component. The SG method reflects the SSB's operational duties within the framework of Islamic institutions' internal governance structures for CG. Shariah compliance procedure, Shariah compliance assessment, Shariah coordination, and Shariah report are all covered in this part, along with the appointment, composition, and competencies of the SSB (Hasan, 2011b).

6.3.1 Appointment

Members of the SSB are typically selected by the BOD or the shareholders at the annual general meeting (AGM). According to the document published by the International Association of Islamic Banks (IAIB), SSB members must not be staff members of banks and must not be subject to the authority of the BOD (Rammal, 2006). Furthermore, the AAOIFI governance standard requires that Shariah Supervisory members of the Board be appointed by shareholders at the AGM rather than by the BOD. The management board cannot nominate or remove members of the SSB since that responsibility rests with the shareholders. If the shareholders form an SSB at the AGM based on the BOD's suggestion, members of that board are welcome to attend BOD meetings to address the ethical implications of the board's choices (Nathan and Ribiere, 2007).

6.3.2 Composition

The current norm for an SSB includes knowledgeable scholars of *fiqh al muamalat* and *usul-al fiqh*. SSBs at various Islamic organizations have varying make-ups. Local and regional scholars serve on the SSBs of specific IFIs (Hasan, 2011a). Scholars from all over the world sit on the SSBs of both international organizations and national governments.

6.3.3 Qualification

Scholars of Shariah and law, more especially *fiqh al muamalat* and *usul-al fiqh*, make for the best SSB members, so goes the argument. This is owing to the fact that the SSB focuses on business matters (Ayub, 2007; BNM, 2019). The AAOIFI governance standards and the IFSB-10 allow for a non-expert in *fiqh al muamalat* to be appointed to the SBP's and BNM's SSBs so that the Boards can better scrutinize and understand banking operations and business operations (Hasan, 2011).

6.3.4 Shariah Compliance Process

The practices of SG vary from one Islamic bank to other. Management, commercial approval, and both pre- and post-implementation audits fall beyond the scope of current SG standards. Shariah-related concerns are often handled by a specialized department or secretariat. The officer in the

Shariah department is mainly responsible for administrative and clerical activities linked to the SSB. This includes, but is not limited to, preparing and maintaining papers to be presented at the SSB's meeting. It is up to the SSB to decide who should be present at the meeting, although it might include the CEO, management, bank officials, legal officers, solicitors, and representatives from the Islamic bank's branches. Whether the challenges at hand are operational, product, legal documents, or something else entirely will influence the scope of participation.

Issues related to Shariah are addressed during SSB meetings. These include the creation and design of new and existing products, as well as their documentation, processes, and investment portfolios. The Islamic bank will provide all relevant materials to the SSB members at least a week before the meeting, giving them plenty of time to review them. The meeting will be presided over by the chairman of the SSB, and decisions will be reached by a show of hands. When an international IFI issues *sukuk*, an SSB may allow decisions to be taken with a simple majority vote. It is customary for an SSB to have one of its members function in an executive capacity. Each member of the administrative board acts as a selection committee, with the authority to decide whether or not to call a meeting to debate a certain topic (McMillan, 2006: 141). In another common scenario, the Shariah officer is given the final say. All relevant parties within the IFI will be informed of the SSB's decision after the meeting and will be expected to abide by it (Hasan, 2011B).

Furthermore, an organizational structure (see Figure 6.1) for a Shariah Secretariat (SS) for the IBs in Bangladesh was suggested in a study undertaken by Alam *et al.* (2022a). The SS will collaborate with management in the proposed framework, monitor Shariah-related concerns, and be responsible for disseminating up-to-date information concerning situations that contravene Shariah principles. A full-time SSB member and Shariah officers from the relevant departments can form the SS. The management is in charge of ensuring that Shariah principles are applied consistently across IBs' operations. The SS should report directly to the SSB and indirectly to management in terms of reporting. They will also help the external auditor to carry out its duties. If any issues are found, the Shariah Secretary or officials should independently notify the SSB so that steps can be taken to address them right away. To strengthen the Shariah department, the management should hire additional Shariah officers with in-depth knowledge of the relevant laws and regulations. For instance, the departments should contain 100% or at least 50% of qualified staff. It is

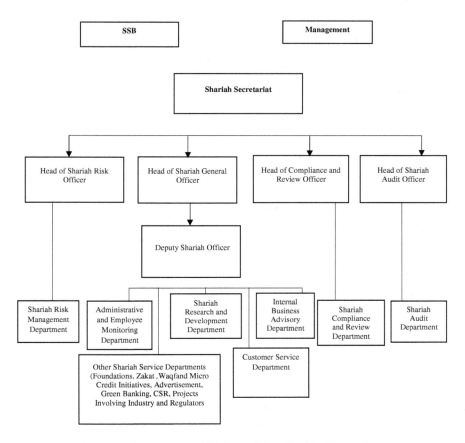

Figure 6.1: Proposed Organizational Framework for Shariah Secretariat.
Source: Alam et al. (2022b).

recommended that the SSB carry out its proper duties in relation to the selection and advancement of the SS and its officers.

Reasons for the establishment of the SS: The reason for the establishment of the SS in an IFI is to assist the SSB in its functions. Since SSB members are not full-time employees of an IB or IFI, there is a need to have competent Shariah professionals at the level of IBs and IFIs as well. In this regard, Aziz and Faizal (2012) observe that since the SSB members do not work like regular executives, the SS and its members should have practical knowledge of *uṣul al-fiqh* and *fiqh al-muamalat* in order to monitor Shariah issues. The SS is also established at the regulatory authority's level to assist the apex Shariah Advisory Council (SAC). For instance, Bank Negara Malaysia (BNM) has established an SS to assist the SAC at the level of the central bank. No literature has provided the precise historical context of the reason for the establishment of the SS. However, what is apparent is that since the formation of SSBs within IFIs, administrative staff have been allocated to ensure the smooth running of the functions of the SAC and the enactment of SGFs. The term "Shariah Secretariat" has been coined to indicate that having ordinary administrative staff to assist SSBs is not sufficient for SSBs to effectively carry out their functions. As such, the function and organ of SS became an important part of the SGF enacted in different parts of the world, especially to carry out the Shariah research function. In this regard, SGF 2010 issued by BNM is the first SGF in which the SS is given much importance (BNM, 2019, paragraphs 7.25 and 7.26). Paragraph 7.25 of SGF 2010 requires IFIs in Malaysia to establish a Secretariat to serve the SSB. SGF 2010 was replaced by the Shariah Governance Policy Document (SGPD) which became effective on April 1, 2020, except for paragraph 12.5. Under part C of the SGPD on the SSB, one paragraph is dedicated to the SS (BNM, 2019, paragraph 14). Paragraph 14.1 of the SGPD clearly states that IFIs must have an SS established to serve the SSB.

6.3.5 Shariah Compliance Review

Four primary elements for effective supervisory control are outlined by the Basel II Committee. (1) banks should have a process for assessing their overall capital adequacy relative to their risk profile and a strategy to safeguard their capital levels; (2) supervisors should examine and assess banks' internal capital adequateness assessments and methods, as well as how well they are able to monitor and ensure compliance with mandated capital ratios, and take appropriate oversight and performance. action if they are not satisfied with the outcome of this process (Kahf, 1998).

In order to verify that all transactions are in accordance with Shariah principles, Islamic organizations, unlike conventional banks, are required to undertake a Shariah review and internal Shariah review process. The former refers to an audit conducted by an independent internal Shariah auditor or as part of an internal examination based on the Shariah rulings, guidelines, and directions issued by the SSB, while the latter describes an audit conducted by the SSB itself. When conducting audits of IFIs, this department often lends a hand to the SSB.

The fundamental purpose of the Shariah review is to guarantee adherence to Shariah principles and the decisions of the SSB. With this in mind, the AAOIFI governance guidelines include a number of steps for Shariah reviews, such as process design, procedure execution, working paper preparation and review, conclusion documentation, and Shariah review report writing (AAOIFI, 2005a). In practice, there is no standardized structure for either the Shariah review process or the Shariah compliance report. According to the IFSB study, more than 90% of 69 IFIs do a Shariah compliance evaluation (IFSB, 2008b: 27). The Shariah review differs from a standard audit in that it is focused on Shariah-related aspects and is guided by Islamic principles, with the primary purpose being to ensure that the leadership team of Islamic banks is discharging its responsibilities while complying with Shariah rules and principles.

Since the Shariah review is concerned with Shariah compliance issues of given items, a robust Shariah internal control system is required for this procedure. Each stage of the Shariah administration process, from ideation to documentation to testing to implementation and review, must be reviewed by an internal auditor as part of the Shariah review process. According to Shariah review practice, most IFIs do not conduct reviews of their goods (IFSB, 2008b: 29). In most IFIs, the Shariah review is either integrated into the overall internal audit process or performed separately from the rest of the audit. When it comes to Shariah review, some IFIs prefer to bring in an outside auditor. Internal reviews are used by 89% of IFIs, whereas external reviews are used by 41% (IFSB, 2008b: 34).

6.3.6 Shariah Audit

An audit was conducted in accordance with Shariah law. The Shariah audit provides its judgment and opinion to the competent authorities after collecting and assessing adequate and reliable information about the operations of an IFI. Both the IFI's operational rules and procedures and its financial dealings are scrutinized during a Shariah audit. Due to the lack of both an unambiguous Shariah audit in practice and a dearth of literature on this issue, the scope and nature of a Shariah audit remain unclear. The AAOIFI's Governance Standards No. 2 (GSIFI 2 of AAOIFI) provides the broadest definition of Shariah audit currently in use, noting, "Shariah review examines whether an IFI follows *shariah* in all of its activities." Contracts, policies, goods, transactions, articles of association, financial statements, reports (especially internal audit and central bank inspection), etc., are all subject to the shariah review at IFIs. The opposite is also true (Sultan, 2007).

All aspects of an audit, from planning to follow-up, must be approved by the SSB. Aboumouamer's (1989) research shows that the majority of SSB members (78%) are involved in pre-audit tasks, while an additional 80% are involved in the actual audit itself, and a further 61% are involved in post-audit tasks. Some SSBs are too tiny to take part in the thorough audits required by the Shariah. They have a limited number of resources and time, and most of them aren't even employees of the individual IFIs. Furthermore, they lack the auditing abilities and operational understanding of IFIs' operations necessary to carry out the auditing responsibility (Banaga *et al.*, 1994). Unless there is a disagreement or difficulty with Shariah-related topics, the SSB will not typically take part in the Shariah auditing process. This calls for the auditor performing the Shariah audit to have enough religious knowledge to spot Shariah's concerns and provide comments on whether or not requirements have been followed.

Alam *et al.* (2023a) outlined (shown in Figure 6.2) that the existing Shariah auditing system of Islamic banks needs to be improved to ensure the implementation of the Shariah rules and guidelines in the operational transactions. They outlined that in order to have a complete and proper Shariah auditing, Islamic banks in Bangladesh have to have the combination of four elements such as: (a) a Shariah audit manual, (b) a sound IT-based audit system, (c) proper monitoring and functional system, and (d) a robust Shariah secretariat or department under the SSB with sufficient supportive manpower inclusive of Shariah executives.

According to Khan (1985) the Shariah auditor will report on matters such as *bakhs* (decrease in product quality), *taff* (causing harm to the other party in weights and measures), *uqd* (contract), *ihtikr* (hoarding), *khiynah* (embezzlements), *isrf* (extravagance), *tanjush* (bidding up prices in an auction by planting a fake bidder), and speculation. The purported Shariah audit Khan proposes purports to cover a wide, nebulous, and intricate auditing space. Actually, the Shariah evaluation includes an audit of *zakah* funds, as well as assessments and observations of Shariah-compliant systems and controls, suggestions for prospective upgrades, and required remedial measures (Aboumouamer, 1989). In the case of a dispute or difference of opinion between the administration and Shariah auditors, individual SSBs may be contacted. Shariah review reports should be given to the SSB, the audit committee of the BOD, and the IFI shareholders in the same way as conventional review reports are (Hasan, 2011b).

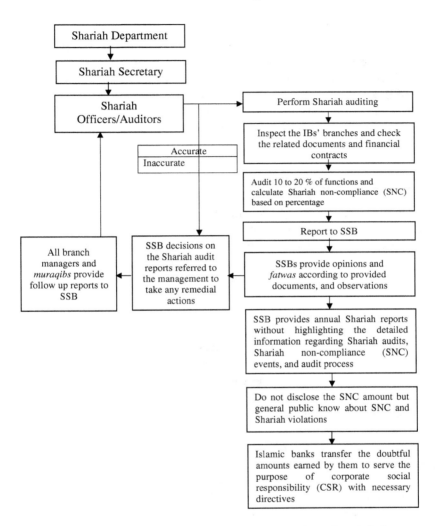

Figure 6.2: Reporting and Auditing Process of Islamic Banks in Bangladesh.
Source: Alam et al. (2023b).

6.3.7 Shariah Coordination

When it comes to SG, the role of the Shariah coordinator is analogous to that of the company secretary. Interaction with the SSB, internal or external review, and other instruments of SG are all coordinated by the Shariah coordinator. Several different Shariah coordination models have

218   *Shariah Governance Systems of Islamic Banks*

been identified and classified according to the following criteria (Dar, 2009): Shariah advisory firm as the outside Shariah coordinator; Shariah advisory firm as internal Shariah coordinator; compliance with Shariah officer; Shariah coordination department; internal Shariah communicating officer; and SSB secretary as Shariah coordinator. A Shariah compliance officer or chairperson of the SSB often handles Shariah coordination. In fact, certain Shariah compliance professionals at IFIs serve as Shariah coordinators and oversee the Shariah review procedure (Hasan, 2011b).

6.3.8 *Shariah Report*

Transparency and honesty are valued in a Shariah-compliant administration. Accountability is a cornerstone of Shariah administration, and as such, Islamic organizations are obligated to be completely transparent and provide accurate data to the public. This is in line with the central message of the Quran, where Allah exhorts his followers, "O believers! The verse from the Holy Quran (2:282) indicates that "when you engage in transactions containing future obligations within an established time frame, transcribe them to writing and have a scribe record them correctly between the parties." All business deals and transactions are encouraged and required to be recorded in writing according to this passage. With regards to SG, this term denotes the SSB's duty to provide a Shariah report on a semiannual or annual basis.

The SSB is obligated to provide an annual report detailing its operations, services, edicts, and statement of adherence to Islamic law. On a regular basis, the Shariah report will be presented to the BOD. Some IFIs present the Shariah report to the BOD and also seek shareholder approval. IFIs only provide the Shariah report to the audit committee 48% of the time and to shareholders 49% of the time (IFSB, 2008b: 35). Whether the SSB had been chosen by the BOD or the shareholders may be reflected in this decision. A statement of Shariah conformity and details about the Islamic bank's responsibilities and offerings are standard fare for the yearly Shariah report (Banaga *et al.*, 1994). The Shariah report, according to Haniffa and Hudaib (2007), should include additional details like the names, pictures, and compensation of the SSB, the number of meetings held, disclosure of defects in the products provided, and recommendations to rectify the defects, including measures taken by management, as a foundation for examining the documentation, a declaration of Shariah legal compliance and the signatures of all SSB members.

While internal Shariah control efficacy is discussed in theory, in practice most Shariah reports focus on product compliance (IFSB, 2008b:48). Instructions for Shariah Conformity in Islamic Banking Institutions of Pakistan lays forth the specifics of what must be included in the Shariah report. The IFI's compliance with Shariah rules and principles will be determined by looking at things like the allocation of funds, profit sharing ratios, profits, and charging of losses, as well as making sure that any profits are distributed in a way that is consistent with Shariah.

The Shariah report must follow the framework outlined in the AAOIFI governance requirements. However, in practice, the Shariah report might look different from year to year, and some SSBs may not even release a report at all. Grais and Pellegrini (2006a) found that only four of thirteen IFIs have published a Shariah report. Maali *et al.* (2006: 285) revealed that only 72% of a sample of 29 institutions submitted a Shariah report. This amounts to 21 organizations. The Shariah report is essential because it attests to an IFI's adherence to Shariah principles and gives the public and interested parties insight into how well the IFI's services and products conform to Shariah standards. The AAOIFI governance requirements require that the SSB publish the annual Shariah assessment in the format prescribed in the Shariah report (Hasan, 2011).

6.4 General Approach to Shariah Governance System

According to the basic approach of the SG system, good governance practice comprises both *ex-ante* and *ex-post* processes. *Ex-ante* procedures include issuing Shariah rulings and doing compliance inspections before a product is made available to customers.

Financial institutions that adhere to Shariah principles would perform an *ex-post* procedure that includes an internal Shariah evaluation and SG monitoring to ensure that its Shariah compliance is consistent and that any risks associated with Shariah compliance are successfully managed. Each IFI should also make sure the SSB has clear terms of reference for its mission and duties, established processes and reporting lines, and a solid grasp of professional ethics and behavior (Hasan, 2011b).

6.4.1 *Competence*

Several methods are proposed to assess whether or not SSBs have the necessary knowledge and abilities, as well as to monitor their progress and development as professionals. The International Financial Institutions have set standards for the qualifications of SSB members. The SSB members of IFIs must have access to continual training and education opportunities. In addition, the performance of the SSBs as a whole and the individual contributions of its members should be formally assessed (Hasan, 2011b).

6.4.2 *Independence*

This section aims to safeguard the SSBs' autonomy, especially in relation to the administration of the IIFS, by drawing attention to the existence of possible conflicts of interest and providing guidance on how they should be handled. The IFSB suggests that the SSB performs a strong and autonomous role of supervision, with the authority to make impartial decisions on Shariah-related issues. The SSB's decision-making process should be independent of any outside influence. For the SSB to carry out its duties, it must be given full, sufficient, and timely information in advance of all meetings and on a continuous basis (Hasan, 2011b).

6.4.3 *Confidentiality*

In order to gain the public's confidence, IFIs must place special emphasis on the sanctity of secrecy among the Shariah's most important governing bodies. Members of the SSB also have a duty to protect the privacy of any company information they may obtain in the course of their work (Hasan, 2011b).

6.4.4 *Consistency*

In order to prevent any disagreements, compliance must be constant. To ensure credibility and confirm the integrity of the SSB, IFIs should emphasize improving the uniformity of the professional conduct of its members via a set of best practices. Financial institutions that adhere to Shariah law should be familiar with the local laws and regulations that apply to the making of Shariah-compliant announcements and decisions. When feasible, it should encourage the convergence of SG principles and guarantee that its SSB strictly follows the aforementioned structure (Kasim *et al.*, 2013).

6.5 Conclusion

This chapter focused on SG models, systems, and SG processes. In addition, this chapter provides different approaches of SG systems.

CHAPTER 7

Model of *Shariah* Supervisory Board and Its Functions

7.1 Introduction

In this chapter, Shariah governance framework in Islamic banks is discussed in detail.

7.2 Institutionalization of Shariah Supervisory Board

The Shariah Supervisory Board (SSB) is a modern addition to Islamic organizations. Sheikh Saleh Kamel is credited for conceptualizing the SSB (Rahman, 2010) as part of the Shariah Governance Framework (SGF) of Islamic organizations, when he established the Dallah Al Baraka Group. The first ever SSB was created in 1976 by the Egyptian Faisal Islamic Bank (Kahf, 2004). When Islamic banking first began, there was no central authority to provide guidance on Shariah law issues to Islamic financial firms. Without instituting a Shariah body as part of their governance systems, the Mitr Ghams Savings Bank opened on July 23, 1963, the Nasser Social Bank in Egypt opened in 1972, and the Dubai Islamic Bank opened in 1975. Although there were no Shariah oversight committees present, it was found that Islamic Financial Institution (IFI) operations were in line with the spirit of Shariah.

With the foundation of the Faisal Islamic Bank of Egypt in 1976 came the formation of the SSB. It was the first Egyptian organization to formally appoint a board of Shariah experts to serve as an SSB (Kahf, 2004). In 1978, the Faisal Islamic Bank of Sudan and the Jordan Islamic Bank did the same; and so did the Kuwait Finance House in 1979, Bank Islam

Malaysia Berhad in 1983, and the Dubai Islamic Bank in 1999. The Islamic Development Bank (IDB) begun building acquaintances with an assortment of Shariah scholars by inviting them for discussion and seeking *fatwas* on *muamalat* issues, despite the fact that it did not have an SSB or designated Shariah council when it was first established (Kahf, 2004). The IDB has also established an SSB.

Abd al-Sami (1988) emphasized the importance of establishing Shariah advisory boards when establishing Islamic banks and "Islamic windows" to reassure consumers and shareholders that Islamic banks are not engaging in activities that are forbidden by Shariah. This is so that any worldwide union of Islamic institutions may serve as evidence of the Shariah advisory board's supreme authority, especially on a global scale. DeLorenzo (2007) argues that it is crucial for mutual funds and unit trusts to include an SSB. A Shariah advisory board is a revolutionary approach to creating an Islamic bank and is one of its fundamental components (Hassan, 2010).

Each Islamic bank will have an SSB whose job it is to review the bank's proposed new products and the types of transactions the bank has conducted to verify they are in line with Islamic law. Until they are approved by the SSB, no new items will be released. In the past, the SSB was made up of religious academics who sometimes lacked a firm grasp of contemporary banking practice and the language used to record financial dealings. This might be a major roadblock in the creation of Islamic financial markets and other innovative businesses. It's encouraging that an attempt is being made to bolster the expertise of the SSB by adding members with banking backgrounds (Ghayad, 2008). It is the responsibility of the SSB to oversee all aspects of Islamic banking to guarantee that they are conducted in accordance with Islamic Shariah law and philosophy (Ghayad, 2008). The SSB is an independent body that works with the IFI's BOD to ensure that the IFI adheres to Islamic law. The SSB is responsible for five main functions, including "[1] ensuring compliance with overall Islamic banking basic concepts, [2] certifying permissible financial products through fatwas, [3] verifying that transactions in accordance with issued *fatwas*, determining and distributing *zakat*, [4] disposing of non-Shariah compliant earnings, and [5] advising on the allocation of income or expenses among shareholders and account for investment holders" (Samra, 2016).

There is also worry that SSB members may struggle to meet all of their obligations across all of the organizations on which they serve due to a lack of competent persons to serve on SSBs. American businesses had

Model of Shariah Supervisory Board and Its Functions   223

an issue with board members sitting on too many boards, which prevented them from meeting their fiduciary obligations (such as the duty of good faith, loyalty, candor, etc.) to any one company. The number of boards on which one individual may sit has been capped at three by several American corporations. A lack of suitably competent people to serve on the SSBs of all current Islamic organizations would result from the adoption of such a criterion. The SSB also raises the issue of supervision. It differs from country to country regarding who oversees SSBs and how they do so. In many countries, especially those where Islamic finance is practiced outside of an Islamic country, the SSB is not formally supervised. Thus, there is no way to guarantee that the *fatwas* issued by a certain SSB are in accordance with Shariah. Members of SSBs are often financially rewarded by the Islamic bank requesting a *fatwa*, which raises the risk that the SSB may rule that a transaction is Shariah-compliant even if it is not. Such actions might confuse conventional and Islamic finance, damaging the former and driving the latter out of business. Furthermore, it is not obvious how differences between management, the Board, and the SSB should be settled or who is accountable for overseeing whom in order to have the "final word." Institutions can't take control of the SSB without outside oversight (Samra, 2016).

The SSB's independence, competence, conflict of interest, anonymity, transparency, disclosure, and the issue of compliance with Shariah and Shariah-based products, as well as the responsibilities of the SSBs, are all important concerns despite the positive development of SG in Islamic banks (Hasan, 2011b).

7.3   Importance of Shariah Supervisory Board

Due to their critical function in monitoring, regulating, and looking into the actions and conduct of IBs, SSBs are required and significant in all IFIs. The creation of Islamic banking products that are in line with Shariah principles, which forbid usury, ambiguity, and suspicion, involves the use of SSBs as well. Customers of Islamic banks feel satisfied and confident just by having SSBs there, which raises their trustworthiness and unintentionally improves their financial success. It is clear that the SSBs have a difficult time finding a specialist who combines knowledge of financial sciences with Fiqh (Islamic law). By providing more Shariah-compliant goods and services, IBs must continue to satisfy client requests and standards. This creates a fresh difficulty for the SSBs.

The required nature of SSB decisions and their independence from conflict management have been the focus of numerous studies and theses, the majority of which contend that the independence and force of SSB decisions are essential. As a result, the reputation of the Islamic bank would unavoidably suffer if this important department, which monitors the bank management's actions, wants, and orientations is inefficient. This is because there may be excesses and irregularities in some areas. As a result, this issue may be connected to the risk of Shariah non-compliance, one of the most significant types of risk for Islamic banks.

Non-compliance with the Shariah laws and principles, as assessed by the Shariah board of the IBs and IFIs, or what the International Financial Services Board (IFSB) or the relevant body in the jurisdiction in which they operate, is characterized as *"shariah* compliance" (IFSB, 2005). Shariah compliance in Islamic banking is also described as a phenomenon that ensures the underlying financial products of the banks are in compliance with the guidelines and laws outlined by the Shariah passed down to Muhammad, the final Prophet of Islam (Ariffin *et al.*, 2007). To do this, the organization's goods and activities must be thoroughly infused with the compliance criteria; a Shariah Board or Advisor or other appropriate system and controls can help (Izhar, 2010). Irresponsible business practices and serious Shariah compliance failures might put your reputation at peril, according to the IFSB (2014). This illustrates the degree to which risk exposure for the Islamic bank could result from SSB action.

7.4   Models of the Shariah Supervisory Board

An important SG structure is the SSB (Grais and Pellegrini, 2006a). To reassure its constituents, banks often form an SSB (Grais and Pellegrini, 2006b). The SSB aids Islamic organizations in effective and Shariah-compliant financial management. If IFIs fail to adhere to Islamic finance principles, it might damage their reputations as well as the reputation of the Islamic finance sector as a whole (Besar *et al.*, 2009; Grais and Pellegrini, 2006a). In a study (Van Gruening and Iqbal, 2008), the SSB is trusted by stakeholders like investors and depositors to deploy their capital in a way that is compliant with Shariah. A standard to govern SSBs is currently being developed by the AAOIFI (Richter, 2010). Right now, SSBs are self-policing.

The board's principal responsibility is to guarantee that the Islamic bank adheres to Islamic values and principles in all aspects of its business (Grassa, 2016). The SSB of the Islamic bank is made up of Shariah academics. This board, which is part of the institution's internal governance structure, acts as an internal control body, bolstering the institution's credibility in the eyes of consumers, shareholders, and so on (Rammal, 2006).

7.4.1 Internal Shariah Supervisory Board

The custom of creating an SSB differs from one nation to another. The lack of consistency in the implementation of SG norms may be traced back to a number of factors, including variations in how different countries address Shariah problems, the scarcity of trained scholars in local areas, and the early or late growth of the Islamic bank in question. It is common practice for Islamic institutions to have an SSB, and in certain places this board's duties have been bolstered by the creation of a Centralized Shariah Supervisory Body (CSSB) (Song and Oosthuizen, 2014). An internal body might be the bank's or the group's SSB.

Individual SSB inside Islamic organizations is the norm rather than the exception. An SSB is often required by an Islamic bank's articles of formation. SSBs may have varying organizational structures on the inside. The SSB's organizational framework is defined by its articles of incorporation. Based on this concept, individual banks may set up their own SSB, apart from those of their parent or group firms. When operating in different countries, each of HSBC Amanah's many branches have their own SSB (Hasan, 2011b). Another concept, with an SSB for a conglomerate of companies, stands in opposition to this one. Although these Islamic organizations engage in international trade, a CSSB ensures that all transactions are conducted in accordance with Islamic law. Since a single SSB cannot manage various Shariah concerns from different jurisdictions at the same time, the mechanism used by the Dallah al-Baraka Group looks ineffectual in the majority of jurisdictions (Hasan, 2011b).

7.4.2 External Shariah Supervisory Boards

Different types of external SSBs include those that operate at the national and international levels, as well as Shariah advisory businesses and independent Shariah advisors. Governments, particularly at the national level, have formed SSBs via the central bank or securities commission (as in Malaysia, Indonesia, Brunei, Pakistan, and Sudan) or through other government organizations (as in Kuwait's Ministry of Awqaf). According to Dar and Azami (2010), the Council of Guardians is solely responsible for Islamic banking and finance in Iran. Here we see an alternative kind of national SSB in action. All of these national SSBs operate as the final arbiters of *fatwas* for IFIs, with the ability to enforce their rulings (Hasan, 2011b).

In contrast, an international SSB is often an independent Shariah authority set up via the collaboration of numerous Muslim nations, such as the AAOIFI and the IDB. Differentiating itself from internal and national SSBs, the AAOIFI SSB is charged with the creation of Shariah standards and the promotion of standardization in SG practice (AAOIFI, 2008). The IDB's SSB offers Shariah advice services internally and contributes to the IFI governance standard-setting process. Both the AAOIFI and the IDB are typically made up of highly respected Shariah experts from all walks of life and all corners of the globe (Hasan, 2011b). All of these scholars have prestigious positions in the Shariah community and are considered top experts in the field of *fiqh al muamalat*.

Other than these, some examples of Shariah advisory firms include the Institute for the Study of Islamic Banking and Insurance (IIBI), the International Organization of Islamic Finance (IIIF), the Islamic Finance and Banking Institute of Malaysia (IBFIM), Yasaar Limited (YL), the Minhaj Shariah Financial Advisory (MSFA), Failaka International relations. (FI), BMB Islamic (BMBI), and Taqwaa Advisory and Shariah Investment Solutions (TASIS). These companies are private businesses unaffiliated with international financial institutions that provide advice and supervision on a wide range of banking and financial matters, particularly those pertaining to Shariah law. Independent parties (like IIBI), international banking organizations (like BMBI and IBFIM), law firms, and individual Shariah experts (like FI, YL, IIIF, and MSFA) all own Shariah advising businesses.

The aforementioned organizations all provide various Shariah consulting services, such as audits, product endorsement, and Shariah assessments. These Shariah advising businesses' major function is to advise clients on how to comply with Islamic law and provide other related services. Consulting and other fees are charged to the IFIs that employ them at rates that are commensurate with the quality and breadth of services

Model of Shariah Supervisory Board and Its Functions 227

provided. Due to the non-binding nature of their work, IFIs are not required to follow the recommendations of Shariah advising companies (Hasan, 2011b).

7.5 The Role and Function Internal of SSB

Legal role: In fact, Islamic banks can't do business as usual unless they adhere to Shariah law. The duty to ensure Shariah compliance rests squarely on the shoulders of the Shariah advisors who serve in a supervisory council, making their mission and function vital.

Tacit role: The SSB is essentially a second government in and of itself. The first concerns the compliance of the board-approved business transactions with Shariah law. The second has to do with whether or not the directors of the bank uphold Shariah law. Monitoring the moral nature of banking's business transactions and product development is not sufficient to ensure the bank's positive image and reputation. The SSB oversees not just the actions of the BOD but also the underlying structures of the organization (Ghayad, 2008).

The SSB's duties should be appropriate to its position as a part of the bank that aids in the accomplishment of the bank's objectives. The board's primary duties include making Shariah pronouncements relevant to the bank's business activities and overseeing the application and implementation of what has been taken from such pronouncements. The role of the SSB is crucial in situations where Shariah non-compliance is brought on by mistake or deliberate wrongdoing by Islamic financial organizations. An internal audit or a review of the contracts and papers distributed to the committee could show Shariah disobedience. The SSB is required to review the transaction's documentation, its execution, and any appendices in order to undertake the audit. Interviews and conversations with the Shariah officer are also necessary for the effective implementation of contracts. Additionally, the author has recommended that the SSB look at the yearly reports, which cover information on profit and loss, deposit accounts (investment, current, and savings), profit distribution, etc. For proper handling of the situation, the Shariah unit must be notified right away of any cases of non-Shariah compliance. The institution's top authority should be informed of the situation, followed by the shareholders if no action is taken. The Supreme Court has the duty to inform the public if no action is taken. One of the SSB's duties is to assess the Shariah compatibility and compliance of each financial transaction in Malaysia's Islamic banking and insurance industries. The Court suggested for the creation an international Shariah council for commercial and financial matters, including representation from all Muslim countries, and this council must work to include all the important Shariah bank experts. Then, they must agree to any general rules and exclusions that apply specifically to their nation (Hassan *et al.*, 2010).

The contribution of Islamic academics to the growth and popularization of Islamic banks was emphasized by Antonio (2001). Among other things, he stated that Islamic scholars' tasks include overseeing how Islamic banks are run, making periodic statements regarding how well products and services adhere to Shariah, conducting in-depth analyses, and making recommendations regarding any new items the bank introduces. In a similar vein, Mudawi (1984) explained that the fundamental functions of an SSB include ensuring that operations adhere to Islamic principles in light of the Western influence on the educational systems of the majority of nations. He added that it would not be necessary to establish the Board if Islamic banking were to operate in a society governed by Shariah law, as the state would have its own organ to issue *fatwas*.

The guidelines stipulate that Shariah advisors on the Islamic Capital Market (ICM) must have adequate experience and exposure in Islamic finance, as well as an understanding of ICM operations and issues. The following have been identified as the primary Shariah oversight areas within ICM:

(a) *Documentation*: The proposal form, contract, agreement, or other relevant documents must go through the Shariah advisors' thorough review and approval process.
(b) *Structuring*: The Shariah consultants must guarantee that the entire transaction involved in the proposed issue complies with Shariah.
(c) *Investment*: The style and manner of the revenue retained by the trustee, as well as the operations carried out with it, must be closely examined for Shariah compliance by the Shariah consultants.
(d) Operational and administrative issues.

Similarly, Salih (2009) has listed five main functions of a Shariah Advisory Board as follows:

(a) To maintain public confidence by adherence to Shariah. The practical supervisory function involves carefully examining all banking activities to make sure that all issued *fatwas* are followed as directed. Advisors on Shariah are expected to offer *fatwas* on business transactions, operations, and product development.

(b) A consultative role before any new product operations are carried out;
(c) Performing an administrative duty by arranging a meeting to discuss Shariah-related issues with management, if necessary;
(d) Academic activities include publishing books and articles, hosting seminars and conferences to explore the difficulties Islamic banks face and the opportunities for their continued development, and teaching bank employees and the general public about the general principles of Islamic commercial law.

According to Haron (1997), there is no uniformity across Islamic banks in terms of the responsibilities and powers of SSBs. However, he noted that these tasks typically fall into three broad categories:

(a) To provide guidelines and offer advice to banks;
(b) To conduct Shariah audits;
(c) To make decisions on matters which have religious repercussions.

Al-Khudairi (1990) provided an overview of the Shariah compliance procedure and divided it into three tiers. The selection and training of the institution's officers to guarantee that they are aware of the nature of Islamic financial operations and secure goods marks at the beginning of the first level. The second level is the internal audit. The third level is the external audit, which also consists of the SSB. This committee is ought to be an impartial, external organization. The author categorizes the duties of the SSB into four groups:

- Reviewing current products on the market to check that all transactions adhere to Shariah and corrective function;
- Reviewing the bank's routine business processes in order to guard against potential non-compliance is a preventive function;
- *Innovative purpose*: To create innovative items that will meet consumer demand;
- *Directive purpose*: To offer recommendations and assistance to improve how the bank operates.

Moreover, integrity in IBs depends on their adherence to Shariah, a defining feature of IBs. The IFSB has stressed the need for Islamic banks to establish procedures to obtain and apply decisions from Shariah scholars and to keep track of their Shariah compliance. Shariah-compliance in Islamic banks should be governed in accordance with recommendations made by the IFSB, which include the following: (i) the establishment of an SSB made up of knowledgeable scholars appointed by shareholders as well as reporting to the BOD, charged with the duty of approving the sale of goods and services and conducting reviews in order to guarantee Shariah-compliance (among other duties); (ii) the establishment of an internal Shariah governance. An important choice must be made about the creation of a Centralized SSB (in addition to SSBs at the bank level) to oversee the SG structure in IBs. By standardizing Shariah judgments, a CSSB may cut down on compliance and Shariah-related expenses for IBs. In secular states where substantive law bans regulator engagement in Shariah concerns, a central SSB might be formed by the regulator, or IBs could be urged to establish such a body collectively. SSBs' responsibilities and reporting lines to IB boards of directors are not standardized. While some of the SSBs the central bank has set up have the power to legislate and adjudicate on Shariah matters, others are just advised on changes to the regulatory framework. Concerning accountability, it is difficult to tell whether SSB members report to the IBs' BOD or not. The bulk of SSB–IB relationships seem to be consultative in nature, with the BOD of the bank ultimately bearing responsibility for Shariah compliance. While this is in line with IFSB Shariah standards, reputational and legal concerns connected with Shariah compliance may be mitigated if SSBs' mandates, responsibility, and independence were clarified (Song and Oosthuizen, 2014).

The literature on SG of Islamic banks (for example, Banaga *et al.*, 1994; Tomkins and Karim, 1987; Ghayad, 2008; Haniffa and Hudaib, 2007) suggests that the SSB would advise on Shariah-related issues of the Islamic banks' activities. Islamic financial services and products (Banaga *et al.*, 1994; Briston and ElAshker, 1986; Alhabshi and Bakar, 2008); providing guidance and developing operational procedures (Alhabshi and Bakar, 2008; Bannaga *et al.*, 1994) advising and developing corporate strategic issues (Alhabshi and Bakar, 2008); and so on are all included in the Shariah Advisory Role of the SSB. When IFIs were originally presented to the Muslim community, the board of the SSB was given credit for legitimizing the business (Siddiqi, 2006). Meanwhile, other scholars have discussed the need for the SSB to balance the desires of shareholders for profits with Shariah compliance with the operations of Islamic banks (Ghayad, 2008; Ahmed, 2011), a task that can be challenging for the SSB. If there is a disagreement between economic considerations and Shariah standards in the creation of an Islamic financial product for sale to consumers, Ahmed (2011) suggested that Shariah principles should take precedence. The SSB has an implied obligation to make sure the Shariah is still being applied and implemented in Islamic banks due to the pervasive effect of the Shariah, which encompasses all elements of Islamic banking operations (Ahmed, 2011). Some of the SSB's previous rulings may become irrelevant due to advancements in the development of Islamic banking operations. Siddiqi (2006) argued that the SSB has the authority to provide a fresh and more relevant Shariah ruling in this case, in accordance with *maqasid al-Shariah* (objectives of the Shariah). Given the ever-changing nature of the Islamic banking sector, it is imperative that the SSB's Shariah advisory role be recognized as flexible and responsive.

The community may have concerns about how to run an Islamic bank or about Islamic banking products, and the SSB must answer these queries (Banaga *et al.*, 1994). The SSB continues to face challenges in the context of contemporary Islamic finance, within which Islamic institutions function. By establishing contemporary Islamic financial goods and services in accordance with their interpretation of Islamic Shariah principles, members of the SSB are tasked with shaping Islamic institutions (Karim, 1996; Tomkins and Karim, 1987; Laldin, 2008). Islamic banks are distinguished from their conventional counterparts by their SSB and the consolidated SSB, as emphasized by Laldin (2008). Furthermore, Laldin (2008) stresses that Islamic banks should be led by the SSB in line with the Shariah principles and that they should not mindlessly imitate conventional banking operations while innovating in contemporary Islamic finance and services. The huge duty that Shariah experts have is justified by the unmatched significance of the SSB (Hassan, 2012).

The SSB's duties and responsibilities are outlined in basic terms in the AAOIFI governance standard. Among these responsibilities is the duty to advise, inspect, and regulate IFIs to ensure they are adhering to Shariah law (AAOIFI, 2005). The Shariah compliance of IFIs' purchases of shares, equities, *sukuk*, and other business avenues can be ensured through the following activities: participation in product development and structuring activities; reviewing and approving matters related to Shariah; issuing *fatwas*; conducting Shariah audits; issuing an annual certification of Shariah compliance (McMillen, 2007); and issuing an annual certification of Shariah compliance. The responsibilities and mandate of each IFI's SSB are specified in the organization's bylaws, as well as in the IFSB principles and AAOIFI governance standards (Hasan, 2011b).

Nevertheless, a typical list of SSB duties in an Islamic financial institution can include the following:

(1) Obtaining *fatwa* approval for the sale of financial instrument items offered by Islamic banks.
(2) Conducting an internal audit of the Shariah internal review unit's implementation of SSB rulings.
(3) Issuing a report every year to shareholders attesting that the bank has operated in accordance with Shariah law.
(4) Determining the amount of *zakat* due and counseling management on how to use the money earned in ways that violate Shariah law to support charitable causes.
(5) Ratifying the allocation of losses and gains to shareholders and investment account holders.
(6) Raising public knowledge of Islamic finance and its goals via outreach, education, and training of Islamic bank personnel in Shariah principles.
(7) Developing new Shariah-compliant products and services (Alkhamees, 2013).
(8) In order to ensure that Islamic banks always act in accordance with Shariah principles, the SSB is tasked with advising the board and providing feedback on Shariah concerns.
(9) The SSB is responsible for approving the Islamic banks' Shariah policies and processes and checking that they adhere to Islamic law.
(10) As part of their responsibilities, Shariah review and Shariah audit must evaluate the work done to guarantee Shariah compliance and guarantee information is included in the annual report.
(11) When a Shariah issue arises in an Islamic bank, the SSB may suggest seeking advice from the SAC.
(12) It is the responsibility of the SSB to present written Shariah views whenever an Islamic bank requests further consultation with the SAC or applies to the Bank for approval of a new product (BNM, 2019).

Alam *et al.* (2021b) stated that in order to meet the demands of the many stakeholders, Islamic banks expect SSB members to offer their opinions on Shariah issues, guidelines, and decisions regarding contemporary banking practices, and to deliver *fatwas* on current issues as presented by management. They should also guarantee Shariah principles and compliance. They can also create and execute SG policies, authorize and develop new products, watch over and monitor banking operations, discover issues

Model of Shariah Supervisory Board and Its Functions

and suggest remedies, and so on. In addition to preparing SG guidelines, ensuring Shariah principles and compliance, monitoring and reviewing all banking activities and functions, evaluating contracts, products, and services, offering opinions on current SG practices, and delivering Shariah resolutions on the overall functions are among the roles and responsibilities carried out by the members of the SSBs.

7.6 The Role and Function of CSSB

SSBs have been established by the central banks or regulatory authorities in Malaysia, Indonesia, Brunei, Pakistan, and Sudan. Establishing an SG structure and developing national policy and judgments for the sector is primarily the purview of a national SSB. According to the IFSB's research into the implementation of Shariah in 69 IFIs across 11 countries (Bahrain, Qatar, Brunei, Iran, Jordan, Indonesia, Malaysia, Pakistan, the United Arab Emirates, Sudan, and Bangladesh), a national Shariah authority's primary function is to establish the SGF, not to issue rulings on individual cases. Despite these results, macro-level SSBs play an important role in the harmonization and standardizing of *fatwa* and serve as the ultimate authority for IFIs (Hasan, 2011b).

Fatwa proclamation by collective *ijtihad*, monitoring (*raqabah*), and review (*mutabaah*) are the three basic aspects of Shariah administration in which the SSB is normally engaged. At the local level, the SSB plays a significant role in providing advice on Shariah matters, ensuring that operations are in line with Shariah principles, recommending and confirming the appropriate paperwork pertaining to the goods and services it sells, as well as internal procedures, manuals, and advertisements, and making sure that all of its decisions are carried out correctly. The SSB is the supreme Shariah authority at the national (macro) level, with the power to create a Shariah-compliant framework for governance and to issue Shariah-compliant policies and industry judgments. Meanwhile, a worldwide SSB like the AAOIFI prioritizes Shariah standardization and improvement (Hasan, 2011b). According to Alam (2022), SSBs should be in charge of providing appropriate Shariah instructions and applications, and CSSBs should oversee and direct all Islamic banks (AAOIFI, 2017). Furthermore, CSSB has the authority to review and update the current Shariah guidelines, rules, and principles as well as the investment and deposit contracts of all Islamic banks. It can also create standard and homogenous guidelines (Alam, 2022; Hossain and Khatun, 2014; Hassan *et al.*, 2017). They can

234   *Shariah Governance Systems of Islamic Banks*

examine each bank's audit functions and determine whether or not they were carried out in accordance with the rules set forth by the central bank. Once all of these tasks have been completed and the results have been analyzed, they can then advise the Islamic banks to correct any errors and raise the standard of Shariah compliance (Alam, 2022). In addition, the CSSB can organize training sessions, conferences, seminars, symposiums, and social awareness campaigns to dispel public misconceptions, enhance the caliber of bankers' applications, and apply Shariah (Alam, 2022). Even though the Shariah process will take a while to implement due to the CSSB's exclusive authority, it will be a flawless process that guarantees each SSB's accountability for carrying out their duties. For their overall work, each SSB will be accountable to the CSSB (BNM, 2019). In cases when the Shariah issues are not being followed by individual banks or the SSB, the CSSB has the authority to take action or address the central bank to resolve the matter.

7.7 The Supervision of Islamic Banking in Practice

Just like in conventional banking, prudential monitoring within an IB framework is necessary to protect the soundness and security of individual IBs and to help offset risks to the stability of the financial system. The supervision of banks has to be done in a way that respects the specifics of IFIs. Administrators must be aware of the challenges associated with IB and the possible outcomes of interactions between IBs and CBs, such as regulatory arbitrage.

In countries that allow both Islamic and traditional financial services, IBs may choose between two different supervisory frameworks. Some countries (Ethiopia, Kazakhstan, Saudi Arabia, Kuwait, Qatar, Kenya, Tunisia, the United Arab Emirates, Turkey, and the United Kingdom, for example) follow the first model, in which both IBs and CBs report to a single supervisory body. In the second model, different parts of a single supervisory body (as in Indonesia, Bahrain, Jordan, Pakistan, Lebanon, and Syria) handle different aspects of regulation. In the initial scenario, all banks (IBs and CBs) are governed by the same set of regulations, but in the second model, IBs may be subject to different regulations from different regulatory bodies. There is usually a great deal of agreement between the different supervisory frameworks in actual use.

Whether or not a certain paradigm of banking supervision is adequate depends on local needs and circumstances. Authorities should be cognizant of the costs connected with any reorganization of a regulatory and supervisory structure and think about implementing less expensive alternatives, such as improving communication, coordination, and information sharing across agencies, despite the fact that the benefits associated with integration have been recognized. In most cases, authorities should look for the most efficient ways to achieve their goals rather than concentrating on the optimal structure of monitoring. Adequate resources (such as sufficient funding, the right abilities, and legitimate people), an appropriate legal foundation, an effectively designed governance framework, and accurate accountability practice are necessary for effective financial supervision.

Shariah compliance is required regardless of whether or whether a given supervisory authority uses a risk-based or traditional approach to monitoring IBs. The regulatory authorities use the same supervision structure and set of procedures for both Islamic and conventional banks. It is typically appropriate to use a Capital-Asset-Management-Earnings-Liquidity-Sensitivity (CAMELS) grading system, but this approach must be modified to account for the specific risks involved in IB, such as those related to Shariah compliance, capital sufficiency, asset quality, and liquidity. It is also necessary to modify the existing stress testing frameworks. To get there, we need better data collection and accounting practice, particularly those that zero in on what makes IBs so special. Islamic banking and Shariah compliance are regulated in a manner that is unique to each supervisor. Generally speaking, the stricter the enforcement of Shariah law is, the more Muslim-dominated a culture is. Strict regulations and increased supervisory monitoring are recommended to limit the risks connected with Shariah compliance and offer sufficient consumer protection in countries where Islamic windows operate.

Improved disclosure and transparency measures for IBs should have the support of regulatory bodies. Guidelines for encouraging good business practices, protecting stakeholders, and taking enforcement action in the case of non-compliance should be developed in accordance with IFSB standards. In practice, approaches to the kind and amount of information that banks must give to regulatory bodies have varied widely among countries. To facilitate remote supervision, all banks in countries where Shariah law is not accepted must provide the same data (including data collected remotely). Additional information on Islamic banking operations and products may be requested from IBs in Shariah law countries with both conventional and IBs in order to evaluate the bank's adherence to Shariah law.

Furthermore, different legal systems use various techniques to provide on-site monitoring. There is a greater emphasis on operational risks and supervisors look at whether there is a discrepancy between the facts on the ground and public representations regarding Shariah compliance at an Islamic bank under the same on-site supervision framework in non-Shariah jurisdictions. If a discrepancy is found, the supervisory authority will evaluate its potential effects on the bank's "systems and controls" and reputational risk management evaluation, as well as on mis-selling, consumer protection, governance, and internal controls. Up to 80% of the supervisory authority's resources are apparently dedicated to ensuring Shariah compliance (and onsite examiners are well-trained and educated about Shariah law) in Shariah law countries where only IBs are authorized.

It is also important to create FSIs for IBs, increase supervisory capability on IB-related concerns, and prioritize consolidated and cross-border supervision. When designing FSIs, it's important to consider how IB works and ensure that all relevant information is made public. This would help interested parties understand the FSIs' calculation process, how they differ from CB FSIs, and how they were included in bank risk assessments. The IFSB and other suppliers of technical assistance should be used to help supervisory authorities in jurisdictions where IBs are situated learn about the specific requirements for supervising IBs. Last but not least, it is recommended that authorities adopt the soon-to-be-released IFSB core principles for IB. Doing so would assist mitigate regulatory arbitrage across countries. Adopting these fundamental principles, which are in line with the Basel fundamental principles for effective bank supervision, would be beneficial for all countries where IBs are monitored either independently or in tandem with CBs (Norat *et al.*, 2014).

7.8 Issues and Challenges of the Shariah Supervisory Board

The Islamic finance business, and its SG structure, in particular, face considerable obstacles and concerns when Islamic financing is practiced beyond international boundaries. Unresolved concerns and challenges must be dealt with properly since compliance with Shariah cannot be jeopardized at any time. Hasan (2011b) found that the Islamic financial industry faces six major concerns and challenges related to the SGF. A properly operating SSB is also supposed to be thorough, timely, consistent, and open in its discussions and judgments. This is relevant to concerns about the impartiality, secrecy, expertise, consistency, and transparency of SSB conducting audits of IFI operations to ensure Shariah compliance.

Lack of clarity regarding how directors should make decisions is one of the challenges associated with viewing the corporation as a social entity. Directors are better equipped to balance competing interests when making crucial decisions for the organization when they are aware that shareholders are their primary obligation. In contrast, stakeholders for IFIs include members of the larger Islamic community, customers who participate in a profit-sharing scheme, recipients of the IFI's *zakat*, and the local communities in which the IFI operates. Islamic finance's most significant stakeholder, according to experts, is Islam itself. Providing directors with direction regarding the corporation's important stakeholders and how to prioritize their interests when faced with difficult decisions is one of the issues IFIs encounter when implementing CG. What rights the stakeholders would have if they object to the IFI's actions is likewise not clear. Would a consumer have the right to question the investment's Islamic nature, for example, if he no longer thought his product was actually Shariah-compliant? To whom would he address this challenge (Chapra and Habib, 2002)? Thus, Tabash *et al.* (2020) stated that the Islamic banks in Bangladesh have an image crisis and are negatively legitimized as they violate Shariah principles.

Having their own SSBs with local Imam and Shariah scholars as members is one of the most important challenges of SG in Islamic institutions. There are instances in which their opinions diverged from those of the world's foremost Shariah advisors. Fiqh al-*Muamalat* is an intricate component of Islamic law that is still in the process of development. Occasionally, local Imams and Shariah scholars may be unfamiliar with the appropriate profundity of Fiqh *Muamalat* concepts. There are numerous Madhabs (schools of Islamic law) with contradictory interpretations of Shariah law throughout the globe. Global Shariah standardization is therefore not always possible. Due to the inherent conflicts of interest among Shariah scholars, the global function of Shariah scholars must be transparent. SG's most challenging issue is Islamic finance's dearth of human capital. In his article, Rahman (2006) argues that the lack of product knowledge and practical banking experience can make it difficult for Shariah Scholars to achieve synchronization between financial products and activities. The conventional governance system differs significantly from the administration of the Islamic bank. Conventional governance or management is not required to adhere to the recommendations or regulations of their legal advisors, whereas Islamic bank management is required to adhere to the decisions and recommendations of their Shariah advisors. The difficulty lies in differentiating between Shariah regulatory, legal, financial, and tax requirements for the development of Islamic finance. In the current evolution of Islamic finance, banks may lose consumers if their new products do not achieve satisfactory growth. A newly introduced product must be devoid of *riba*, *zulm*, and *gharar*. It is essential for banks to receive sanctions from their Shariah scholars before launching new products. Due to a dearth of knowledgeable human capital, it is possible that the majority of Shariah scholars lack familiarity with such proceedings. Since stringent Shariah regulations may impede the rapid development of Islamic finance, flexibility is provided for "exceptional need." The challenges of SG are moving toward innovation and providing Islamic-based services and products while competing with conventional products that have reached maturity. It can be challenging to perform an exhaustive Shariah compliance audit of the operations of a fully fledged Islamic financial institution while maintaining confidentiality.

7.8.1 *Independence of Shariah Supervisory Board*

The independence of the SSB is an imporatnt contested topic. One problem is that IFIs pay the members of the SSB, which may lead to a conflict of interest if those individuals were to approve of dubious or illegal practices only to keep their jobs (Rammal, 2006: 207). The credibility of IFIs hinges on the supposed independence of the SSB, which is not entirely accurate because members of the SSB are expected to be anchored in moral beliefs and religious values. However, an appropriate structure in the form of a policy or regulation is still required. It's to be expected that as the Islamic financial business grows exponentially, so will the number of competing *fatwas*. Because of this, learning more about the method used to appoint the SSB is crucial.

Aboumouamer (1989) found that of the 41 members of the SSB questioned, 75% thought that the Board's power is drawn from the shareholders and that the Board's connections with its executives and directors were confined to coordination and advising responsibilities. No firm conclusions can be drawn from this study; rather, it serves to show the BOD's viewpoint on the selection of the SSB. Another study, this one done in 1996 by the International Institute of Islamic Thought, seems to show a different picture, finding that the BOD, rather than the shareholders, made approximately 80% of the nominations to the SSB. These two studies debunk the common assumption that an IFI's SSB can only be really independent if it is selected by the shareholders, showing instead that the practice of selecting the board varies widely across IFIs.

In and of itself, the argument that the SSB's impartiality may be ensured by its selection by the company's shareholders falls flat. A member of the SSB may be appointed by the shareholders, but the BOD can still have input into the process. In its place, it is worthwhile to notice the recommendations made by Grais and Pellegrini (2006a), who provide three methods for addressing the problem of the SSB's lack of autonomy. The approaches appear to revolve around giving the SSB equivalent authority to that held by independent directors in the audit committee (Hasan, 2011b). This includes clearly outlining the board's responsibilities and powers in the articles of association, giving the board sufficient powers, and granting the board the appropriate organizational status and audit responsibilities.

Here, independence is not letting the opinions of others influence or change your own. This is possible because of the organization's reliability and objectivity. The independence of the SSB is crucial to achieving the core purpose of IFIs, which is Shariah compliance, and to increase public faith in the conformity of IFIs to Shariah rules and principles. In order to preserve the board's impartiality, participants of the SSB ought not to defer to the assessment of others on is important of Shariah supervision; they also shouldn't work for the same IFI or have any hand in the management or day-to-day operations of the IFIs. Alam and Miah (2021) found the SSBs of Islamic banks in Bangladesh are not independent in performing their Shariah activities.

7.8.2 Competence, Conflict of Interest, and Confidentiality

The majority of SSB members (76.6% according to a study of Islamic banking practice) are educated and qualified, but only 8.6% have knowledge of both Shariah and business law, and only 11.4% have knowledge of Shariah, law, and economics. A further survey found that only 92% of the members of 41 SSBs had formal training in Islamic law, while 60% had studied non-religious topics. This finding suggests that some individuals have doubts about the broad range of standards and qualifications met by the SSB. There is also a lack of coordination and standardized curricula (McMillen, 2006) with regard to the education of SSB members. The efficiency of the SSBs' work may depend on the individual in this role, who must have the requisite professional expertise and education in addition to Shariah competence in order to make substantive and tangible Shariah judgments. SSB members of Islamic banks lack proficient qualifications.

For a long time now, Shariah scholars in Kuwait, Saudi Arabia, Bahrain, Qatar, and the United Arab Emirates have enjoyed the unfettered ability to serve on SSBs. In reality, as is evident from the standard procedure in many countries, there is no prohibition on members of an SSB sitting on the boards of other IFIs. There are now questions about conflict of interest and secrecy that cast a poor light on the SSB. When the same consultants who sit on the central bank's SSB additionally work for the IFI in question, a conflict of interest and breach of confidentiality may arise when a new Islamic banking product of the IFI is presented for approval to the SSB. Due to the conflicting nature of the SBS's and the Shariah Advisor's contractual responsibilities, the Shariah Advisor may not serve on both the SSB and the IFI's BOD. Alam (2022) suggested that SSB should not be members of multiple banks and CSSB members shall not sit in institutional SSBs.

7.8.3 *Disclosure and Transparency*

Openness and honesty are fundamental tenets of SG. Since the al-Qur'an forbids concealing evidence, IFIs must be completely transparent if they want to be compliant with Shariah. The IFSB states that IFIs must guarantee that their financial and non-financial reporting adhere to generally accepted accounting standards and Shariah principles (IFSB, 2006: 5). Information sharing is now low, as seen by the numerous SG practice; even information on Shariah decisions is hardly available to the public.

Both Grais and Pellegrini (2006a) and Maali *et al.* (2006: 285) conducted surveys that draw attention to the drawbacks of the current practice of disclosing information, particularly the Shariah report. Despite the fact that the Shariah report is essential for demonstrating the IFI's adherence to Islamic principles and for informing the public and interested parties of the degree to which the IFI's services and goods comply with Shariah criteria, many IFIs nevertheless choose to disregard it. Hasan (2011) contends that the greatest SG system should permit complete openness and

Model of Shariah Supervisory Board and Its Functions 241

transparency as a result. Alam (2022) suggested that Islamic banks should disclose all relevant Shariah compliance and non-compliance information to their stakeholders.

7.8.4 *Shariah-Compliant vs Shariah-Based*

Intense debate has been sparked by numerous criticisms of the current practice of Islamic finance, especially regarding the question of whether or not something is Shariah-compliant or Shariah-based. The latter can be characterized as complying with the Shariah objectives and spirit, while the former refers only to the legal aspects of Shariah law. Proponents of the Shariah-based approach believe that Islamic financial goods and services must be concerned not only with conformity with Islamic law but also with the *maqasid* Shariah (Dar, 2009), even if there is no exact definition of Shariah-compliant and Shariah-based. Shariah-compliant goods are Islamic financial instruments that were not developed for the mainstream market, according to a second line of reasoning (ISRA, 2009: 2). Product innovation is very important for developing *maqasid* Shariah-compliant financial systems, according to Siddiqi (2008).

There is no difference between Shariah-compliant and Shariah-based goods, say some academics. To be considered Shariah-compliant, Shariah-based, or Shariah-tolerant, a financial product must be free of interest, uncertainty, wagering, and forbidden things, and it must also meet the contractual requirements (ISRA, 2009: 2). In contrast, the Shariah-based approach is described by Dar (2009a: 10–12) as including two components: strict adherence to Shariah principles and the discharge of one's societal duties. There are three types of Islamic financial products that he identifies: those that are Shariah-tolerant, like *tawarruq* and *bay-al inah*; those that are Shariah-compliant, like *murbahah*-based short selling and *arbun*-based short selling; and those that are Shariah-based, like *waqf*-based financial products, *zakah*, Islamic private equity, and Islamic venture capitalists. This system classifies Islamic financial items according to how closely they adhere to Shariah. The SG structure may be impacted by the variety of interpretations of Shariah-compliant and Shariah-based goods. SG will be restricted to the legal formalities of Islamic financial instruments if compliance with the Shariah is the main consideration.

If social obligation, the interest of the public, and *malahah* are included in IFIs' activities, the SG structure expands and becomes more nuanced. Currently, IFIs must take into account Shariah compliance as well as their

242   *Shariah Governance Systems of Islamic Banks*

social duties in order to be in line with the Shariah-based strategy. Since this broadens the application and intent of the SG structure, it may have implications for IFIs.

7.8.5 *Consistency*

Given the variation in Islamic financial practice between countries, conflicting *fatwas* or Shariah declarations are possible and might shake faith in the sector. For the purpose of consistency, there has to be continual work to unify Shariah requirements. Shariah harmonization has benefits and drawbacks, but it might help bring the Islamic banking sector closer to the degree of uniformity that is essential to its success.

Furthermore, the adoption of the AAOIFI Shariah criteria will ensure the enforceable nature of transactions and standardize Islamic financial practices across countries. Bruneian, Jordanian, and Qatari IFIs were the most enthusiastic for Shariah adoption, followed by Sudanese and Indonesian IFIs. IFIs from Malaysia, Pakistan, and the United Arab Emirates were less enthusiastic. About 65% of the surveyed IFIs also fail to recognize the relevance of the AAOIFI Shariah requirements.

The choice to embrace global standards is one that is political, despite the fact that SG practice need shared and strict norms. The future of Islamic finance will be determined in large part by political will, as seen by current practice. In the meanwhile, it's important to look at things from different angles as they pertain to the unique political, economic, and legal climates of different countries. The IFSB views that no "single paradigm" or "perfect fit for all" exists is instructive here. IFIs should have a set of satisfactory, effective, and high SG standards capable of maintaining their credibility and mitigating Shariah's failure to comply with risks (Hasan, 2011b) if external as well as internal variables of certain countries are toward the adoption of such Shariah standards.

7.8.6 *The Remit of Various Institutions of Shariah Supervisory Boards*

It is possible that a lack of coordination and administrative overlap would result from the creation of SSBs in several types of IFIs and at the national level. IFIs may need to go through many tiers of SSBs to have their products approved. The Shariah-based system of government that exists in Malaysia might serve as a model. It is common practice for IFIs to seek the advice of both their own SSB and the national Shariah consultative council before releasing a new Islamic financial product. If the transaction includes Islamic capital market products, the IFI will need approval from the CSSBs. For IFIs, this drawn-out process might mean higher costs in terms of time and resources spent and perhaps the appearance of competing *fatwas*.

Insufficient dialogue amongst SSBs hinders efforts to standardize procedures and policies, according to the IFSB study. IFSB (2008) reports that only 65% of SSBs interact with other IFIs' SSBs, and only 45% of individual IFI-level SSBs contact with the CSSB. Given this shortcoming, the SGF must be able to address the mission of SSBs by coordinating Shariah at both the institutional and country levels.

7.8.7 The Commitment of Dedicated, Qualified Directors Who Understand and Can Assess Shariah

Compliance would allow for more efficient governance and protect the business sector from reputational risks. When assessing and encouraging the growth of Shariah-compliant financial services, the credentials and expertise of Shariah advisers are crucial. Without it, the shareholders/BOD might abandon Shariah principles in favor of short-term profits/gains. Having Shariah experts on the board would discourage putting profits before religious tenets. The licensing step is crucial from a regulatory perspective since the licensing body needs clear proof of the sponsorship's commitment to Islamic banking.

7.8.8 Demarcation of Responsibility and Accountability between Board, Management, and SSB

The demarcation problem between the SSB and the management/BOD is analogous to the separation of powers separating the BOD and the Management in a traditional bank. It seems to reason that the Shariah consultant will go into most areas of the business given the religious underpinnings of the company. However, rather than meddling in day-to-day operations, the SSB's role may be confined to certifying the fundamental structure of goods and other specific activities. Although traditional bank advisors are more common, Shariah advisors must be the norm. Since the most eminent Shariah scholars are already recognized on the SSBs of different institutions, there is a pressing need to increase both the number and expertise of Shariah scholars working in the financial sector. To this end, the State Bank of Pakistan has taken the lead by requiring all financial institutions to select a single Shariah Scholar in line with the Fit and Proper Criteria. This has led to the appointment of Shariah consultants by all of the authorized IFIs, and the practice is spreading to new institutions. This strategy also guarantees that these advisors will be accessible around the clock to assist and supervise the organizations.

7.8.9 Investment Policy to Comply with Shariah Criteria

Companies engaged in *non-halal* activities are ineligible for investment by an IFI, whether through financing or the purchase of shares. This adds a new dimension to the CG responsibilities of the IFIs' Board and management. The investment policy, which must be Shariah-compliant, is part of the overarching corporate strategy that must be approved by the Board.

7.8.10 Investors' Protection

According to the Mudaraba concept, the IAH, in the role of Rabb-ul-Mal, bears the risk of the invested money provided by the IFI, in the role of Mudarib. This means that IAHs are subject to the same risk of capital loss as IFI shareholders due to their status as investors in the IFI. Given that the IAH would be more risk averse than IFI owners, the supervisory authorities should play a role in defending the IAH's interests *vis-à-vis* the shareholders of IFIs when it comes to their rights and preserving against combining of funds and/or disputes of interest of shareholders. Central banks providing deposit insurance schemes might construct Shariah-compliant deposit insurance networks to provide an additional layer of protection for depositors of IFIs while preserving the stability of the financial system.

7.8.11 Financing

When it comes to finance, the safety of the invested money depends on the business's management whether the funds have been invested via a Musharaka or Mudaraba. Using Musharaka or Mudaraba, IFIs should keep a close eye on the businesses they fund. The role of IFIs in the management of these kinds of firms should be long-term and active, rather than short-term and transactional. IFIs need industry expertise in order to properly evaluate business risk and keep tabs on these companies' activities.

7.8.12 Harmonization of Shariah Rulings

The lack of uniformity in the interpretation of Shariah law across different countries and areas is one of the obstacles faced by the Islamic banking sector. Different schools of thinking on the same subject might bring interesting variety, but they can also lead to public misunderstanding. If the Islamic financial services business is able to achieve global harmony, its diversity may become a strength, enabling it to meet the demands of a wide range of consumers. AAOIFI has taken the lead by developing Shariah standards that have been approved by 14 leading Shariah experts from different parts of the world. Shariah conformity and new product development may both benefit from the international spread of these standards. It is also necessary for the central banks/regulatory agencies that keep an eye on Islamic financial firms to organize their own SSB to help them with things like rulemaking and reconciling competing interpretations of Shariah law.

7.8.13 Vigilance and Oversight of the Supervisor

The role of the supervisor in a cryptocurrency bank is just as important as it is in a traditional bank. Having a framework in place to oversee Shariah compliance is crucial to ensuring the continued success and growth of the Islamic financial system in accordance with Islamic law (Akhtar, 2006).

7.8.14 The Absence of Proper Shariah Governance

Not only has the business of Islamic banking and finance been self-regulating from its start, without the monitoring or participation of genuinely independent authorities, but it also confronts challenges owing to a lack of viable SG. Despite the Fiqh Academy, the largest group of modern Shariah scholars, declaring Tawarruq to be wholly forbidden, the industry-based regulatory body AAOIFI has introduced a standard for this product. To exclude unqualified SSB members, the Islamic Financial Service Board (IFSB) has avoided the subject of creating governance rules for SSBs (Aljarhi, 2009). This shows how ineffective and unreliable industry self-regulation has been. Since the main problem facing Islamic banking is the legitimacy of its offerings and their closeness to normal banking products, the involvement of central banks has also proved ineffectual. Because of the parallels between conventional banking goods and Islamic

246 *Shariah Governance Systems of Islamic Banks*

banking products, central banks are unlikely to be pleased with Islamic banks providing truly Islamic products. Central banks are likely to be unhappy if IFIs provide genuine Islamic goods because of the dangers these products pose to the economy. Therefore, there has to be a level playing field when it comes to Shariah regulation, and any Shariah regulating body should be wholly apart from Islamic banks (Abozaid, 2016).

7.8.15 *Accountability*

The absence of institutional institutions to ensure that board members are held accountable presents another problem for the IFIs with CG. Members of the SSB and the general BOD are also subject to this requirement for responsibility. Due to several of the issues raised above, there aren't many safeguards in place to make sure a bank genuinely complies with Shariah when it says its products are compatible. Furthermore, the Islamic world has not completely evolved the role of governments and central banks in creating and enforcing CG standards (Chapra and Habib, 2002).

7.9 Conclusion

Similarly important to CG is the concept of SG, which is used to assess whether or not Islamic financial transactions are in line with Shariah's conclusions and principles (Haqqi, 2014). By lowering Shariah non-compliance concerns and, in the long term, helping to maintain financial stability, the new SG structure will increase stakeholder trust and the credibility of the Islamic financial sector.

The credibility of IFIs would be bolstered by the implementation of effective SG. These concerns must be dealt with in this Shariah-based system of government. Harmonizing and improving SG practice requires adherence to the AAOIFI governance requirements and the IFSB governing principles. Many problems with SG are hoped to be solved by the standards. Based on what has been discussed above, it would seem that there is room for improvement in the current SG structure that is intended to foster the growth of the Islamic financial sector. In order to identify problems and give guidance for SG optimal practice in IFIs, this situation necessitates more study and investigation of the level of SG practice across countries (Hasan, 2011b).

CHAPTER 8

Shariah Risk Management and Compliance System

8.1 Introduction

The public's trust in Islamic Financial Institutions (IFIs) with regard to their adherence to Shariah principles in practice may be bolstered by the Shariah governance (SG) system's emphasis on moderation and fairness in financial transactions (Wilson, 2009). IFIs want to please their shareholders, of course, but they also want to earn the respect and trust of the people who use their services. The public's faith in the goods' legality and legitimacy may suffer if there is no oversight mechanism or governing structure in place. The *ex-ante* and *ex-post* Shariah compliance procedures of the Shariah Governance Framework (SGF) will boost the credibility of 87 IFIs. Alam *et al.* (2020b, 2020d; 2021b, 2022a, 2023a, 2023b) and Alam (2022) highlighted that Islamic banks in Bangladesh are not following Shariah principles which damage their image and reputation.

Shariah non-compliance risk is a special kind of risk faced only by IFIs, and it is this risk that the SG structure is designed to mitigate. According to the IFSB-3, "Shariah non-compliance risk" is "the danger that results from IFIs' inability to be in accordance with the principles and regulations of Shariah established by the SSB or the appropriate governing body in the area of authority in which IFIs operate" (IFSB, 2006: 26). As an example of the operational and regulatory risk posed by Shariah non-compliance, Delorenzo (2007) uses *fatwa* rejection and differences. Shariah risk is further subdivided by Iqbal and Mirakhor (2007) into two subcategories: Shariah non-compliance risk and Islamic financial product risk that deviates from industry norms.

We observe the importance of Shariah non-compliance risk to the Islamic finance sector in the case of declining *sukuk* issuance, as demonstrated by the Malaysian High Court's assessment of the BBA issue and the disagreement over *The Investment Dar Company KSCC vs. Blom Developments Bank Sal* (2009) EWHC 3545 and the OIC Fiqh Academy's statement on the illegality of *tawarruq* (Ch). 90 Despite the influence of several factors, Sheikh Muhammad Taqi Usmani's assertion that 85% of possibly Shariah-compliant *sukuk* in the Gulf are non-compliant has damaged public confidence in the legitimacy and Islamicity of *sukuk*. The revelation of the *tawarruq* financial instrument's inadmissibility could have significant ramifications for IFIs given how widely accessible it is. Additionally, when the BBA facility's profit-sharing structure was taken before the Malaysian High Court, a knowledgeable judge ruled that it was improper. Since more than 80% of Islamic financial facilities in Malaysia are built on the BBA concept, this virtually spelled the end for IFIs.

The Islamic banking industry finds it challenging to implement the vast and complex SGF. Non-compliance with Shariah law presents a distinct threat to IFIs. The possibility of failure to comply with Shariah standards poses a threat to IFIs. The IFSB (2006) outlined that SGF provides a method of managing risks, especially those associated with Shariah non-compliance, liquidity, return on investment, and other areas of concern. There is a potential for operational and regulatory concerns to develop from the various intellectual views. Three prominent examples include a ruling against *tawarruq* by the Organization of the Islamic Conference (OIC) Fiqh Academy, a ruling against bay *bithamanajil* by the Malaysian high court, and a statement by the chairman of the AAOIFI SSB rejecting *sukuk* issuances, which is the main objective of SG. The AAOIFI accounting guidelines confirm the need to be open and honest about an IFI's financial standing. Shariah risk is an element of operational risk, and according to the International Financial Services Board (2002), it can only be managed properly with a competent and adequate SGF. Therefore, an SGF helps IFIs minimize Shariah non-compliance risks, which might cost them credibility and money. In an SG structure, IFIs rely on Shariah consultants for guidance on Shariah-related issues. Financial activity and earnings are closely tracked. Advisors may do more than just draw up items and contracts; they can also serve as impartial arbiters in cases where

Shariah law is at issue. Performing Shariah audits for IFIs is the most crucial duty.

8.2 The Risk Profile in Islamic Financial Intermediation

Risks associated with the intermediation process make it difficult for IFIs to remain competitive and satisfy the interests of their many constituencies (including depositors, stockholders, and government regulators). Islamic banks might better manage risk and compete with conventional banks with the help of a robust risk management competence, a business-friendly institutional climate, and an efficient regulatory framework. In addition, these factors would allow them to establish the genuine groundwork for Islamic financial intermediation and reap the advantages that flow from it. In this part, this section reviews the operational IFI's risk profile in light of the theoretical framework. Islamic institutions, in theory, would be more stable than traditional banks. This competitive edge is due to the fact that both banks and investment depositors share in the risks associated with the banking industry. This risk-sharing tenet directly embraces market discipline. Any negative effect on the returns on an Islamic bank's assets is assumed to be borne by the bank's owners and investment depositors in the theoretical model (Baldwin *et al.*, 2002; Khan and Ahmed, 2001). Participants of the sharing of profits investment accounts in the Islamic system communicate the financial institution's earnings and decreases alongside the shareholders and are therefore exposed to the risk of departing all or a portion of the initial investment they made, whereas consumers within traditional banking systems have a fixed assertion on the returns to the assets of the financial institution because they are paid an agreed-upon rate of interest in addition to their guaranteed the head office regardless of the bank's profitability.

In practice, the risk-sharing benefit is "neutralized" when Islamic banks with hybrid systems offer their investment holders of accounts of a competitive "market" return regardless of their real performance and profitability. As a result, equity investors face a business risk as their rewards are diverted. The gap between theory and practice is also shown in the shift away from profit-sharing and loss-sharing (PLS) initiatives like Mudaraba and Musharaka and toward alternative modalities of financing like *ijara* and *murabaha*. This shift is probably the result of cautious asset allocation and susceptibility because of liquid debts. Because of this, short-term, low-profit, and safe trade-related activities tend to dominate

Figure 8.1: Risk Profile in the Operational Activities of IFI.
Source: Modified from El-Hawary et al. (2004). World Bank Policy Research Working Paper 3227.

asset portfolios, leaving less capital available for longer-term, higher-profit, and riskier investments.

The dangers that operational IFI faces are summarized in Figure 8.1. Risks may be broken down into the following five broad categories: transactional, operational, treasury, governance, and fundamental. IFIs have unique risks depending on their balance sheet composition and the types of contracts they implement.

It has been argued that the PLS aspect of Islamic financing creates new risks for the sector. According to AAOIFI (1999), misplaced commercial risk occurs when an Islamic bank is compelled to provide a larger rate of return to its investment depositors than what is required under the "actual" requirements of the investment agreement. A policy an Islamic bank imposes on its own to prevent customers from cashing out their investment accounts and putting their money somewhere else. As a result, the bank may have to sacrifice part or all of the income it would otherwise distribute to its shareholders during times of economic stress. The International Islamic Bank for Investment and Reconstruction in Egypt did not pay any dividends to its stockholders throughout the mid- to late-1980s, instead gave the money to customers with investment accounts.

At the other end of the range of business hazards, "withdrawal risk" is important to consider. That's because conventional and IFIs provide formidable competition for IFIs (Khan and Ahmed, 2001). Because depositors at an Islamic bank would get a lower rate of return than those at conventional banks, the Islamic bank may lose customers to the competition. The bank's brand value would suffer as a result of withdrawals of this magnitude. The danger that a bank would run out of money is known as solvency risk (Greuning and Bratanovic, 2003), and it's another kind of business risk.

The fiduciary risk inherent in IFIs is distinct in type since it is a direct result of the PLS feature of Islamic financing. According to AAOIFI (1999), fiduciary risk is the danger of being held legally liable for a violation of the investment contract due to non-compliance with Shariah standards or mishandling of investors' assets. The breach of the bank's fiduciary obligation to its depositors would result in direct losses, and the subsequent drop in the market price of the bank's publicly traded shares would result in indirect losses. This outcome, as will be described further, ought to indirectly impose market regulation on Islamic institutions.

Furthermore, the bank's image would suffer if carelessness or malfeasance occurred. If depositors lose trust and withdraw their money, even a healthy Islamic bank might go down. The danger of economic loss owing to fiduciary risk affects both stockholders and investment deposits because of the possibility that they may not get their expected portion of the bank's profits. For instance, if the bank were to invest in assets that did not comply with Shariah law, any profits would be given to charity.

By allowing depositors to cash out their funds, shareholders to sell shares, and authorities to take necessary measures in the event of any mismanagement or misconduct, disclosure of data promotes discipline in the markets and enables different stakeholders to safeguard their own interests. However, differences in accounting approaches across Islamic organizations have made it more difficult to compare, standardize, and disclose the financial health of these organizations. This reduces the potential impact of market discipline and increases uncertainty. Basel Committee for Banking Supervision, September 1998, defines transparency as "the public disclosure of trustworthy and up-to-date data that enables users of that knowledge to make an accurate evaluation of a bank's financial standing and achievement, company operations, risk outline, and risk management practice." Consequently, losses are more likely to be incurred as a consequence of bad judgments made with little or wrong information when there is a lack of transparency.

Operational risk, often known as the risk associated with internal processes comprising people and systems, is a subset of governance risk. Specifically, Islamic banks are vulnerable to losses due to the possibility of human error (Khan and Ahmed, 2001). In 1998, the Dubai Islamic Bank lost $50 million due to an internal control problem when a bank executive did not follow the firm's loan conditions. A total of $138 million, or 7% of the bank's total deposits, were withdrawn in a single day because of this (Warde, 2000). This is in addition to the operational risk of using software and communication technologies that aren't designed with Islamic institutions in mind (tech risk) (Khan and Ahmed, 2001).

Neither Islamic nor conventional banks need a supportive institutional setting and an efficient regulatory framework to function. Islamic banks face systemic risks from institutional, legal, and regulatory challenges because of this lack of support. The absence of agreement among Fiqh experts on the contractual principles governing financial transactions poses a significant threat to financial institutions. Some scholars of Islamic law (Fiqh) hold that a buyer is legally bound by the terms of a *murabaha* or *Istisna* contract after an order is placed and a commitment fee is paid, while others disagree (Khan and Ahmed, 2001). This may add to possible litigation concerns and raise Islamic institutions' vulnerability to counter-party risks arising from the ambiguity of contracts. Relatedly, there is a lack of uniformity in the financial reporting, auditing process, and accounting practice of Islamic organizations due to divergent interpretations of the underlying Shariah regulations. As we've seen, this makes it difficult to understand and compare their financial statements.

The lack of competent litigation and dispute resolution mechanisms and the lack of standard agreements for Islamic financial instruments also pose a threat to the business climate. Increased vulnerability to counterparty failure and delinquency risks is associated with Islamic banks' inability to effectively execute contractual agreements (Khan and Ahmed, 2001). Although fines for late payments are forbidden by Shariah law, some institutions nonetheless employ them as a deterrent and put the money toward good causes.

Banks do face regulatory risk and potential penalties when they are negligent or make mistakes in complying with rules. However, this risk may be the consequence of lax oversight or a lack of regulatory openness (Khan and Ahmed, 2001). In nations with both an Islamic and a conventional banking system, regulatory risk may also exist for Islamic financial firms. Moreover, there may be a general lack of clarity on the relevant laws due to differences that exist among the SSB of specific IFIs within each country and between the regulatory authorities of different countries.

Because of their restricted access to money, Islamic institutions are particularly vulnerable to liquidity risk, which may negatively impact the effectiveness of treasury management. Since borrowing is forbidden by Shariah law and there is no active interbank money market, Islamic banks lack extensive options for successfully handling their liquidity position, which can lead to problems such as an excess of cash that must be made for investments or a deficiency of cash which needs to be financed (Maroun, 2002). IFIs have been able to put their surplus capital to use via short-term trade financing and the secured commodities *murabaha*. However, IFIs do not have a reliable means of making up for a scarcity of cash.

These reasons have made it more difficult for Islamic banks to invest in long-term, often less liquid, but more lucrative assets in order to meet withdrawal demands from depositors, which has raised their dependence on liquidity risk and severely affected their profitability. Secondary markets for trading long-term securities have not developed due to a lack of Shariah-compliant products, trained market makers, and information and data transmission. Long-term Mudaraba investment documents, for example, might benefit the bank and the investor by facilitating secondary market trading rather than direct redemption with the issuing bank. The International Islamic Financial Market (IIFM) and Liquidity Management Centre (LMC) were set up to help IFIs better manage their liquidity needs in this respect.

Credit risk is another issue that affects Islamic financial firms. Some Islamic financial arrangements carry this danger. Islamic institutions are more vulnerable to credit risk because they lack comprehensive credit risk assessment processes and the requisite competence. When an Islamic bank delivers a payment under a bay Muajjal contract or provides assets under a *murabaha* transaction before receiving payment, it exposes itself to the risk of loss by dealing with a counter-party. The bank runs the risk in Bay Salam and Istisna contracts that the items won't be delivered on time or at all, or won't be of the quality promised. Salam agricultural contracts may be subject to extra pricing risks, such as storage of inventory fees (Khan and Ahmed, 2001).

There are moral hazard concerns when PLS projects include Mudaraba as an asset. While the *rabb-ul-mal* (IFI) takes the hit in the case of a loss, the Mudaraba (those receiving the monies) are not obligated to take any certain measures or put in any specific amount of effort on IFI's behalf. Funders of international financial institutions (IFIs) may take advantage of this situation (Lewis and Algaoud, 2002). Furthermore, the bank has no authority over or say in the management of the project in any way. Both the initial capital and any possible profit share will be lost by the bank if the entrepreneur's books show a loss.

If an Islamic bank signs a Mudaraba contract in the role of the *rabb-ul-mal*, or principal, and the *mudarib*, or agent, then the bank may face principal–agent difficulties. Since the higher consumption is partly paid by the bank while the business owner enjoys the advantages on the whole, the user of the money (*mudarib*) may be motivated to increase spending on projects and consume non-pecuniary benefits at the price of pecuniary returns. On the liability side, a similar problem develops when investors deposit Mudaraba monies into an IFI investment account. As was indicated before, this raises the danger of breach of fiduciary duty.

In Musharaka, the moral hazard issue is reduced since the *musharik*'s money is also at stake. In addition, the problem of informational asymmetry would be mitigated by equity partnership since the IFI would have the opportunity to take part in the management of the project in which it is investing. However, the Musharaka asset class has a cost due to adverse selection, which calls for rigorous screening, information gathering, and oversight. The cost of intermediation for IFIs would rise as they would need to analyze and negotiate PLS provisions for each Musharaka contract. Due to the challenges of *mudaraba* and *musharaka*, international financial institutions (IFIs) normally invest only a tiny portion of their money in these types of assets. Therefore, IFIs may be forced to invest more heavily in risky asset-backed securities and have fewer opportunities to diversify their holdings.

There is a market risk associated with Murabaha contracts that Islamic organizations must consider. The value of the bank's Murabaha contract fluctuates in response to changes in the underlying benchmark interest rate. Financing options like Murabaha are often priced in relation to the underlying market interest rate, London Interbank Offered Rate (LIBOR). This risk is especially real for IFIs since their markup rate is locked in for the length of the contract whereas the benchmark rate is subject to market fluctuations (Baldwin *et al.*, 2002; Khan and Ahmed, 2001). Since certain contracts provided by Islamic banks include delayed trading, the value of the currency in which receivables are due may devalue or the denomination in which payments are due may appreciate (Khan and Ahmed, 2001), posing an extra transaction risk.

By minimizing their overall risk exposure, IFIs may strengthen their competitive standing in the global market. The potential impact of Islamic institutions might be reduced in the absence of effective risk management procedures. Adequate resources must be allocated to the discovery, measurement, and development of risk management strategies. Integrating a deep understanding of Shariah law with cutting-edge risk management practices is crucial for creating cutting-edge risk reduction and hedging products.

8.3 Shariah Risk and Possible Implications

8.3.1 *Shariah Risk Definition*

When internal procedures, people, and systems are insufficient or fail due to external events, operational risk arises. This is according to the Basel Committee on Banking Supervision's (BCBS) definition of operational risk. Risks to an organization's strategy or reputation are not included in this definition (BCBS, 2011). One of the unique operational problems of Islamic organizations is Shariah risk. Shariah compliance risk is "the risk of failing to comply deriving from an absence of an Islamic bank's internal procedures and personnel," according to Archer and Haron (2007). The danger that an Islamic finance deal might be contested on the basis that it goes against Islamic law is what is called Shariah risk (Balz, 2008). An IFI faces Shariah risk when its actions violate Shariah principles as established by the SSB or the competent authorities in the applicable jurisdiction. Since we are focused on monetary damages, the aforementioned description does not include non-monetary or immaterial losses. However, Muslims believe that spiritual losses would lessen God's blessings, which will have a negative effect on the IFI's financial status. Quantifying these losses, however, is very difficult, if not impossible.

8.3.2 *Possible Shariah Risk Implications*

Debt exposure: Without adequate management, Shariah risk may undermine trust among stakeholders including customers, investors, savers, and workers (IDB and IFSB, 2007). As a consequence, there is a possibility of customers defaulting on their bank loans. Customers may be uncooperative for a number of reasons, including a feeling that the agreement that they engaged in has been nullified on Shariah grounds, mistrust in the institution's procedures, or a sense of betrayal. If the contract is nullified owing to Shariah breaches, the bank will have to report no revenue from the associated transaction since the money was earned illegally (AAOIFI, 2010). The SSB would then disperse this cash to other charity organizations via an account it manages.

Aspects of lawful risk and conformity: Risks associated with Shariah might lead to problems with the law and regulatory compliance. There is a common tendency to conflate these two types of threats. Contrarily, violation of rules and regulations is a common source of compliance risk, whereas non-compliance with contracts is a common source of legal risk.

"The risk that arbitration, unfavorable judgments, or arrangements that turn out to be illegal could disrupt or negatively affect the bank's operations or condition," as defined by the BCBS (2001). To be more precise, "credit risk" can be defined as "the risk of loss to an institution that is mainly brought about by an incorrect transaction; or an assertion (including a defense to an assert or a counterclaim) being brought; or an additional occurrence happening that results in an obligation for the institution or an additional loss [. . .]; or malfunctioning to take the necessary steps in order to safeguard assets [. . .] possessed by the institution; or a change in law" (McCormick, 2010: 479). Compliance risk, on the other hand, is defined by the BCBS as "the risk of legal or regulation penalties, material monetary damage, or loss of credibility that a bank may suffer as a consequence of its failure to adhere to the regulations, laws, rules, associated the organization standards, and descriptions of conduct necessary to its banking activities" (BCBS, 2005: 7).

Banks that profess to follow Shariah principles in their constitution and/or articles of the organization but don't really do so may risk legal action from disgruntled shareholders and depositors. Falsely advertising services in the United Kingdom are prohibited according to the Trade Descriptions Act of 1968, for example. Making false or misleading representations about a product or service with the goal of earning financial gain is also prohibited under the Fraud Act of 2006. This is an example of a situation where the law is in danger because of Shariah law. Other factors that undermine market discipline include the difficulty courts have in understanding Shariah terms and the potential unenforceability of Shariah transactions in secular law countries (DeLorenzo and McMillen, 2007). When a bank is required by its regulator to create competent internal SG structures but fails to do so, the bank faces compliance risk as a result of Shariah risk. The bank may face fines or perhaps lose its license if it is found to have broken the rules. IFIs in Malaysia are required by law to act in accordance with Shariah at all times. It also requires IFIs to alert the central bank within 30 days of discovering Shariah-incompliant activities and present a plan to remedy the matter within the same time frame. A violation of these rules might result in a maximum sentence of 8 years in jail and/or a fine of up to 25 million ringgit (about $8 million).

Threat to one's good name: This is "the probability that adverse publicity about a bank's corporate practice and affiliations will cause a decline in the bank's reputation for honesty and fair dealing" (BCBS, 2001). The general population is heavily involved in banking activity. Therefore, a bank's performance depends on earning and keeping their trust and confidence (Leventis et al., 2013). Particularly important to the success of an Islamic bank is its reputation for upholding Shariah law in all of its dealings (Archer and Haron, 2007). Loss of depositors and other stakeholders due to rumors of Shariah breaches may have a negative effect on the bank's position in the marketplace, availability, and revenue (IFSB, 2005).

Market danger: Any equities held by an Islamic bank that become Shariah-incompliant due to factors such as a debt-to-market capitalization ratio in excess of 30% must be liquidated. There might be a loss if this happens while the equity is worth less than what was paid for it.

Finally, depending on the size of the Islamic banking industry in the country (AAOIFI, 2010; Ali, 2003; El-Hawary et al., 2004; IFSB, 2007a; Izhar, 2010; CBO, 2012), the aforementioned Shariah risk and its implications may result in the withdrawal of funds, higher expenses to attract deposits, both immediate and secondary financial losses, liquidity issues, bank runs, bank failure, and financial instability. It might also damage an industry that values its reputation among its constituents (IFSB, 2007b). Shariah risk and its possible ramifications are shown in Figure 8.2.

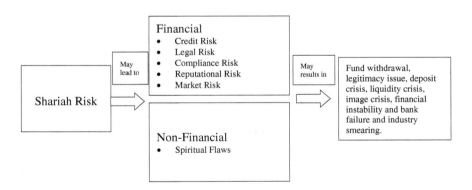

Figure 8.2: Possible Implications of Shariah Risk.
Source: Modified from Ginena (2014).

8.3.3 Shariah Risk Causes and Events

Once Shariah danger has been detected, its probable origins and effects must be determined. Three internal causes (people, internal processes, and systems) and one external cause (external events) account for operational risk, as defined by BCBS.

8.3.4 People

Risk of fatwa: The chance that a *fatwa* is wrong, imprecise, or too complicated might affect a bank's SSB (DeLorenzo, 2007). A *fatwa* may be incorrect for a variety of reasons. One such SSB is one that incorrectly reads a given set of circumstances as meaning something different (Ginena, 2014).

The lack of research or carelessness may have led to this: The SSB may be misinformed, for instance, if it evaluates a product idea submitted by the bank's manufacturing team without first consulting legal counsel. Therefore, in order for an SSB to get an accurate and comprehensive knowledge of problems and issue the right *fatwa*, coordinated meetings bringing together key department officials for discussion of a product or problem are required. If an SSB irresponsibly announces a *fatwa* without sufficient thought and is subsequently proved to be erroneous, Hammad (2007) believes that it should be held liable for bank losses stemming from such carelessness. A mistaken picture of a situation may also result from intentional misrepresentation by top executives or other workers, with the goal of misleading the SSB. A *fatwa* might be wrong if the SSB doesn't have enough expertise. Furthermore, workers may misunderstand the intent of those who granted the *fatwa* if the document is too vague or lacks adequate specifics (Ginena, 2014). In addition, the absence of a clear mechanism for implementing such a *fatwa* might lead to unforeseen implementation mistakes. Errors in execution may also occur from a *fatwa* that is too complicated or written in highly nuanced juristic language that practitioners are unable to understand (DeLorenzo, 2007).

Data manipulation and fabrication: This is yet another situation that might violate Shariah law. This is particularly the case if the user is not prevented from doing transactions in the required sequence by Shariah constraints in the bank's IT system (Ginena, 2014). For instance, the bank could have a *murabaha* module with pre-set accounting entries for different parts of a *murabaha* transaction, but it might not include a control function that stops the user from completing the sale of the commodity without entering the payment for it from the vendor. This creates room for human mistakes and the possibility of forged documents. If a finance officer makes this unfortunate mistake, he or she may try to cover it up by changing the sequence of events by making the purchase contract's date come before the sale's closing date. Since a bank cannot sell before it acquires legal title, the agreement to sell would be null and invalid if such a fake were found. Gains from such a deal wouldn't count toward the threshold for inclusion (Ginena, 2014).

Non-compliance with guidelines and the use of unauthorized items, processes, or contracts: Launching something without SSB clearance would be far more disastrous than breaking transactional procedures, since it may lead to their departure and public disgrace. The SSB and the legal counsel complement each other in their examination of legal papers; neither could execute its jobs effectively without the other. Without consultation between these groups, a contract may be invalid because it contains terms that contradict Shariah principles (Ginena, 2014).

Due to a lack of preparation, equipment, and attention to detail: Another possible Shariah risk element is insufficient internal people in the Shariah coordination department. This is because department staff may have considerably more on their plates than they can handle, which might lead to activities like Shariah audits of transactions being neglected or completed inadequately. The situation may be made worse since most regulatory authorities do not mandate that Islamic institutions have internal Shariah auditors. Bank losses might be exacerbated by employees who have not received proper training on the Shariah-compliant components of transactions. Employees need this training so they can adequately answer customers' questions about the thought process behind a specific step in a transaction. However well-staffed and trained a bank may be, human error nevertheless poses a threat to Shariah compliance (Ginena, 2014).

Miscommunication: In cases when the parties speak different languages, there is even another possible Shariah-inciting element. Using non-professional translators to bridge the language gap between Shariah experts who only speak Arabic and attorneys who only know English might lead to erroneous interpretations and decisions. Is it, as an alternative, realistic to hire a professional interpretation for each meeting and have each document translated? Contracts for sukuk are notoriously lengthy

260 *Shariah Governance Systems of Islamic Banks*

(sometimes exceeding 100 pages), making this process tedious, time-consuming, and expensive (Ginena, 2014).

No clear division of work: The same body should not be in charge of conflicting tasks like legalization and audits, since this would provide it cover to hide Shariah infractions. Employees who sign purchase orders for the bank ought to remain separated from those who sign lease or sale agreements with consumers in order to minimize Shariah risk (Ginena, 2014).

A key member of the team has left the company: The departure of a key person, such as the organization's internal Shariah coordination head, may potentially pose a threat to the organization in terms of Shariah compliance. If the division is dependent on this individual, no records have been kept, and everything is disorganized, this could represent the situation. For instance, there was a lack of archiving for *fatwa*, outlining for Shariah-related components of procedures, and recording of general knowledge. The internal Shariah planning team looks at previous SSB *fatwas* for guidance when making decisions in similar cases. What if, however, the departing important figure never recorded any *fatwa* in the company's records? Others in the workplace may try to remember the *fatwa*, but doing so presents a danger associated with Shariah law due to the possibility of memory lapses. Here, we may provide an example to illustrate the second possible source of Shariah-related risk (Ginena, 2014).

8.3.5 *Processes*

Incomplete or ambiguous methods, guidelines, or roles and duties: It is possible for Shariah breaches to emerge if processes, rules, procedures, and duties are not clearly defined. Lack of standardization might lead to inefficiency. Processes, rules, and procedures must be reviewed and updated on a periodic basis to account for changes in the law, regulations, and in the industry that may have an impact on Shariah-related parts of operations and transactions. The SSB may need to reevaluate any of its prior recommendations or *fatawa* in light of the aforementioned changes and make any required adjustments. The bank might be held liable for fines if transactions don't follow instructions. This periodic review is also important for making sure that the latest SSB recommendations and *fatawa* are included in existing practice (Ginena, 2014).

Poorly implemented Shariah-compliant internal mechanisms for governance: Inadequate Shariah compliance controls are the result of underestimating the need to create appropriate internal SG procedures, which may have disastrous effects. Failure may also occur from putting these systems in place but not making sure the right tools are employed to do the job. It is thus not negligible on the part of regulatory organizations to guarantee that institutions have made necessary plans and are well prepared (Hasan, 2012).

Inadequate honesty and transparency: Stakeholders may fail to identify Shariah infractions if there is insufficient information or openness. As a result, interested parties could not notice a latent Shariah risk until it's too late. This is a predicament that has become all too common since the financial crisis. Hasan (2012) argues that SSBs' yearly reports to their stakeholders often fail to provide enough openness about even the most fundamental matters, which include the number of sessions attended, resolutions passed, goods authorized, etc. After looking through the annual reports of seven Islamic banks between 2002 and 2004 (Haniffa and Hudaib, 2007) found that just one had revealed the compensation paid to its SSB.

Most current SSB decisions are unsupported by evidence, therefore greater openness is required to allow stakeholders to analyze *fatawa* and the scraps of evidence that were used to produce them (Hasan, 2012). Some trading partners are seeking SSB merchandise and contract certifications before committing to deals in order to mitigate Shariah's risk. Many Islamic organizations have yet to publish such texts online or distribute their own *fatawa*. The public may see the bank as being secretive as a result of the increased opacity regarding Shariah issues (Haniff and Hudaib, 2007). For CG to be successful, transparency is a must (BCBS, 2006). This would bring us one step closer to market discipline and let consumers hold the SSB, BOD, and upper management responsible for their mistakes (BCBS, 2006).

Use of a designated charitable account, revenue sharing, and monetary segregation: If money is disallowed because it violates Shariah, that money goes to a good cause. Auditors must keep a tight eye on this account, which might be worth millions of dollars, to ensure that management isn't artificially inflating earnings that will have to be written down later. It is also important to verify that the donated money went to worthy organizations. A second problem involving accounts is the sharing of profits from P and L-managed investment accounts. The bank takes on substantial Shariah risk by treating these financial accounts as earnings or losses and choosing to manage them on a fixed-interest basis. The last difficulty relating to financial documents is the segregation of a conventional bank's finances from those of its Islamic window (the division of a conventional bank that provides Islamic banking services). When it comes to Islamic investment accounts, it is unlawful for an Islamic window to collect deposits, use that money in its regular activities, and then deliver the equivalent profits to the investors. This concludes the discussion of the internal factors that pose a threat due to Shariah law (Ginena, 2014).

8.3.6 *Systems*

System defects include anomalies in the accounting process or system, a lack of product modules, inaccurate reporting, and the use of unauthorized software. The bank's IT system's accounting entries and transaction procedures should mirror those detailed in the product manuals that were authorized by the SSB (Ginena, 2014). Otherwise, there may be a threat to Shariah from contradictions shown by disparities. SSBs should not only assess product legal paperwork but also the IT system modules that maintain records for and incorporate transactions, to ensure end-to-end conformity. It's possible that not all of the accounting entries, system settings, and other modules agree with Shariah law. Therefore, lawyers need an understanding of accounting so that they can tell the difference between legal and illegal transactions. The linked problem is that the present banking system is inadequate, necessitating the manual entry of accounting transactions. From a Shariah and an accounting perspective, this is risky since it invites fraud and mistakes. It's more difficult and takes more time to generate reports. The lack of these system reports, the inaccuracy of the information supplied in them, or the insufficiency of the knowledge presented in them might lead to ill-informed judgments that represent a danger associated with Shariah (Ginena, 2014).

We had a problem with an inept vendor, slow service, a frustrating user interface, and a faulty system. Conventional banking information technology providers perceive an opportunity to join a new market sector by providing Islamic finance modules due to the fast growth of the Islamic finance industry. However, if suppliers lack the necessary expertise and guidance from subject matter experts when building their modules, potentially risky system choices that violate Shariah may be created. The problem may be made much worse by a lack of user-friendliness in a system module or by late vendor support. Inaccuracies in a system create problems from a Shariah perspective.

8.3.7 *External Causes*

Shariah risk may also be influenced by factors outside of the control of Islamic banks. We will now talk about a few of the most typical things that happen in the outside world.

Risk of fatwa: This may also be the case if an Islamic financial institution hires a Shariah advisory consulting business rather than forming a separate SSB. There would still be the previously described risks associated with *fatwas*, and maybe even more. Possible conflicts of interest may arise when a legal professional is both a shareholder in the Shariah advising business and a member of the firm's SSB. If the jurist is also a shareholder in the Shariah advice company, would it influence the severity of his *fatawa* (Ginena, 2014)?

Incompetent Shariah advising company whose auditing, advisory services, and permitting functions are at odds with one another. Shariah risk may also arise from two external occurrences that are on the same issue as Shariah advice firms. The first is using a Shariah advising company that hasn't been around long enough to establish a track record and may make easily preventable mistakes. The second issue is the possibility for bias when one firm provides *fatawa*, auditing, and consultancy to the same Islamic bank. The financial auditing profession learned the hard way from many tragic company catastrophes the dangers of offering competing services like audits and consultation. Given that Shariah advice businesses also provide a potentially contradictory service — legalization through *fatawa* issuance — these principles are equally relevant to them (Ginena, 2014).

Lack of clarity in Shariah governance laws and regulations: Regulators play a crucial part in SG because of the risk of instability (Ahmed, 2011; IDB and IFSB, 2007). IFSB (2007a) suggests that regulators should demand banks show they have corporate SG structures in place to deal with Shariah risks. We have found that if SG standards are weak or nonexistent, banks may ignore SG concerns, exposing themselves to Shariah risk. This may also occur when legal requirements are unclear (Ginena, 2014).

Threats associated with Shariah may still exist despite attempts to reduce them. This might be because the Islamic bank has outgrown its internal SG structure, or because new gaps have emerged that have yet to be filled. Even yet, procedures for continuous improvement should make sure that infractions like this are dealt with quickly and are kept to a minimum. The potential occurrences of Shariah risk for BCBS are shown in Figure 8.3 and categorized pursuant to the four sources of operational risk. To do this, we first assign values between 1 and 10 to two key dimensions — the probability (L) of the event happening and the possibility of a negative effect (I) on the bank — and then compare the results. Because some disasters are more catastrophic than others, their potential damage is evaluated. The risk score (R) for an incident is then calculated by multiplying L by its impact (I). Any incident with a higher R-value should be treated with increased caution. The next step is to assess the degree to which the bank is prepared to mitigate the Shariah risk associated with such an occurrence. It's referred to as the "P-value." To get the cumulative (C) score, we divide the R-value for each occurrence by its associated P-value. At last, the order of occurrences is determined by a cumulative score, with the greatest score having priority. In order to ease comparisons across potential risk factors, the grid additionally keeps track of accumulated scores for each potential risk factor (Ginena, 2014).

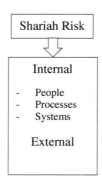

Figure 8.3: Shariah Risk Events Grouped under the Four BCBS Operational Risk Causes.
Source: Modified from Ginena (2014).

8.3.8 *The Responsibility of the BOD and Senior Management*

The BOD must keep an eye on Shariah risk as part of its duty to oversee risk management, and it must know how it will affect the bank, its goals, and its stakeholders down to the last detail. The BOD of an IFI is tasked with ensuring that the institution's operations are fully compliant with Shariah principles, as well as assessing and managing the institution's exposure to Shariah risk (AAOIFI, 2010; CBO, 2012). According to a study by AAOIFI (2010), the IFI's audit and governance committee could help the BOD keep an eye on Shariah compliance. This board shall assess the completeness of Shariah controls and evaluate the performance of the SG structure on a regular basis. It must also respond to questions and suggestions made by the SSB, internal and external auditors, Shariah auditors, and government agencies (Ginena, 2014).

The BOD is responsible for appointing a qualified SSB, acknowledging the SSB's authority to make its own choices, and staying out of the way so as not to jeopardize the SSB's impartiality and independence. Each year, the BOD should assess the SSB's effectiveness in light of the IFSB's recommended performance metrics and address any potential conflicts of interest that may have arisen. However, without the approval of the shareholders and perhaps the regulator, the BOD may not fire any member of the SSB. The purpose of this policy is to protect SSB members from any improper influence from the BOD. All policies pertaining to Shariah should be approved by the BOD after consultation with the SSB, and the BOD should also supervise their implementation. It also needs to make sure that employees know what they're responsible for in terms of Shariah compliance and that they can voice any concerns they may have about the company's approach to Shariah without fear of retaliation (BNM, 2019).

In addition to implementing policies and plans and performing tasks specified by the BOD, senior management is also responsible for effective internal SG, which controls Shariah risk (AAOIFI, 2010). Furthermore, they are accountable for establishing an organizational framework that establishes authority and accountability lines, developing processes and systems to implement SG arrangements developed by the BOD, and delegating appropriate responsibilities to qualified individuals. Establishing complying with Shariah as an overarching requirement for all policies, procedures, and activities, educating staff on Shariah specifications, and providing ongoing Shariah risk training to key stakeholders are all the responsibilities of senior management (BNM, 2019). It is the responsibility of management to create and follow Shariah-compliant policies and procedures. Furthermore, they must follow protocol in the event of non-compliance, as well as provide a precise, comprehensive, and timely publication to the SSB and Shariah auditors, refer all Shariah-related questions and concerns to the SSB, and implement all rulings and decisions made by the Board (BNM, 2019). Management's responsibilities when they become aware of Shariah-inconsistent behavior include alerting the internal Shariah auditor, stopping the behavior in question, fixing the problem by implementing recommendations from the internal Shariah auditor and possibly the SSB and taking steps to prevent a recurrence (CBO, 2012).

8.3.9 *Role of Banking Supervisors*

Protecting the stability of the financial system is important to banking authorities. As part of their dedication to stability, Islamic banks must identify, quantify, assess, monitor, report on, and control or minimize shariah risk (CBO, 2012). Additionally, regulators must ensure that Islamic banks uphold their obligation to conduct business in accordance with Shariah principles and that any negligence on their part doesn't harm customers who are drawn to these institutions primarily because of the values and goals they uphold. As a result, the IFSB (2007a) advises authorities to give financial firms internal Shariah compliance structures. However, the standard-setter acknowledges that due to the various legislative structures regulating the countries in which Islamic banks operate, different regulators would have varying opinions on what they can and cannot do in terms of SG (IFSB, 2009). Additionally, the IFSB is aware that different Islamic organizations would have different demands depending on things like size. If authorities are unable to accomplish the aforementioned, they should investigate whether institutions have implemented policies and controls to ensure Shariah conformity (Ginena, 2014).

Administrators must first equip themselves with the information, methodologies, tools, and competence required to assess the BOD and senior management's grasp of and adherence to their SG duties. A comprehensive examination of the following may be performed for such an assessment:

- Interactions between its members and the BOD and the sufficiency of information exchanged;
- Internal review reports and external review evaluations of the framework;

- Interactions between the SSB and the BOD and the SSB and employees of the framework;
- Internal SG arrangements and the extent to which they are documented, reviewed, updated, and communicated.

The IFSB backs a supervisory effort to publish standards for judging the experience and honesty of candidates for seats on the SSB. Furthermore, IFIs should detail how they choose and appoint their SSB members, how they deal with emergencies like the unexpected death of a board member, and how they assess the performance of the SSB and their own internal Shariah coordinating staff (IFSB, 2007a).

In order to promote transparency and mitigate Shariah risk, regulators may mandate that Islamic banks publish monthly SG reports including matters such as SSB resolutions, Shariah audit findings, and internal SG improvements (Ginena, 2014). Along with keeping regulators up-to-date on developments at the bank, these documents will stress the need for sound governance to the BOD and upper management. When regulators find problems, they should demand that institutions fix them by a certain date. To keep stakeholders updated, to give transparency into the bank's SG system, and to encourage Shariah market discipline, the IFSB (2007b) recommends that banks provide both qualitative and quantitative statements on SG.

Bank Negara Malaysia (BNM), for instance, took the initiative to draft the Islamic Financial Services Act of 2013 to ensure continued financial stability and Shariah compliance. Part four of the Act is named "Shariah requirements" and is broken down into three subparts: shariah compliance, SG, and a Shariah compliance audit. It is the licensee's obligation to guarantee Shariah compliance, and the Act mandates that the BOD give weight to the recommendations of the SSB and the CSSB, the regulatory counterpart of the SSB. For the purpose of harmonizing Islamic legal views, BNM is granted authority under Clause 29 of the Act to develop Shariah-related norms, provided that it does so in line with SAC decisions or recommendations or gives effect to them. In addition, BNM has been given the right to create non-SAC-reviewable operational SG criteria. Creating the framework for internal Shariah compliance activities and dealing with any other Shariah compliance-related issues are all part of the board's, management's, and the SSB's Shariah compliance obligations. Institutions, BOD, CEOs, execs, and SSB members must all adhere to the requirements. Therefore, organizations should develop internal policies that directors, officials, and SSB members will follow. If an organization or person is not compliant with the requirements, they risk the aforementioned consequences (Ginena, 2014).

8.4 Risk Management in Islamic Financial Institutions

IFIs face six distinct types of risk, as defined by the IFSB in their "Guiding Principles of Risk Management for Institutions (other than Insurance institutions)": investment risk, credit risk, market risk, operational risk, rate of return risk, and liquidity risk. This article will analyze how Shariah Compliance Audits are used by IFIs for operational risk management. The broad concepts and particular hazards described above are included in the 15 principles presented in "Guiding Principles of Risk Management for Institutions (including but not limited to Insurance Institutions)" (IFSB, 2005).

General Principle: First and foremost, an IFI must have a robust risk administration and reporting structure in place. To guarantee that the supervisory authority obtains sufficient risk reporting, the procedure should take into account the measures needed to comply with Shariah norms and principles.

8.4.1 *Credit Risk*

Principle 1: An IFI must have a plan for obtaining funding. Shariah-compliant instruments take into account the numerous credit risks that may occur throughout the lifecycle of a financing transaction.

Principle 2: Before settling on an acceptable Islamic financing instrument, IFI should conduct a due diligence evaluation with regard to counterparties.

Principle 3: IFIs must have reliable methods for assessing and reporting the risk of credit associated with each kind of Islamic financing.

Principle 4: IFIs must use credit risk management strategies that are suitable for each kind of Islamic finance and are compatible with Shariah law (IFSB, 2005).

8.4.2 Equity Investment Risk

Principle 1: IFIs should have proper risk management and communication mechanisms in place, taking into account the unique features of equity investments like *Mudarabah* and *Musharakah*.

Principle 2: To analyze the possible effects of their valuation procedures on profit estimates and allocations, IFIs must adhere to and make sure they are adequate and consistent. The techniques must be agreed upon by both the IFI and the *Mudarib* and/or *Musharakah* stakeholders.

Principle 3: IFIs should have a well-defined and established exit strategy for their equity investment operations, including the extension of time and redemption requirements for *Mudarabah* and *Musharakah* investments, with the permission of the institution's Shariah Board (IFSB, 2005).

8.4.3 Market Risk

Principle 1: IFI should put in place an appropriate structure for market risk management (which incorporates reporting) with regard to all assets held, including those that lack an immediate market and/or are subject to extreme price fluctuations (IFSB, 2005).

8.4.4 Liquidity Risk

Principle 1: Liquidity vulnerabilities with respect to each type of current account and unconstrained and controlled investment accounts must be taken into consideration on a separate and overall basis by the IFI's liquidity management system (including reporting).

Principle 2: The liquidity risk taken on by an IFI must be proportional to the availability of Shariah-compliant funds available to it (IFSB, 2005).

8.4.5 Rate of Return

Principle 1: For IFI to evaluate the possible effects of market conditions on investment account holder (IAH) return rates relative to predicted rates of return, a thorough risk management and reporting mechanism must be implemented (IFSB, 2005).

Principle 2: If relevant, IFI should put in place a system for handling the business risk that results from relocation (IFSB, 2005).

8.4.6 *Operational Risk*

Principle 1: To guarantee adherence to Shariah principles, IFIs need reliable mechanisms and controls, such as a Shariah Board or Advisor.

Principle 2: All fund providers' interests must be protected by the proper processes set up by the IFI (IFSB, 2005).

CHAPTER 9

Shariah Audit System

9.1 Introduction

Shariah audit is one of the key elements of the Shariah governance (SG) framework of Islamic Financial Institutions (IFIs). It provides reassurance to IFI stakeholders that all goods, services, and operational activities adhere to Shariah principles (Haniffa and Hudaib, 2010; Alam *et al.*, 2019b, 2022b; Bank Negara Malaysia (BNM), 2019). In order to achieve Shariah compliance, Shariah audit makes sure that the SG rules and policies created within the IFIs' functions are followed (Kamaruddin and Hanefah, 2017). A more comprehensive definition of Shariah audit was given by Haniffa (2010), who defined it as a systematic process of objectively gathering and assessing evidence regarding claims about religious and socioeconomic actions and events in order to determine the extent to which those claims and the applicable financial reporting framework correspond, taking into account the criteria recommended by the SSB and Shariah principles. The results are then communicated to all relevant parties.

9.2 What is Shariah Audit?

The advent of IFIs necessitated the development of a new auditing component known as Shariah audit. Surprisingly, however, just one description of Shariah audit cannot be found in the literature, which may be owing to a lack of significant concentration on this issue area (Sultan, 2007). Different authors have different interpretations of what a Shariah audit entails; some say it's an examination of an organization's products, processes, and people to spot potential violations of Shariah law (e.g., Sultan, 2007), while others say Shariah auditors perform all the duties of traditional auditors with an additional layer of Shariah expertise. In this work, we use the latter definition, which states that Shariah auditors who are well-versed in both Islamic law and conventional auditing practice are the optimum candidates to perform audits of Islamic organizations. We shall elaborate after doing a brief literature research on this subject. Abdel-Magid's (1981) foundational research regarding the accounting behaviors of Islamic banks lays the groundwork for the discussion of Islamic-specific accounting and auditing systems. In this work, he elaborates on the Islamic Shariah system and explains why alternative accounting methods are required for banking transactions that adhere to Shariah standards. The first works in this area, therefore, proposed a theoretical structure for the Islamic accounting of Islamic financial instruments. The number of papers expanded on what Abdel Magid had established. For instance, in Al-Obji (1989), the author elaborated on the differences between Islamic and Western banking practices with regard to accounting. Heakal (1989) provides a similar conceptualization of the areas of difference between the accounting practice of Islamic and Western banking systems.

Certain transactions or accounting concerns often become the topic of later studies. For instance, Gambling and Karim (1991) contended that the historical cost is insufficient for determining a company owner's *zakah* duty and that balance sheet assets must be properly categorized to ascertain whether wealth is susceptible to *zakah*. Murabahah transactions raise a number of accounting questions, which Al-Jalf (1996) investigated. The AAOIFI was set up in 1991 to provide IFIs with accounting, auditing, and CG standards (Napier, 2009).

Khan's (1985) analysis of early Islamic auditing practices is one of the first works to offer an Islamic auditing paradigm. Auditing in accordance with the tenets of Shariah is said to have been performed by the Prophet Muhammad (PBUH) and his companions by Khan (1985, 2001). Therefore, suggestions for Shariah auditing shouldn't be seen as radically new ideas. Khan (1985) offered an auditing paradigm based on early Islamic empire practice that would work best in an Islamic economy. In an Islamic economy, according to Khan's definition of a Shariah audit, auditors are responsible to both the management of the company and the community at large. In other words, auditors are tasked with determining whether or not a company's financial accounts are in accordance with Shariah law, in the spirit of '*amrbilma'rufwanahi'analmunkar*' (enjoining the appropriate and banning the improper). In a significant work, Karim (1990) argued that since Islam does not create such a distinction, there should be none between religious and financial auditors. As a result, auditors in an Islamic economy should be knowledgeable about both financial reporting issues and issues relating to Shariah's social and ethical principles. As a result, knowledge of the numerous diverse religious laws that have an impact on an Islamic bank's financial affairs as well as accounting principles that are compliant with Islamic law must be established as a foundation for those who conduct financial audits for IFIs or Islamic businesses.

Banaga *et al.* (1994), who studied the connection between corporate governance (CG) and independent auditing in IFIs, pointed out that Shariah-compliance assessments make a Shariah auditor's role in an IFI distinct from the position of a traditional auditor. However, they discovered that Shariah auditing is deficient in practice since external auditors do not examine concerns of Shariah compliance owing to a lack of expertise. Furthermore, the SSBs' independence in producing audit reports based on Shariah law is often questioned. Understanding between religious and accounting professionals in Bahrain was studied by Hood and Bucheery (1999). Surveys showed that financial and religious auditors in Bahrain could not understand the responsibilities of the other. Since Islamic institutions are intended to function in line with an Islamic worldview defined by divine revelations, Khan (2001) claimed elsewhere that it is reasonable for the auditing system to be different from the Western one. Their duty is to the Islamic community, whose values and interests may vary from one's own. Furthermore, Ibrahim and Yaya (2005) state that, unlike traditional auditing, Shariah audits are supposed to meet the higher Shariah goals (Maqasid Shariah). In general, there aren't many studies that look at auditing from an Islamic viewpoint, and much of the literature in this area focuses on a critical analysis of the future of Islamic accounting and the part AAOIFI plays in it. In an effort to compile a list of papers that are of interest to the field of Shariah auditing, studies on the role, functions, responsibility, and independence of Shariah advisors are categorized separately from those that highlight auditing issues in Islamic banks (Al-Abji, 1989; Siddiqui, 2000) and those that attempt to investigate the theoretical foundation of auditing from an Islamic perspective (e.g., Harahap, 2002; Khan, 1985; Briston and El-Ashker, 1986). Business processes, guidelines, and methods; contracts and agreements; accounting systems and reporting; management of human resources; social activities and contributions and advertisement and advertising; reports and circulars; zakat calculation and payment; computerized systems; are all considered part of the Shariah audit in Islamic institutions for the purposes of this chapter. Standard-making organizations are the home of AAOIFI Governance.

In this study, we advocate for a Shariah audit, which may best be described as a standards-explanatory "Shariah review". Standard No. 2 of the AAOIFI Governance Framework defines Shariah review as an investigation into whether or not an IFI abides by Shariah principles in its day-to-day operations. Everything from legal documents to financial statements to reports (including those from internal and central bank inspections and circulars) is fair game for this scrutiny (Section 3.2 of the GSIFI-2 AAOIFI Standards (2004)).

There are a number of writers, such as Briston and El-Ashker (1986), Karim (1990), and Hood and Bucheery (1999), who classify SSB members as religious auditors and compare their work to that of Shariah auditors. However, SSBs present focus on technical compliance elements of finance contracts, i.e., what is acceptable and what is not, fails to capture the fundamental core of Shariah audit (Rosly, 2010). In addition, after delivering views *ex-ante*, Shariah advisers often do not do an *ex-post* evaluation of the product. Numerous studies have raised doubts about SSBs' expertise and objectivity in doing Shariah audits. However, it has been questioned whether or not external auditors have the requisite experience and qualifications in the subject of Shariah. In light of the fact that traditional auditors' statements are restricted to monetary activities and occurrences, we maintain that it is impossible for them to undertake a Shariah audit of the organization. As was also said before, the present SSB Shariah advisers do not do a full Shariah audit.

9.3   Why Do We Need Shariah Audit?

All organizations functioning in a realm regulated by an Islamic worldview face a special risk due to instances of Shariah disobedience, which is presumably why a Shariah audit is necessary. There is a pressing need to establish a Shariah auditing framework due to the growth of the worldwide Islamic banking and finance business. As we saw in the preceding section, the implication of this study is that the existing independent auditors and SSB members are not doing a thorough Shariah audit. Products, enabling technology, operational processes, personnel, documents and contracts, rules and procedures, and any other endeavor necessitating commitment to

Shariah principles all provide potential non-compliance concerns, as stated by Sultan (2007).

The consequences of violating Shariah may be severe, both in the here and now for the organization at fault and in the hereafter for the people guilty of the transgression. Most Islamic fund providers may only utilize Shariah-compliant banking services out of principle; if they decide to litigate over a breach of Shariah, the financial institution might lose investors' money and face severe liabilities (Archer and Karim, 2007). Shariah compliance criteria should be implemented throughout the board of an Islamic company and in all of its goods and operations, as emphasized by Archer and Karim (2007). Based on the enlightened goals established by Shariah (Maqasid Shariah), which prioritize societal benefits over individual benefits, Greuning and Iqbal (2008) argue that Islamic institutions would be able to accomplish a higher level of CG objectives if they opted for Shariah audits. Traditional Islamic socioeconomic institutions like *zakah* (obligatory charity), *waqf* (Islamic endowments), and other associated Islamic organizations are seeing a renaissance, as Ibrahim (2008) points out. Considering the growing number of Islamic organizations that must follow the Shariah in everything that they do, it makes sense to create a Shariah audit framework that can accommodate their specific needs. By reducing concerns about Shariah compliance risks in institutions, regular Shariah audits may help the sector grow and attract more investors. The majority of Malaysian accountants, auditors, academicians, and Shariah scholars polled support for the creation of a separate Shariah auditing profession with its own set of regulations.

Bank Negara Malaysia, the nation's central bank, made an attempt to promote Shariah compliance and openness. The four pillars of the structure that IFIs must create to ensure Shariah compliance and research are Shariah review, Shariah risk management, Shariah audit, and Shariah research. According to new rules published by the State Bank of Pakistan, Shariah advisers and external auditors must cooperate to audit and verify profit/loss distributions for Mudarabah-based deposits in IFIs. These initiatives are restricted to the banking industry, but they demonstrate how crucial Shariah auditing is for Islamic organizations. It is reasonable to conclude that Shariah auditing is a field that is ready to be developed because it will not only benefit Muslim societies but also its all-encompassing social welfare fundamentals can only benefit everyone in the world by ensuring that we manage our businesses to promote human and environmental social security.

9.4 Characteristics of Shariah Audit

Shariah auditing has four major characteristics:

(1) The scope of a Shariah audit is significantly greater and it is regarded as a social role.
(2) Financial statements must be prepared in accordance with the SSB's regulation guidelines.
(3) When generating the financial statements of IFIs, AAOIFI standards, as well as international and national auditing norms and procedures, should be followed.
(4) Shariah auditors must be well-versed in Islamic laws and values.

9.5 Objectives and Scopes of Shariah Audit

From these definitions, it is clear that a Shariah audit is conducted to verify that an IFI is acting in accordance with Shariah principles. In reality, this is what Shariah audit is all about. The purpose of an audit of an IFI is to allow the auditor to provide an opinion on whether or not the IFI's financial statements have been prepared in accordance with the applicable *fatwas*, rulings, and guidelines issued by the IFI's SSB, with the accounting standards of the AAOIFI, with national accounting standards and practice, and with the corresponding laws and regulations of a nation in which the IFI operates. In addition to demonstrating righteousness, integrity, reliability, fairness, honesty, the declaration of independence, neutrality, competence as a professional, due care, anonymity, professional conduct, and technical standards (Yaacob, 2012), the auditors performing this audit must also abide by the Code of Conduct for Professional Accountants. The definition and function of a Shariah audit simplify the process of comprehending its scope. It's more comprehensive than a regular audit since it checks for Shariah compliance as well. This in no way suggests that the monetary parts of a transaction would be ignored during a Shariah audit. The financial accounts of the IFI would be the first target of a Shariah audit, as stated by Rahman (2008). It would guarantee that all monetary dealings are properly recorded and accounted for and that the rights and obligations arising from different contracts are reflected therein. Furthermore, it would guarantee conformity with relevant standards like Bank Negara's guidelines, AAOIFI's requirements, etc. It's worth noting, nevertheless, that Shariah is a fairly general phrase that includes financial dealings along with every other aspect of life. According to Hameed (2008), this results in SSBs reducing Shariah observance to the mere formality of ensuring that financial contracts correspond to the SSB's fatwas (opinions) on whether or not a certain transaction is lawful. So, he argues, a more all-encompassing strategy is required, one that considers "business policies, processes and procedures, agreements and contracts, financial systems and reporting, management of human resources, social activities and investments, advertising and promotional activities, reports and announcements, *zakat* estimation and making a payment, and IT systems" (Hameed, 2008).

In addition, according to Yaacob and Dongla (2012), auditing is crucial for establishing trust among a company's many stakeholder groups and maintaining corporate responsibility. "The auditing of IFI encompass a broad extent," as opposed to the focus of a traditional audit on the financial statements' conformance with GAAP and other relevant requirements. As stated by Yaacob and Donglah (2012), "to attain the *maqasid* as Shariah, auditors/Shariah auditors must attest that management has complied not only with the appropriate requirements but also the Shariah foundation in all transactions." Islamic auditing, as described by Yahya and Mahzan (2012), is more comprehensive than traditional auditing in which the auditor reports directly to the firm owner and is not bound by any religious standards. A Shariah auditor, on the other hand, "would incorporate an alternate strategy and objective, namely preserving Shariah principles, in light of Islamic teaching." Khan (as reported in Yahya and Mahzan, 2012) also emphasizes this greater reach when he says, "The scope of auditing in an Islamic context is significantly broader than that of standard auditing." It would go beyond the standard idea of competence and authority to report on the social and economic dimensions of corporate organizations. This is due to the fact that Shariah principles and the core values of Islamic society provide the basis for auditing in Islam.

The SSB now has a relatively restricted interpretation of the word *shariah* in terms of technical conformity of financial transactions, despite the fact that the term *shariah* is highly inclusive. Business strategy (a), Operations (b), Procedures (c), Agreements (d), Finance (d), Human Resources (e), Charities (f), Environmental Consequences of (g), Marketing (h), Public Relations (i), Reporting (j), and *zakat* (k) (l) Computer Networks Programs for various uses, etc. (Sultan, 2007) laid out the four areas of focus for Shariah auditing in IFIs.

(1) The financial accounts of the IBs are examined by the Shariah auditor to ensure that they were recorded in conformity with both national and international Shariah regulations. *Aspects of Islamic banks' operations*: The types of business that an Islamic bank engages in are examined

278   *Shariah Governance Systems of Islamic Banks*

through a Shariah audit. It consists of (1) Examining the reports produced by the Shariah Supervisory Council, (2) Policies and procedures of Islamic bank activities, (3) Operation processes, (4) Contracts, and (5) Memorandum of Articles of Association (SSB).

(2) The Shariah audit of an Islamic bank would look at the bank's internal operations, including its management of both its staff and its assets. This guarantees that an Islamic bank has the right organizational structure and qualified employees to do business in accordance with Islamic Shariah.

(3) Systems of Information and Communication Technology Shariah audits must extend to Islamic banks' IT infrastructures. It's crucial to check whether Islamic banks are equipped with the right IT and other current technology to do business in accordance with Islamic Shariah.

9.6   Issues in Shariah Audit

As was previously said, the vast bulk of Shariah audit's scholarly potential remains unexplored. As a result, it's not unexpected that there are so many problems with it. At the outset, the independence of Shariah auditors is the most critical feature of Shariah audit. The principle of independence is fundamental to both Western and Islamic auditing practices. However, in certain IFIs, representatives of the SSB who do audits are paid for their services by the institution being audited. That is to say, they conduct internal audits on themselves, which may lead to concerns about bias and conflicts of interest. This is because, although following Shariah law, SSB members do not follow a professional code. Although AAOIFI has an established code of ethics that its members must follow, the organization has not developed a structure to guide its members as they carry out their responsibilities (Kassim, 2009). In addition, Hameed (2008) deals with the topic of whether or not SSB members are qualified to perform Shariah audits. He claims that the members of SSB are not eligible to function as auditors because they lack the appropriate training and credentials, even if they are qualified to make fatwas about the legality or otherwise of any financial instrument. The IFAC code of ethics (Hameed, 2008) also recognizes the "self-review threat" that is created when an auditor serves in both the advisory and auditing capacities throughout product development. It is important to note, however, that in many countries, including Malaysia, members of the Shariah board do not take part in the Shariah audit process since it is outside of their purview and duties. However, they communicate with one another to resolve certain open questions for the auditors. Finally, Rahman (2008) highlights specific details from SSB's studies that prove Islamic bank practices are in full accordance with Shariah.

The SSB, in contrast, is not even tasked with auditing in the same way that financial auditors are. They are solely responsible for the acceptance of goods and services. Financial auditors have extensive education, qualifications, training, and experience is what the author emphasizes. They are free to conduct audits in accordance with professional standards and with complete objectivity in exchange for payment. However, despite the fact that SSB members are accomplished Shariah scholars, they lack formal accreditation in the field and are not provided with sufficient training. Responsibility among SSB members is a related concern. Their main duty is to "advise" the bank on how to comply with Shariah law in its dealings with customers. Interestingly, according to their report, they are in charge of Shariah compliance "assurance". An interesting fifth issue arises from this scenario; the SSB's responsibility for Shariah non-compliance. Muneeza and Hassan (2011), who first brought this up, argue that existing law remains quiet on the implications of malpractice responsibility for SSB members. The general public may mistakenly believe that Shariah scholars cannot be sued for carelessness by their clients, thus it's important to establish whether or not this is indeed the case. Perhaps IFSA (2013) has already dealt with this problem. However, the authors bring up an interesting additional concern by arguing that the sector would be hampered by a lack of knowledge if Shariah Board members are allowed to be prosecuted by their customers. As a result, it is more practical to state that Shariah experts may only be sued in the most dire of situations (Muneeza and Hassan, 2011). There are still deep-seated problems that require fixing in the framework of the Shariah audit.

9.7 Professional Accounting Qualifications: Critical Economic Perspectives

9.7.1 Background Analysis

Universities seldom granted accounting degrees prior to the 1960s (Kitchen and Parker, 1980). As a consequence, people studied professionally in their spare time utilizing mail-order manuals to hone their accounting skills. It wasn't until the 1960s that accounting was offered as a degree program at UK institutions (Solomons and Berridge, 1974). However, professional accounting organizations continued to exert influence over the accounting field, and this trend has only accelerated as colleges seek "accreditation" for their degrees. University accounting degrees mimicked professional credentials closely (in terms of learning strategies, norms, and regulations) so that students may acquire the most possible exemptions from professional exams. The loss of more global consideration of the social effects of these practices and procedures is the price that must be paid, say Sikka and Willmott (2002). In 2003, the International Federation of Accountants (IFAC) had 155 member organizations from 113 countries. Of these, 61 (39% of the total) were based in the 41 nations (36% of the total) that were once a part of the British Empire (Parker, 2005). In the literature, many writers (Carnegie and Parker, 1999; Parker, 1989; Chua and Poullaos, 1998; Annisette, 2000) contend that an imperial component is necessary to fully comprehend the international accounting profession. The problem was first brought to light in one of the early publications by Johnson and Caygill (1971).

British professional accounting organizations had an early impact because of the transfer of British-qualified accountants to other countries, especially Commonwealth states, as revealed by Johnson and Caygill (1971). The presence of these accountants would be crucial in establishing regulatory bodies in these countries. On the other hand, following WWII, British accounting associations started spreading their exams over the world. At the time, the two biggest exporters were the Chartered Institute of Management Accountants (CIMA) and the Association of Certified Public Accountants (ACCA). This has led some to claim that the shipment of British accounting credentials to members in other countries is more significant than the export of British accountants themselves.

British professional accounting organizations CIMA and ACCA have been the subject of an in-depth analysis by Briston and Kedslie (1985). According to their research, between 1969 and 1989, CIMA and ACCA had increases in membership of 164% and 167%, respectively; the bulk of these increases may be attributed to the export of their certifications. The percentage of South and East Asians who joined ACCA increased more than any other region. There were 199 members of ACCA in SEA in 1969; by 1995, there were 11,319 members. Around 62% of ACCA's worldwide membership was based in South East Asia in 1995. These numbers attest to the deep institutional linkages that exist between ACCA and Hong Kong, Malaysia, and Singaporean professional accounting associations. Historically, the majority of CIMA's international members have come from South Asia, particularly Pakistan, India, and Sri Lanka. South East Asia, on the other hand, had more CIMA members than South Asia had by 1995 (31.6% of the total foreign membership), and this shift occurred as

Shariah Audit System   281

early as 1985. Overall, the two British accounting associations have made great achievements in exporting their credentials abroad, with the bulk of international members hailing from developing countries.

9.7.2 *Critical Economic Perspectives*

From a vital economic vantage point, developing nations (or OIC countries in our case, since almost all of them are developing) may benefit greatly from importing accounting credentials from Western organizations. Due to the high cost of examinations, course materials, textbooks, etc., local institutions in poor countries are often pushed to focus on preparing students for foreign credentials rather than creating a curriculum tailored to the local community's requirements (Briston and Kedslie, 1985). There is a lot written on the problems that arise when developing countries adopt Western accounting practices that aren't suited to their needs.

The situation has not improved despite the accounting organizations' best efforts to attract as many students and members as possible via extensive advertising campaigns. Senior management discusses growth and opportunities much like any other for-profit business. In the goals of these professional groups, the public interest viewpoint of accounting and auditing seems to have taken a second seat. The Association of Certified Fraud Examiners (ACCA) said in 1991, "The changing political environment in South Africa is going to provide the Association of Certified Fraud Examiners with new opportunities." This new function will first take the form of "an all-encompassing education and training program for the development of nonwhites' skills" (Briston and Kedslie, 1985). When a CEO talks about "new opportunities," he or she is talking about increasing profits by selling into untapped areas. Continuing, we read, "Mr Phillips [Chairman of the International Affairs Committee] additionally commended the substantial level of ACCA infiltration in China, and the considerable effort put in by the secretariat to forge links there notwithstanding significant language and cultural barriers." The term "penetration" suggests that these credentials may be sold to businesses and exported to other countries. Briston and Kedslie (1985) wonder how the Chinese might profit from a British professional organization given the substantial linguistic and cultural hurdles.

We do not suggest in this research that developing countries should avoid acquiring credentials from the West. Instead, we argue that accounting organizations have become for-profit businesses that rely on international service exports to fund domestic operations. Given that

British accounting groups have won Queen's Awards for export successes throughout the years (the ACCA body won its first in 1996), this charge is no longer baseless. This has led to a competitive environment in which professional accounting organizations like ACCA, CIMA, ICAEW, etc., all try to win over new students and members via a variety of advertising campaigns. Bakre (2004) and Yapa (2006), who examined the impact of Western accounting organizations on the accounting profession in Jamaica and Sri Lanka, provide two case studies that lend credence to this claim. To localize accounting education and professional activity throughout the 1950s and 1970s, the Institute of Chartered Accountants of Jamaica (ICAJ) tried, and ultimately failed, as detailed by Bakre (2004). The author claims that this effort was met with resistance by powerful minority members of the profession who had close ties to ACCA, while ACCA itself was reluctant to lose this market. As a result, once localization failed, the ACCA and its prominent minority members dominated the booming Jamaican accounting industry (February 10, 1999 ACCA Newsletter).

Yapa (2006) explains the financial toll taken by Sri Lanka (a former British colony) as a result of adopting British accounting standards. CIMA's yearly student membership was $54 in 1997, while registration was $30 and exams cost between $27 and $47 for each paper (depending on the level of the test). Additionally, it was highly recommended that students invest in pre-made study packages curated by British test specialists. As a result, Sri Lanka sends the United Kingdom almost $1 million in yearly accounting student fees. In addition, each of the almost a thousand "fellows" and "associates" who represent CIMA in the United States must pay a yearly fee to remain in good standing. It has been estimated that CIMA gets about £200,000 annually. The same situation applies to ACCA. Although Yapa's (2006) numbers are from 1997, the growth of student enrolment and participation in these groups has been steady. Developing countries send a lot of money to British accounting groups every year in the form of dues, registration fees, and test costs. It should come as no surprise, therefore, that various writers in the literary canon have offered critiques of imperialism and politics as an explanation for this occurrence. The majority of underdeveloped nations, as Perera (1989: 42) observes, "had little opportunity to establish accounting systems that accurately reflected local requirements and conditions." Their current systems are mostly elaborations on models established elsewhere, especially by capitalist Western countries like the UK and the US. Colonial powers, powerful capitalists, and international businesses all had a hand in imposing these institutions.

Worse still, OIC nations have made insufficient efforts to fight the infiltration of Western professional accounting organizations into the Islamic financial industry. Next, we show how a new breed of accountants and auditors, versed in Western accounting concepts but with an eye toward auditing Islamic financial organizations, is emerging thanks to the combination of ACCA and CIMA certificates with degrees and diplomas in Islamic finance. There are serious economic ramifications for the countries of the Organization of Islamic Cooperation (OIC) if Western accounting firms are allowed into the Islamic financial industry. Our main point is that OIC members need their own Shariah accounting and auditing professional firm to meet the needs of IFIs by offering thorough Shariah audit services. Following this, the study analyzes the present Shariah accounting and auditing credentials provided by different organizations throughout the world and explains why they fall short of what is needed for a comprehensive Shariah audit.

9.7.3 Shariah Accounting/Auditing Qualifications: A Market Gap

We return to our argument, briefly discussed in Section 9.2, that certain writers believe SSB members to be religious auditors and associate their function to that of Shariah auditing (for examples, see Briston and El-Ashker (1986), Abumouamer (1989), Karim (1990), and Hood and Bucheery (1999)). It is unusual to find an auditor who is competent for the role and who was educated in Anglo-American accounting and auditing concepts, in contrast to the SSB members/advisors who are well-equipped to issue fatwas or Islamic judgments on the permissibility of items. However, there are traditional auditors who are members of professional associations but who are not equipped to do Shariah audits due to their lack of familiarity with Islamic law. Therefore, we argue that a new breed of Islamic accountants and auditors versed in both Western and Islamic frameworks is necessary.

9.7.4 Shariah Accounting and Auditing Qualifications in the Market

For those who are interested in auditing the financial accounts of IFIs, we will now look at the present Shariah accounting and auditing standards. There is a seemingly endless supply of Islamic finance certifications, diplomas, certificates, and executive courses; nevertheless, we only take into consideration credentials that are deemed (or stated) to be similar to or near to professional accounting qualifications. As a result, we restricted our search to individuals who have earned accreditation as Islamic auditors and/or accountants. For the purposes of this chapter, we picked six schools whose curricula were most probable to generate Shariah auditors. Each company's website and prospectus were combed through to assemble the information displayed here. Although it is far from complete, this examination of prerequisites is an important first step that might stimulate more research.

9.7.4.1 *Accounting and Auditing Organization for Islamic Financial Institutions (AAOIFI)*

The AAOIFI was established in Bahrain in 1991 as an Islamic international autonomous non-profit corporation with the mission of creating accounting and auditing standards as well as governance, ethics, and Shariah guidelines for the Islamic financial sector. Currently, it offers the Chartered Islamic Professional Accountants (CIPA) program and the Chartered Shariah Adviser and Auditor (CSAA) program for professional growth. A candidate who completes the CIPA program will have the technical understanding as well as the professional abilities in accountancy required by international Islamic banks and financial institutions, while a candidate who completes the CSAA program will have the knowledge and skills required by the industry to ensure Shariah compliance and review processes are followed. The Bank Negara Malaysia (Central Bank of Malaysia) created the worldwide hub for Education in Islamic Finance (INCEIF) in December 2005 as part of the Malaysian Government's effort to boost Malaysia's reputation as a worldwide Islamic finance hub. It's the only place in the world where you can get a master's degree in Islamic finance. Its flagship Chartered Islamic Finance Professional (CIFP) degree educates students in a variety of Takaful and capital market-related Islamic banking practices. The Association of Chartered Islamic Finance Professionals (ACIFP) was also founded on May 7, 2008 to support the initiative.

9.7.4.2 *CIMA*

CIMA's Islamic finance certifications are the first offered by any professional chartered accounting organization. The three tiers of participation are designed to accommodate professionals with varying degrees of familiarity with Islamic finance. There are three levels of certification offered by CIMA in Islamic finance: a certificate, a diploma, and an advanced diploma. The CIMA advanced diploma in Islamic finance (CADIF) was named "most exceptional Islamic training module" at the 2011 KLIFF Islamic finance honors.

9.7.4.3 *LSBF*

With an emphasis on the theoretical as well as the practical consequences of Shariah banking and Islamic financial management, the London School of Business and Finance provides a dual ACCA/MSc Finance and Investment (Islamic Finance and Banking) degree.

9.7.4.4 *BIBF*

The Bahrain Institute of Banking and Finance established its Centre for Islamic Finance in 1997 with aid from AAOIFI and financial backing from the Central Bank of Bahrain. The Advanced Diploma in Islamic Commercial Jurisprudence (ADIC), which is meant to prepare students for careers in Shariah compliance and Shariah supervision in Islamic Banking, and the Advanced Diploma in Islamic Finance, which is meant to enhance employment prospects for students already working in the banking industry but who want to specialize in Islamic finance, are the two professional certifications it offers.

9.7.4.5 *EIIF*

Over 20,000 paying customers in 44 countries use the services of the Ethica Institute of Islamic Finance (EIIF), which is situated in Dubai, United Arab Emirates. Both the CIFE (Certified Islamic Finance Executive) and the ACIFE (Advanced CIFE in Islamic Accounting) are available through Ethica. The AAOIFI standard is the gold standard in Islamic banking, and Ethica's certification is the only online curriculum that fully conforms with it.

9.7.5 *Limitations and Market Gap*

We found the following design problems that preclude the creation of a comprehensive Shariah auditor after examining the course structures, modules taught, period of instruction, articles/internship requirements, and other essential features of each of the aforementioned programs:

AAOIFI: Differentiating between the roles of a CIPA and a CSAA. Candidates for CIPA learn the skills they'll need to work as auditors for IFIs, while those for CSAA learn the skills they'll need to sit on the SSB boards of IFIs. It falls short of what is needed to train competent auditors who are also familiar with Shariah concepts. Furthermore, it is clear that the curricula only provide instruction in AAOIFI's standards and principles, rather than providing instruction in IFRS or GAAP. Given the very low level of acceptance of AAOIFI standards in the Islamic world, this is not ideal.

The emphasis of the training at INCEIF is on Islamic financial concepts rather than on accounting and auditing as such. It is possible that the Certified Islamic Financial Professional (CIFP) curriculum is not seen as a specialist certificate on par with professional accounting qualifications, despite its careful design to cover all areas of Islamic finance, especially Shariah. Initially, the CIFP curriculum featured a course called Shariah Audit and Compliance, but it has since been removed. While it is encouraging that ACIFP has been established, the Certified Islamic Financial Planner designation may be seen more as an entry-level certificate for a career in the Islamic financial business, and ACIFP as an opportunity for networking for CIFP graduates.

CIMA: The Chartered Institute of Management Accountants offers courses that enable existing practitioners and qualified accountants and auditors with an understanding of Shariah. These courses are not recognized as professional Shariah accounting and auditing qualifications; nevertheless, they do give a good foundation in Islamic accounting and auditing. They like to help those who already have more traditional accounting qualifications, such as the ACCA or CIMA. Also, if Western accounting organizations start providing Islamic accounting and auditing courses, and this method becomes popular, it might have negative economic consequences for the Islamic world in the form of outflows of foreign currency reserves to these entities.

As was previously mentioned, the completion of a standard ACCA certificate is a prerequisite to LSBF. Although it might lead to the development of conventional auditors with an understanding of Islamic financial difficulties, this course would be economically harmful to the Muslim world.

A diploma from the BIBF is intended to provide a comprehensive education for work in the SSB or other general IFI roles, hence it is a rather broad field. These degrees are not sufficient on their own to practice public accounting or auditing. However, they might be useful additions for a candidate who already has Western accounting credentials.

Brief, four-month EIIF certification programs introduce students to key concepts in Islamic accounting. In and of itself, they provide little to no value, yet they could help a candidate who already has accounting memberships. They also sign up for AAOIFI's standards, which are not widely used in the Muslim world, and get training on them. At last, there is a chance that the course may skimp on discussing how to conduct an audit and review according to Shariah law.

As was previously indicated, there is an appetite for a professional accounting and auditing certification that prepares students to perform a comprehensive audit of the yearly financial statements of IFIs, particularly those that pertain to Sharia law. Conventional auditors now review the annual accounts of IFIs, while Shariah advisers provide a separate report on the IFI's Shariah compliance procedures. An "Association of Chartered Shariah Accountants and Auditors" (ACSAA) that caters to IFIs' needs and reduces the economic costs of purchasing Western accounting qualifications that might not be fully appropriate for domestic needs is something that every country aspiring to be an Islamic finance hub (e.g., Malaysia, Saudi Arabia, the United Arab Emirates, Qatar, etc.) should set up. The next part explains how and why Malaysia may profit economically from forming the ACSAA organization, and why it should take the lead in doing so.

9.7.6 *External Shariah Audit*

After an internal Shariah audit, an independent evaluation is necessary to ensure Shariah compliance in the IBI environment. In this context, it is obligatory for Islamic banking institutions (IBIs) to undergo an independent Shariah audit once the SGF has been implemented. This audit's purpose is to verify that the activities of the IBI comply with Shariah norms and principles. The scope of this audit is confined to evaluating Shariah compliance in contracts, transactions, and financial arrangements in the following order:

(a) All the instructions, regulations, and guidelines of the State Bank of Pakistan regarding Shariah Compliance and the AAOIFI Shariah standards adopted by SBP.
(b) The Fatawas and ruling issued by the SSB of the State Bank of Pakistan.

(c) The Islamic Financial Accounting Standards (IFAS) notified by the Securities and Exchange Commission of Pakistan (SECP):

Figure 9.1 illustrates the external Shariah audit structure. The external auditors will compile a report on the Shariah compliance environment for the BOD that will be included in the yearly financial statements based on an assessment of the IBI's activities, contracts, etc. AAOIFI (2008) further claims that the annual financial audit will ensure Shariah compliance at IBI, negating the necessity for a separate external Shariah audit.

9.7.7 Ethical and Divine Qualities of an Auditor

9.7.7.1 Qualities of an Auditor from an Ethical Perspective

Ethics can be defined as the permissible behavior of human beings in society. To make auditing permissible in society, professionals adhere to a set of ethical guidelines. The fundamental components of professional codes of ethics are a general statement of acceptable conduct and specific guidelines for identifying unacceptable behavior.

There are five principles of professional ethics:

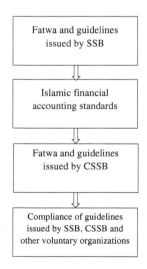

Figure 9.1: External Shariah Audit Structure.
Source: Modified from Shahzad et al. (2017).

(1) An auditor ought to be impartial and independent. He should do the audit with integrity.
(2) The auditor must be able to adhere to the industry's technical standards and maintain his auditing proficiency.
(3) The auditor should be neutral and fair when conducting the audit. He should attend to the clients as much as his obligations permit.
(4) A good working connection between auditors is essential.
(5) As a member of a human community, an auditor is required to uphold the public interest.

9.7.7.2 *Qualities of an Auditor from an Islamic Perspective*

AAOIFI's "Code of Ethics for Professional Accounts" shall be followed by the auditor. According to Islamic law, an auditor must perform the following duties:

First and foremost, an auditor must be moral. Integrity is of the utmost importance for an auditor. This trait pervaded the whole prophetic movement. Hazrat Umar (RA) would not let certain individuals do business because they lacked the competence required to operate a company successfully. Sincerity and hard effort are essential qualities to have while employed by another person, business, or organization. Ihsan, which translates to "profitability and efficiency," is our fifth value. Islam mandates that we offer our all at all times. Iklas (Sincerity): No one can do a good job if they are not honest about their intentions. If someone is genuine, he will put up his very best effort. Auditor objectivity stems from an understanding of the audit's scope and purpose. An auditor's professional competence is essential. He needs much instruction and direction in order to succeed. The auditor's ability to keep information secret is crucial to the success of his audit.

9.8 Shariah Audit Evidence

9.8.1 *Definition of Audit Evidence and Its Main Features*

Auditors carefully gather data regarding a company's health and then weigh that evidence to reach a conclusion. All evidence gathered during an audit serves as the foundation for a conclusion or assessment. Evidence obtained during an audit is the basis on which a conclusion or judgment is formed. For the purposes of an audit, evidence is any piece of information that may be utilized as a basis for making observations and drawing conclusions. As stated in the Audit Manual published by the Public Service Commission

290 Shariah Governance Systems of Islamic Banks

of Canada in 2005, it "provides persuasive evidence in favor of a fact or an argument under consideration." Contrast the weight of audit evidence with that of legal evidence. As a consequence, the auditor is able to reach an acceptable level of confidence in his conclusion. Audit evidence seldom allows for 100% assurance. However, legal evidence is a sort of rigorous proof that is more definite and certain than audit evidence (Hayes *et al.*, 2005). Substantially excellent audit evidence should have the following qualities: (1) *Adequate*: Adequate does not need submitting a complete audit trail. This means there has to be enough evidence for the auditor to reach a conclusion. (2) *Appropriateness*: Whereas sufficiency evaluates the total amount of audit evidence, proportionality evaluates its quality. In other words, it evaluates the dependability and relevance of audit data in identifying misstatements and compliance breaches. For the auditor to rely on audit evidence in making his judgment, it must be (3) *Dependable*: Achieving perfect dependability is illogical. Therefore, it is necessary that the proof be persuasive rather than absolute. (4) The kind of evidence should be appropriate for the question being asked. If you want to be sure that your stock levels are accurate, for instance, you need to have a physical verification. Audit evidence, unlike legal proof, is not expected to be incontestable. If the auditor thinks the evidence is strong, that's good enough. Most conclusions are formed with just a little quantity of evidence. Hayes *et al.* (2005) claim that if the evidence is consistent across several sources, it is more convincing. In addition to the above, the following criteria might be helpful for determining the reliability of audit evidence: To begin, it is better to rely on written evidence rather than personal testimony. Second, it's preferred to use evidence that has come from a variety of different places or is of a unique kind. The original papers are always better than any reproductions made of them. Third, outside evidence is more reliable than data collected inside. Last but not least, indirect evidence is inferior to direct evidence gathered by the auditor by own personal inspection, etc.

9.8.2 *Sources and Techniques of Audit Evidence*

Audit evidence can be obtained from two primary sources: primary and secondary (Audit Manual Public Service Commission of Canada, 2005).

Initial evidence: This is the information personally gathered by auditors. Auditors can collect the information themselves using techniques such as interviews, surveys, observation, and investigation. When selecting one or more of these techniques to collect data, the auditor must possess the requisite skills and knowledge to implement them.

Indirect evidence: There are two categories of secondary evidence: information garnered by the audited entity and information gathered by third parties. Due to the fact that every business entity maintains records of its daily transactions, it generates an abundance of auditable data. Similarly, external authorities, such as regulators, possess substantial information about the entity that can serve as auditable evidence.

An auditor has the following options as techniques for collecting audit evidence:

- Inquiry
- Observation
- Inspection
- Recalculation
- Confirmation and
- Analytical procedures

9.8.3 *Documentation of Audit Evidence*

The actual pieces of evidence are often included in the paperwork. Not all papers reviewed nor the information gathered from them in great detail are to be copied and filed. It should be sufficient, for instance, to specify which document was studied and how to identify and find that document if the evidence comprises a company's financial records. The supporting documentation, or "working papers," should also be well-organized and simple to locate. These records should include either the evidence itself or a summary of the evidence studied so that readers may draw the same conclusions as the auditor. Evidence documenting relies heavily on the auditor's professional judgment and expertise (Audit Manual Public Service Commission of Canada, 2005).

9.9 Shariah Audit Methodology Examination, Reporting and Documentation Phase

9.9.1 *Shariah Audit Methodology*

9.9.1.1 *Planning Phase*

Since a Shariah audit is a "systematic process," it's important to get the layout right from the start. To pass the auditor's inspection, it has to be well "planned" and built. After careful preparation, the next step is to conduct an "examination." The reporting phase follows the implementation of Shariah audits and is the natural conclusion to the previous two. The last step of a Shariah audit is to compile an audit report, which serves as evidence of compliance with Shariah requirements. The following are crucial components of any Shariah audit plan:

Understanding the business of IFI: Financial institutions and the businesses they serve are not interchangeable. Some organizations support large-scale government and non-government programs, while others serve a larger clientele of people and businesses. Therefore, it is essential for a Shariah auditor to understand the scope and character of the IFI's operations. Retail banking for individual customers may be a significant part of an Islamic bank's business model. In addition to mortgage and other consumer loans, this kind of IFI may also provide credit card services. Any audit plan comprising methodologies and processes acceptable for the audit of project finance will do if a Shariah auditor is charged with auditing a retail banking IFI. As a result, the Shariah auditor has to learn about the IFI's operations before making any judgments.

Understanding the contracts appropriate for the business: When compared to domestic banks, IFIs have a different approach to business and have a distinct set of guiding principles. Islamic financial organizations emphasize trade, whereas conventional financial organizations like banks concentrate on lending and borrowing. Therefore, instead of lending or borrowing money, IFIs make purchases and sales with their clients. This is typical of Islamic retail businesses like banks. When it comes to consumer banking and personal finance, a Shariah auditor may conclude that the *murabaha* contract is the most applicable and widespread. Project funding is often handled via *salam, istisna*, and *ijarah* contracts, whereas equity financing is typically handled through *musharakah* and Mudharabah contracts. It would be detrimental for an IFI to create a plan for auditing that emphasizes *murabaha* transactions given that project financing is the core business function of the organization. However, an audit method that places more focus on *salam* and *istisna* would be inappropriate when the IFI serves a wider clientele.

Identifying the appropriate evidence-gathering techniques: The next step of organizing a Shariah audit is to determine the most suitable strategies that can be used to gather evidence with the goal to form a conclusion about the IFI's Shariah compliance status, which is dependent on the auditor's understanding of the nature and objectives of the IFI's business and the fundamentals and sequence of the applicable agreements used by the IFI to achieve these objectives. Since IFIs' contracts are different from those used by other businesses, it is only natural that different auditing methods would be better suited to this task. IFIs mostly engage in buying and selling rather than lending and borrowing, thus they need tools that can support this element of their operation. A site visit, if judged required by the auditor, might prove preferable to alternative techniques in the event of project funding, for example.

Developing a proper audit plan: It is essential to create an adequate audit strategy in light of these choices after understanding the IFI's activities and choosing the best methods for evidence gathering (Sultan, 2007). An audit plan is a list of the key tasks the auditor will complete throughout the auditing process. It outlines the goals of every activity that makes up this procedure. It also explains the methods that will be used to accomplish these goals. In a nutshell, the audit plan is the first, most important step that establishes the goals for the entire auditing process.

9.9.2 *Examination Phase*

The question of whether or not to do real fieldwork is a key one in the audit technique. The accomplishment of the whole process depends on the examination, which is the actualization of the first audit plan. During this phase of the audit, choosing the best method for gathering audit evidence is crucial. The auditor may choose one or more tools from a wide range of auditing methods. A Shariah auditor typically has the option of using the flow interview, the statistical walkthrough, or questionnaires. Several of these instruments may be chosen or given priority for a variety of reasons. For instance, it will depend on the reason for the audit. In a similar vein, certain methods will be more appropriate than others for IFI because of the nature of their company. This choice will also be affected by the ease with which some of these methods may be implemented, the lack of others, and the supremacy of certain methods, such as direct observation.

9.9.3 *Reporting Phase (Nature of the Audit Report)*

An audit report is often extremely short, consisting of just a few lines at most. The audit report is quick and to particular, thus the components it

294 *Shariah Governance Systems of Islamic Banks*

includes are concise and to the point as well, excluding fluff and extraneous information. While the report's format may vary from auditor to auditor, the following Audit Form No. 1 should always be included in any respectable Shariah audit report:

AUDIT FORM NO. 1

Murabaha/Musawama of Cars/Vehicles/Goods/Real Estate/Buildings/Land

Auditing branch #:

Transaction carried out in the following quarter: Q1/Q2/Q3/Q4

Type of Transaction:
1- *Murabaha* for the Purchase Orderer (Obligatory Promise) ☐

2- *Musawama* ☐

Customer Name:

A/C No:

Transaction No:

Title deed before purchase in the name of:

Title deed after purchase in the name of:

Sale invoice in the name of:

S/N	Document Name	Document used? ☑ Or ☒	Date/ Time	Data complete? ☑ Or ☒	Signatures fulfilled? ☑ Or ☒	Document approved? ☑ Or ☒
1	Quotation					
2	Purchase request and promise to buy					
3	*Murabaha/musawama* (for companies) MOU					
4	Authorization to charge fees					
5	Purchase contract					
6	Final purchase invoice					
7	Sale contract (*Musawama/Murabaha*)					
8	Form (permission to examine and accept delivery of item of sale)					
9	Insurance policy (*takāful*)					
10	Transferring the title deed in the name of customer					
11	Arrears payment notification					
12	Arrears and penalty payment notification					
13	*Takāful* insurance cancellation notification					

Shariah Audit System

After reviewing the *sharī'ah* controls for *murabaha/musawama*, check that the procedures are *sharī'ah*-compliant as follows:

Tick ☑ when the condition is fulfilled, ☒ when the condition is not fulfilled, ☐ when the condition does not apply for this case.

1. Check that the documents are approved by the *sharī'ah* supervisory board (SSB) (   )
2. Check that the data and signatures are complete (   )
3. Check that the customer is independent from the supplier by comparing the sale and purchase contracts against the commercial registration of the customer (   )
4. Check that there is no contract between the supplier and the customer by reviewing the quotation and ensuring that it does not include a statement saying "the customer paid a down payment" and that no contract is signed between the two parties (   )
5. Check, in case a contract is found between the customer and supplier, that such contract is voided by an official letter from the supplier (   )
6. Check that the goods of sale are not gold or silver (   )
7. Check that the purchase order and promise and the purchase and sale contracts are electronically timed (   )
8. Check that the bank did not charge fees more than the tariffs agreed to with the customer by reviewing the authorization to debit fees, the *murabaha/musawama* (for companies) MOU, the financing calculation and the accounting entries in the automated system (   )
9. Check that the bank did not take a down payment from the customer before finalizing the sale through the accounting entries in the automated system – it is permissible to take a margin of seriousness before sale (   )
10. Check that the bank did not benefit from the margin of seriousness, if found, more than the actual damages (difference between the promised sale price and the actual sale price in the market) in case of the customer not complying with their promise to purchase the good (   )
11. Check that the purchase orderer who has been assigned as an agent on behalf of the bank has not sold the good(s) to him/herself, but that the bank has sold it to the person (   )

29. Check, through the transaction's documents, that if the bank sold goods to the customer in foreign currency then voided the contract and initiated another sale in local currency that the goods subject to the sale existed at the time of the latter sale and that they were in the same condition as per the initial contract (   )
30. Check, through the *murabaha* contract and accounting entries, that in case of agreement to pay the *murabaha* liabilities in a currency that is different from the currency of the outstanding liabilities, that this is done using the exchange rate of the repayment day and that the entire debt that will be paid in foreign currency is repaid on spot basis (   )

Observations and Remarks: ....
....
....
....
....
....
....
....

Supporting evidence attached?	☐
Field *Sharī'ah* Auditor: Signature	**Audit date: -----/-----/ 20**

***Sharī'ah* Audit Department's Comments:**

....
....
....
....
....
....
....

Should the observation be stated in the final report?	☐
Head of *Sharī'ah* Audit: Signature	**Audit date: -----/-----/ 20**

Management's Response & Plan of Action:

....
....
....
....
....
....
....

Name:	**Signature:**	**Date: -----/-----/ 20**

9.9.4 *Audit Documentation Phase*

The audit documentation serves as the foundation for the auditor's judgments and is the main source of evidence for his report. In addition, it gives a written evaluation of the work's standard and quality and backs up the auditor's findings with documentation. The term "working papers" or "work papers" can also refer to documentation related to an audit. These records detail the auditor's general activity throughout the auditing process as well as the findings and judgments he reached based on the audit evidence. Both paper and electronic formats are acceptable for presenting this information (Hayes *et al.*, 2005). Working papers have many different uses.

(1) Planned and executed effectively, and the necessary reference information and detail should be included.

(2) Demonstrating that the auditor's opinion is valid and compliant with the applicable regulatory requirements.

(3) The supervisory authorities determine whether the entire audit procedure is effective and reliable for their own objectives, similar to tax authorities.

What information should or should not be included in the working documents depends on the auditor's professional judgment. While it is impossible to include every point, it is also challenging to omit any points that should be included in these documents. As a general rule, the auditor should add any information necessary for another auditor with no prior experience and knowledge of the entity to comprehend the audit work performed. They should justify the decision that has already been made.

9.10 Challenges in Implementing Shariah Audit

Shariah auditing in Islamic banking entails gathering evidence and reporting on whether the activities of Islamic institutions comply with Islamic Shariah. This auditing should be performed by a skilled, independent, and capable auditor. There must be established criteria upon which an auditor can conduct an audit of an Islamic bank. To ensure Shariah conformance, the Shariah auditor audits the objective (financial information) and subjective (Shariah information) aspects of Islamic banking.

Shariah audit proof: Gathering audit evidence is the first difficult task a Shariah auditor must complete. Shariah audit evidence is essentially any data that the auditor uses to assess whether the Islamic bank under audit correctly complies with Islamic Shariah rules. Information appraisal depends on the type of information. The authority of the Islamic bank under audit and the auditor may decide together on the standards for evaluating subjective data. However, the auditor may follow the SSB's (documented) rules.

To find out if an Islamic bank is following Shariah guidelines, data is gathered for a Shariah audit. The auditor may use a variety of information sources, including computerized transaction data, auditor observations, oral evidence from the auditee, and written correspondence between the bank and its customers. Auditors must gather enough data to assess the bank's compliance with Islamic Shariah.

Shariah auditing methodology: Critical to Shariah auditing is the development of a systematic and exhaustive audit program. If auditing procedures are documented as a list, the audit program may be considered Shariah-compliant. There must be a separate Shariah audit program for legal documentation and operational procedures. An audit program scrutinizes a particular area of audit.

Shariah auditors who are both qualified and objective are in short supply. In order to audit an Islamic bank, a Shariah auditor must possess at least two specific qualifications: (1) the ability to do audits in conformity with accepted auditing standards; and (2) familiarity with Islamic Shariah. It is incredibly rare to see these two attributes together. The Shariah auditor must, nevertheless, be sane. In order to create skilled Shariah auditors, there is currently no institution that offers education and training in both auditing and Islamic Shariah. The following two requirements must be taught and acquired by a Shariah auditing institution in order for it to be recognized as a separate profession: (1) Shariah understanding of Islamic Banking and Finance and (2) knowledge of accounting and auditing. Both accountants and Shariah experts are welcome to join this organization. This organization will play a crucial role in the future development of Shariah auditing as a unique profession.

9.11   Conclusion

Islamic finance is unquestionably characterized by adherence to Shariah. It serves as the backbone of the entire sector and was the original goal. One of the crucial tools for achieving Shariah compliance is Shariah audit, a rapidly growing field of study.

Assuring adherence to Shariah is the aim. This chapter discusses the Shariah audit, audit process, challenges, methodology, and reporting process.

CHAPTER 10

Shariah Reporting and Disclosure System

10.1 Introduction

Shariah governance reporting (SGR) outlines that developing effective SG mechanisms and practicing transparency in reporting allow Islamic Financial Institutions (IFIs) to rebuild public confidence, achieve business objectives, and ensure growth consistency (Ab Ghani *et al.*, 2023; Elamer *et al.*, 2020). Additionally, SGR streamlines IFIs' business, affairs, and activities to fulfill regulatory requirements as well as ensures the prevalence of *Shariah* standards in internal policies and procedures (Ferriswara *et al.*, 2022; Laldin and Furqani, 2018). Several emerging studies have identified multiple reasons for the need for SGR in IFIs (Elghuweel *et al.*, 2017). First, reporting of products, services, operations, and governance information through annual reports allows stakeholders to assess institutional compliance with the *Shariah* principles, the level of internal control, SG practices, and credibility of financial information (Alam *et al.*, 2022b; Kasim *et al.*, 2013). Second, transparency in SGR boosts shareholders, board of directors (BODs), and management's confidence by preserving IFIs' integrity and reputation (Mukhibad *et al.*, 2022). Third, SGR represents IFIs' capability to understand and interpret the *Shariah* rules and principles to ensure the implementation of *Shariah* principles in every business activity which would allow them to conform to religious requirements (Garas and Pierce, 2010; Muhammad *et al.*, 2021).

10.2 Islamic Social Reporting

Islamic principles of social responsibility advocate for transparency in business dealings, since the public has the right to know how a company's actions impact them (Baydoun and Willett, 1997). Complete disclosure, as defined by Haniffa and Hudaib (2002), requires the firm to provide only information that is both relevant and trustworthy in order to let external users make an educated economic and religious choice. One of the main aims of Islamic social reporting is to disclose whether or not an organization complies with the Shariah law. According to Maali *et al.* (2006) and Sulaiman *et al.* (2011), Islamic social reporting should help Muslim decision-makers fulfill their religious obligations by disclosing not only whether a company corresponds with the Shariah principles but also how the company's commercial activities could negatively impact the users. According to Haniffa and Hudaib (2002), Islamic social reporting goes beyond the norms of social disclosure by considering the company's spiritual obligations as well as those imposed by society at large about the company's role in the economy. The upshot is a more open and honest corporate environment, since Muslim decision-makers have access to information that meets their religious needs. In order to increase their ethical responsibility and trustworthiness, Islamic banks must be transparent.

In order to meet their social obligations, IFIs might include Shariah-related information in their annual reports, as suggested by Raman and Bukair (2013). Islamic institutions should provide both required and optional information in their yearly reports to give customers more trust in their religious choices. Multiple studies (Haniffa, 2002; Baydoun and Willet, 2000; Ousama and Fatima, 2010; Maali *et al.*, 2006; Farook *et al.*, 2011) argue that the annual reports of the Islamic banks should devote more space to social issues like *zakat*, charity, profit sharing, the environment, social activities, and employees. The annual report additionally has to include details on the Board and the SSB's composition and decision-making processes including the members' educational backgrounds, professional expertise, and independence.

Based on the facts, this chapter aims to elaborate on the sources of development of Islamic banking reporting based on the Accounting and Auditing Organization for Islamic Financial Institutions (AAOIFI) standards, the harmonization of Islamic accounting standards with International Financial Reporting Standards (IFRS), alternatives of Islamic corporate reporting, and the accounting policies of Islamic banks in many countries. Secondly, this chapter tries to formulate the components that

Shariah Reporting and Disclosure System 301

should be reported by Islamic banks in order to increase the degree of accountability. Thirdly, this chapter also tries to evaluate the existing Islamic banking reporting components in order to measure the gap between expectations and realities.

10.3 The Roles of AAOIFI

The AAOIFI is an Islamic international autonomous not-for-profit corporate body that prepares accounting, auditing, governance, ethics, and Shariah standards for IFIs and industries.

Until now, AAOIFI has issued a total of 117 standards in the areas of Shariah, accounting, auditing, ethics, and governance for international Islamic finance. It is supported by a number of institutional members, including central banks and regulatory authorities, financial institutions, accounting and auditing firms, and legal firms from over 45 countries (www.aaoifi.com). As an independent international organization, AAOIFI is supported by institutional members (200 members from 45 countries, so far) including central banks, IFIs, and other participants from the international Islamic banking and finance industry worldwide.

AAOIFI has gained assuring support for the implementation of its standards, which are now adopted in the Kingdom of Bahrain, Dubai International Financial Centre, Jordan, Lebanon, Qatar, Sudan, and Syria. The relevant authorities in Australia, Indonesia, Malaysia, Pakistan, the Kingdom of Saudi Arabia, and South Africa have issued guidelines that are based on AAOIFI's standards and pronouncements.

The objectives of AAOIFI are as follows: (a) to develop accounting and auditing thoughts relevant to IFIs; (b) to disseminate accounting and auditing thoughts relevant to IFIs and its applications through various media; (c) to prepare, promulgate, and interpret accounting and auditing standards for IFIs; and (d) to review and amend accounting and auditing standards for IFIs.

The objectives of financial accounting for Islamic banks and financial institutions are as follows: (a) to determine the rights and obligations of interested parties; (b) to safeguard entity assets and rights of others; (c) to contribute to the enhancement of managerial productive capacities; (d) to provide useful information to make legitimate decisions; (e) to encourage Shariah compliance; and (f) to distinguish prohibited earnings and expenditure.

The Statement of Financial Accounting (SFA) No. 1 stated that financial reports for IFIs, which are directed mainly to external users, should provide the following types of information:

(1) Information about the Islamic bank's compliance with the Shariah precepts.

(2) Information about the separation of prohibited earnings and expenditures.

(3) Information about the Islamic bank's economic resources and related obligations.

(4) Information about the determination of *zakah* on Islamic banks' funds and the purpose of the disbursement.

(5) Information about the estimation of cash flows that might be realized from dealing with Islamic banks, the timing of those flows, and the risk associated with their realization. This is related to the prediction of Islamic bank's ability to generate income in order to distribute profits to equity and investment account holders.

(6) Information about the ability of Islamic banks to safeguard the third parties' funds through various investment schemes.

(7) Information about the Islamic bank's discharge of its social responsibilities.

Karim (1999) explained that AAOIFI had an extensive due process that governed the production of its accounting and auditing standards. The due process included the vetting of the juristic suitability of the proposed standards by AAOIFI's Shariah Board. It also provided interested parties with the opportunity to express their opinion on the standards before the Board finally approved them. This is made possible by the holding of public hearings to discuss the exposure drafts. It is the practice of AAOIFI to hold a public hearing on the same exposure drafts in two countries.

Karim (1999) argued that AAOIFI did not have the power to force IFIs to implement the standards it promulgates. AAOIFI had, therefore, pursued a strategy of having its standards implemented by cooperating with concerned governmental and professional agencies, namely central banks and bodies that are responsible for implementing accounting standards. For instance, the supervisory authorities in Bahrain and Sudan had asked Islamic banks to adhere AAOIFI's standards in preparing their 1998 financial statements. Some Islamic banks in other countries (e.g., Malaysia and Saudi Arabia) have also started voluntarily to use AAOIFI's accounting standards to prepare their financial statements. Furthermore, international rating agencies have also started to take AAOIFI's standards into consideration when rating Islamic banks.

However, Harahap (2003) noted that due to a lack of accepted standards for annual report disclosure, Islamic organizations still use accepted

Shariah Reporting and Disclosure System 303

disclosure standards for conventional annual reports. Even though AAOIFI had been established, the accounting standards (that includes disclosure) were mostly based on conventional accounting concepts. Therefore, Harahap tried to search the Islamic values inside AAOIFI's accounting standards. Haniffa and Hudaib (2001) argued that the conceptual framework for Islamic accounting should be based on Shariah. According to them, the objectives of Islamic accounting are to assist in achieving socio-economic justice (Al-falah) and recognize the fulfillment of obligation to God, society, and individuals concerned. In addition, it is a form of worship by parties involved in economic activities such as accountants, auditors, managers, owner, government, etc.

From this basis, Haniffa and Hudaib (2001) divided the accounting into two aspects: technical and human. Technical Islamic accounting needed measurements for *zakah* thereby understanding how profit was distributed. For disclosure aspects, Islamic accounting should clearly state how the institution is fulfilling its duties and obligations according to Shariah, e.g., lawful dealings, *zakah* to beneficiaries, *sadaqah* (charities/gifts), wages, and the achievement objective of business venture and protecting the environment. On the other hand, the human aspects of Islamic accounting should be based on morality, ethics and Divine law, and accountability.

Harahap (2003) argued that according to AAOIFI there were some items concerning Islamic value information items must be disclosed:

(1) Basic information about the Islamic bank.
(2) Unusual supervisory restriction.
(3) Earning of expenditure prohibited by Shariah.
(4) The method used by the Islamic bank to allocate investment profits (loss) between unrestricted investment account holders or their equivalent and the Islamic.
(5) Bank as a Mudarib or as an investor with its own funds.
(6) Statement of changes in restricted investments.
(7) Statement sources and uses of funds in the *zakah* and charity fund.
(8) Statement of sources and uses of funds in the Quard fund.

10.4 Harmonization of Islamic Accounting Standards with IFRS

The globalization of business has created an impact on the international accounting standards. The international standard setters have to face challenges to accommodate the need for a single international accounting standard for all companies around the world in order to simplify the process of financial reporting. Therefore, the International Accounting Standards Board (IASB), an independent standard-setting board, tried to propose IFRS in order to develop and promote a single set of high-quality, understandable, and international financial reporting standards for general-purpose financial statements. They claimed that 113 countries around the world require and permit IFRS reporting for companies. Moreover, they implemented IFRS on January 1, 2012 and encouraged all member countries to adopt the standards gradually.

The IASB was established in 2001 by the International Accounting Standards Committee (IASC). IASC was created in 1973 between the professional accountancy bodies in nine countries and from 1982 its membership comprised all the accountancy bodies who were members of the International Federation of Accountants (IFAC). The principal significance of the IASC was to encourage national accounting standard setters around the world to improve and harmonize national accounting standards. The members of the IASC who were Professional Accountancy Bodies of the world delegated the responsibility to the IASC Board. The IASC Board was responsible for all activities including standard-setting activity. The standards adopted by the IASC Board were known as the International Accounting Standards (IAS).

10.4.1 *The International Accounting Standards Board*

The IASB is responsible for all standard-setting activities, including the development and adoption of IFRS. The IASB comprises 14 members that are to be increased to 16 members. The members of the board are a mix of practical experience in standard-setting process, or as a user, or accounting, academia, or from the preparer community. The constitution also makes it amply clear that the work of the IASB will not be invalidated by its failure at any time. It would also not have its representation in accordance with the geographical allocation laid down in the constitution. Members of the IASB are appointed for a term of up to 5 years, renewable once. When the IASC Foundation was first constituted, the IASB adopted all IAS issued by the previous IASC. The existing IAS continues to be operative till the extent it has not been amended or withdrawn by the IASB. New standards issued by the IASB are called the IFRS. Collectively IFRS includes both IAS and IFRS.

10.4.2 The Roles of IASB

The main aim of IASB is to develop a single set of high-quality, understandable, and enforceable accounting standards to help participants in the world's capital markets and other users make economic decisions. Furthermore, the other objectives of IASB are as follows: (a) to formulate and publish accounting standards and to promote their worldwide acceptance; (b) to work on the improvement and standardization of regulations, accounting standards, and procedures; and (c) the IASB does not appear to believe that the many reasons provided as to why different nations should have different accounting standards (e.g., tied to differences in culture, religion, and so forth) outweigh the benefits of international standardization.

One of its short-term aims is to merge the national accounting standards and the IAS. Moreover, the long-term aim of global uniformity is to have a single set of accounting standards for all listed and economically significant business enterprises. This process is also supported by the International Organization of Securities Commission (IOSCO) which is working with IAS/IFRS to achieve widespread acceptance. They together developed a plan such that compliance with IAS/IFRS will allow an organization to have securities listed in all global markets.

10.4.3 The Challenges for Islamic Accounting Standards

The implementation of IFRS has made the existence of Islamic accounting standards a little overlooked because the concepts of IFRS do not directly accommodate the uniqueness of transactions in IFIs. IFRS which was derived from conventional accounting worldview acknowledges some concepts that were not relevant to the Islamic accounting approach, for example: time value of money, substance over form, and conservatism. Therefore, accounting standard setters from several countries who are concerned with efforts to implement IFRS by making adjustments to the local character as well as the uniqueness of the Islamic financial industry joined to form The Asian-Oceanian Standard-Setters Group (AOSSG).

The AAOSG has been formed to discuss the issues and share the experiences on the adoption of IFRS and to contribute to the development of a high-quality set of global accounting standards. Some of the objectives of this group are as follows: (a) to promote the adoption of, and convergence with, IFRS by jurisdiction in the region; (b) to promote consistent application of IFRS by jurisdictions in the region; (c) to coordinate input from the region to the technical activities of the IASB; and (d) to cooperate with governments and regulators and other regional and international organizations to improve the quality of financial reporting in the region.

One of the important working groups that is relevant to the development of Islamic accounting standards is The Working Group on The Financial Reporting relating to Islamic Finance. This group is led by Malaysia and its members are Australia, China, Dubai, Indonesia, Korea, Pakistan, and Saudi Arabia. Unfortunately, the AAOIFI is not a part of this group despite its significant contribution to the development of Islamic accounting standards. The objective of the Islamic Finance Working Group is to facilitate AOSSG members by providing input and feedback to the IASB on the adequacy and appropriateness of proposed and existing IFRS to Islamic financial transactions and events. The working group takes into consideration that there may be variations in interpretations and practices of Islamic finance in different jurisdictions.

The differing approaches to accounting for Islamic financial transactions can generally be attributed to opposing views on two main points of contention: (a) the acceptability of reflecting a time value of money in reporting an Islamic financial transaction and (b) the conventional approach of recognizing and measuring the economic substance of a transaction, rather than its legal form. Some of the issues in applying IFRS to Islamic financial transactions that have been discussed by the group are as follows: (1) recognition of profit in sales contracts for Murabaha, Salam, and Istisna; (2) derecognition in Sale and Buy Back Agreements (SBBA); (3) the recognition of transaction fees whether all at once or throughout the financing period; (4) the classification of Shirkah-based placements and accounts; (5) profit equalization reserves (PER) and investment risk reserve (IRR); (6) accounting treatment of Ijarah; (7) assets transferred to a special purpose entity; (8) Sukuk valuation; (9) applying IFRS 4 to Takaful; (10) classification and measurement of Qardh; and (11) presentation of financial statements of Takaful entities.

The absence of AAOIFI in the AAOSG Working Group is a setback in the development of the Islamic accounting standards since AAOIFI acts as the initiator for formulating high-quality standards for IFIs. A low-level adoption of AAOIFI accounting standards should be overcome with an active involvement of AAOIFI by cooperating with countries that develop the Islamic financial industry such as Indonesia, Malaysia, Pakistan, Dubai, and Saudi Arabia. However, AAOIFI has recognized that some of the approaches in shaping the Islamic accounting standards were derived from conventional accounting approaches. Thus, many of the Financial Accounting Standards (FAS) issued by AAOIFI do not appear in conflict with IFRS as that are merely requirements for additional disclosure and presentation.

10.5 The Alternative Components for Islamic Banking Reports

There are many studies regarding the way Islamic institutions report their financial and non-financial accountability to God and stakeholders. Baydoun and Willet (2000) tried to develop a theory about the form and the content of the financial information that should be included in Islamic financial statements. They proposed Islamic Corporate Reports (ICRs) as the modification of the form of a conventional Western set of financial statements. This model used assumptions that Islamic accounting should encourage social accountability and follow a rule of full disclosure based on Shariah. ICRs can be referred to criticize the framework for financial reports of Islamic banks released by the Islamic Financial Accounting Standard Board (IFASB) in two aspects. Some additional information should be included in financial statements and the form of income statement that still adopted Western Financial Accounting Standards (WFASs) needs to be adjusted. They argued that ICRs should be added by current value balance sheets because *zakah* was levied based on the current value of assets, surplus to the requirements of the firm, and that current value information was necessary for the calculation of shares in Mudharabah contract. Therefore, the components of ICRs, as amended from the IFASB form, would be added by the financial position statement using the current value basis (see Figure 10.1).

Moreover, Baydoun and Willett (2000) encouraged the substitution of income statements by using Value Added Statement (VAS). The argument of this proposal was that VAS places more emphasis on the cooperative nature of economic activities and less on competitive aspects. This was consistent with the religious principle of fair and considerate trading specified in Shariah. Baydoun and Willet (2000: 84) argued that VAS rearranged the information in the income statement, giving more weight to the shares of groups other than owners in the fruits of the firm's activities.

Haniffa (2002) asserted that Islamic social disclosure practice should be different from conventional social reporting because the information items that need to be emphasized are different. She suggested the use of

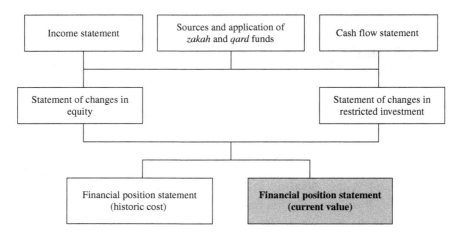

Figure 10.1: Form of ICRs as Amended of IFASB.
Source: Islamic Financial Accounting Standard Board (IFASB).

the Shariah framework in developing the Islamic Social Reports (ISRs) that fulfills both accountability and transparency objectives as it addresses the relationship between man and God, man and man, and also man and nature. Haniffa (2002) suggested two objectives and ethical statements of ISRs that are as follows: (a) to demonstrate accountability to God and community; and (b) to increase transparency of business activities by providing relevant information in conformance to the spiritual needs of Muslims decision-makers. She also proposed ethical principles and contents of ISR based on five themes: finance and investment, product, employees, society, and environment (see Table 10.1).

Hameed and Yaya (2003) tried to elaborate on the development of the practices and discussions of the application of social and environmental accountability in Western countries, which were in line to some extent with the Shariah principles. The study aimed to develop Islamic corporate reporting for any Muslim business organization particularly for Islamic banks, which are still searching for a practical form of Islamic accounting even now. Their study began to expose the characteristics and the problems of mainstream accounting which were stated by Laughlin and Gray (1988) such as: (1) restricted to accounting entities; (2) accounting only for the economic activities that relate to those entities; (3) only recording those economic events which have already or will generate some cash equivalent; and (4) assumed to be for a particular set of individuals typically

Shariah Reporting and Disclosure System 309

Table 10.1:   Summary of Ethical Principles and Contents of ICR.

Theme	Ethics	Content
Finance and investment	*Tawhid* *Halal vs Haram* *Wajib*	**Riba activities:** Identify activities and % profit contribution **Gharar activities:** Identify activities and % of profit contribution **Zakah:** Amount and beneficiaries
Product	*Tawhid* *Halal vs Haram*	Nature of product/service Identify activities and % of profit contribution
Employees	*Tawhid* *Adil* *Amanah*	Wages **Nature of work:** Religious provisions; holiday and leave; working hours Education and training Equal opportunities
Society	*Tawhid* *Ummah* *Amanah* *Adl*	**Sadaqah:** Amount and beneficiaries **Waqf:** Type and value **Qard Hassan:** Amount and beneficiaries
Environment	*Tawhid* *Khilafah* *Mizan* *Akhirah* *I'tidal vs Israf*	**Use of resources:** Description and amount Conservation of environment: Description and amount spent

Source: Modified from Haniffa (2002: 136).

investors and others with a purely financial interest and involvement with the accounting entity. Then, they explained the problematic issues in accounting according to Gray (1994) such as: (1) the extent and ubiquity of its practice; (2) economic consequences; (3) social and socio-political consequences; and (4) environmental implications.

Hameed and Yaya (2003) searched the alternative accounting practices from the previous researches as follows: potential social responsibility (Bowen, 1953), the lack of the level of social responsibility exercised by American corporations (Drucker, 1965), potential link between social responsibility and accounting (Linowes, 1972), social responsibility accounting adopted by Deutsche Shell Reports (Schreuder, 1979), environmental accountability (Perks, 1993), employee-related reporting (Gray *et al.*, 1996), and value-added report (Belkaoui, 1999).

Hameed and Yaya (2003) tried to evaluate the contemporary accounting and reporting for Muslim business organizations. They reviewed four annual reports from Islamic banks in Malaysia and Indonesia especially in the context of Shariah, social, and environmental disclosures. They concluded that Shariah, social, and environmental disclosures were not sufficiently reported by the existing Islamic institutions. The disclosures were only at the stage of explanatory notes. These were just like news reports on the activities without being accompanied by a plan to achieve better performances in compliance with Shariah and social-environmental objectives.

10.6 Conclusion

In light of these results, this chapter scrutinizes a broader perspective of reporting on Islamic banking that involves many aspects that are relevant to the development of an ideal format for reporting on Islamic banking. This idea comes from the assumption that Islamic banks around the world do not have standardization in the reporting model, even AAOIFI as the initiator in the development of accounting standards for IFIs does not have the authority to encourage Islamic banks to implement its standards. Moreover, the attempts of IASB in promoting IFRS would affect the AAOIFI's roles since Islamic banks will choose the more appropriate and relevant accounting standards for their future development and relation with other institutions.

Therefore, this chapter covers many disclosure issues in Islamic banks such as the accounting standards that are used by some Islamic banks in the Middle East and in other areas in the Asian region, the content of annual reports of both financial and non-financial issues including Shariah, social, and environmental disclosures. Moreover, the discussion regarding harmonization or standardization of accounting standards for Islamic banks is also relevant in order to understand the challenges, faced particularly by the AAOIFI.

Appendix

First author papers on Shariah governance:

Alam, M. K. (2021). Rationality of fourth party in legitimacy theory: Shariah governance of Islamic financial institutions. *Journal of Islamic Accounting and Business Research, 12*(3), 418–438; *Scopus Q3, ESCI, Web of Science (IF: 2.3), ABDC C and CABS 2.* Bingley: Emerald Insight.

Alam, M. K. (2022). A proposed centralized Shariah governance framework for Islamic banks in Bangladesh. *Journal of Islamic Accounting and Business Research, 13*(2), 364–389; *Scopus Q2, ESCI, Web of Science (IF: 2.3), ABDC C and CABS 2.* Bingley: Emerald Insight.

Alam, M. K., & Miah, M. S. (2021). Independence and effectiveness of Shariah Supervisory Board of Islamic banks: Evidence from emerging economy. *Asian Review of Accounting, 29*(2), 173–191; *Scopus Q2, CABS 2, ABDC B, and ESCI, Web of Science.* Bingley: Emerald Insight.

Alam, M. K. & Uddin, A. H. M. E. (2023). Legal and Regulatory Frameworks for Sharī'a Governance Practices in the Islamic Banking Industry of Bangladesh. *Mizanü'l-Hak: Journal of Islamic Sciences, 2023*(17), 663-688. https://doi.org/10.47502/mizan.1332588. Published by Izmir Kâtip Çelebi University.

Alam, M. K., & Thakur, O. A. (2022). Why does Bangladesh require a centralized Shariah governance framework for Islamic banks? *Journal of Nusantara Studies (JONUS), 7*(1), 24–42. *(ESCI, Web of Science).* Universiti Sultan Zainal Abidin, Malaysia.

Alam, M. K. & Miah, M. S. (2024). Do Islamic banks use institutional theory in the light of Shariah governance? Empirical evidence from a Muslim dominant country. *Heliyon*, 10(2), e24252. https://doi. org/10.1016/j.heliyon.2024.e24252 (Science Citation Index Expanded (SCIE), Web of Science and Scopus Q1). Published by both cell.com/ Heliyon and ScienceDirect; IF: 4.

Alam, M. K., Ahmad, A. U. F., Ahmed, M. U., & Uddin, M. S. (2023). Shariah audit of Islamic Banks in Bangladesh: The present practice and the way forward. *Journal of Applied Accounting Research, 24*(5), 986–1003; *Scopus Q1, ABDC B, CABS 2 and ESCI, Web of Science.* Bingley: Emerald Insight.

Alam, M. K., Tabash, M. I., Thakur, O. A., Rahman, M. M., Siddiquii, M. N., & Hasan, S. (2023). Independence and effectiveness of Shariah Department officers to ensure Shariah compliance: Evidence from Islamic banks in Bangladesh. *Asian Journal of Accounting Research, 8*(1), 15–26; *Scopus Q2 and ABDC C.* Bingley: Emerald Insight.

Alam, M. K., Islam, M. S., Islam, F. T., Tabash, M. I., Sahabuddin, M., & Alauddin, M. (2022). One regulator: Diversified Shariah governance practices, why? *Asian Journal of Accounting Research, 7*(3), 332–343; *Scopus Q2 and ABDC C.* Bingley: Emerald Insight.

Alam, M. K., Ahmad, A. U. F., Muneeza, A., Tabash, M. I., & Rahman, M. A. (2022). Proposing an organizational framework for Sharī'ah Secretariat of Islamic banks in Bangladesh. *ISRA International Journal of Islamic Finance, 14*(1), 107–118; *Scopus Q2, ABDC C, and ESCI, Web of Science.* Bingley: Emerald Insight.

Alam, M. K., Miah, M. S., Siddiquii, M. N., & Hossain, M. I. (2020). The influences of board of directors and management in Shariah governance guidelines of the Islamic banks in Bangladesh. *Journal of Islamic Accounting and Business Research, 11*(9), 1633–1647. *Scopus Q2, ESCI, Web of Science (IF: 2.3), ABDC C and CABS 2.* Bingley: Emerald Insight.

Alam, M. K., Ahmad, A. U. F., & Muneeza, A. (2022). External sharī'ah audit and review committee *vis-a-vis* Sharī'ah compliance quality and accountability: A case of Islamic banks in Bangladesh. *Journal of Public Affairs, 22*(1), 1–10; *Scopus Q1, ABDC B and ESCI, Web of Science.* Hoboken: John Wiley & Sons Inc.

Alam, M. K., Islam, F. T., & Runy, M. K. (2021). Why is Shariah governance framework important for Islamic banks? *Asian Journal of Economics and Banking, 5*(2), 158–172.

Alam, M. K., Karbhari, Y., & Rahman, M. M. (2021). Adaptation of new institutional theory components in Shariah governance practice, structure and process. *Journal of Business, Economics and Environmental Studies*, *11*(1), 5–15.

Alam, M. K., Rahman, S. A., Hossain M. S., & Hosen, S. (2019). Shariah governance practices and regulatory problems of Islamic insurance companies in Bangladesh. *International Journal of Academic Research in Business and Social Sciences*, *9*(1), 109–124. *(Peer Reviewed Journal)*.

Alam, M. K., Rahman, M. M., Runy, M. K., Adedeji, B. S., & Hassan, M. F. (2022). The influences of Shariah governance mechanisms on Islamic banks performance and Shariah compliance quality. *Asian Journal of Accounting Research*, *7*(1), 2–16; *Scopus Q2 and ABDC C*. Bingley: Emerald Insight.

Alam, M. K., Rahman, S. A., Tabash, M. I., Thakur, O. A., & Hosen. S. (2021). Shariah Supervisory Boards of Islamic banks in Bangladesh: Expected duties and performed roles and functions. *Journal of Islamic Accounting and Business Research*, *12*(2), 258–275; *Scopus Q3, ESCI, Web of Science (IF: 2.3), ABDC C and CABS 2*. Bingley: Emerald Insight.

Alam, M. K., Rahman, S. A., Thakur, O. A., Bashir, M. A., & Hosen, S., (2020). The reasons behind the absence of a comprehensive Shariah governance framework of the Islamic banks in Bangladesh. *International Journal of Economics and Business Administration*, *8*(1), 134–145; *Scopus Q2*. Bingley: Emerald Insight.

Alam, M. K., Rahman, S. A., Mustafa, H., Shah, S. M., & Hossain M. S. (2019). Shariah governance framework of Islamic banks in Bangladesh: Practices, problems and recommendations. *Asian Economic and Financial Review*, *9*(1), 118–132; *Scopus Q3 and ABDC C*. Bingley: Emerald Insight.

Alam, M. K., Tabash, M. I., Hassan, M. F., Hassan, N., & Javed, A. (2021). Shariah governance systems of Islamic banks in Bangladesh: A comparison with global practices. In A. Rafay (Ed.), *Money Laundering and Terrorism Financing in Global Financial Systems* (Chapter 11: 261–279). PA: IGI Global.

Alam, M. K., Rahman, S. A., Mustafa, H., Shah, S. M., & Rahman, M. M. (2019). An overview of corporate governance models in financial institutions. *International Journal of Management and Sustainability*, *8*(4), 181–195; *Scopus Q4*. Bingley: Emerald Insight.

Alam, M. K., Mustafa, H., Uddin, M. S., Islam, M. J., Mohua, M. J., & Hassan, M. F. (2020). Problems of Shariah governance framework and its mechanisms: An empirical investigation of Islamic banks in Bangladesh. *Journal of Asian Finance, Economics and Business*, *7*(3), 265–276; *Scopus Q4 and ESCI, Web of Science*. Bingley: Emerald Insight.

Alam, M. K., Rahman, M. M., Islam, F. T., Adedeji, B. S., Mannan, M. A., & Sahabuddin, M. (2021). The practices of Shariah governance systems of Islamic banks in Bangladesh. *Pacific Accounting Review*, *33*(4), 505–524; *Scopus Q2, ABDC B, CABS 1 and ESCI, Web of Science*. Bingley: Emerald Insight.

Alam, M. K., Tabash, M. I., Thakur, O. A., Sahabuddin, M., Hosen, S., & Hassan, M. F. (2020). A central Shariah regulatory authority for the Islamic Banks in Bangladesh: Legalization or formation. *Journal of Asian Finance, Economics and Business*, *7*(1), 91–100; *Scopus Q4 and ESCI, Web of Science*. Bingley: Emerald Insight.

Karbhari, Y., Alam, M. K., & Rahman, M. M. (2020). Relevance of application of institutional theory in Shariah governance of Islamic banks. *PSU Research Review*, *5*(1), 1–15; *Scopus Q4 and CABS 1*. Bingley: Emerald Insight.

Tabash, M. I., Alam, M. K., & Rahman, M. M. (2022). Ethical legitimacy of Islamic banks and Shariah governance: Evidence from Bangladesh. *Journal of Public Affairs*, 22(2), e2487; *Scopus Q1, ABDC B and ESCI, Web of Science*. Hoboken: John Wiley & Sons Inc.

Tumewang, Y. K., Supriani, I., Dewi, H. R., & Alam, M. K. (2024). A Hybrid Review on Sharia Governance Studies from 2001 to 2022. *Journal of Islamic Accounting and Business Research.* https://doi.org/10.1108/JIABR-11-2022-0319 (**Scopus Q2, ESCI, Web of Science (IF: 2.3), ABDC C and CABS 2**). Published by Emerald Insight (EarlyCite).

Other authors' publications on *Shariah* and corporate governance:

Azid, T. & Nodel, A. A. (2018). Determinants of *Shariah* governance disclosure in financial institutions: Evidence from Saudi Arabia. *International Journal of Ethics and Systems (Humanomics)*, *35*(2), 207–226.

Azid, T. *et al.* (2019). *Research in Corporate and Shariah Governance in the Muslim World: Theory and Practice*. Bingley: Emerald Publishing, Bingley.

Azid, T. *et al.* (2021). *Monetary Policy, Islamic Finance, and Islamic Corporate Governance: An International Overview*. Bingley: Emerald Publishing.

Azid, T. *et al.* (2021). Monetary policy, Islamic finance, and Islamic corporate governance: An introductory note. In Azid, T. *et al.* (Eds.), *Monetary Policy, Islamic Finance, and Islamic Corporate Governance* (pp. 1–12). Bingley: Emerald Publishing.

Azid, T. *et al.* (2021). Monetary policy and good governance in Islamic framework: A concluding note. In Azid, T. *et al.* (Eds.), *Monetary Policy, Islamic Finance, and Islamic Corporate Governance* (pp. 323–328). Bingley: Emerald Publishing.

Faruq, A. U., & Rehman, S. (2019). Corporate social responsibility in Islamic banks' practice: Evidence from Bangladesh. In Azid, T. *et al.* (Eds.), *Research in Corporate and Shariah Governance in the Muslim World: Theory and Practice* (pp. 305–314). Bingley: Emerald Publishing.

Hassan, R., Faruq, A. U., & Sen, S. P. (2021). Governance structure affecting dividend policy in Malaysia: Theoretical perspective. In Azid, T. *et al.* (Eds.), *Monetary Policy, Islamic Finance, and Islamic Corporate Governance* (pp. 233–246). Bingley: Emerald Publishing.

Nodel, A. A., & Azid, T. (2019). Voluntary disclosure of *Shariah* governance of Islamic financial institutions in Saudi Arabia. In Azid, T. *et al.* (Eds.), *Research in Corporate and Shariah Governance in the Muslim World: Theory and Practice.* Bingley: Emerald Publishing, pp. 141–152.

Nodel, A. A., & Azid, T. (2021). The impact of the Board of Directors characteristics on regulation compliance: An evaluation of the Board of Directors effectiveness. *Journal of Governance and Regulation, 10*(4), 93–103.

Rehman, S., & Faruq, A. U. (2021). Governance of Islamic financial institutions: The case of Bangladesh. In Azid, T. *et al.* (Eds.), *Monetary Policy, Islamic Finance, and Islamic Corporate Governance* (pp. 291–302). Bingley: Emerald Publishing.

Tanin, T. I., Faruq, A. U., & Farooq, M. O. (2021). What determines bank profitability? Empirical evidence from Turkish banking sector. In Azid, T. *et al.* (Eds.), *Monetary Policy, Islamic Finance, and Islamic Corporate Governance* (pp. 247–266). Bingley: Emerald Publishing.

References

AAOIFI (1999). Accounting, Auditing and Governance Standards for Islamic Financial Institutions. Manama, Bahrain. http://aaoifi.com/standard/accountingstandards/?lang=en.

AAOIFI (2008). Accounting, Auditing and Governance Standards for Islamic Financial Institutions. Manama, Bahrain. http://aaoifi.com/standard/accountingstandards/?lang=en.

AAOIFI (2009). Accounting, Auditing and Governance Standards for Islamic Financial Institutions. Manama, Bahrain. http://aaoifi.com/standard/accountingstandards/?lang=en.

AAOIFI (2017). Governance Standards for IFIs, No. 8, "Central Shariah Board" Bahrain, AAOIFI. Accounting and Auditing Organization for Islamic Financial Institution. http://aaoifi.com/standard/accounting-standards/?lang=en.

AAOIFI (2018). Accounting, Auditing and Governance Standards for Islamic Financial Institutions. Manama, Bahrain. http://aaoifi.com/standard/accountingstandards/?lang=en.

AAOIFI (2021). Accounting and Auditing Organization for Islamic Financial Institutions (2010), Governance Standards for Islamic Financial Institutions, AAOIFI, Bahrain. http://aaoifi.com/standard/accountingstandards/?lang=en.

Ab Ghani, N. L., Mohd Ariffin, N., & Abdul Rahman, A. R. (2023). The extent of mandatory and voluntary shariah compliance disclosure: Evidence from Malaysian Islamic financial institutions. *Journal of Islamic Accounting and Business Research*, *15*(1) https://doi.org/10.1108/JIABR-10-2021-0282.

Abdalla, R. M., Saleh, A., Kumar, N., & Ann, J. H. (2012). The evaluation of chief executive officer performance: A stakeholder theory perspective. *World*, *2*(4), 121–137.

Abdel-Magid, M. F. (1981). The theory of Islamic banking: Accounting implications. *International Journal of Accounting*, *17*(1), 79–102.

Abdullah, M. F., & Ab Rahman, A. (2017). Shariah governance of Islamic banks in Bangladesh issues and challenges. *Journal of Islamic Economics, Banking and Finance*, *13*(3), 82–94.

Abdullah, M. F., Amin, R., & Ab Rahman, A. (2017). Is there any difference between Islamic and conventional microfinance? Evidence from Bangladesh. *International Journal of Business and Society, 18*(S1), 97–112.

Abdullah, W. A. W., Percy, M., & Stewart, J. (2015). Determinants of voluntary corporate governance disclosure: Evidence from Islamic banks in the Southeast Asian and the Gulf Cooperation Council regions. *Journal of Contemporary Accounting & Economics, 11*(3), 262–279.

Abedifar, P., Molyneux, P., & Tarazi, A. (2013). Risk in Islamic banking. *Review of Finance, 17*(6), 2035–2096.

Abeysekera, I. (2010). The influence of board size on intellectual capital disclosure by Kenyan listed firms. *Journal of Intellectual Capital, 11*(4), 504–518.

Abhayawansa, S., & Abeysekera, I. (2009). Intellectual capital disclosure from sell-side analyst perspective. *Journal of Intellectual Capital, 10*(2), 294–306.

Aboagye-Otchere, F., Bedi, I., & Kwakye, T. O. (2012). Corporate governance and disclosure practices of Ghanaian listed companies. *Journal of Accounting in Emerging Economies, 2*(2), 140–161.

Aboumouamer, F. M. (1989). *An Analysis of the Role and Function of Shariah Control in Islamic Banks.* Cardiff: University of Wales.

Abozaid, A. (2016). The internal challenges facing Islamic finance industry. *International Journal of Islamic and Middle Eastern Finance and Management, 9*(2), 222–235.

Abuhmaira, M. A. (2006). *The Impact of "AAOIFI" Standards on the Financial Reporting of Islamic Banks: Evidence from Bahrain.* Wales: University of South Wales (United Kingdom).

Abu-Tapanjeh, A. M. (2009). Corporate governance from the Islamic perspective: A comparative analysis with OECD principles. *Critical Perspectives on Accounting, 20*(5), 556–567.

Adams, C. A., Hill, W. Y., & Roberts, C. B. (1998). Corporate social reporting practices in Western Europe: Legitimating corporate behaviour? *The British Accounting Review, 30*(1), 1–21.

Adan, I. A. (2017). *Factors Influencing Growth of Client Base of Fully Fledged Islamic Banks in Kenya* (Doctoral dissertation).

Aerts, K., Matthyssens, P., & Vandenbempt, K. (2007). Critical role and screening practices of European business incubators. *Technovation, 27*(5), 254–267.

Agrawal, A., & Knoeber, C. R. (1996). Firm performance and mechanisms to control agency problems between managers and shareholders. *Journal of Financial and Quantitative Analysis, 31*(3), 377–397.

Aguilera, R. V. (2009). A comparative analysis of corporate governance systems in Latin America: Argentina, Brazil, Chile, Colombia, and Venezuela. In *Corporate Governance in Developing Economies* (pp. 151–171). Boston: Springer.

Aguilera, R. V., & Jackson, G. (2003). The cross-national diversity of corporate governance: Dimensions and determinants. *Academy of Management Review, 28*(3), 447–465.

Ahmad, A. (1984). A macro model of distribution in an Islamic economy. *Journal of King Abdulaziz University: Islamic Economics, 2*(1).

Ahmad, N. N. N., & Sulaiman, M. (2004). Environment disclosure in Malaysia annual reports: A legitimacy theory perspective. *International Journal of Commerce and Management, 14*(1), 44–58.

Ahmad, S., & Omar, R. (2016). Basic corporate governance models: A systematic review. *International Journal of Law and Management, 58*(1), 73–107.

Ahmed, H. (1992). The historiography of Islam in Ethiopia. *Journal of Islamic Studies, 3*(1), 15–46.

Ahmed, H. (2002). Financing microenterprises: An analytical study of Islamic microfinance institutions. *Islamic Economic Studies, 9*(2), 1–38.

Ahmed, H. (2011). Maqasid al-Shariah and Islamic financial products: A framework for assessment. *ISRA International Journal of Islamic Finance, 3*(1), 149–160.

Ahmed, M., Mahmood, A. N., & Islam, M. R. (2016). A survey of anomaly detection techniques in financial domain. *Future Generation Computer Systems, 55*, 278–288.

Ajili, H., & Bouri, A. (2018). Assessing the moderating effect of Shariah Board on the relationship between financial performance and accounting disclosure. *Managerial Finance, 44*(5), 570–589.

Akhtar, S. (2006). Syariah compliant corporate governance. In *Keynote Address by the Governor of the State Bank of Pakistan at the Annual Corporate Governance Conference, Dubai, United Arab Emirates* (pp. 243–283).

Akinpelu, O. A. (2012). Corporate governance framework in Nigeria: An international review. Bloomington, USA: iUniverse, Inc.

Al-Abji, K. A. F. (1989). Developing the responsibility of the auditor to meet the requirements of investment in Islamic banks. *Islam Today, 7*, 32–50.

Alam, M. K. (2019). Development of a centralized Shariah governance framework for Islamic banks in Bangladesh, PhD Thesis, Universiti Putra Malaysia.

Alam, M. K. (2021). Rationality of fourth party in legitimacy theory: Shariah governance of Islamic financial institutions. *Journal of Islamic Accounting and Business Research, 12*(3), 418–438.

Alam, M. K. (2022). A proposed centralized Shariah governance framework for Islamic banks in Bangladesh. *Journal of Islamic Accounting and Business Research, 13*(2), 364–389.

Alam, M. K., & Miah, M. S. (2021). Independence and effectiveness of Shariah Supervisory Board of Islamic Banks: Evidence from emerging economy. *Asian Review of Accounting, 29*(2), 173–191.

Alam, M. K., & Thakur, O. A. (2022). Why does Bangladesh require a centralized Shariah governance framework for Islamic banks? *Journal of Nusantara Studies (JONUS), 7*(1), 24–42.

Alam, M. K., Ahmad, A. U. F., & Muneeza, A. (2022a). External Shariah audit and review committee vis-a-vis Shariah compliance quality and accountability: A case of Islamic banks in Bangladesh. *Journal of Public Affairs, 22*(1), 1–10.

Alam, M. K., Islam, F. T., & Runy, M. K. (2021a). Why is Shariah governance framework important for Islamic banks? *Asian Journal of Economics and Banking, 5*(2), 158–172.

Alam, M. K., Karbhari, Y., & Rahman, M. M. (2021e). Adaptation of new institutional theory components in Shariah governance practice, structure and process. *Journal of Business, Economics and Environmental Studies*, 11(1), 5–15.

Alam, M. K., Ahmad, A. U. F., Ahmed, M. U., & Uddin, M. S. (2023a). Shariah audit of Islamic Banks in Bangladesh: The present practice and the way forward. *Journal of Applied Accounting Research*, 24(5), 986–1003.

Alam, M. K., Miah, M. S, Siddiquii, N., & Hossain, M. I. (2020d). The Influences of board of directors and management in Shariah governance guidelines of the Islamic banks in Bangladesh. *Journal of Islamic Accounting and Business Research*, 11(9), 1633–1647.

Alam, M. K., Ahmad, A. U. F., Muneeza, A., Tabash, M. I. & Rahman, M. A. (2022b). Proposing an organizational framework for Shariah Secretariat of Islamic banks in Bangladesh. *ISRA International Journal of Islamic Finance*, 14(1), 107–118.

Alam, M. K., Rahman, M. M., Runy, M. K., Adedeji, B. S., & Hassan, M. F. (2022d). The influences of Shariah governance mechanisms on Islamic banks performance and Shariah compliance quality. *Asian Journal of Accounting Research*, 7(1), 2–16.

Alam, M. K., Rahman, S. A., Mustafa, H., Shah, S. M., & Hossain M. S. (2019b). Shariah governance framework of Islamic banks in Bangladesh: Practices, problems and recommendations. *Asian Economic and Financial Review*, 9(1), 118–132.

Alam, M. K., Rahman, S. A., Mustafa, H., Shah, S. M., & Rahman, M. M. (2019a). An overview of Corporate Governance Models in financial institutions. *International Journal of Management and Sustainability*, 8(4), 181–195.

Alam, M. K., Ab Rahman, S., Tabash, M. I., Thakur, O. A., & Hosen, S. (2021b). Shariah supervisory boards of Islamic banks in Bangladesh: Expected duties and performed roles and functions. *Journal of Islamic Accounting and Business Research*, 12(2), 258–275.

Alam, M. K., Rahman, S. A., Thakur, O. A., Bashir, M. A., & Hosen, S., (2020c). The reasons behind the absence of a comprehensive Shariah governance framework of the Islamic banks in Bangladesh. *International Journal of Economics and Business Administration*, 8(1), 134–145.

Alam, M. K., Tabash, M. I., Hassan, M. F., Hassan, N., & Javed, A. (2021c). Shariah governance systems of Islamic banks in Bangladesh: A comparison with global practices. In A. Rafay (Ed.), *Money Laundering and Terrorism Financing in Global Financial Systems* (Chapter 11: 261–279). PA: IGI Global.

Alam, M. K., Islam, M. S., Islam, F. T., Tabash, M. I., Sahabuddin, M., & Alauddin, M. (2022c). One regulator: Diversified Shariah governance practices, why? *Asian Journal of Accounting Research*, 7(3), 332–343.

Alam, M. K., Tabash, M. I., Thakur, O. A., Rahman, M. M., Siddiquii, M. N., & Hasan, S. (2023b). Independence and effectiveness of Shariah department officers to ensure Shariah compliance: Evidence from Islamic banks in Bangladesh. *Asian Journal of Accounting Research*, 8(1), 15–26.

Alam, M. K., Tabash, M. I., Thakur, O. A., Sahabuddin, M., Hosen, S., & Hassan, M. F. (2020a). A Central Shariah Regulatory Authority for the Islamic Banks in Bangladesh: Legalization or formation. *Journal of Asian Finance, Economics and Business, 7*(1), 91–100.

Alam, M. K., Mustafa, H., Uddin, M. S., Islam, M. J., Mohua, M. J., & Hassan, M. F. (2020b). Problems of Shariah governance framework and its mechanisms: An empirical investigation of Islamic banks in Bangladesh. *Journal of Asian Finance, Economics and Business, 7*(3), 265–276.

Alam, M. K., Rahman, M. M., Islam, F. T., Adedeji, B. S., Mannan, M. A., & Sahabuddin, M. (2021d). The practices of Shariah governance systems of Islamic banks in Bangladesh. *Pacific Accounting Review, 33*(4), 505–524.

Al-Baluchi, A. E. (2006). *The Impact of AAOIFI Standards and Other Bank Characteristics on the Level of Voluntary Disclosure in the Annual Reports of Islamic Banks.* Surrey: University of Surrey (United Kingdom).

Aldrich, H. E., & Fiol, C. M. (1994). Fools rush in? The institutional context of industry creation. *Academy of Management Review, 19*(4), 645–670.

Alhabshi, S. M., & Bakar, M. D. (2008). Survey on Shariah board of institutions offering Islamic financial services across jurisdictions. *Islamic Finance: Surveys on Global Legal Issues and Challenges*, 167–206.

Al-Jalf, A. (1996). *The Accounting Methodology for Murabaha Transactions in Islamic Banks.* Cairo: The International Institute of Islamic Thought.

Al-Jarhi, M. (2009). *Institutional Tawarruq: A Products of Ill Repute in Islamic Finance.* Munich: MPRA.

Aljifri, K. (2008). Annual report disclosure in a developing country: The case of the UAE. *Advances in Accounting, 24*(1), 93–100.

Alkhamees, A. (2013). The impact of Shariah governance practices on Shariah compliance in contemporary Islamic finance. *Journal of Banking Regulation, 14*, 134–163.

Al-Khudairi, M. (1990). *Crisis Management: An Integrated Economic and Administrative Approach to Resolving Crises.* Cairo: Madbouly Library.

Allais, M. (1993). Les conditions monétaires d'une économie de marchés: des enseignements du passé aux réformes de demain: The monetary conditions of an economy of markets: From the teaching of the past to the reforms of tomorrow. *Revue D'économie Politique*, 317–367.

Allen, F., & Zhao, M. (2007). The corporate governance model of Japan: Shareholders are not rulers. *PKU Business Review, 36*(7), 98–102.

Al-Mehmadi, F. B. S. B. (2004). *The External Reporting Needs of Investors in Islamic Banks in Saudi Arabia: An Exploratory Study of Full Disclosure* (Doctoral dissertation, University of Dundee).

Almutairi, A. R., & Quttainah, M. A. (2017). Corporate governance: Evidence from Islamic banks. *Social Responsibility Journal, 13*(3), 601–624.

Alnabsha, A., Abdou, H. A., Ntim, C. G., & Elamer, A. A. (2018). Corporate boards, ownership structures and corporate disclosures. *Journal of Applied Accounting Research, 19*(1), 20–41.

Al-Nasser Mohammed, S. A. S., & Muhammed, J. (2017). The relationship between agency theory, stakeholder theory and Shariah supervisory board in Islamic banking: An attempt towards discussion. *Humanomics, 33*(1), 75–83.

Al-Obji, K. (1989). *Islamic Financial Institutions' Accounting.* Al-Farouq Publication, PK.

Angelides, P., & Thomas, B. (2011). *The Financial Crisis Inquiry Report: Final Report of the National Commission on the Causes of the Financial and Economic Crisis in the United States,* NY. Government Printing Office.

Annisette, M. (2000). Imperialism and the professions: The education and certification of accountants in Trinidad and Tobago. *Accounting, Organizations and Society, 25*(7), 631–659.

Ansoff, H. I. (1987). The emerging paradigm of strategic behavior. *Strategic Management Journal, 8*(6), 501–515.

Antonio, M. S. (2011). Islamic microfinance initiatives to enhance small and medium enterprises in Indonesia: From historical overview to contemporary situation. *Journal of Indonesian Islam, 5*(2), 313–334.

Archer, S., & Karim, R. A. A. (1997). Agency theory, corporate governance, and the accounting regulation of Islamic banks. *Research in Accounting Regulation, 2,* 97–114.

Archer, S., & Karim, R. A. A. (2007). Specific corporate governance issues in Islamic banks. *Islamic Finance: The Regulatory Challenge, 394,* 310.

Archer, S., & Karim, R. A. A. (2009). Profit-sharing investment accounts in Islamic banks: Regulatory problems and possible solutions. *Journal of Banking Regulation, 10,* 300–306.

Archer, S., & Karim, R. A. A. (2014). The IILM short-term *sukūk* for liquidity management: A success story in enhancing financial stability. *SEACEN Financial Stability Journal, 3*(1), 11–23.

Archer, S., Karim, R. A. A., & Al-Deehani, T. (1998a). Financial contracting, governance structures and the accounting regulation of Islamic banks: An analysis in terms of agency theory and transaction cost economics. *Journal of Management and Governance, 2*(2), 149–170.

Archer, S., Karim, R. A. A., & Al-Deehani, T. (1998b). Financial contracting, governance structures and the accounting regulation of Islamic banks: An analysis in terms of agency theory and transaction cost economics. *Journal of Management and Governance, 2*(2), 149–170.

Ariffin, N. M., Archer, S., & Karim, R. A. A. (2007). Transparency and market discipline in Islamic banks. *Islamic Economics and Finance, 153.*

Arshad, Z. (1997). Islamic financial systems. *Finance & Development, 34*(2), 42–45.

Arshad, S., & Wardhany, N. (2012). The role of Shariah Board in Islamic Banks: A case study of Malaysia, Indonesia and Brunei Darussalam. *Islamic Finance in a Challenging Economy Moving Forward.* In 2nd ISRA Colloquium.

Ashforth, B. E., & Gibbs, B. W. (1990). The double-edge of organizational legitimation. *Organization Science, 1*(2), 177–194.

Asutay, M. (2007). A political economy approach to Islamic economics: Systemic understanding for an alternative economic system. *Kyoto Bulletin of Islamic Area Studies, 1*(2), 3–18.

Audit Manual Public Service Commission of Canada (2005). https://publications. gc.ca/site/eng/280444/publication.html.

Ayub, M. (2007). *Understanding Islamic Finance*. West Sussex: John Wiley and Sons Ltd.

Ayuso, S., & Argandoña, A. (2009). Responsible corporate governance: Towards a stakeholder board of directors? *IESE Business School Working Paper No. 701*. https://papers.ssrn.com/sol3/papers.cfm?abstract_id=1349090#.

Azid, T., Asutay, M., & Burki, U. (2007). Theory of the firm, management and stakeholders: An Islamic perspective. *Islamic Economic Studies, 15*(1).

Aziz, A. F., & Faizal, A. (2012). Shariah governance: Challenges ahead. *Munich Personal RePec Archive (MPRA) Paper*, 1–25.

Azzam Wajeeh, I., & Muneeza, A. (2012). Strategic corporate governance for sustainable mutual development. *International Journal of Law and Management, 54*(3), 197–208.

Baiman, S., & Verrecchia, R. E. (1996). The relation among capital markets, financial disclosure, production efficiency, and insider trading. *Journal of Accounting Research, 34*(1), 1–22.

Bakar, M. D. (2008). Hedging instruments in Islamic finance. In *Kertas Kerja 7th conference of the Shariah Boards of Islamic Financial Institutions*. The Accounting and Auditing Organization for Islamic Financial Institutions (AAOIFI), Bahrain (pp. 24–27).

Bakre, O. (2001). An emergence and development of the accountancy profession in developing countries: The case of Jamaica. Unpublished Ph.D. Dissertation, University of Essex, England.

Baldwin, K., Dar, H. A., & Presley, J. R. (2002). On determining moral hazard and adverse selection in the Islamic firm. *Theoretical Foundations of Islamic Economics*, 145.

Bälz, K. (2008). Sharia risk. *How Islamic Finance Has Transformed Islamic Contract Law*, MA, USA.

Banaga, A., Ray, G. H., & Tomkins, C. (1994). *External Audit and Corporate Governance in Islamic Banks: A Joint Practitioner-Academic Research Study*. London: Avebury, Hants.

Bandsuch, M. R., Pate, L. E., & Thies, J. (2008). Rebuilding stakeholder trust in business: An examination of principle-centered leadership and organizational transparency in corporate governance. *Business and Society Review, 113*(1), 99–127.

Barca, F., & Becht, M. (Eds.). (2001). *The Control of Corporate Europe*. Oxford: OUP.

Barth, J. R., Caprio Jr, G., & Levine, R. (2004). Bank regulation and supervision: What works best? *Journal of Financial Intermediation, 13*(2), 205–248.

Basel Committee on Banking Supervision (2001). *Customer Due Diligence for Banks*. Switzerland: BCBS.

Basel Committee on Banking Supervision (2005). *Compliance and the Compliance Function in Banks*. Switzerland: BCBS.

Basel Committee on Banking Supervision (BCBS) (2006). *Enhancing Corporate Governance for Banking Organizations*. Switzerland: BCBS.

Basel Committee on Banking Supervision (BSBS) (2011). *Principles for the Sound Management of Operational Risk*. Switzerland: BCBS.

Bauwhede, H. V., & Willekens, M. (2008). Disclosure on corporate governance in the European Union. *Corporate Governance: An International Review, 16*(2), 101–115.

Baydoun, N., & Willett, R. (1997). Islam and accounting: Ethical issues in the presentation of financial information. *Accounting, Commerce and Finance: The Islamic Perspective Journal*, 1(1), 1–25.

Baydoun, N., & Willett, R. (2000). Islamic corporate reports. *Abacus, 36*(1), 71–90.

Beasley, M. S., Carcello, J. V., Hermanson, D. R., & Neal, T. L. (2009). The audit committee oversight process. *Contemporary Accounting Research, 26*(1), 65–122.

Beck, T., & Demirguc-Kunt, A. (2006). Small and medium-size enterprises: Access to finance as a growth constraint. *Journal of Banking & Finance, 30*(11), 2931–2943.

Beekun, R. I., & Badawi, J. A. (2005). Balancing ethical responsibility among multiple organizational stakeholders: The Islamic perspective. *Journal of Business Ethics, 60*, 131–145.

Belal, A. R., Abdelsalam, O., & Nizamee, S. S. (2015). Ethical reporting in Islamic Bank Bangladesh Limited (1983–2010). *Journal of Business Ethics, 129*(4), 769–784.

Belkaoui, A, R. (1999). *Value Added Reporting and Research*. London: Quorum Books.

Berger, B. (Ed.). (1991). *The Culture of Entrepreneurship* (pp. 1–12). San Francisco: ICS Press.

Berger, P. L., & Luckmann, T. (2017). Social interaction in everyday life. In *Communication Theory* (pp. 86–101). London: Routledge.

Berle, A. A., & Means, G. G. C. (1991). *The Modern Corporation and Private Property*. New Jersey: Transaction Publishers.

Berle, A., & Means, G. (1932). *The Modern Corporate and Private Property*. New York: McMillian.

Berry, M. A., & Rondinelli, D. A. (1998). Proactive corporate environmental management: A new industrial revolution. *Academy of Management Perspectives, 12*(2), 38–50.

Besar, M. H. A. H., Sukor, M. E. A., Muthalib, N. A., & Gunawa, A. Y. (2009). The practice of Shariah review as undertaken by Islamic banking sector in Malaysia. *International Review of Business Research Papers, 5*(1), 294–306.

Beseiso, F. H. (2014). Central banks' role in shaping the future of Islamic banking. In *The Developing Role of Islamic Banking and Finance: From Local to Global Perspectives* (pp. 3–30). Leeds: Emerald Group Publishing Limited.

Beyer, A., Cohen, D. A., Lys, T. Z., & Walther, B. R. (2010). The financial reporting environment: Review of the recent literature. *Journal of Accounting and Economics, 50*(2–3), 296–343.

Bhagat, S., & Bolton, B. (2008). Corporate governance and firm performance. *Journal of Corporate Finance, 14*(3), 257–273.

Bhattacharya, U., & Dittmar, A. (2004). Costless versus costly signaling in capital markets: Theory and evidence. In *FIRS Conference on Banking, Insurance and Intermediation in Capri in May 2004*.

Bhatti, M., & Bhatti, I. (2009). Development in legal issues of corporate governance in Islamic finance. *Journal of Economic and Administrative Sciences*, *25*(1), 67–91.

Bhatti, M., & Bhatti, M. I. (2010). Toward understanding Islamic corporate governance issues in Islamic finance. *Asian Politics & Policy*, *2*(1), 25–38.

Bitektine, A. (2011). Toward a theory of social judgments of organizations: The case of legitimacy, reputation, and status. *Academy of Management Review*, *36*(1), 151–179.

Black, B. S., Jang, H., & Kim, W. (2006). Predicting firms' corporate governance choices: Evidence from Korea. *Journal of Corporate Finance*, *12*(3), 660–691.

BNM (2010). *Shariah Governance Framework for Islamic Financial Institutions (BNM/RH/GL 012-3)*. Kuala Lumpur: Bank Negara Malaysia.

BNM (2019). *Shariah Governance Policy Document, Bank Negara Malaysia, Kuala Lumpur*. https://www.bnm.gov.my/index.php?ch557andpg5140and ac5835andbb5file (Accessed October 4, 2023).

Boatright, J. R. (1999). Does business ethics rest on a mistake? *Business Ethics Quarterly*, *9*(4), 583–591.

Boot, A. W., & Thakor, A. V. (1993). Self-interested bank regulation. *The American Economic Review*, 206–212.

Borham, A. J. (2013). Malaysian experience in implementation of the banking and financial transactions without riba. *International Journal of Research in Social Science*, *3*(2), 1–10.

Bowen, H. (1953). *Social Responsibilities of the Businessman*. New York: Harpened Row.

Boyd, B. (1990). Corporate linkages and organizational environment: A test of the resource dependence model. *Strategic Management Journal*, *11*(6), 419–430.

Boyd, B. K. (1995). CEO duality and firm performance: A contingency model. *Strategic Management Journal*, *16*(4), 301–312.

Bradley, J. C., Waliczek, T. M., & Zajicek, J. M. (1999). Relationship between environmental knowledge and environmental attitude of high school students. *The Journal of Environmental Education*, *30*(3), 17–21.

Braiotta Jr, L., & Zhou, J. (2006). An exploratory study of the effects of the Sarbanes–Oxley Act, the SEC and United States stock exchange(s) rules on audit committee alignment. *Managerial Auditing Journal*, *21*(2), 166–190.

Brammer, S., Millington, A., & Rayton, B. (2007). The contribution of corporate social responsibility to organizational commitment. *The International Journal of Human Resource Management*, *18*(10), 1701–1719.

Branco, M. C., & Rodrigues, L. L. (2006). Communication of corporate social responsibility by Portuguese banks: A legitimacy theory perspective. *Corporate Communications: An International Journal*, *11*(3), 232–248.

326 *Shariah Governance Systems of Islamic Banks*

Bratanovic, S. (2003). *Analyzing and Managing Banking Risk: A Framework for Assessing Corporate Governance and Financial Risk*. World Bank Group.

Brignall, S., & Modell, S. (2000). An institutional perspective on performance measurement and management in the "new public sector". *Management Accounting Research, 11*(3), 281–306.

Briston, R., & El-Ashker, A. (1986). Religious audit: Could it happen here? *Accountancy, 98* (1118), 113–127.

Briston, R., & Kedslie, M. (1985). Must smaller firms continue to lose out? *Accountancy (March)*, 163–164.

Brown, L. D., & Caylor, M. L. (2006). Corporate governance and firm valuation. *Journal of Accounting and Public Policy, 25*(4), 409–434.

Brudney, V. (1985). Corporate governance, agency costs, and the rhetoric of contract. *Columbia Law Review*, 1403–1444.

Buchanan, J. M., & Tullock, G. (1965). *The Calculus of Consent: Logical Foundations of Constitutional Democracy* (Vol. 100). University of Michigan Press, Ann Arbor, Michigan.

Burgess, J. (1902). *Political Science and Comparative Constitutional Law*. Boston: Ginn.

Cader, S. A. (2007). The glass has yet to become full. *Islamic Finance News, 4*(20), 18.

Caldwell, C., & Karri, R. (2005). Organizational governance and ethical systems: A covenantal approach to building trust. *Journal of Business Ethics, 58*, 249–259.

Campbell, D. J. (2000, March). Legitimacy theory or managerial reality construction? Corporate social disclosure in Marks and Spencer Plc corporate reports, 1969–1997. *Accounting Forum, 24*(1), 80–100.

Carmona, S., & Ezzamel, M. (2006). Accounting and religion: A historical perspective. *Accounting History, 11*(2), 117–127.

Carnegie, G. D., & Parker, R. H. (1999). Accountants and empire: The case of co-membership of Australian and British accountancy bodies, 1885 to 1914. *Accounting, Business & Financial History, 9*(1), 77–102.

Carpenter, V. L., & Feroz, E. H. (2001). Institutional theory and accounting rule choice: An analysis of four US state governments' decisions to adopt generally accepted accounting principles. *Accounting, Organizations and Society, 26*(7–8), 565–596.

Carroll, A. (1993). *Business and Society: Ethics and Stakeholder Management*. Cincinnati: South-Western Publishing.

Carroll, A. B., & Buchholtz, A. K. (1999). *Business and Society: Ethics and Stakeholder Management*. 4th Ed. London: International Thomson.

Carroll, A. B., & Buchholtz, A. K. (2008). Educating students in corporate governance and ethics. *Advancing Business Ethics Education*, 285–304.

Carruthers, B. G. (1995). Accounting, ambiguity, and the new institutionalism. *Accounting, Organizations and Society, 20*(4), 313–328.

Central Bank of Oman (2012). *Islamic Banking Regulatory Framework, CBO, Oman*. Chapra.

Cernat, L. (2004). The politics of banking in Romania: Soft loans, looting and cardboard billionaires. *Government and Opposition, 39*(3), 451–475.

Chami, M. R., Khan, M. M. S., & Sharma, M. S. (2003). *Emerging Issues in Banking Regulation.* Washington, D.C.: International Monetary Fund.

Chapra, M. U. (1985). *Towards a Just Monetary System* (Vol. 8). Herndon: International Institute of Islamic Thought (IIIT).

Chapra, M. U. (1992). *Islam and the Economic Challenge* (No. 17). Herndon: International Institute of Islamic Thought (IIIT).

Chapra, M. U. (2004). Mawlana Mawdud's contribution to Islamic economics. *The Muslim World, 94*(2), 163–180.

Chapra, M. U. (2007). The case against interest: Is it compelling? *Thunderbird International Business Review, 49*(2), 161–186.

Chapra, M. U., & Ahmed, H. (2002). *Corporate Governance in Islamic Financial Institutions.* Jeddah: Islamic Development Bank.

Chapra, M. U., & Khan, T. (2000). *Regulations and Supervision of Islamic Banks.* Jeddah: Islamic Research and Training Institute (IRTI).

Cheffins, B. R. (2001). Does law matter? The separation of ownership and control in the United Kingdom. *The Journal of Legal Studies, 30*(2), 459–484.

Cheffins, B. R. (2009). Did corporate governance "fail" during the 2008 stock market meltdown? The case of the S&P 500. *The Business Lawyer, 65*(1), 1–65.

Cheffins, B. R. (2011). The history of modern US corporate governance: Introduction. In Mike Wright, Donald Siegel, Kevin Keasey and Igor Filatotchev (Eds.), *Edward Elgar's Corporate Governance in the New Global Economy Series. Oxford Handbook of Corporate Governance.* Oxford: Oxford University Press, Oxfordshire, UK.

Chen, S., Chen, X. I. A., & Cheng, Q. (2008). Do family firms provide more or less voluntary disclosure? *Journal of Accounting Research, 46*(3), 499–536.

Choudhury, M. A., & Alam, M. N. (2013). Corporate governance in Islamic perspective. *International Journal of Islamic and Middle Eastern Finance and Management, 6*(3), 180–199.

Choudhury, M. A., & Alam, M. N. (2019). Corporate governance in Islamic perspective. In *Research in Corporate and Shariah Governance in the Muslim World: Theory and Practice* (pp. 27–42). Bradford: Emerald Publishing Limited.

Choudhury, M. A., & Hoque, M. Z. (2004). *An Advanced Exposition of Islamic Economics and Finance.* New York: Edward Mellen Press.

Choudhury, M. A., & Hoque, M. Z. (2006). Corporate governance in Islamic perspective. *Corporate Governance: The International Journal of Business in Society, 6*(2), 116–128.

Choudhury, M. A., & Malik, U. A. (1992). *The Foundations of Islamic Political Economy.* New York: St. Martin's Press.

Chowdhury, N., & Shaker, F. (2015). Shariah governance framework of the Islamic banks in Malaysia. *International Journal of Management Sciences and Business Research, 4*(10).

Chua, W. F., & Poullaos, C. (1998). The dynamics of "closure" amidst the construction of market, profession, empire and nationhood: An historical analysis of an Australian accounting association, 1886–1903. *Accounting, Organizations and Society, 23*(2), 155–187.

Ciancanelli P., & Gonzalez J. A. R. (2001). Corporate governance in banking: A conceptual framework, *Working Paper.*

Claessens, S. (2006). Corporate governance and development. *The World Bank Research Observer, 21*(1), 91–122.

Clarke, T. (2004). Theories of corporate governance. *The Philosophical Foundations of Corporate Governance, Oxon, 12*(4), 244–266.

Clarkson, M. E. (1995). A stakeholder framework for analyzing and evaluating corporate social performance. *Academy of Management Review, 20*(1), 92–117.

Clarkson, P., Guedes, J., & Thompson, R. (1996). On the diversification, observability, and measurement of estimation risk. *Journal of Financial and Quantitative Analysis*, 31, 69–84.

Clegg, S. R. (2019). Radical revisions: Power, discipline and organizations. In *Postmodern Management Theory* (pp. 73–91). Routledge.

Clendenin, W. D. (1972). Company presidents look at the board of directors. *California Management Review, 14*(3), 60–66.

Coase, R. H. (1993). *The Nature of the Firm (1937).* Oxford: Oxford University Press.

Coase, R. H., & Fowler, R. F. (1937). The pig-cycle in Great Britain: An explanation. *Economica, 4*(13), 55–82.

Coffee Jr, J. C. (1984). Market failure and the economic case for a mandatory disclosure system. *Virginia Law Review*, 717–753.

Cohen, S., Janicki-Deverts, D., & Miller, G. E. (2007). Psychological stress and disease. *JAMA, 298*(14), 1685–1687.

Coles, J. W., McWilliams, V. B., & Sen, N. (2001). An examination of the relationship of governance mechanisms to performance. *Journal of Management, 27*(1), 23–50.

Collier, P. M. (2008). Stakeholder accountability: A field study of the implementation of a governance improvement plan. *Accounting, Auditing and Accountability Journal, 21*(7), 933–954.

Colyvas, J. A., & Powell, W. W. (2006). Roads to institutionalization: The remaking of boundaries between public and private science. *Research in Organizational Behavior, 27*, 305–353.

Cooke, T. E., & Sawa, E. (1998). Corporate governance structure in Japan — Form and reality. *Corporate Governance: An International Review, 6*(4), 217–223.

Cormier, D., Ledoux, M. J., & Magnan, M. (2011). The informational contribution of social and environmental disclosures for investors. *Management Decision, 49*(8), 1276–1304.

Cormier, D., Aerts, W., Ledoux, M. J., & Magnan, M. (2009). Attributes of social and human capital disclosure and information asymmetry between managers and investors. *Canadian Journal of Administrative Sciences, 26*(1), 71–88.

Courpasson, D. (2000). Managerial strategies of domination. Power in soft bureaucracies. *Organization Studies, 21*(1), 141–161.

Covaleski, M. A., & Dirsmith, M. W. (1988). An institutional perspective on the rise, social transformation, and fall of a university budget category. *Administrative Science Quarterly, 33*, 562–587.

Covaleski, M. A., Dirsmith, M. W., & Michelman, J. E. (1993). An institutional theory perspective on the DRG framework, case-mix accounting systems and health-care organizations. *Accounting, Organizations and Society, 18*(1), 65–80.

Curado, C., Henriques, L., & Bontis, N. (2011). Intellectual capital disclosure payback. *Management Decision, 49*(7), 1080–1098.

Czarniawska-Joerges, B. (1989). The wonderland of public administration reforms. *Organization Studies, 10*(4), 531–548.

Dacin, M. T., Goodstein, J., & Scott, W. R. (2002). Institutional theory and institutional change: Introduction to the special research forum. *Academy of Management Journal*, 45(1), 45–56.

Daily, C. M., Dalton, D. R., & Cannella, J. A. (2003). Corporate governance: Decades of dialogue and data. *Academy of Management Review, 28*(3), 371–382.

Daniel, W. E. (2003). Corporate governance in Indonesian listed companies — A problem of legal transplant. *Bond Law Review, 15*, i.

Dar, H. (2009). Models of Sharia Advisement in Islamic Finance. *Al Watan Daily*. http://jesr.alwatan.com.kw/Default.aspx?MgDid5786239&pageId5163.

Dar, H. A., & Presley, J. R. (2000). Lack of profit loss sharing in Islamic banking: Management and control imbalances. *International Journal of Islamic Financial Services, 2*(2), 3–18.

Darmadi, S. (2013). Board members' education and firm performance: Evidence from a developing economy. *International Journal of Commerce and Management, 23*(2), 113–135.

Davis, D. R., & Moore, W. H. (1997). Ethnicity matters: Transnational ethnic alliances and foreign policy behavior. *International Studies Quarterly, 41*(1), 171–184.

Davis, G. F. (2005). New directions in corporate governance. *Annual Review of Sociology, 31*, 143–162.

Davis, G. F., & Useem, M. (2002). Top management, company directors, and corporate control. *Handbook of Strategy and Management, 9*(3), 232–258.

Davis, J. H., Schoorman, F. D., & Donaldson, L. (1997). Davis, Schoorman, and Donaldson reply: The distinctiveness of agency theory and stewardship theory. *Academy of Management Review, 22*(3), 611.

Davis, G. F., & Thompson, T. A. (1994). A social movement perspective on corporate control. *Administrative Science Quarterly, 39*(1), 141–173.

De Villiers, C., & van Staden, C. J. (2006). Can less environmental disclosure have a legitimising effect? Evidence from Africa. *Accounting, Organizations and Society, 31*(8), 763–781.

Deegan, C. (2002). Introduction: The legitimising effect of social and environmental disclosures — A theoretical foundation. *Accounting, Auditing & Accountability Journal, 15*(3), 282–311.

Deegan, C., & Rankin, M. (1996). Do Australian companies report environmental news objectively? An analysis of environmental disclosures by firms prosecuted successfully by the Environmental Protection Authority. *Accounting, Auditing & Accountability Journal, 9*(2), 50–67.

Deegan, C., Rankin, M., & Tobin, J. (2002). An examination of the corporate social and environmental disclosures of BHP from 1983–1997: A test of legitimacy theory. *Accounting, Auditing & Accountability Journal, 15*(3), 312–343.

Deephouse, D. L. (1996). Does isomorphism legitimate? *Academy of Management Journal, 39*(4), 1024–1039.

Delener, N. (1994). Religious contrasts in consumer decision behaviour patterns: Their dimensions and marketing implications. *European Journal of Marketing, 28*(5), 36–53.

DeLorenzo, L. C. (2012). Missing faces from the orchestra: An issue of social justice? *Music Educators Journal, 98*(4), 39–46.

DeLorenzo, Y., & McMillen, M. (2007). Law and Islamic finance: An interactive analysis. In Archer, S. and Abdel Karim, R. (Eds.), *Islamic Finance: The Regulatory Challenge* (pp. 132–197). Singapore: John Wiley & Sons.

Delorenzo, Y. T. (2007). Sharī'ah compliance risk. *Chicago Journal of International Law, 7*(2), 397–408.

DeLorenzo, Y. T., & McMillen, M. J. (2007). Law and Islamic finance: An interactive analysis. *Islamic Finance: The Regulatory Challenge*, 132–197.

Demirag, I., & Tylecote, A. (1992). The effects of organizational culture, structure and market expectations on technological innovation: A hypothesis. *British Journal of Management, 3*(1), 7–20.

Demirgüç-Kunt, A., & Huizinga, H. (1999). Determinants of commercial bank interest margins and profitability: Some international evidence. *The World Bank Economic Review, 13*(2), 379–408.

Denis, D. K., & McConnell, J. J. (2003). International corporate governance. *Journal of Financial and Quantitative Analysis, 38*(1), 1–36.

Dharwadkar, R., George, G., & Brandes, P. (2000). Privatization in emerging economies: An agency theory perspective. *Academy of Management Review, 25*(3), 650–669.

Dignam, A., & M. Galanis, (2009). *The Globalization of Corporate Governance.* Farnham: Ashgate.

DiMaggio, P. (1998). The relevance of organizational theory to the study of religion. In N. J. Demerath, P. D. Hall, T. Schmitt, & R. H. Williams (Eds.), *Sacred Companies* (p. 161). Oxford: Oxford University Press.

DiMaggio, P., & Powell, W. (1983). The iron cage revisited: Collective rationality and institutional isomorphism in organizational fields. *American Sociological Review, 48*(2), 147–160.

DiMaggio, P., & Powell, W. (1991). *The New Institutionalism in Organizational Analysis.* Chicago: University of Chicago Press.

Dittmar, A., Mahrt-Smith, J., & Servaes, H. (2003). International corporate governance and corporate cash holdings. *Journal of Financial and Quantitative Analysis, 38*(1), 111–133.

Donaldson, L. (1990). A rational basis for criticisms of organizational economics: A reply to Barney. *Academy of Management Review, 15*(3), 394–401.

Donaldson, L., & Davis, J. H. (1991). Stewardship theory or agency theory: CEO governance and shareholder returns. *Australian Journal of Management, 16*(1), 49–64.

Donaldson, T., & Preston, L. E. (1995). The stakeholder theory of the corporation: Concepts, evidence, and implications. *Academy of Management Review, 20*(1), 65–91.

Dowling, J., & Pfeffer, J. (1975). Organizational legitimacy: Social values and organizational behavior. *Pacific Sociological Review, 18*(1), 122–136.

Drori, I., & Honig, B. (2013). A process model of internal and external legitimacy. *Organization Studies, 34*(3), 345–376.

Drucker. P. (1965). Is business letting young people down? *Harvard Business Review*, Nov/Dec.

Du Plessis, E. (2005). *The Advertised Mind: Ground-breaking Insights into How our Brains Respond to Advertising.* New York: Kogan Page Publishers.

Du Plessis, J. J., A. Hargovan & J. Harris, (2018). *Principles of Contemporary Corporate Governance.* Port Melbourne: Cambridge University Press.

Duarte, J., Han, X., Harford, J., & Young, L. (2008). Information asymmetry, information dissemination and the effect of regulation FD on the cost of capital. *Journal of Financial Economics, 87*(1), 24–44.

Durisin, B., & Puzone, F. (2009). Maturation of corporate governance research, 1993–2007: An assessment. *Corporate Governance: An International Review, 17*(3), 266–291.

Durnev, A., & Han, K. E. (2002). The interplay of firm-specific factors and legal regimes in corporate governance and firm valuation. Paper presented in *Dartmouth's Center for Corporate Governance Conference: Corporate Governance*, Tuck School of Business, July, pp. 12–13.

Dusuki, A. W. (2008). What does Islam say about corporate social responsibility. *Review of Islamic Economics, 12*(1), 5–28.

Dusuki, A. W. (2011). *Ethical and Social Responsibility Models for Islamic Finance.* ISRA Research Report. Kuala Lumpur: ISRA.

Easley, D., de Prado, M. L., & O'Hara, M. (2016). Discerning information from trade data. *Journal of Financial Economics, 120*(2), 269–285.

Eisenhardt, K. M. (1989). Agency theory: An assessment and review. *Academy of Management Review, 14*(1), 57–74.

Elasrag, H. (2014). Corporate governance in Islamic finance: Basic concepts and issues. 1–98. https://dx.doi.org/10.2139/ssrn.2442014.

El-Hawary, D., Grais, W., & Iqbal, Z. (2004). *Regulating Islamic Financial Institutions: The Nature of the Regulated.* Washington, DC: World Bank Policy Research Working Paper.

Elamer, A. A., Ntim, C. G., & Abdou, H. A. (2020). Islamic governance, national governance, and bank risk management and disclosure in MENA countries. *Business & Society, 59*(5), 914–955.

El-Gamal, M. A. (2006). *Islamic Finance: Law, Economics, and Practice.* Cambridge: Cambridge University Press.

Elghuweel, M. I., Ntim, C. G., Opong, K. K., & Avison, L. (2017). Corporate governance, Islamic governance and earnings management in Oman: A new empirical insights from a behavioural theoretical framework. *Journal of Accounting in Emerging Economies*, *7*(2), 190–224.

El-Hawary, D., & Grais, W. (2004). *Regulating Islamic Financial Institutions: The Nature of the Regulated* (Vol. 3227). Washington, DC: World Bank Publications.

Elsbach, K. D., & Sutton, R. I. (1992). Acquiring organizational legitimacy through illegitimate actions: A marriage of institutional and impression management theories. *Academy of Management Journal*, *35*(4), 699–738.

Elzahar, H., Hussainey, K., Mazzi, F., & Tsalavoutas, I. (2015). Economic consequences of key performance indicators' disclosure quality. *International Review of Financial Analysis*, *39*, 96–112.

Errico, L., & Sundararajan, V. (2002). Islamic financial institutions and products in the global financial system: Key issues in risk management and challenges ahead. IMF Working Paper No. 02/192. https://ssrn.com/abstract=1930788.

Errico, M. L., & Farahbaksh, M. M. (1998). *Islamic Banking: Issues in Prudential Regulations and Supervision*. International Monetary Fund. IMF Working Paper No. 98/30.

Ewmi, P. F. (2005). Three models of corporate governance from developed capital markets. *Lectures on Corporate Governance*, *12*, 1–14.

Fama, E. F. (1980). Agency problems and the theory of the firm. *Journal of Political Economy*, *88*(2), 288–307.

Fama, E. F., & Jensen, M. C. (1983a). Agency problems and residual claims. *The Journal of Law and Economics*, *26*(2), 327–349.

Fama, E. F., & Jensen, M. C. (1983b). Separation of ownership and control. *The Journal of Law and Economics*, *26*(2), 301–325.

Farinha, J. (2003). Dividend policy, corporate governance and the managerial entrenchment hypothesis: An empirical analysis. *Journal of Business Finance & Accounting*, *30*(9–10), 1173–1209.

Farook, S., Kabir Hassan, M., & Lanis, R. (2011). Determinants of corporate social responsibility disclosure: the case of Islamic banks. *Journal of Islamic Accounting and Business Research*, *2*(2), 114–141.

Farrington, J., & Farrington, C. (2005). Rural accessibility, social inclusion and social justice: Towards conceptualisation. *Journal of Transport Geography*, *13*(1), 1–12.

Faruki, K. A. (1962). *Islamic Jurisprudence*. Karachi: National Book Foundation.

Faruqi, I. I. R. A. (1982). Islam and the Theory of Nature. *Islamic Quarterly*, *26*(1), 16.

Ferrer, R. C., & Ferrer, G. J. (2011). The relationship between profitability and the level of compliance to the international financial reporting standards (IFRS): An empirical investigation on publicly listed corporations in the Philippines. *Academy of Accounting and Financial Studies Journal*, *15*(4), 61–82.

References

Ferriswara, D., Sayidah, N., & Agus Buniarto, E. (2022). Do corporate governance, capital structure predict financial performance and firm value? (empirical study of Jakarta Islamic index). *Cogent Business & Management*, *9*(1), 2147123.

Fianna, J., & Grant, K. (2005). The revised OECD principles of corporate governance and their relevance to non-OECD countries. *Corporate Governance as an International Review*, *13*, 127–136.

Filatotchev, I., Stephan, J., & Jindra, B. (2008). Ownership structure, strategic controls and export intensity of foreign-invested firms in transition economies. *Journal of International Business Studies*, *39*, 1133–1148.

Fine, G. A., & Sandstrom, K. (1993). Ideology in action: A pragmatic approach to a contested concept. *Sociological Theory*, *11*, 21–38.

Fiss, P. C. (2008). Institutions and corporate. In *The Sage Handbook of Organizational Institutionalism* (Vol. 389).

Fligstein, N. (2001). Social skill and the theory of fields. *Sociological Theory*, *19*(2), 105–125.

Fohlin, C. (2004). *The History of Corporate Ownership and Control in Germany*. C. Fohlin.

Fombrun, C. J., & Gardberg, N. (2000). Who's tops in corporate reputation? *Corporate Reputation Review*, *3*, 13–17.

Fotiuh, H. A. (2010). *Corporate Governance in Islamic Finance*. www.articleslash. net/Finance/555054__Corporate-Governance-in-Islamic-Finance.html.

Franks, J. and C. Mayer, (1997). Corporate ownership and control in the UK, Germany, and France. *Journal of Applied Corporate Finance*, *9*(4), 30–45.

Freeman, R. E. (1984). *Strategic Management: A Stakeholder Approach*. Boston, Mass: Pitman.

Gales, L. M., & Kesner, I. F. (1994). An analysis of board of director size and composition in bankrupt organizations. *Journal of Business Research*, *30*(3), 271–282.

Gallego-Álvarez, I., García-Sánchez, I. M., & Rodríguez-Dominguez, L. (2010). The influence of gender diversity on corporate performance. *Spanish Accounting Review*, *13*(1), 53–88.

Gallhofer, S., & Haslam, J. (1994). Accounting and the Benthams: Accounting as negation?. *Accounting, Business & Financial History*, *4*(2), 239–274.

Gambling, T., & Karim, R. A. A. (1991). *Business and Accounting Ethics in Islam*. London: Mansell Publishing Limited.

Gambling, T., Jones, R., & Karim, R. A. A. (1993). Credible organizations: Self-regulation v. external standard-setting in Islamic banks and British charities. *Financial Accountability & Management*, *9*(3), 195–207.

Garas, S. N. (2012). The conflicts of interest inside the Shari'a supervisory board. *International Journal of Islamic and Middle Eastern Finance and Management*, *5*(2), 88–105.

Garas, S. N., & Pierce, C. (2010). Shari'a supervision of Islamic financial institutions. *Journal of Financial Regulation & Compliance*, *18*(4), 386–407.

Gaur, S. S., Bathula, H., & Singh, D. (2015). Ownership concentration, board characteristics and firm performance: A contingency framework. *Management Decision, 53*(5), 911–931.

Ghayad, R. (2008). Corporate governance and the global performance of Islamic banks. *Humanomics, 24*(3), 207–216.

Gilson, R. J. (2001). Globalizing corporate governance: Convergence of form or function. *The American Journal of Comparative Law, 49*(2), 329–358.

Ginena, K. (2014). Sharīʿah risk and corporate governance of Islamic banks. *Corporate Governance, 14*(1), 86–103.

Ginena, K., & Hamid, A. (2015). *Foundations of Shariah Governance of Islamic Banks.* Chichester, West Sussex: John Wiley & Sons.

Gintzburger, G., & Saïdi, S. (2010). From inventory to monitoring in semi-arid and arid rangelands. *Range and Animal Sciences and Resource Management, 2*, 237–273.

Gordon, L. A., Loeb, M. P., & Sohail, T. (2010). Market value of voluntary disclosures concerning information security. *MIS Quarterly*, 567–594.

Graham, J., Amos, B., & Plumptre, T. (2003). Principles for good governance in the 21st century. *Policy Brief No. 15*, Institute on Governance, Ottawa.

Grais, W. M., & Pellegrini, M. (2006a). Corporate governance in institutions offering Islamic financial services: Issues and options. *World Bank Policy Research Working Paper 4052*, World Bank.

Grais, W. M., & Pellegrini, M. (2006b). Corporate governance and Shariah compliance in institutions offering Islamic financial services. *World Bank Policy Research Working Paper 4054*, World Bank.

Grassa, R. (2013). Shariah supervisory system in Islamic financial institutions: New issues and challenges: A comparative analysis between Southeast Asia models and GCC models. *Humanomics, 29*(4), 333–348.

Grassa, R. (2016). Corporate governance and credit rating in Islamic banks: Does Shariah governance matters? *Journal of Management & Governance, 20*, 875–906.

Grassa, R., & Matoussi, H. (2014). Corporate governance of Islamic banks: A comparative study between GCC and Southeast Asia countries. *International Journal of Islamic and Middle Eastern Finance and Management, 7*(3), 346–362.

Gray, R., Kouhy, R., & Lavers, S. (1995). Corporate social and environmental reporting: a review of the literature and a longitudinal study of UK disclosure. *Accounting, Auditing & Accountability Journal, 8*(2), 47–77.

Gray, R., Owen, D., & Adams, C. (1996). *Accounting and Accountability: Changes and Challenges in Corporate Social and Environmental Reporting.* London: Prentice-Hall.

Gray. H. R. (1994). Corporate reporting for sustainable development: Accounting for sustainability in 2000 AD. *Environmental Values, 3*(1), 17–45.

Gray, R., Owen, D., & Adams, C. (1996). *Accounting and Accountability: Changes and Challenges in Corporate Social and Environmental Reporting.* London: Prentice-Hall.

Greenough, W. C., & Clapman, P. C. (1980). Role of independent directors in corporate governance. *Notre Dame Law Review* Seligman, *56*, 916.

Greenwood, R., & Hinings, C. R. (1996). Understanding radical organizational change: Bringing together the old and the new institutionalism. *Academy of Management Review, 21*(4), 1022–1054.

Greenwood, R., Suddaby, R., & Hinings, C. R. (2002). Theorizing change: The role of professional associations in the transformation of institutionalized fields. *Academy of Management Journal, 45*(1), 58–80.

Gregory, H. J. (2000). The globalization of corporate governance. *Global Counsel, 5*, 52–65.

Guo, L., Smallman, C., & Radford, J. (2013). A critique of corporate governance in China. *International Journal of Law and Management, 55*(4), 257–272.

Guthrie, J., & Parker, L. D. (1989). Corporate social reporting: A rebuttal of legitimacy theory. *Accounting and Business Research, 19*(76), 343–352.

Hagendorff, J., Collins, M., & Keasey, K. (2007). Bank governance and acquisition performance. *Corporate Governance: An International Review, 15*(5), 957–968.

Hameed, S. (2008). The case for Islamic auditing. *International Accountant*, 41, May 2008.

Hameed, S. A. (2009). Software engineering ethical principles based on Islamic values. *Journal of Software, 4*(6), 563–570.

Hameed, S., & Yaya, R. (2003). The Future of Islamic corporate reporting: Lessons from alternative Western accounting report. In *International Conference on Quality Financial Reporting and Corporate Governance*. Kuala Lumpur.

Hameed, S., Ade, W., Bakhtiar, A., Nazli, dan Sigit, P. (2004). *Alternative Disclosure dan Performance for Islamic Bank's*. Saudi Arabia: Dahran.

Hamid, A. A., Haniff, M. N., Othman, M. R., & Salin, A. S. A. P. (2011). The comparison of the characteristics of the Anglo-Saxon governance model and the Islamic governance of IFIs. *Malaysian Accounting Review, 10*(2), 1–12.

Hamid, S., Craig, R., & Clarke, F. (1993). Religion: A confounding cultural element in the international harmonization of accounting? *Abacus, 29*(2), 131–148.

Hammad, N. (2007). *Contemporary Islamic Jurisprudence on Monetary and Banking Transactions*. Damascus: Dar Al-Qalam.

Hamza, H. (2013). Sharia governance in Islamic banks: Effectiveness and supervision model. *International Journal of Islamic and Middle Eastern Finance and Management, 6*(3), 226–237.

Handelman, J. M., & Arnold, S. J. (1999). The role of marketing actions with a social dimension: Appeals to the institutional environment. *Journal of Marketing, 63*(3), 33–48.

Haniffa, R. (2002). Social reporting disclosure: An Islamic perspective. *Indonesian Management & Accounting Research, 1*(2), 128–146.

Haniffa, R. (2010). *Auditing Islamic Financial Institutions. Islamic Finance: Instruments and Market*. QFinance, 109–112, London: Bloomsbury Information Limited, UK.

Haniffa, R. M., & Cooke, T. E. (2002). Culture, corporate governance and disclosure in Malaysian corporations. *Abacus, 38*(3), 317–349.

Haniffa, R. M., & Cooke, T. E. (2005). The impact of culture and governance on corporate social reporting. *Journal of Accounting and Public Policy, 24*(5), 391–430.

Haniffa, R., & Hudaib, M. (2001, February). A conceptual framework for Islamic accounting: The Shari'a paradigm. In *Accounting, Commerce and Finance: The Islamic Perspective International Conference IV, New Zealand* (pp. 12–14), Edward Elgar, Cheltenham, UK.

Haniffa, R., & Hudaib, M. (2006). Corporate governance structure and performance of Malaysian listed companies. *Journal of Business Finance & Accounting, 33*(7–8), 1034–1062.

Haniffa, R., & Hudaib, M. (2007). Exploring the ethical identity of Islamic banks via communication in annual reports. *Journal of Business Ethics, 76*, 97–116.

Haniffa, R., & Hudaib, M. (2010). Islamic finance: From sacred intentions to secular goals? *Journal of Islamic Accounting and Business Research, 1*(2), 85–91.

Haniffa, R., & Hudaib, M. A. (2002). A theoretical framework for the development of the Islamic perspective of accounting. *Accounting, Commerce and Finance: The Islamic Perspective Journal, 6*(1/2), 1–71.

Haqqi, A. R. A. (2014). Shariah governance in Islamic financial institution: An appraisal. *US-China Law Review, 11*, 112.

Harahap, M. Y. (2002). Pembahasanpermasalahan dan penerapan KUHAP penyidikan dan penuntutan Edisikedua.

Harahap, S. (2003). The disclosure of Islamic values–annual report. The analysis of Bank Muamalat Indonesia's annual report. *Managerial Finance, 29*(7), 70–89.

Haridan, N. M. (2016). Quality of Shariah compliance assurance in Malaysian Islamic banks post implementation of Shariah governance framework. Master thesis, Putra Business School.

Haridan, N. M., Hassan, A. F. S., & Karbhari, Y. (2018). Governance, religious assurance and Islamic banks: Do Shariah boards effectively serve? *Journal of Management and Governance, 22*(4), 1015–1043.

Haron, S. (1997). Determinants of Islamic bank profitability: Some evidence. *Journal Pengurusan, 16*(1), 33–46.

Haron, S., & Wan Azmi, W. N. (2009). Islamic finance and banking system: Philosophies, principles and practices. Kuala Lumpur; New York: McGraw Hill.

Hart, O. (1995). Corporate governance: Some theory and implications. *The Economic Journal, 105*(430), 678–689.

Harzi, A. (2012). *The Impact of Basel III on Islamic Banks: A Theoretical Study and Comparison with Conventional Banks.* Chapters of books published by the Islamic Economics Institute, KAAU or its faculty members, pp. 591–610.

Hasan, A. B. (2007). Optimal Sharia governance in Islamic finance, paper presented at the Financial Regulators Forum in Islamic Finance - Global Islamic Finance Forum (GIFF), Kuala Lumpur, Malaysia, March.

Hasan, Z. (2008, June). Corporate governance of Islamic financial institutions. In *Conference on Malaysian Study of Islam, Lamperter, United Kingdom.*

Hasan, Z. (2009). Regulatory framework of Shariah governance system in Malaysia, GCC Countries and the UK. *Kyoto Bulletin of Islamic Area Studies*, 3–2.

Hasan, Z. (2010). Corporate governance in Islamic financial institutions: An ethical perspective. In *Proceeding of the Conference on the Future of Faith in the Era of Globalization.*

Hasan, Z. (2011a). A survey on Shariah governance practices in Malaysia, GCC countries and the UK: Critical appraisal. *International Journal of Islamic and Middle Eastern Finance and Management*, *4*(1), 30–51.

Hasan, Z. (2011b). Sharīʻah governance in Islamic financial institutions in Malaysia, GCC countries and the UK (Doctoral dissertation, Durham University).

Hasan, Z. (2012). *Shariah Governance in Islamic Banks*. Edinburgh: Edinburgh University Press.

Hasan, Z. (2014). *Islamic Banking and Finance: An Integrative Approach*. Oxford: OUP Catalogue.

Hassan, A. F. S. (2012). An empirical investigation into the role, independence and effectiveness of Shariah boards in the Malaysian Islamic banking industry. PhD Thesis, University of Cardiff.

Hassan, M. K., & Dicle, M. F. (2005). Basel II and regulatory framework for Islamic banks. *Journal of Islamic Economics, Banking and Finance*, *1*(1), 1–16.

Hassan, M. K., & Chowdhury, A. (2004). Islamic banking regulations in light of Basel II. *The American Journal of Islamic Social Sciences*, *27*, 1.

Hassan, M. K., & Lewis, M. K. (2007). Islamic banking: An introduction and overview. *Handbook of Islamic Banking*, Cheltenham, UK. *38*.

Hassan, M. K., Ullah, M. H., & Khanam, R. (2017). Shariah governance practices in Bangladesh in Ali, N. (Ed.), *Shariah Governance Systems and Practices in a Globalized World*. Leeds: Emerald Insight, West Yorkshire, England.

Hassan, R., Othman, A. A., Omar, M. N., Napiah, M. D. M., Abdullah, M. A., Arifin, M., ... & Karim, M. S. A. (2017). Shariah risk management process for Islamic financial institutions in the context of Shariah governance framework 2010. *UUM Journal of Legal Studies*, *8*, 1–15.

Hassan, R., Abdullah, N. I., Hassan, A., Ibrahim, U., Sawari, M. F. M., Abd. Aziz, A., & Triyanta, A. (2011). *A Comparative Analysis of Shariah Governance in Islamic Banking Institutions Across Jurisdictions*. Kualal Lumpur: International Shariah Research Academy for Islamic Finance.

Hayes, R., Dassen, R., Schilder, A., & Wallage, P. (2005). *Principles of Auditing. An Introduction to International Standards on Auditing*. 2nd Ed. Prentice Hall.

He, Y., Tian, Z., & Chen, Y. (2007). Performance implications of nonmarket strategy in China. *Asia Pacific Journal of Management*, *24*(2), 151–169.

Heakal, S. (1989). The conceptual difference between financial accounting for Islamic banks and financial accounting for Western commercial banks, *Paper*

Prepared for the Follow Up Committee for Accounting Standards for Islamic Banks, IDB, Jeddah.

Healy, P. M., Hutton, A. P., & Palepu, K. G. (1999). Stock performance and intermediation changes surrounding sustained increases in disclosure. *Contemporary Accounting Research, 16*(3), 485–520.

Heath, J., & Norman, W. (2004). Stakeholder theory, corporate governance and public management: What can the history of state-run enterprises teach us in the post-Enron era? *Journal of Business Ethics, 53*, 247–265.

Hendry, K., & Kiel, G. C. (2004). The role of the board in firm strategy: Integrating agency and organisational control perspectives. *Corporate Governance: An International Review, 12*(4), 500–520.

Henry, D. (2010). Agency costs, ownership structure and corporate governance compliance: A private contracting perspective. *Pacific-Basin Finance Journal, 18*(1), 24–46.

Hidayah, N. (2014). *Religious Compliance in Islamic Financial Institutions* (Doctoral dissertation, Aston University).

Higgs, D. (2003). *Review of the Role and Effectiveness of Non-Executive Directors* (pp. 1–120). London: Stationery Office.

Hill, C. W., & Jones, T. M. (1992). Stakeholder-agency theory. *Journal of Management Studies, 29*(2), 131–154.

Hillman, A. J., Cannella, A. A., & Paetzold, R. L. (2000). The resource dependence role of corporate directors: Strategic adaptation of board composition in response to environmental change. *Journal of Management Studies, 37*(2), 235–256.

Hillman, A. J., Keim, G. D., & Luce, R. A. (2001). Board composition and stakeholder performance: Do stakeholder directors make a difference? *Business & Society, 40*(3), 295–314.

Hirschey, M., Kose, J., & Anil, M. (2009). Corporate governance and firm performance. *Journal of Corporate Finance, 6*.

Hoepner, A. G., Rammal, H. G., & Rezec, M. (2011). Islamic mutual funds' financial performance and international investment style: Evidence from 20 countries. *The European Journal of Finance, 17*(9–10), 829–850.

Holder-Webb, L., Cohen, J., Nath, L., & Wood, D. (2008). A survey of governance disclosures among US firms. *Journal of Business Ethics, 83*, 543–563.

Hood, K. L., & Bucheery, R. (1999). The interaction of financial and religious (Islamic) auditors with reference to the audit expectation gap in Bahrain. *Accounting, Commerce and Finance: The Islamic Perspective Journal, 3*(1), 25–58.

Hossain, M., & Taylor, P. J. (2007). The empirical evidence of the voluntary information disclosure in the annual reports of banking companies: The case of Bangladesh. *Corporate Ownership and Control, 4*(3), 111–125.

Hossain, M., Perera, M. H. B., & Rahman, A. R. (1995). Voluntary disclosure in the annual reports of New Zealand companies. *Journal of International Financial Management & Accounting, 6*(1), 69–87.

Hossain, M. S., & Yahya, S. B. (2017). Developing a conceptual framework of corporate community development practices of Islamic banks in Bangladesh:

An institutional perspective. *Journal of Internet Banking and Commerce,* *22*(1), 1–20.

Huber, G. P., & Glick, W. H. (Eds.). (1993). *Organizational Change and Redesign: Ideas and Insights for Improving Performance.* Oxford: Oxford University Press, USA.

Huse, M. (2005). Corporate governance: Understanding important contingencies. *Corporate Ownership & Control, 2*(4), 41–50.

Huther, J., & Shah, A. (1998). *Applying a Simple Measure of Good Governance to the Debate on Fiscal Decentralization* (Vol. 1894). Washington, DC: World Bank Publications.

Ibrahim, E. N. M., Hamzah, W. N. I. I. W., Taslim, J., & Adnan, W. A. W. (2010). Evaluating trust elements in the context of Islamic based informational websites. In *2010 International Conference on User Science and Engineering (i-USEr)* (pp. 268–272). IEEE.

Ibrahim, S. H. M., & Yaya, R. (2005). The emerging issues on the objectives and the characteristics of Islamic accounting for Islamic business organizations. *Management & Accounting Review (MAR), 4*(1), 74–92.

IFSB (2005). *Guiding Principles of Risk Management for Institutions (Other Than Insurance Institutions) Offering Only Islamic Financial Services.* Kuala Lumpur: IFSB.

IFSB (2006). *Guiding Principles on Corporate Governance for Institutions Offering Only Islamic Financial Services (Excluding Islamic Insurance (Takaful) Institutions and Islamic Mutual Funds).* Kuala Lumpur: International Service Board.

IFSB (2008). *Survey on Shariah Boards of Institutions Offering Islamic Financial Services Across Jurisdictions.* Kuala Lumpur: IFSB.

IFSB (2009). *Guiding Principles on Shariah Governance Systems for Institutions Offering Islamic Financial Services.* Kuala Lumpur: Islamic Financial Services Board.

IFSB (2014). *Guiding Principles on Shariah Governance Systems for Institutions Offering Islamic Financial Services.* Kuala Lumpur: Islamic Financial Services Board.

IFSB (2023). The Islamic Financial Services Board (IFSB). https://www.ifsb.org/.

Iftikhar, A. R., Bhatti, H. N., Hanif, M. A., & Nadeem, R. (2009). Kinetic and thermodynamic aspects of Cu (II) and Cr (III) removal from aqueous solutions using rose waste biomass. *Journal of Hazardous Materials, 161*(2–3), 941–947.

Iqbal, Z., & Mirakhor, A. (2004). Stakeholders model of governance in Islamic economic system. *Islamic Economic Studies, 11*(2), 44–63.

Iqbal, M., & Mirakhor, A. (2007). An introduction to Islamic finance: Theory and practice. Chichester: John Wiley & Sons.

Islamic Development Bank (IDB) and Islamic Financial Services Board (IFSB) (2007). *Islamic Financial Services Industry Development: Ten-year Framework and Strategies.* Kuala Lumpur: IFSB.

340   *Shariah Governance Systems of Islamic Banks*

Islamic Financial Services Board (2007a). *Guidance on Key Elements in the Supervisory Review Process of Institutions Offering Islamic Financial Services.* Kuala Lumpur: IFSB.

Islamic Financial Services Board (2007b). *Disclosures to Promote Transparency and Market Discipline for Institutions Offering Islamic Financial Services.* Kuala Lumpur: IFSB.

ISRA (2009). Shariah Compliant versus Sharī'ah Based Products. ISRA Bulletin, 2, 2.

Izhar, H. (2010). Identifying operational risk exposures in Islamic banking. *Kyoto Bulletin of Islamic Area Studies, 3*(2), 17–53.

Jacoby, W. G. (2000). Issue framing and public opinion on government spending. *American Journal of Political Science*, 750–767.

Jagadeesan, R., Jeffrey, A., Pitcher, C., & Riely, J. (2009). Towards a theory of accountability and audit. In *Computer Security–ESORICS 2009: 14th European Symposium on Research in Computer Security, Saint-Malo, France, September 21–23, 2009. Proceedings 14* (pp. 152–167). Berlin Heidelberg: Springer.

Jamali, D., Safieddine, A. M., & Rabbath, M. (2008). Corporate governance and corporate social responsibility synergies and interrelationships. *Corporate Governance: An International Review, 16*(5), 443–459.

Jensen, M. (2001). Value maximisation, stakeholder theory, and the corporate objective function. *European Financial Management, 7*(3), 297–317.

Jensen, M. C. (1993). The modern industrial revolution, exit and the failure of internal control systems. *Journal of Finance, 48*(3), 831–880.

Jensen, M. C., & Meckling, W. H. (1976). Theory of the firm: Managerial behaviour, agency costs, and ownership structure. *Journal of Financial Economics*, 3(4), 305–350.

Jesover, F., & Kirkpatrick, G. (2005). The revised OECD principles of corporate governance and their relevance to non-OECD countries. *Corporate Governance: An International Review, 13*(2), 127–136.

John, K., & Senbet, L. W. (1998). Corporate governance and board effectiveness. *Journal of Banking & Finance, 22*(4), 371–403.

Johnson, C., Dowd, T. J., & Ridgeway, C. L. (2006). Legitimacy as a social process. *Annual Review of Sociology, 32*, 53–78.

Johnson, R. A., & Greening, D. W. (1999). The effects of corporate governance and institutional ownership types on corporate social performance. *Academy of Management Journal, 42*(5), 564–576.

Johnson, T. J., & Caygill, M. (1971). The development of accountancy links in the Commonwealth. *Accounting and Business Research, 1*(2), 155–173.

Judge, T. A., Cable, D. M., Boudreau, J. W., & Bretz Jr, R. D. (1995). An empirical investigation of the predictors of executive career success. *Personnel Psychology, 48*(3), 485–519.

Kahf, M. (1982a). Saving and investment functions in a two sector Islamic economy. In Ariff, M. (Ed.), *Monetary and Fiscal Economics of Islam.* Jeddah: International Centre for Research in Islamic Economics.

Kahf, M. (1982b). Fiscal and monetary policies in an Islamic economy. In Ariff, M. (Ed.), *Monetary and Fiscal Economics of Islam*. Jeddah: International Centre for Research in Islamic Economics.

Kahf, M. (2004). Islamic economics: What went wrong. *Islamic Development Bank Roundtable on Islamic Economics: Current State of Knowledge and Development of the Discipline*, Jeddah May, 26, 27.

Kahf, M. (2006). Maqasid Al-Shariah in the Prohibition of Riba and Their Implication for Modern Islamic Finance. In: *IIUM International Conference on Maqasid al- Shariah*. Kuala Lumpur.

Kalbers, L. P., & Fogarty, T. J. (1998). Organizational and economic explanations of audit committee oversight. *Journal of Managerial Issues*, 129–150.

Kamla, R. (2009). Critical insights into contemporary Islamic accounting. *Critical Perspectives on Accounting, 20*(8), 921–932.

Kamla, R., Gallhofer, S., & Haslam, J. (2006). Islam, nature and accounting: Islamic principles and the notion of accounting for the environment. *Accounting Forum, 30*(3), 245–265.

Kamali, M. H. (2000). *Islamic Commercial Law: An Analysis of Futures and Options*. Cambridge: The Islamic Texts Society.

Kamali, M. H. (2008). *Shariah Law: An Introduction*. London: Simon and Schuster.

Kamaruddin, M. I. H., & Hanefah, M. M. (2017). Enhancing Shariah audit practices in Islamic financial institutions in Malaysia. *Journal of Modern Accounting and Auditing, 13*(11), 457–470.

Karbhari, Y., Muye, I., Hassan, A. F. S., & Elnahass, M. (2018). Governance mechanisms and efficiency: Evidence from an alternative insurance (Takaful) market. *Journal of International Financial Markets, Institutions and Money, 56*, 71–92. https://doi.org/10.1016/j.intfin.2018.02.017.

Karbhari, Y., Alam, M. K., & Rahman, M. M. (2020). Relevance of application of institutional theory in Shariah governance of Islamic banks. *PSU Research Review, 5*(1), 1–15.

Karim, R. A. A. (1990a). The independence of religious and external auditors: The case of Islamic banks. *Accounting, Auditing & Accountability Journal, 3*(3), 34–44.

Karim, R. A. A. (1990b). Standard setting for the financial reporting of religious business organisations: The case of Islamic banks. *Accounting & Business Research, 20*(80), 299–305.

Karim, R. A. A. (1999). Accounting in Islamic financial institutions. *Accounting and Business Magazines*, July-August 1999.

Karim, R. A. A. (2001). International accounting harmonization, banking regulation, and Islamic banks. *The International Journal of Accounting, 36*(2), 169–193.

Kasim, N. B., Ibrahim, S. H. M., & Sulaiman, M. (2009). Shariah auditing in Islamic financial institutions: Exploring the gap between the "desired" and the "actual". *Global Economy and Finance Journal, 2*(2), 127–137.

Kasim, N., NuHtay, M. S. N., & Salman, S. A. (2013). Shariah governance for Islamic capital market: A step forward. *International Journal of Education and Research, 1*(6), 1–14.

Kasim, R. S. R., & Shamsir, N. F. M. (2012). Innovative governance framework for global Islamic microfinance institutions. In *2012 International Conference on Innovation Management and Technology Research*.

Kay, J. and Silberston, A. (1995). Corporate governance. *National Institute Economic Review, 153*(1), 84–97.

Kayed, R. N., & Mohammed, K. (2009). Unique risks of Islamic modes of finance: Systemic, credit and market risks. *Journal of Islamic Economics, Banking and Finance, 5*(3), 9–34.

Keasey, K., Thompson, S., & Wright, M. (1997). Introduction: The corporate governance problem-competing diagnoses and solutions. In Keasey, K., Thompson, S. and Wright, (Eds.), *Corporate Governance, Economic, Management, and Financial Issues* (pp. 1–17). Oxford: Oxford University Press.

Kent, P., & Stewart, J. (2008). Corporate governance and disclosures on the transition to international financial reporting standards. *Accounting & Finance, 48*(4), 649–671.

Kesner, I. F., & Johnson, R. B. (1990). An investigation of the relationship between board composition and stockholder suits. *Strategic Management Journal, 11*(4), 327–336.

Khadaroo, M. I. (2005). An institutional theory perspective on the UK's Private Finance Initiative (PFI) accounting standard-setting process. *Public Management Review, 7*(1), 69–94.

Khan, F. (2010). How 'Islamic' is Islamic banking? *Journal of Economic Behavior & Organization, 76*(3), 805–820.

Khan, M. A. (1987). Methodology of Islamic economics. *International Journal of Economics, Management and Accounting, 1*(1), 1–15.

Khan, M. F. (2007). Setting standards for Shariah application in the Islamic financial industry. *Thunderbird International Business Review, 49*(3), 285–307.

Khan, M. S., & Mirakhor, A. (1986). The framework and practice of Islamic banking. *Finance and Development, 23*(3), 32–41.

Khan, T., & Ahmed, H. (2001). *Risk Management: An Analysis of Issues in Islamic Financial Industry (Occasional papers)* (No. 91). The Islamic Research and Teaching Institute (IRTI).

Khir, K., Gupta, L., & Shanmugam, B. (2008). *Longman Islamic Banking: A Practical Perspective*. Malaysia: Pearson Malaysia Sdn Bhd.

Kim, J., & Mahoney, J. T. (2005). Property rights theory, transaction costs theory, and agency theory: an organizational economics approach to strategic management. *Managerial and Decision Economics, 26*(4), 223–242. https://doi.org/10.1002/mde.1218.

Kitchen, J., & Parker, R. H. (1980). Accounting thought and education: Six English pioneers.

Kostova, T., & Roth, K. (2002). Adoption of an organizational practice by subsidiaries of multinational corporations: Institutional and relational effects. *Academy of Management Journal, 45*(1), 215–233.

Kostova, T., & Zaheer, S. (1999). Organizational legitimacy under conditions of complexity: The case of the multinational enterprise. *Academy of Management Review*, *24*(1), 64–81.

Krishnan, L. (2010). The antithesis between civil law and Islamic law in a pluralistic society. *Jurnal Syariah*, *18*(2), 401–414.

La Porta, R., Lopez-de-Silanes, F., Shleifer, A., & Vishny, R. (2002). Investor protection and corporate valuation. *The Journal of Finance*, *57*(3), 1147–1170.

Laeven, L., & Levine, R. (2008). Complex ownership structures and corporate valuations. *The Review of Financial Studies*, *21*(2), 579–604.

Lahsasna, A. (2011). Fatwa and its Shariah methodology in Islamic finance. *Journal of Fatwa Management and Research*, *2*(1), 133–179.

Laldin, M. A. (2008). Islamic financial system: The Malaysian experience and the way forward. *Humanomics*, *24*(3), 217–238.

Laldin, M. A., & Furqani, H. (2018). Islamic Financial Services Act (IFSA) 2013 and the Sharī'ah-compliance requirement of the Islamic finance industry in Malaysia. *ISRA International Journal of Islamic Finance*, *10*(1), 94–101.

Lambert, R., Leuz, C., & Verrecchia, R. E. (2007). Accounting information, disclosure, and the cost of capital. *Journal of Accounting Research*, *45*(2), 385–420.

Laughlin, R., & Gray, R. (1988). *Financial Accounting: Method and Meaning*. Florida: Taylor & Francis.

Lawrence, T., Suddaby, R., & Leca, B. (2011). Institutional work: Refocusing institutional studies of organization. *Journal of Management Inquiry*, *20*(1), 52–58.

Lawrence, T. B., & Suddaby, R. (2006). 1.6 institutions and institutional work. *The Sage Handbook of Organization Studies*, 215–254.

Lazonick, W., & O'Sullivan, M. (2000). Innovation, and Economic Performance, 1–147.

Lee, C. S., & Ma, L. (2012). News sharing in social media: The effect of gratifications and prior experience. *Computers in Human Behavior*, *28*(2), 331–339.

Leuz, C., & Verrecchia, R. E. (2000). The economic consequences of increased disclosure. *Journal of Accounting Research*, *38*, 91–124.

Leventis, S., Dimitropoulos, P., & Owusu-Ansah, S. (2013). Corporate governance and accounting conservatism: Evidence from the banking industry. *Corporate Governance: An International Review*, *21*(3), 264–286.

Levine, R. (2004). *The Corporate Governance of Banks: A Concise Discussion of Concepts and Evidence* (Vol. 3404). Washington, DC: World Bank Publications.

Lewis, M. K. (1999). *The Globalization of Financial Services*. London: Edward Elgar Publishing.

Lewis, M. K. (2005). Islamic corporate governance. International association for Islamic economics. *Review of Islamic Economics*, *9*(1), 5–29.

Lewis, M. K., & Algoud, L. M. (2001). *Islamic Banking*. Chelteham, UK and Northampton.

Licht, A. N., Goldschmidt, C., & Schwartz, S. H. (2005). Culture, law, and corporate governance. *International Review of Law and Economics, 25*(2), 229–255.

Lindblom, C. K. (1994). The implications of organizational legitimacy for corporate social performance and disclosure. In *Critical Perspectives on Accounting Conference*, New York, 1994.

Linowes, D. F. (1972). An approach to socioeconomic accounting. Conference Board Record, November.

Lorsch, J. W., & MacIver, E. (1989). *Pawns or Potentates: The Reality of America's Corporate Boards*. Boston: Harvard Business School Press.

Luoma, P., & Goodstein, J. (1999). Stakeholders and corporate boards: Institutional influences on board composition and structure. *Academy of Management Journal, 42*(5), 553–563.

Lynall, M. D., Golden, B. R., & Hillman, A. J. (2003). Board composition from adolescence to maturity: A multitheoretic view. *Academy of Management Review, 28*(3), 416–431.

Maali, B., Casson, P., & Napier, C. (2006). Social reporting by Islamic banks. *Abacus, 42*(2), 266–289.

Mace, M. L. G. (1971). *Directors: Myth and Reality*. Boston: Division of Research Graduate School of Business Administration Harvard University.

Macey, J. R. (2004). Efficient capital markets, corporate disclosure, and Enron. *Cornell Law Review, 89*, 394.

Macey, J. R., & O'hara, M. (2003). The corporate governance of banks. *Economic Policy Review, 9*(1), 1–17.

Macey, J. R., & Miller, G. P. (1997). Universal banks are not the answer to America's corporate governance "problem": A look at Germany, Japan, and the US. *Journal of Applied Corporate Finance, 9*(4), 57–73.

Magalhã Es, R., & Al-Saad, S. (2013). Corporate Governance: *The International Journal of Business* in society Corporate governance in Islamic financial institutions: The issues surrounding unrestricted investment account holders. *Humanomics The International Journal of Business in Society, 13*(1), 39–57.

Majeed, S., Aziz, T., & Saleem, S. (2015). The effect of corporate governance elements on corporate social responsibility (CSR) disclosure: An empirical evidence from listed companies at KSE Pakistan. *International Journal of Financial Studies, 3*(4), 530–556.

Maliah, S., Shani, G., & Stern, R. (2015). Privacy preserving pattern databases. In *Proceedings of the 3rd Distributed and Multiagent Planning (DMAP) Workshop of ICAPS* (Vol. 15, pp. 9–17).

Mallin, A. (2007). *Corporate Governance*. Oxford, UK: Oxford University Press.

Mallin, C., Farag, H., & Ow-Yong, K. (2014). Corporate social responsibility and financial performance in Islamic banks. *Journal of Economic Behavior & Organization, 103*, S21–S38.

Mannan, M. A. (1984). *Abstracts of Researchers in Islamic Economics*. Jeddah: International Centre for Research in Islamic Economics.

Manning, B. (1958). *Livingston: The American Stockholder*. New York: J. B. Lippincott Co.

Maroun, Y. (2002). *Islamic Innovation and Management Regulation.*

Marshall, A. (1920). *Principles of Economics.* London: Macmillan.

Martinez, R. J., & Dacin, M. T. (1999). Efficiency motives and normative forces: Combining transactions costs and institutional logic. *Journal of Management, 25*(1), 75–96.

Martynova, M., & Renneboog, L. (2011). Evidence on the international evolution and convergence of corporate governance regulations. *Journal of Corporate Finance, 17*(5), 1531–1557.

Maurer, J. K. (1971). *Readings in Organizational Theory: Open System Approaches.* New York, NY: Random House.

Mawdadi, A. (1974). Tafhim al-Quran: An understanding of Quran. *Urdu Digest Printers, Lahore.*

Mawdudi, A. (1986). The Prohibition of Interest in Islam. *Al–Islam* June.

McCormick, R. (2010). *Legal Risk in the Financial Markets.* Oxford: Oxford University Press.

McDonald, L. M., & Rundle-Thiele, S. (2008). Corporate social responsibility and bank customer satisfaction: A research agenda. *International Journal of Bank Marketing, 26*(3), 170–182.

McMillen, M. J. (2007). Shariah-compliant project finance: An overview, including structures. *Journal of Islamic Economics, Banking and Finance, 3*(1), 1–45.

Meek, G. K., Roberts, C. B., & Gray, S. J. (1995). Factors influencing voluntary annual report disclosures by US, UK and continental European multinational corporations. *Journal of International Business Studies, 26,* 555–572.

Meier, H. H., & Meier, N. C. (2014). Corporate governance: An examination of US and European models. *Corporate Ownership & Control, 11*(2), 347–351.

Merton, R. C. (1995). A functional perspective of financial intermediation. *Financial Management, 24*(2), 23–41.

Metawa, S. A., & Almossawi, M. (1998). Banking behavior of Islamic bank customers: Perspectives and implications. *International Journal of Bank Marketing, 16*(7), 299–313.

Meyer, J. W., & Rowan, B. (1977). Institutionalized organizations: Formal structure as myth and ceremony. *American Journal of Sociology, 83*(2), 340–363.

Meyer, J. W., & Rowan, B. (1991). Institutionalized organizations: Formal structure as myth and ceremony. In Powell, W. and DiMaggio, P. (Eds.). *The New Institutionalism in Organizational Analysis* (pp. 41–62). Chicago: University of Chicago Press.

Meyer, J. W., & Scott, W. R. (1983). *Organizational Environments: Ritual and Rationality.* Beverly Hills: Sage.

Meyer, J. W., Scott, W. R., & Deal, T. (1983). Research on school and district organization. *The Dynamics of Organizational Change in Schools,* 409–425.

Meyer, K. E. (2004). Perspectives on multinational enterprises in emerging economies. *Journal of International Business Studies, 35,* 259–276.

Minhas, I. (2012). *Shariah Governance Model (SGM) and Its Four Basic Pillars.* Islamic Finance News Malaysia published by Kuala Lumpur: Red Money Publication.

Minsky, H. P. (1982). *The Financial-Instability Hypothesis: Capitalist Processes and the Behavior of the Economy.* Berlin: The Jerome Levy Economics Institute of Bard College.

Mittal, R. K., Sinha, N., & Singh, A. (2008). An analysis of linkage between economic value added and corporate social responsibility. *Management Decision, 46*(9), 1437–1443.

Mizushima, T. (2014). Corporate governance and Shariah governance at Islamic financial institutions: Assessing from current practice in Malaysia. *Reitaku Journal of Interdisciplinary Studies, 22*(1), 59–84.

Mollah, S., & Zaman, M. (2015). Shariah supervision, corporate governance and performance: Conventional vs. Islamic banks. *Journal of Banking & Finance, 58*, 418–435.

Monks, R. A., & Minow, N. (2011). *Corporate Governance.* Hoboken: John Wiley & Sons.

Monks, R. A. G., & Minow, N. (1995). Corporate governance on equity ownership and corporate value. *Journal of Financial Economics, 20*(3), 293–315.

Morin, R. & Jarrell, S. (2001). *Driving Shareholders Value: Value-Building Techniques for Creating Shareholder Wealth.* Sydney: McGraw-Hill Publishers.

Morris, D. W. (1987). Ecological scale and habitat use. *Ecology, 68*(2), 362–369.

Mostepaniuk, A. (2017). Corporate governance. In L. Emeagwali (Ed.). *Corporate Governance and Strategic Decision Making* (pp. 1–21). Intech Open. Rijeka - Croatia. https://www.intechopen.com/books/corporate-governance-and-strategic-decision-making.

Mudawi, A. B. Y. (1984). Islamic Banks Problems and Prospects: Islamic Banking Evaluation of Experience. In *International Seminar on Islamic Banking. Islam Abad, Pakistan.*

Muhammad, R., Azlan Annuar, H., Taufik, M., Nugraheni, P., & Ntim, C. G. (2021). The influence of the SSB's characteristics toward sharia compliance of Islamic banks. *Cogent Business & Management, 8*(1), 1929033.

Mukhibad, H., Yudo Jayanto, P., Sfvuryarini, T., & Bagas Hapsoro, B. (2022). Corporate governance and Islamic bank accountability based on disclosure — A study on Islamic banks in Indonesia. *Cogent Business & Management, 9*(1), 2080151.

Mülbert, P. O. (2009). Corporate governance of banks. *European Business Organization Law Review (EBOR), 10*(3), 411–436.

Muneeza, A., & Hassan, R. (2011). Legal obstacles in Shariah corporate governance of Islamic financial institutions in Malaysia. *Journal of King Abdulaziz University: Islamic Economics, 24*(2), 1–15.

Muneeza, A., & Hassan, R. (2014). Shariah corporate governance: The need for a special governance code. *Corporate Governance, 14*(1), 120–129.

Nadzri, F., & Aida, F. (2009). Roles and impacts of accounting and auditing organization for Islamic financial institutions (AAOIFI) in dealing with the accounting and disclosure of Zakah and interest (Riba). A thesis submitted to Auckland University of Technology in Partial Fulfilment of the Requirements for the Degree of Master of Business.

Napier, C. (2009). Defining Islamic accounting: Current issues, past roots. *Accounting History*, *14*(1–2), 121–144.

Napier, C. J. (2006). Accounts of change: 30 years of historical accounting research. *Accounting, Organizations and Society*, *31*(4–5), 445–507.

Nathan, S., & Ribière, V. (2007). From knowledge to wisdom: The case of corporate governance in Islamic banking. *Vine*, *37*(4), 471–483.

Nienhaus, V. (2007). Governance of Islamic banks. In M. Kabir Hassan and Mervyn, K. Lewis (Eds.), *Handbook of Islamic Banking* (pp. 128–143). Cheltenham, UK and Northampton, MA, USA: Edward Elgar.

Nier, E., & Baumann, U. (2006). Market discipline, disclosure and moral hazard in banking. *Journal of Financial Intermediation*, *15*(3), 332–361.

Norat, M. M., Mejia, A. L., Aljabrin, S., Awad, R., & Song, M. I. W. (2014). *Regulation and Supervision of Islamic Banks* (No. 2014/219). International Monetary Fund.

North, D. C. (1990). A transaction cost theory of politics. *Journal of Theoretical Politics*, *2*(4), 355–367.

Nwanji, T. I., & Howell, K. E. (2007). Shareholdership, stakeholdership and the modern global business environment: A survey of the literature. *Journal of Interdisciplinary Economics*, *18*(4), 347–361.

O'Dwyer, B. (2002). Managerial perceptions of corporate social disclosure: An Irish story. *Accounting, Auditing & Accountability Journal*, *15*(3), 406–436.

Obid, S. N. S., & Naysary, B. (2014). Toward a comprehensive theoretical framework for Shariah governance in Islamic financial institutions. *Journal of Financial Services Marketing*, *19*(4), 304–318.

Ocasio, W., & Joseph, J. (2005). Cultural adaptation and institutional change: The evolution of vocabularies of corporate governance, 1972–2003. *Poetics*, *33*(3–4), 163–178.

Odenius, J. (2008). *Germany's Corporate Governance Reforms: Has the System Become Flexible Enough? (No. 8-179)*. Washington, DC: International Monetary Fund.

OECD. (2004). *OECD Principles of Corporate Governance*. https://www.oec d.org/corporate/ca/corporategovernanceprinciples/31557724.pdf (Accessed January 31, 2023).

Ogden, S., & Clarke, J. (2005). Customer disclosures, impression management and the construction of legitimacy: Corporate reports in the UK privatised water industry. *Accounting, Auditing & Accountability Journal*, *18*(3), 313–345.

Okumura, A. (2004). A Japanese view on corporate governance. *Corporate Governance: An International Review*, *12*(1), 3–4.

Okumuş, H. S., & Genc, E. G. (2013). Interest free banking in Turkey: A study of customer satisfaction and bank selection. *European Scientific Journal*, *9*(16), 1–12.

Oliver, C. (1991). Strategic responses to institutional processes. *Academy of Management Review*, *16*(1), 145–179.

Oliver, C. (1997). Sustainable competitive advantage: Combining institutional and resource based views. *Strategic Management Journal, 18*(9), 697–713.

Onagun, A. I., & Mikail, A. (2013, February). Shariah governance system: A need for professional approach. In *Sharia Economics Conference* (pp. 71–80).

Oseni, U. A., Ahmad, A. U. F., & Hassan, M. K. (2016). The legal implications of "Fatwāshopping" in the Islamic finance industry: Problems, perceptions and prospects. *Arab Law Quarterly, 30*(2), 107–137.

Othman, N. (2016). A preface to the Islamic personality psychology. *International Journal of Psychological Studies, 8*(1), 20–27.

Othman, R., & Ameer, R. (2015). Conceptualizing the duties and roles of auditors in Islamic financial institutions. *Humanomics, 31*(2), 201–213.

Ouchi, W. G., & Johnson, J. B. (1978). Types of organizational control and their relationship to emotional well-being. *Administrative Science Quarterly,* 293–317.

Ousama, A. A., & Fatima, A. H. (2010). Voluntary disclosure by Shariah approved companies: an exploratory study. *Journal of Financial Reporting and Accounting, 8*(1), 35–49.

Ozkan, N. (2007). Do corporate governance mechanisms influence CEO compensation? An empirical investigation of UK companies. *Journal of Multinational Financial Management, 17*(5), 349–364.

Parasuraman, A., Zeithaml, V. A., & Berry, L. L. (1985). A conceptual model of service quality and its implications for future research. *Journal of Marketing, 49*(4), 41–50.

Parker, J. (2005). Cooperation and conflict: An analysis of political legitimacy claims in lobbying for education for sustainable development. *Contemporary Politics, 11*(2–3), 169–177.

Parker, R. H. (1989). Importing and exporting accounting: The British experience. *International Pressures for Accounting Change,* Prentice Hall London, 7–29.

Parsons, T. (1956). Suggestions for a sociological approach to the theory of organizations. *Administrative Science Quarterly, 1*(1), 63–85.

Parsons, T. (1960). *Structure and Process in Modem Societies.* Glencoe: Free Press.

Pasiouras, F., Tanna, S., & Zopounidis, C. (2009). The impact of banking regulations on banks' cost and profit efficiency: Cross-country evidence. *International Review of Financial Analysis, 18*(5), 294–302.

Patten, D. M. (2005). The accuracy of financial report projections of future environmental capital expenditures: A research note. *Accounting, Organizations and Society, 30*(5), 457–468.

Pennings, J. M. (1980). *Interlocking Directorates: Origins and Consequences of Connections among Organizations' Board of Directors.* Hoboken: Jossey-Bass.

Perera, M. H. B. (1989). Towards a framework to analyze the impact of culture on accounting. *The International Journal of Accounting, 24*(1), 42–56.

Perrow, C. (1986). Economic theories of organization. *Theory and Society, 15*(1/2), 11–45.

Perks, R. W. (1993) *Accounting and Society*. Hampshire: The Chapman and Hall series in Accounting and Finance, Cengage Learning Emea.

Pesqueux, Y., & Damak-Ayadi, S. (2005). Stakeholder theory in perspective. *Corporate Governance: The International Journal of Business in Society, 5*(2), 5–21.

Pfeffer, J. (1972). Interorganizational influence and managerial attitudes. *Academy of Management Journal, 15*(3), 317–330.

Pfeffer, J. (1981). Management as symbolic action: The creation and maintenance of organizational paradigms. In Cummings, L. and Staw, B. (Eds.). *Research in Organizational Behavior*, 13 (pp. 1–52). Greenwich: JAI Press.

Pfeffer, J., & Salancik, G.R. (1978). *The External Control of Organizations: A Resource Dependence Approach*. New York: Harper and Row Publishers.

Platonova, E., Asutay, M., Dixon, R., & Mohammad, S. (2018). The impact of corporate social responsibility disclosure on financial performance: Evidence from the GCC Islamic banking sector. *Journal of Business Ethics, 151*, 451–471. https://doi.org/10.1007/s1055_1-016-3229-0.

Pratt, J. W., & Zeckhauser, R. (1985). *Principals and Agents: The Structure of Business*. Brighton: Ouchi Harvard Business School Press.

Prowse, S. (1997). Corporate control in commercial banks. *Journal of Financial Research, 20*(4), 509–527.

Pryor, F. L. (2007). The economic impact of Islam on developing countries. *World Development, 35*(11), 1815–1835.

Rafay, A., & Sadiq, R. (2015). Problems and issues in transformation from conventional banking to Islamic banking: Literature review for the need of a comprehensive framework for a smooth change. *City University Research Journal, 5*(2), 315–326.

Rahajeng, D. (2012). The effectiveness of Sharī'ah supervisory board roles in Islamic banks. https://dx.doi.org/10.2139/ssrn.2357831.

Rahman, A. R. A. (1998). Issues in corporate accountability and governance: An Islamic perspective. *American Journal of Islam and Society, 15*(1), 55–69.

Rahman, A. R. A. (2010). Islamic microfinance: An ethical alternative to poverty alleviation. *Humanomics, 26*(4), 284–295.

Rajan, R. G., & Zingales, L. (2001). The influence of the financial revolution on the nature of firms. *American Economic Review, 91*(2), 206–211.

Raman, A. A., & Bukair, A. A. (2013). The influence of the Shariah supervision board on corporate social responsibility disclosure by Islamic banks of Gulf Co-operation Council countries. *Asian Journal of Business and Accounting, 6*(2), 65–104.

Rammal, H. G. (2006). The importance of Shariah supervision in Islamic financial institutions. *Corporate Ownership and Control, 3*(3), 204–208.

Rammal, H. G., & Parker, L. D. (2013). Islamic banking in Pakistan: A history of emergent accountability and regulation. *Accounting History, 18*(1), 5–29.

Rashid, M. H. U., Khanam, R., & Ullah, M. H. (2022). Corporate governance and IFSB standard-4: Evidence from Islamic banks in Bangladesh. *International Journal of Islamic and Middle Eastern Finance and Management, 15*(1), 1–17.

Rashidah, A. R., & Faisal, D. (2012). Introduction to corporate governance from Islamic perspective. *Humanomics, 28*(3), 220–231.

Richter, C. (2013). The Egyptian Muslim Brotherhood movement and its media strategies: The mobilising effect of religion in contentious politics. In *Religious Actors in the Public Sphere* (pp. 167–191). London: Routledge.

Rindova, V. P., Pollock, T. G., & Hayward, M. L. (2006). Celebrity firms: The social construction of market popularity. *Academy of Management Review, 31*(1), 50–71.

Roberts, R. W. (1992). Determinants of corporate social responsibility disclosure: An application of stakeholder theory. *Accounting, Organizations and Society, 17*(6), 595–612.

Rowley, T. J. (1997). Moving beyond dyadic ties: A network theory of stakeholder influences. *Academy of Management Review, 22*(4), 887–910.

Ruef, M., & Scott, W. R. (1998). A multidimensional model of organizational legitimacy: Hospital survival in changing institutional environments. *Administrative Science Quarterly*, 877–904.

Ruigrok, W., Peck, S. I., & Keller, H. (2006). Board characteristics and involvement in strategic decision making: Evidence from Swiss companies. *Journal of Management Studies, 43*(5), 1201–1226.

Ryan, L. V., & Schneider, M. (2003). Institutional investor power and heterogeneity: Implications for agency and stakeholder theories. *Business & Society, 42*(4), 398–429.

Sacconi, L. (2006). A social contract account for CSR as an extended model of corporate governance (I): Rational bargaining and justification. *Journal of Business Ethics, 68*, 259–281.

Safieddine, A. (2009). Islamic financial institutions and corporate governance: New insights for agency theory. *Corporate Governance: An International Review, 17*(2), 142–158.

Salacuse, J. W. (2003). Corporate governance, culture and convergence: Corporations American style or with a European touch. *Law and Business Review of the Americas, 9*, 33.

Salih, M. (Ed.). (2009). *Interpreting Islamic Political Parties.* Berlin: Springer.

Samra, E. (2016). *Corporate Governance in Islamic Financial Institutions.* http://chicagounbound.uchicago.edu/international_immersion_program_pap ers?utm_source=chicagounbound.uchicago.edu%2Finternational_immersion_ program_papers%2F20&utm_medium=PDF&utm_campaign=PDFCover Pages.

Sarea, A. M. (2012). The level of compliance with AAOIFI accounting standards: Evidence from Bahrain. *International Management Review, 8*(2), 27–32.

Scapens, R. W. (2006). Understanding management accounting practices: A personal journey. *The British Accounting Review, 38*(1), 1–30.

Schilling, F., (2001). Corporate governance in Germany: The move to shareholder value. *Corporate Governance: An International Review, 9*(3), 148–151.

Schreuder, H. (1979). Corporate social reporting in the Federal Republic of Germany: an overview. *Accounting, Organizations and Society, 4*(1–2), 109–122.

Schur, L., Kruse, D., & Blanck, P. (2005). Corporate culture and the employment of persons with disabilities. *Behavioural Sciences and the Law, 23*(1), 3–20.

Schwartz, V. E. (1976). Privileges under the Federal Rules of Evidence-A Step Forward. *University of Pittsburgh Law Review, 38*(1), 79–95.

Scott, J. (1997). *Corporate Business and Capitalist Classes* (p. 300). Oxford: OUP.

Scott, K. (1999). Institutions of corporate governance. *Journal of Institutional and Theoretical Economics, 155*(1), 3–13.

Scott, K. (2003). The role of corporate governance in South Korean economic reform. In Joel M. Stern and Donals H. Chew, Jr. (Eds.), *The Revolution in Corporate Finance* (4th Ed., pp. 519–534). London: Blackwell Publishing.

Scott, J. C. (1985). *Weapons of the Weak: Everyday Forms of Peasant Resistance.* New Haven: Yale University Press.

Scott, L. M. (1994). Images in advertising: The need for a theory of visual rhetoric. *Journal of Consumer Research, 21*(2), 252–273.

Scott, W. R. (1975). Organizational structure. In *Annual Review of Sociology.* Vol. 1, edited by Alex Inkeles (pp. 1–20). Palo Alto: Annual Reviews.

Scott, W. R. (1987). The adolescence of institutional theory. *Administrative Science Quarterly,* 32(4), 493–511.

Scott, W. R. (1995). *Institutions and Organizations.* Thousand Oaks: Sage.

Scott, W. R. (2004). Reflections on half a century of organizational psychology. *Annual Review of Sociology,* 30, 1–21.

Scott, W. R. (2008). *Institutions and Organizations: Ideas and Interests.* Thousand Oaks: Sage.

Scott, W. R. (2014). *Institutions and Organizations: Ideas, Interests, and Identities.* Thousand Oaks: Sage.

Seligman, J. (1987). Sheep in wolf's clothing: The American Law Institute principles of corporate governance project. *George Washington Law Review, 55,* 325.

Selvaggi, M., & Upton, J. (2008). Governance and performance in corporate Britain. ABI Research Paper, No. 7.

Selznick, P. (1949). *TVA and the Grass Roots.* California: University of California Press.

Shafii, Z., Salleh, S., & Shahwan, S. H. (2010). Management of Shariah non-compliance audit risk in the Islamic financial institutions via the development of Shariah compliance audit framework and Shariah audit programme. *Kyoto Bulletin of Islamic Area Studies, 3,* 3–16.

Shafii, Z., Abidin, A. Z., Salleh, S., Jusoff, K., & Kasim, N. (2013). Post implementation of shariah governance framework: The impact of shariah audit function towards the role of shariah committee. *Middle East Journal of Scientific Research.*

Shaharuddin, A. (2011). Shariah governance of Malaysian Islamic banking institutions. *Talaa Journal of Islamic Finance,* 14(2), 1–20.

Shahrier, N. A., Ho, J. S. Y., & Gaur, S. S. (2018). Ownership concentration, board characteristics and firm performance among Shariah-compliant companies. *Journal of Management and Governance,* 22(3), 1–24.

Shahwan, A., Bailey, C., Shekerdemian, L., & Harvey, A. S. (2010). The prevalence of seizures in comatose children in the pediatric intensive care unit: A prospective video-EEG study. *Epilepsia, 51*(7), 1198–1204.

Shahzad, M. A., Saeed, S. K., & Ehsan, A. (2017). Sharī'ah audit and supervision in sharī'ah governance framework: Exploratory Study of Islamic Banks in Pakistan. *Business & Economic Review, IM Sciences, Peshawar, 9*(1), 103–118.

Shane, S., & Stuart, T. (2002). Organizational endowments and the performance of university start-ups. *Management Science, 48*(1), 154–170.

Shanmugam, B., & Zahari, Z. R. (2009). *A Primer on Islamic Finance*. Charlottesville: Research Foundation Publications, CFA Institute.

Sharma, A. (2011). Corporate governance and board effectiveness. *International Journal of Computational Engineering & Management, 13*(1), 116–124.

Sherer, P. D., & Lee, K. (2002). Institutional change in large law firms: A resource dependency and institutional perspective. *Academy of Management Journal, 45*(1), 102–119.

Sheu, H. B., Lent, R. W., Brown, S. D., Miller, M. J., Hennessy, K. D., & Duffy, R. D. (2010). Testing the choice model of social cognitive career theory across Holland themes: A meta-analytic path analysis. *Journal of Vocational Behavior, 76*(2), 252–264.

Shleifer, A., & Vishny, R. W. (1997). A survey of corporate governance. *The Journal of Finance, 52*(2), 737–783.

Shrives, P. J., & Brennan, N. M. (2015). A typology for exploring the quality of explanations for non-compliance with UK corporate governance regulations. *The British Accounting Review, 47*(1), 85–99.

Siddiqi, M. N. (1981). *Muslim Economic Thinking: A Survey of Contemporary Literature*. United Kingdom: Islamic Foundation.

Siddiqi, M. N. (1983). *Issues in Islamic Banking*. Islamic Foundation, Leicester, London, UK.

Siddiqi, M. N. (2004). *Riba, Bank Interest and the Rationale of Its Prohibition*. Jeddah: Islamic Research and Training Institute.

Siddiqi, M. N. (2006). Islamic banking and finance in theory and practice: A survey of state of the art. *Islamic Economic Studies, 13*(2), 1–48.

Siddiqi, M. N. (2008). Obstacles of research in Islamic economics. *Journal of King Abdulaziz University: Islamic Economics, 21*(2), 1–21.

Siddiqui, D. A. (2000). A comparative analysis of the Islamic and the Western models of news production and ethics of dissemination. In *Annual Convention of the International Association of Media and Communication Research, Nanyang Technical University, Singapore* (pp. 16–20).

Siepel, J., & Nightingale, P. (2014). Anglo-Saxon governance: Similarities, difference and outcomes in a financialised world. *Critical Perspectives on Accounting, 25*(1), 27–35.

Sikka, P. N., & Willmott, H. C. (2002). Commentary — Beyond Reductionism in Critical Accounting Research. *Accounting and the Public Interest, 2*(1), 88–93.

References

Simon, H. A. (1964). On the concept of organizational goal. *Administrative Science Quarterly*, 1–22.

Smith, A. (1993). *An Inquiry into the Nature and Causes of the Wealth of Nations*. Indianapolis: Hackett.

Sole, J. A. (2007). Introducing Islamic banks into conventional banking systems. IMF Working Paper No. 07/175. https://papers.ssrn.com/sol3/papers.cfm?abstract_id=1007924#.

Solomon, J. (2007). *Corporate Governance and Accountability*. 2nd Ed. Hoboken: John Wiley & Sons, Ltd.

Solomons, D., & Berridge, T. M. (1974). *Prospectus for a Profession: The Report of the Long Range Enquiry into Education and Training for the Accountancy Profession*. Advisory Board of Accountancy Education, Stanford, CA, USA.

Song, M. I., & Oosthuizen, C. (2014). *Islamic Banking Regulation and Supervision: Survey Results and Challenges*. Washington, DC: International Monetary Fund.

Sori, Z. M., Mohamad, S., & Shah, M. (2015). Shariah governance practices in Malaysian Islamic financial institutions. http://dx.doi.org/10.2139/ssrn.2579174.

Soualhi, Y. (2016). Models of Shariah governance across jurisdictions. ISRA — Thomson Reuters Islamic Commercial Law Report 2016, pp. 22–25.

Sourial, M. S. (2004). Corporate governance in the Middle East and North Africa: An overview. https://dx.doi.org/10.2139/ssrn.508883.

Spence, M. (1978). Job market signaling. In *Uncertainty in Economics* (pp. 281–306). Academic Press, Canada.

Staden, C. V. (2015). The influence of corporate social responsibility disclosure on share prices. *Pacific Accounting Review*, *27*(2), 208–228.

Stanley, M. (2008). Implementing corporate governance for Islamic finance. *Finance Network*. www.financenetwerk.nl/files/articles/90.Pdf.

Stoker, G. (1998). Governance as theory: Five propositions. *International Social Science Journal*, *50*(155), 17–28.

Suchman, M. C. (1995). Managing legitimacy: Strategic and institutional approaches. *Academy of Management Review*, *20*(3), 571–610.

Sulaiman, M., Abd Majid, N., & Ariffin, N. M. (2011). Corporate governance of Islamic financial institutions in Malaysia. In Paper presented at the *Proceedings of the 8th International Conference on Islamic Economics and Finance*. Islamic Research and Training Institute (IRTI).

Sultan, S. A. M. (2007). *A Mini Guide to Shariah Audit for Islamic Financial Institutions — A Primer*. CERT Publications Sdn Bhd, Kuala Lumpur, Malaysia.

Sundarajan, V., & Errico, L. (2002). International monetary fund. *Journal of Development Economics*, *67*(2), 1–20.

Swidler, A. (1986). Culture in action: Symbols and strategies. *American Sociological Review*, *51*, 273–286.

Tabash, M. I., Alam, M. K., & Rahman, M. M. (2022). Ethical legitimacy of Islamic banks and Shariah governance: Evidence from Bangladesh. *Journal of Public Affairs*, *22*(2), 1–23.

Tam, O. (2000). Models of corporate governance for Chinese companies. *Corporate Governance: An International Review, 8*(1), 52–64.

The Cadbury Code (1992). *Report of the Committee on the Financial Aspects of Corporate Governance: The Code of Best Practice.* London: Gee Professional Publishing.

The Combined Code. (1998). The London Stock Exchange Limited, June, London, UK.

The Combined Code on Corporate Governance, (2003). Financial Reporting Council, July, London.

The King Report. (2002). The King report on corporate governance for South Africa, King committee on corporate governance, Institute of Directors in Southern Africa, Parktown, South Africa.

Thompson, L. (1990). Negotiation behavior and outcomes: Empirical evidence and theoretical issues. *Psychological Bulletin, 108*(3), 515.

Thompson, R. F. (1967). Foundations of Physiological Psychology, Harper and Row: New York.

Tinker, T. (2004). The Enlightenment and its discontents: Antinomies of Christianity, Islam and the calculative sciences. *Accounting, Auditing & Accountability Journal, 17*(3), 442–475.

Tomkins, C., & Karim, R. A. A. (1987). The Shariah and its implications for Islamic financial analysis: An opportunity to study interactions among society, organization, and accounting. *The American Journal of Islamic Social Sciences, 4*(1), 101–115.

Tost, L. P. (2011). An integrative model of legitimacy judgments. *Academy of Management Review, 36*(4), 686–710.

Tsai, M. C., Lai, K. H., & Hsu, W. C. (2013). A study of the institutional forces influencing the adoption intention of RFID by suppliers. *Information & Management, 50*(1), 59–65.

Tumewang, Y. K., Supriani, I., Dewi, H. R., & Alam, M. K. (2023). A hybrid review on Sharia governance studies from 2001 to 2022. *Journal of Islamic Accounting and Business Research.* Vol. ahead-of-print No. ahead-of-print. https://doi.org/10.1108/JIABR-11-2022-0319.

Turnbull, S. (2000). Corporate governance: Theories, challenges and paradigms. *Gouvernance: Revue Internationale, 1*(1), 11–43.

Uddin, M. H., Ullah, M. H., & Hossain, M. M. (2013). An overview on the basics of Islamic audit. *European Journal of Business and Management, 5*(28), 9–17.

Ullah, M. H. (2013). Compliance of AAOIFI guidelines in general presentation and disclosure in the financial statements of Islamic banks in Bangladesh. *International Journal of Social Science Research, 1*(2), 111–123.

Ullah, M. H., Khanam, R., & Tasnim, T. (2018). Comparative compliance status of AAOIFI and IFSB standards: An empirical evidence from Islami Bank Bangladesh Limited. *Journal of Islamic Accounting and Business Research, 9*(4), 607–628.

Ullah, S., & Lee, K. H. (2012). Do customers patronize Islamic banks for Shari'a compliance? *Journal of Financial Services Marketing, 17*, 206–214.

Ullah, S., Harwood, I. A., & Jamali, D. (2016). "Fatwa repositioning": The hidden struggle for Shari'a compliance within Islamic financial institutions. *Journal of Business Ethics, 149*(4), 895–917.

Ulrich, D., & Barney, J. B. (1984). Perspectives in organizations: Resource dependence, efficiency, and population. *Academy of Management Review, 9*(3), 471–481.

Under Secular Bankruptcy Laws: A Case Study of Arcapita Bank Under US Chapter 11. *Islamic Banking: Growth, Stability and Inclusion,* 127–148.

UNDP. (1997). Governance for sustainable human development: A UNDP policy document. https://digitallibrary.un.org/record/492551?ln=en.

Van Buskirk, A. (2012). Disclosure frequency and information asymmetry. *Review of Quantitative Finance and Accounting, 38,* 411–440.

Van Greuning, H., & Iqbal, Z. (2008). *Risk Analysis for Islamic Banks.* Washigton, DC: World Bank Publications.

Venardos, A. M. (2005). Islamic banking in Malaysia. *World Scientific Book Chapters,* 154–171.

Vinnicombe, T. (2010). AAOIFI reporting standards: Measuring compliance. *Advances in Accounting, 26*(1), 55–65.

Vinten, G. (2001). Shareholder versus stakeholder — Is there a governance dilemma? *Corporate Governance: An International Review, 9*(1), 36–47.

Vogel, F. E., & Hayes, S. L. (1998). *Islamic Law and Finance: Religion, Risk, and Return* (Vol. 16). London: Brill.

Von Staden, A. (2012). The democratic legitimacy of judicial review beyond the state: Normative subsidiarity and judicial standards of review. *International Journal of Constitutional Law, 10*(4), 1023–1049.

Waddock, S. A., Bodwell, C., & Graves, S. B. (2002). Responsibility: The new business imperative. *Academy of Management Perspectives, 16*(2), 132–148.

Wahab, N. A., & Rahman, A. R. A. (2013). Determinants of efficiency of zakat institutions in Malaysia: A non-parametric approach. *Asian Journal of Business and Accounting, 6*(2), 33–64.

Wang, Q., Wong, T. J., & Xia, L. (2008). State ownership, the institutional environment, and auditor choice: Evidence from China. *Journal of Accounting and Economics, 46*(1), 112–134.

Warde, I. (2010). *Islamic Finance in the Global Economy.* Edinburgh: Edinburgh University Press.

Weber, M. (1978). *Economy and Society: An Outline of Interpretive Sociology.* California: University of CA Press.

Weick, K. E., & Quinn, R. E. (1999). Organizational change and development. *Annual Review of Psychology, 50*(1), 361–386.

Wells, H. (2009). The birth of corporate governance. *Seattle University Law Review, 33,* 1247.

Williamson, O. (1985). *The Economic Institutions of Capitalism.* New York: Free Press.

Williamson, O. (1991a). Strategizing, economizing, and economic organization. *Strategic Management Journal, Winter Special Issue, 12,* 75–94.

Williamson, O. (1991b). Comparative economic organization: The analysis of discrete structural alternatives. *Administrative Science Quarterly*, 36, 269–296.

Williamson, O. E. (1975). Markets and hierarchies: Analysis and antitrust implications: A study in the economics of internal organization. University of Illinois at Urbana-Champaign's Academy for Entrepreneurial Leadership Historical Research Reference in Entrepreneurship.

Williamson, O. E. (1979). Transaction-cost economics: The governance of contractual relations. *The Journal of Law and Economics*, *22*(2), 233–261.

Williamson, O. E. (1981). The economics of organization: The transaction cost approach. *American Journal of Sociology*, *87*(3), 548–577.

Williamson, O. E. (1984). The economics of governance: Framework and implications. *Journal of Institutional and Theoretical Economics*, (H. 1), 195–223.

Williamson, O. E. (1998). The institutions of governance. *The American Economic Review*, *88*(2), 75–79.

Willoughby, W. (1896). *An Examination of the Nature of the State*. New York: Macmillan.

Wilson, J. O., Casu, B., Girardone, C., & Molyneux, P. (2010). Emerging themes in banking: Recent literature and directions for future research. *The British Accounting Review*, *42*(3), 153–169.

Wilson, R. (2009). Shariah governance for Islamic financial institutions. *ISRA International Journal of Islamic Finance*, *1*(1), 59–75.

Wilson, W. (1889). *The State and Federal Governments of the United States*. Boston: D.C. Heath.

Wolfensohn, J. D. (1999). A battle for corporate honesty. *The Economist: The World in, 1999*, *29*(1), 38.

World Bank (2013). *The Case for Corporate Governance: What Is Corporate Governance?* Washington DC: World Bank.

Wu, J. L. (1994). *Modern Companies and Enterprise Reform*. Tianjin: Tianjin Renmin Chubanshe.

Yaacob, H., & Donglah, N. K. (2012). Shariah audit in Islamic financial institutions: The postgraduates' perspective. *International Journal of Economics and Finance*, *4*(12), 224–239.

Yahya, Y., & Mahzan, N. (2012) The role of internal auditing in ensuring governance in Islamic financial institutions (IFI). In *3rd International Conference on Business and Economic Research (3rd ICBR 2012)*.

Yamak, S., & Süer, Ö. (2005). State as a stakeholder. *Corporate Governance: The International Journal of Business in Society*, *5*(2), 111–120.

Yapa, P. S. (2006). Cross-border competition and the professionalization of accounting: The case of Sri Lanka. *Accounting History*, *11*(4), 447–473.

Yeo, R. K., & Youssef, M. A. (2010). Communicating corporate image into existence: The case of the Saudi banking industry. *Corporate Communications: An International Journal*, *15*(3), 263–280.

Yoshikawa, T., & Phan, P. H. (2005). The effects of ownership and capital structure on board composition and strategic diversification in Japanese corporations. *Corporate Governance: An International Review*, *13*(2), 303–312.

Zada, N., Lahsasna, A., Mahomed, Z., & Saleem, M. Y. (2017). Chapter 11: Islamic finance insolvencies under secular bankruptcy laws: a case study of Arcapita Bank under US. In Alam, N. and Rizvi, S. A. R. (Eds.) *Islamic Banking: Growth, Stability and Inclusion* (pp. 127–148). Singapore: Springer Nature.

Zaher, T. S., & Hassan, M. K. (2001). A comparative literature survey of Islamic finance and banking. *Financial Markets, Institutions & Instruments, 10*(4), 155–199.

Zahra, S. A., & Pearce, J. A. (1989). Boards of directors and corporate financial performance: A review and integrative model. *Journal of Management, 15*(2), 291–334.

Zahra, S. A., & Pearce II, J. A. (1990). Determinants of board directors' strategic involvement. *European Management Journal, 8*(2), 164–173.

Zaidi, J. A. (2008). Shari'a harmonization, regulation and supervision. Paper presented at the AAOIFI. *World Bank Annual Conference on Islamic Banking and Finance*, Manama.

Zald, M. N. (1969). The power and functions of boards of directors: A theoretical synthesis. *American Journal of Sociology, 75*(1), 97–111.

Zelditch, M. (2001). Processes of legitimation: Recent developments and new directions. *Social Psychology Quarterly, 64*(1), 4–17.

Zelditch Jr, M., & Walker, H. A. (1984). Legitimacy and the stability of authority. *Advances in Group Processes, 1*, 1–25.

Zimmerman, M. A., & Zeitz, G. J. (2002). Beyond survival: Achieving new venture growth by building legitimacy. *Academy of Management Review, 27*(3), 414–431.

Zollo, M., & Freeman, E. (2010). Re-thinking the firm in a post-crisis world. *European Management Review, 7*(4), 191.

Zucker, L. G. (1987). Institutional theories of organization. *Annual Review of Sociology, 13*, 443–464.

Zysman, J. (1983). *Governments, Markets, and Growth: Financial Systems and the Politics of Industrial Change*. Ithaca: Cornell University Press.

Index

A

a national Shariah advisory committee nor any other agency is the final arbiter, 208

AAOIFI and the IFSB, 72

AAOIFI governance standards, 211

absence of sound governance, 6

acceptability of reflecting, 306

accepted as supreme guides, 114

account a wider set of stakeholders, 97

accountability and stakeholder trust, 14

accountability in Islam, 133

accountable to broader groups of stakeholders, 1

Accounting and Auditing Organization for Islamic Financial Institutions (AAOIFI), 301

acquisition of scarce and vital supplies, 30

addressing internal conflicts of interest, 98

adherents of the faith, 132

advise the Islamic banks to correct any errors and raise the standard, 234

agency problem, 100

all information necessary, 134

all relevant Shariah compliance and non-compliance information, 241

all stakeholders in ensuring the company's long-term viability and equitable distribution of resources, 40

Anglo-Saxon and European models, 5

appoint Shariah officers, 83

attain legitimacy in order to survive, 121

B

Bank Negara Malaysia, 76

bank's image, 251

bank-based or bank-led approach, 37

best practices, 7, 104

BOD is accountable to shareholders, 5

BOD is responsible, 81

BOD is ultimately responsible for overseeing the business and affairs, 16

BOD, and the top management, 39

business ethics and managerial responsibility, 21

C

CB-affiliated SSB, 194

Central Shariah Supervisory Board (CSSB), 233

centralized SSB, 128

certain social situations, 123

CG varies, 6

committed to maintaining and expanding economic development, 73

company's owner and the managerial staff as an agent, 19

confirm Shariah compliance, and monitor the functions of the banks, 75

confirming Shariah compliance, 103

conflict of interest, 3

conflict of interest between the parties, 20

conformity of IFIs to Shariah rules and principles, 239

consistent with Islamic principles, 93

constituents or broader environment, 124

cooperative and pro-organizational, 21

corporate controversies, 6

corporate image, 115

corporate management (control), 3

crashes and scandals, 1

credit risk, 253

credit-based financial system, 10

crucial resource, 132

CSSB members shall not sit in institutional SSBs, 240

cultural-cognitive, 110

D

damage their reputations, 127

deliberate acceptance of specific actions and convictions by social actors, 126

dependency concept, 118

depositor protection and ownership concentration, 32

direct and control the administration, 3

disclosure has beneficial effects, 28

due to less accountability, 87

E

economic devastation, 7

effective SG mechanisms and practicing transparency, 299

efficient collaboration among management and owners, 21

efforts made to regulate the sector, 43

encourage transparency, justice, and responsibility, 15

ensure Shariah compliance, 287

ensure transparency, objectivity, and responsibility, 59

ensuring Shariah compliance, 60

entity's actions are acceptable, appropriate, or desirable within a socially established framework of norms, values, beliefs, and jurisdictions, 122

establishing trust, 277

establishment of a more solid SG structure, 79

ethically and socially responsible identity, 132

evaluate business risk, 244

ex-ante and ex-post processes, 219

excessive uncertainty, 69

explain the correlation between openness and business value, 27

external SSBs include, 225

externally granted legitimacy, 127

F

family and state capitalism, 10

family members, 37

fatwa shopping, 204

fiduciary, 98

fiduciary responsibility, 3

fiduciary risk inherent, 251

fiqh al muamalat and usul-al fiqh, 211

five main functions, 228

formalized set of values and procedures, 2

framework of laws, contracts, and cultural standards, 2

fundamentally about leadership, 57

G

gain legitimacy and influence, 107
gathering and assessing evidence, 271
greater corporate transparency, 27
guarantee adherence to Shariah
principles and the decisions of the
SSB, 215
guarantees, 115

H

Harahap (2003), 303
high incidence of conflicts, 35
highlights operational rules and
processes for organizations, 96

I

IBs and IFIs in implementing all
religious requirements, 207
identical practices, 106
IFI's operations are compliant with
Shariah, 161
IFIs fail, 127
IFRS and to contribute to the
development of a high-quality set
of global accounting standards, 305
IFSB-10 allow, 211
IFSB-9, 59
implement Shariah principles, 75
implementation of the laws and
regulations, 177
improper and weak governance, 7
incorporating multiple organizational
functions, 3
independence, competence, 223
independent entities, 209
independent evaluation, 287
independent regulation, 46
information asymmetries, 100
information given by enterprises may
mitigate, 26
insufficient internal people, 259
integrity of Shariah principles, 60
interaction between managers and
shareholders, 97
interdependent relationships, 177

internal and external, 126
internal and outside legitimacy, 126
internal mechanisms' dependence on
resources, 119
International Accounting Standards
Board (IASB), 306
investor trust, 7
Islamic law, 59
Islamic Shariah, 71
Islamic Shariah principles, 66
isomorphic processes, 105

J

justify their actions, 24

L

lack of uniformity, 245
leads to less mispricing, 27
legalization through *fatawa* issuance,
263
legitimacy over efficiency, 105
less interference from regulators,
209

M

management board and a supervisory
board, 36
managers must disclose all financial
and non-financial information,
25
Maqasid al-Shariah, 60
measure how transparency impacts a
company's worth, 28
members of multiple banks, 240
mimetic pressures, 96
minimizing agency costs and
protecting, 99
Mit Ghamr Savings Bank, 138
monitor Shariah compliance, 69
monitoring banking activities,
103

N

nexus for a contracting relationship,
22

362   *Shariah Governance Systems of Islamic Banks*

no regulations or laws exist that set
down SG, 208
no representation from outside
shareholders, 38

O

obligation of accountors, 25
operational risk, 251
operational rules and processes for
organizations, 96
operations of Islamic banks, 115
Organization for Economic
Co-operation and Development
(OECD), 3
organizational legitimacy, 121
ownership and monitoring process,
100

P

perception or assumption, 122
planning to follow-up, must be
approved by the SSB, 216
position on the SG structure remains
unclear, 208
pressure, 107
principals (shareholders) and agents
(management), 3
promote a sound code of mechanism,
6
promoting the stability of the
financial system, 13
protecting the interests of
shareholders, 42
provide opinions on Shariah issues,
guidelines, and decisions regarding
modern banking, practices, and
delivery of *fatwas*, 179
public misconceptions, enhance the
caliber of bankers' applications, 234
public trust and acceptance, 130
public's trust and confidence, 127

Q

Quran, the Sunnah, Ijma', and
Qiyaa', 64

R

reassurance, 271
recognizing and measuring the
economic substance, 306
regulatory, normative, and coercive,
96
relationship, 2
religious aspects of company
activities, 91
religious obligations, 300
religious requirements, 299
required and optional information,
300
resource dependence, 110
resource management and strategy
formulation, 30
responsibilities and powers of SSBs,
229
responsibility and accountability, 84
responsible to God, 101
review and update the current
Shariah guidelines, rules, and
principles, 233
review the bank's proposed new
products and the types of
transactions, 222
right and reliable allocation of the
owner's investment, 39
rights of the stakeholders, 90
rights to all stakeholders, 78
risk of fatwa, 263
roles and responsibilities for every
party, 112

S

safeguard the rights of all
stakeholders, 3
same interests as shareholders, 101
separate advantages, rights, and
liabilities, 2
separation of business finances and
owners, 28
separation of ownership and control, 3
separation of stewardship and
ownership, 101

Index

set of guidelines and procedures, 59
SG guidelines, 179
SG practices, 179
shareholders have a more significant role in decision-making, 37
Shariah compliance, 74, 224
Shariah coordinator, 217
Shariah governing council, 41
Shariah law, 91
Shariah non-compliance risk, 247
Shariah officers, 81
Shariah officers and their responsibilities, 124
Shariah secretariat (SS), 212
Shariah Supervisory Board (SSB), 91
Shariah supervisory members, 211
Shariah-compliant financial operations, 71
Shura, 60
signaling costs, 26
social players, 123
socially accountable, 25
sole proprietorships due, 29
SSB into four groups, 229
SSB is often required, 225
SSB is responsible for guiding, assessing, and monitoring Islamic banking operations, 128
SSB is responsible for supervising, 103
SSB to oversee all aspects, 222
SSB under a Centralized format, 194
SSB's autonomy, 80
SSB's duty, 129

SSBs of different institutions, 193
stakeholders' interests, 33
strict adherence to Islamic law and principles, 91
strong CG may have a positive impact, 6
system for directing and controlling organizations, 3

T

Tawhid and the Shuratic process, 85
Tawhidic epistemological paradigm, 61
that their operations are fully compliant with Shariah law, 73
the principal–agent model, 34
transaction costs arising, 30
transparency, 80
transparency and honesty, 218
trusted by stakeholders, 131
two-tiered, 194

U

understand and interpret the *Shariah* rules and principles, 299
uniformity of SG processes and resolutions, 197
use of regulations to strengthen the SG system, 209

W

welfare of society, 13
World Bank, 2013, 5

www.ingramcontent.com/pod-product-compliance
Lightning Source LLC
Jackson TN
JSHW050833240225
79191JS00007B/15